For Marge & George,

Greetings!

Paul L. Weiss

1992

JOSEPHUS
The Essential Writings

Other books by Paul L. Maier

A Man Spoke, A World Listened

Pontius Pilate

First Christmas

First Easter

First Christians

The Flames of Rome

(ed.) *The Best of Walter A. Maier*

(ed., with G. Cornfeld) *Josephus, The Jewish War*

JOSEPHUS
The Essential Writings

A Condensation of
Jewish Antiquities and *The Jewish War*

Translated and Edited

by

Paul L. Maier

Illustrated

KREGEL PUBLICATIONS
Grand Rapids, Michigan 49501

Cover design: Don Ellens, adapted from the photograph of a statue of Augustus addressing his troops (see page 257).

All photo credits: Paul L. Maier

The publisher gratefully acknowledges the permission of The Paternoster Press, Ltd. for the use of several genealogical/dynastic charts, adapted from F. F. Bruce – *Israel and the Nations.*

Library of Congress Cataloging-in-Publication Data

Josephus, Flavius.
 Josephus: The Essential Writings.

 Includes bibliographies.
 Contents: Jewish Antiquities—War of the Jews.
 1. Jews—History—To A.D. 70. 2. Jews—History—Rebellion, 66-73. I. Maier, Paul L. II. Josephus, Flavius. De bello Judaico. English. 1988. III. Title.

DS116.J7413 1988   909'.04924   87-26261

ISBN   0-8254-2964-1 (pbk.)
ISBN   0-8254-2963-3 (hb.)

4 5 6 7 8 Printing/Year 94 93 92 91

Printed in the United States of America

For
Krista and Katie

Acknowledgments

Special appreciation is due Philip P. Stoner, of Kregel Publications, who shared the vision of a readable Josephus; David P. Robin, of Waldo Library, Western Michigan University, for compiling the Index; and the Burnham–Macmillan Fund, for a Fellowship which supported this research.

CONTENTS

PART II • The Jewish War

INTRODUCTION

Apart from the Bible itself, Flavius Josephus is by far the most important historical source illuminating the entire biblical era, and for some New Testament personalities, he is an even more comprehensive source. In terms of sheer quantity of data, Josephus provides probably 300 times as much information about Herod the Great as does the Gospel of Matthew, for example, or ten times as much about Pontius Pilate. He also furnishes fascinating perspectives on such other biblical figures as Archelaus, Herod Antipas, the two Agrippas, Felix, and Festus, as well as intriguing sidelights on John the Baptist, Jesus' half-brother James, and Jesus himself.

The value of the Jewish historian is less for the Old Testament, but grows dramatically for the intertestamental era until he becomes absolutely indispensable for understanding the whole political, social, intellectual, and religious background of the New Testament era. Jesus is cited in two famous passages in Josephus' *Antiquities*, one of which had been interpolated but is now restored to what is most probably the original form. The fact that Josephus was born in Jerusalem only four years after the crucifixion of Jesus and wrote about the time the Gospels were composed adds to his value as a virtual eyewitness of events in the later New Testament era.

Small wonder, then, that the venerable Whiston translation of Josephus (1737) used to stand next to the Bible on so many library shelves in the English-speaking world with quasi-scriptural authority. But today, alas, few readers have the patience to plow through the 80,000 lines in Josephus' *Jewish Antiquities* and *War*, the equivalent of nearly a dozen average-sized volumes. Scholars continually use Josephus as reference, of course, but hardly anyone simply *reads* Josephus now, which is more the pity, since his works are not only crucial to an understanding of the first century, but engrossing literature in their own right. This condensation is an attempt to reverse that trend and to offer Josephus' two great historical works in a chronological and literary whole, as well as in a digestible unit. The only previous digest of which I am aware is the one by William Shepard in now-antiquated English.

No one is more wary or critical of condensations than I: so often they surrender too much significant material, debasing their usefulness. Accordingly, the goal in these pages has been *to exclude nothing that has important intrinsic value or bearing on the biblical account.* All the most pivotal passages in Josephus are presented word for word, and I would hope that even scholars might find this abridgment useful as a reference tool or literary map through the maze of material Josephus supplies.

The Life of Josephus

Born in A.D. 37, Josephus was the son of a priest named Matthias and a mother who descended from the royal Jewish family of the Hasmoneans. Evidently he was a precocious lad, for Josephus claims:

> About age fourteen, I won universal acclaim for my love of letters, so much so that the chief priests and the city leaders regularly came to me for exact information on some particulars in our laws. (*Vita*, 9)

This passage from his autobiography typifies a strain of conceit in Josephus which would be intolerable today, but was not unknown to a Cicero before him or to Renaissance sorts after him.

Two years later, he began studying the principal Jewish sects—the Pharisees, Sadducees, and Essenes—favoring the last when he lived for three years in the wilderness as a disciple of a hermit named Bannus. But he abandoned such austerity at age nineteen, when he returned to Jerusalem and joined the Pharisees, for whom, however, he later extended some criticism.

In A.D. 64 he traveled to Rome to intercede in behalf of some Jewish priests whom Felix, the Judean procurator, had sent to Nero for trial. En route, he was shipwrecked on the Adriatic, and only 80 of the some 600 passengers aboard were rescued, the first in a series of harrowing escapes for Josephus. In Rome, he was introduced to the empress Poppaea through a Jewish actor, who was one of her favorites, and succeeded in his mission through her intervention. During this visit, Josephus was profoundly impressed with the magnificence and power of the imperial city, the start of his Romanophile tendencies.

When he returned to Judea, the land was on the verge of revolt against Rome, and Josephus, unable to restrain his countrymen, joined the rebellion reluctantly and was appointed commander in

Galilee. Before Roman forces arrived, he trained his army, secured provisions, and fortified some of the cities, using Jotapata as his stronghold when Vespasian conquered Galilee with his legions. After a siege of 47 days, Jotapata fell, but Josephus hid in a cave with some of the townspeople, who vowed death rather than submission. All killed each other except for Josephus and another survivor, who emerged from the cavern and surrendered. Brought before Vespasian, Josephus would probably have been punished but for his prediction that Vespasian would soon become emperor. When this prophecy was fulfilled, Josephus was freed of his chains.

From this point on, he became a client of Vespasian and his sons Titus and Domitian, adding their family name "Flavius" to his own. For the rest of the war he served the Romans as mediator and interpreter, appealing to his countrymen to lay down their arms and save their city and temple against the obvious military superiority of Rome. Because of such efforts, as well as the circumstances of his survival at Jotapata, many of his fellow Jews vilified Josephus as a coward and turncoat, an attitude which persists in some Jewish circles to the present day. Many, however, are prone to overlook unpleasantries in the man for the value of his works.

After the war, Josephus returned to Rome with the Flavians to enjoy their patronage for the rest of his life. Awarded gifts by Titus, he settled in the former mansion of Vespasian with Roman citizen's rights as well as an imperial pension, from which he could devote himself to a literary career. His domestic life was not as successful—his first marriage was by command of Vespasian, his second wife deserted him, and he divorced the third—but he had five sons. When he died, soon after A.D. 100, he was honored with a statue at Rome.

The Writings of Josephus

Although they may claim not to do so, most historians write with some bias, and Josephus especially so, making his partiality easy to adjust for in weighing the ultimate truth of his prose. Following would be his principal prejudices, aside from a lofty appreciation of himself: 1) Jews have a proud and cultured history, as well as the highest form of religious belief; 2) Romans, however, now enjoy God's favor because of the apostasy and villainy of the Jewish Zealot leaders and their insurrectionary followers, whom Josephus regularly styles as bandits or brigands. Accordingly, Vespasian and Titus are heroized as sterling sorts who can do no wrong, while John of Gischala, Simon bar-Giora, and other rebel leaders are vilified as miscreants who can do no right. Bias, however, need not connote falsehood, and if even a fraction of the enormities reported of the latter are true, the Zealot leaders emerge as rogues to any reasonable reading, despite recent efforts to rehabilitate them.

Another fault in Josephus is one he shares with most of the ancient historians: a propensity to exaggerate, particularly with numbers. Casualty lists after some of the battles are so impossibly high that even to note such overstatements would clutter too many pages in the text. The reader must also discount such hyperboles as, for example, the claim that so much blood was shed in Jerusalem during its conquest that streams of gore extinguished fires there. Exaggeration, however, was so common a conceit among most of the ancient sources, that if a Herodotus could claim Xerxes invaded Greece with a total force of 5,283,220, Josephus may have felt it unwise to provide accurate figures if such inflation was common fare at the time.

Other faults of his include digressions from his theme—for which, however, we can be very grateful, since many are gems of information—as well as some contradictory statements made in his various works, particularly *Antiquities* and *War*. His egotism and opportunism have already been cited.

Credits, however, heavily outweigh the deficits. Josephus remains our sole surviving source for so much extra-biblical information that no listing would do the man justice. He also sheds significant light on Roman military and siege tactics, as well as some unique detail on the Julio-Claudian emperors. He knows how to sustain interest, involve dialogue, deliver graphic portrayal, exemplify with the specific, and generally delight the reader with the color, drama, and excitement of Palestine in various eras while avoiding none of the horror of its conquests or intramural strife. He also excels in his geographical and architectural descriptions of the land and its structures in antiquity—areas sometimes scanted in Scripture—and his accuracy is being progressively affirmed today by archaeological excavations.

Josephus' earliest work is *The Jewish War*, even though, for chronological reasons, it is placed last in this condensation. Published in Greek in A.D. 77 or 78 from the Aramaic in which he composed it, the *War* comprises seven books, the first of which epitomizes Jewish history from Maccabean times to the death of Herod as background for the start of the Jewish revolt against Rome in A.D. 66. The last six books detail the struggle itself and its aftermath. His sources include intertestamental literature, a life of Herod written by Nicolas of Damascus, his own wartime experiences along with those of Jewish and Roman colleagues, and the Roman imperial archives. Josephus' Greek-speaking amanuensis-translator added stylistic touches from classical authors. Because it was written under Flavian auspices, this is the most pro-Roman of any of Josephus' writings, and was likely intended as a warning to rebels anywhere in the Greek-speaking East to desist from their intentions. A Slavonic version of the *War* exists, but its variations and sensationalizing addenda render it suspect for most scholars.

About seventeen years later, in 93–94, Josephus published his other great work, the *Jewish Antiquities*, an extremely ambitious history of the Jews, from the Creation to the outbreak of war with Rome, demonstrating for the Greco-Roman reader the ancient, lofty, and reasonable beliefs and culture of Judaism. Comprising twenty books, the first ten carry the account up to the Babylonian Captivity, while the last ten continue the history from the return of the Jews under Cyrus to A.D. 66.

Josephus' model was Dionysius of Halicarnassus and his *Roman Antiquities*, also in twenty books, while his sources for *Antiquities*, beyond those cited above for *War*, include Scripture via the Greek Septuagint, apocryphal documents, haggadic traditions, the Greco-Roman historians, and an important collection of edicts and imperial documents affecting the Jews. Befitting his literary maturity, the tone of *Antiquities* is less impassioned and pro-Roman than the earlier *War*, and includes more valuable detail on the decades in the first century preceding the war with Rome which had been somewhat telescoped in the *War*. Here the famed references to Jesus are found, which are translated word for word with annotation where they appear in the text of *Antiquities* XVIII, 63 and XX, 200.

Josephus attached his autobiography, the *Vita*, as an appendix to the *Antiquities*. In this brief work, he defends himself against charges of a rival historian, Justus of Tiberias, who accused him of helping incite the revolt against Rome. It focuses primarily on Josephus' half-year as commander in Galilee.

Finally, he also wrote *Against Apion*, a classic defense of Judaism not only to oppose the slanders of Apion, an anti-Semitic rhetorician from Alexandria, but to answer all the Egyptian and Greek calumnies against the Jews and their culture. Conversely, he demonstrates the failure of Gentile religion and morality versus the high standards of the Mosaic code.

This Condensation

As indicated, nothing of central significance has been surrendered in this abridgment, while the necessary reduction was made in the following areas:

1. The lengthy—and obviously contrived—harangues Josephus places in the mouths of generals addressing their troops before great battles, or by prophets to their people after great transgressions—a familiar device Josephus learned from Thucydides and other Greco-Roman historians.
2. Excurses Josephus makes on various peripheral matters.
3. Some of the activities of the Jews in Egypt and Mesopotamia.
4. The texts of the many similar edicts and proclamations cited by Josephus.
5. Data not unique to Josephus, but which he drew from Scripture or Greco-Roman sources.

6. General detail that can readily be condensed without forfeiting meaning.

Lengthy omissions are indicated by brackets in the text. Brackets also denote an occasional word or phrase added to the text for purposes of clarification.

Only major deviations between Josephus and Scripture are noted. The many minor differences anyone familiar with the Old and New Testaments will readily recognize, and nearly all such variations were made by Josephus to accommodate his Hellenistic readers in the following ways:

1. Haggadic and rabbinical elaborations are added as embellishments to the scriptural record.
2. Old Testament episodes embarrassing to Judaism, such as Tamar (Genesis 38), Miriam's leprosy (Numbers 12), and the bronze serpent (Numbers 21) are omitted.
3. Anthropomorphisms in the Old Testament are exchanged for allegory in the mode of Philo of Alexandria, and more intellectualism is ascribed to the patriarchs. Abraham, for example, goes to Egypt more to debate the wise men there, and less because of famine.

Marginal references are to the full Greek text of Josephus, which is most conveniently available to scholars in the volumes of the *Loeb Classical Library*—with English translation and excellent critical notes (Harvard, Heinemann, 1956 ff.)—and to the general public in the veteran William Whiston translation (Kregel, Baker, 1960 ff.). Separate editions of *The Jewish War* have been published by G. A. Williamson (Penguin, 1959) and a lavishly illustrated text and commentary by G. Cornfeld (Zondervan, 1982). Correlations between the references in this text and Whiston are listed on pages 748 ff. of the Kregel edition. Marginal references are abbreviated as **A:** for *Antiquities,* and **W:** for *War.*

Most proper names in the text are spelled as they appear in the Old and New Testaments, rather than Josephus' Greek, to establish identity and avoid confusion. Chapter divisions and titles are mine, but many follow the segmentation of Josephus. Dates in the margins are those which can be determined with reasonable certainty either from Josephus' context or general ancient history.

In his Prologue to the *War,* Josephus claims to have written "for lovers of the truth and not to gratify my readers." He easily accomplishes also the latter, for no one has provided a better overview of the entire biblical era. If Josephus had not existed, *all* our Bible dictionaries and commentaries would be substantially smaller. His works are simply indispensable to any student of Scripture. But at a time when Bible study almost always focuses on individual books of the Bible, the whole panorama from Creation to the destruction of Jerusalem in A.D. 70 is usually obscured. These pages are one attempt to redress that imbalance and broaden the view.

PAUL L. MAIER

Western Michigan University
May, 1988

PART I

JEWISH ANTIQUITIES

1
BEGINNINGS

Those who write histories are prompted by various motives. A I,1
This work was undertaken not to display literary skill, win
fame, or please the powerful, but, as a participant in some of the
events, I intended to refute those whose writings were falsifying
the truth and to benefit those ignorant of important affairs.

This narrative will cover our entire ancient history: the origin
of the Jews, the fortunes that overtook them, the great Lawgiver
who taught them piety and virtue, and all their wars through
long ages before their final conflict with Rome. Because such a
theme is so broad, I wrote about the last in the *War*,* a separate
volume. The principal lesson in these pages is this: those who
conform to God's will prosper and are happy, but those who
depart from His laws end in disaster.

Our lawgiver, Moses, was born 2,000 years ago. When he
established his laws, he did not follow fables or begin with the
rights of man, as others have done, but rather elevated their
thoughts to God and the creation of the world. I will first
mention what Moses has said regarding the creation, as I find it
recorded in the sacred books.

The Creation

In the beginning, God created the heaven and the earth. The A I,27
earth was hidden in thick darkness when God commanded that
there be light. He divided the light from the darkness, which He
named night, and the former, day. On the second day, He set

---

* Part II of this book, *The Jewish War.*

the heaven above the universe, surrounding it with ice and making it moist and rainy to benefit the earth. On the third day, He founded the earth, on which plants and seeds grew from the soil, and He poured the sea around it. On the fourth, He arranged the sun, moon, and stars in the heaven, regulating their movement and courses to indicate the seasons. The fifth day, He generated in the deep and in the air the creatures that swim or fly, uniting them in order to multiply their kind. The sixth day, He formed the four-footed creatures, male and female, and on this day He also created man. On the seventh day, God rested from His labor; therefore we also pass this day in repose and call it the Sabbath, which means "rest" in Hebrew.

Moses writes about the formation of man as follows: "God fashioned man from the dust of the earth and breathed into him spirit and soul." This man was called Adam, which in Hebrew signifies "red," since he was made from the red earth, for this is the color of virgin soil. And God showed Adam the male and female of the living creatures, giving them the names by which they are still called to this day.* Since Adam had no female consort and looked with astonishment at the other creatures which had their mates, God took one of Adam's ribs while he slept and formed woman from it. In Hebrew, woman is called *essa* [*issha*], but the name of that first woman was Eve, which means "Mother of all living."

A I,40   Now, in the park which God had planted to the east, He directed that Adam and his wife should eat of all plants except the tree of wisdom, warning that if they touched it, they would be destroyed. At that time, all living creatures spoke a common language, and a serpent maliciously lured the woman into tasting of the tree of wisdom, promising a blissful existence equal to that of a god. She tasted the tree's fruit, and persuaded Adam to do so also. Now aware that they were naked, they covered themselves with fig leaves. When God entered the garden, Adam tried to excuse himself by blaming Eve, and she accused the serpent. God told Adam that the earth would no longer produce anything of itself except in return for grinding toil. He punished Eve through childbirth, and deprived the serpent of speech, putting poison under its tongue. He also removed its feet so that it would have to wiggle along the ground. Then God removed Adam and Eve from the garden to another place.

Cain was born to them, whose name means "acquisition," as well as Abel, meaning "nothing." They also had daughters.

---

* In Genesis 2:20, Adam, not God, names the animals. This is the first of many variations between the biblical text and Josephus, too numerous to list in notation.

Abel, the younger, was virtuous and lived as a shepherd. Cain, on the other hand, was depraved and greedy, and he plowed the soil. In his sacrifices to God, Cain brought the fruits of the earth. Abel offered up milk and the firstborn of his flocks, a sacrifice which God preferred, since it was produced by nature, not human ingenuity. Angry at God's preference, Cain killed his brother and hid his corpse. God confronted Cain with the crime, cursed him to the seventh generation, and expelled him from that land with his wife. He also put a mark on him, assuring Cain that he would not be attacked by any beast or man.

After a long journey, Cain settled with his wife at a place called Nod, where he had children. Indulging in every form of vice and violence, he grew rich and ended the simple life by inventing weights and measures. He was the first to set up boundaries in the land and to build a city, forcing his clan to live behind its fortifications. He called the city Anocha after his eldest son Enoch, whose offspring were also depraved.

Adam, meanwhile, longed for children, and at age 230 he fathered Seth, as well as many other children. The virtuous descendants of Seth discovered the science of astronomy. To prevent their findings from perishing in the destruction by fire and deluge predicted by Adam, they inscribed them on two pillars, one of brick and the other of stone. The latter exists to this day in the land of Seiris.

Noah and the Flood

For seven generations, these people continued believing in A I,72 God as master of the universe, but then they fell into vice and depravity. Some, born of angels who had consorted with women, resembled the audacious giants of Greek mythology. Noah urged them to mend their ways, but he feared they would murder him, so he left the country, taking his entire family. God therefore decided to destroy mankind and create another race exempt from vice, and reduce their life term to 120 years. He gave Noah the idea of constructing an ark four stories tall, 300 cubits long, 50 wide, and 30 deep. He embarked on it with his family, as well as the male and female of every creature, some of them being numbered by sevens. The ark had strong sides and roof, and the catastrophe took place when Noah was 600 years old, 2,262 years after the birth of Adam.

Rain poured down incessantly for 40 days, covering the earth to the depth of 15 cubits. After the rain stopped, the flood continued for 150 days, until the water level started dropping, beginning with the seventh day of the seventh month. When the ark settled on a mountain top in Armenia, Noah released a raven to see if any part of the earth had emerged from the flood, but the bird returned to Noah. A week later, he sent out a dove, and it returned marked with clay and an olive branch in its mouth. Noah released the animals from the ark seven days later, sacrificed to God, and feasted with his family. The Armenians call that spot "the Landing Place," and they show its remains to this day.

This flood and the ark are mentioned by Berosus the Chaldean, who writes: "A portion of the vessel still survives in Armenia on the mountain of the Cordyaeans, and people carry off pieces of the bitumen as talismans." Nicolas of Damascus relates the story as follows: "In Armenia there is a great mountain called Baris, where many refugees found safety at the time of the flood, and one man on an ark landed at the summit, and remains of the timber were long preserved."

Afraid that God might annually inundate the earth, Noah offered burnt sacrifice and prayer, to which God responded: "Never again will water overwhelm the earth. And I exhort you not to shed human blood, but punish those guilty of such a crime. You may eat other living creatures as you see fit, for I have made you master of all, but not their blood, for the soul is within it. Moreover, I will confirm our truce by displaying my bow," by which He meant the rainbow.

Noah lived another 350 happy years after the flood, and died at the age of 950.

The Tower of Babel

A I,109   Shem, Japheth, and Ham, the three sons of Noah who had been born a century before the deluge, became the first to descend from the mountains to the plains, setting an example for others who had stayed in the heights for fear of flood. They settled on the Plain of Shinar, and grew so numerous that God counseled them to send out colonies. In their disobedience, they imagined that God was trying to divide them and make them vulnerable to attack! So they followed Nimrod, the grandson of Ham, who set up a tyranny and began building a tower higher than any water could reach in case God ever wanted to flood the earth again.

With many hands at work, a strong, broad tower went up quickly, built of baked bricks and cemented with bitumen. God, however, threw them into discord by making them speak different languages, so they could not understand one another. The site where they erected the tower is now called Babylon from the confusion of their speech, for the Hebrews call confusion

Baked bricks mortared with bitumen, the building materials for the tower of Babel, were used as late as Nebuchadnezzar's Babylon in the sixth century B.C. The bricks in these ruins are still joined.

"babel." This is also confirmed by the Sibyl in these words: "When all men spoke a common language, some of them built a very high tower, thinking to mount it to heaven. But the gods sent winds against it, overturned the tower, and gave a distinct language to every man."

From then on, the people were dispersed in colonies everywhere, as God led them, so that every continent was occupied, and some crossed the sea in ships and settled on the islands. Japheth, son of Noah, had seven sons who settled the territory between the river Tanais [the Don] and across Europe to Gadeira [Cadiz]. The children of Ham held the territory from Syria and Lebanon through Judea to Africa and the lands along the sea [the Mediterranean]. A curse fell on the children of Canaan, son of Ham, because Ham had once mocked his father Noah when he lay nude in a drunken slumber.

Noah's son Shem had five sons, who settled Asia as far as the Indian Ocean, starting at the Euphrates. His great-great-grandson was Heber, after whom the Jews were originally called Hebrews. In turn, Heber's great-great-great-grandson was Terah, a shepherd living in Chaldea, who at 70 years of age became the father of Abraham.

2
THE PATRIARCHS

Abraham

Tenth in descent from Noah, Abraham was born 992 years A I,148 after the flood. He had two brothers, Nahor and Haran, but Haran died and was buried in a city called Ur of the Chaldees. He left a son named Lot, and two daughters, Sarah and Milcah. Nahor married his niece Milcah, and had many sons and daughters, while Abraham married Sarah, and since he had no children, he adopted his nephew Lot as his son.

Hating Chaldea because of Haran's death, Terah and his family all migrated to Haran in Mesopotamia, where Terah died and was buried at age 205. The duration of human life continued to be diminished until the birth of Moses, when the age limit set by God was 120 years, the length of Moses' life.

When Abraham was 75 years old, he left the land of Chaldea, by the command of God, and went into another country called Canaan. He was the first to declare boldly that God, the creator of the universe, is one, and that the sun, moon, and stars had no inherent power of their own. Because of these opinions, the Chaldeans rose against him, and so he emigrated to Canaan with God's help. Berosus states: "In the tenth generation after the flood, a great and just man lived among the Chaldeans, well versed in celestial lore." Nicolas of Damascus also writes: "Abram reigned (in Damascus), an invader from the Chaldees. But not long afterward, he left for Canaan, where he settled. . . . A village near Damascus is called after him, 'Abram's Abode.'"

For many years, Abraham lived in peace and plenty in Canaan. Then a famine broke out, and Abraham, learning that in

Egypt there was prosperity, took Sarah there. While in Egypt, he talked with the priests and other men, showing them their error in worshiping false gods. He also taught them many things he had learned in Chaldea, including arithmetic and astronomy, and the Egyptians later taught these sciences to the Greeks.

Much of Abraham's route from Ur through Haran into Canaan was along the Euphrates River, shown here next to the ruins of Babylon.

As soon as the famine in Canaan was over, Abraham returned there. Because his servants frequently quarreled with those of Lot about the lands on which to pasture their flocks, Abraham decided to make a fair division. He told Lot that he could go to any part of the land he preferred and Abraham would take the rest for himself. Lot chose the country around the river Jordan, near Sodom. Abraham moved to Hebron, and took all the land around it.

A I,171   Later, the people of Sodom were attacked and defeated by the Assyrians, who took many of them away to their own land as captives. Among these was Lot himself, who had fought as an ally of the Sodomites. When Abraham learned what had happened, he determined to help them. After pursuing them for five days, he came upon the Assyrians in the night at a place called Dan. They had been making merry, and were now drunk or asleep. Abraham and his 318 servants attacked them and killed many, while the rest ran away. He released the prisoners from their bonds, and all returned home rejoicing. On their way, Melchizedek, the king of Salem, who was also a priest of God, came out to meet them. He supplied Abraham and his army with provisions, and while they were all eating and drinking, he praised Abraham and blessed him. Abraham gave him one-tenth of the spoils, and Melchizedek accepted the gift.

When the king of Sodom saw Abraham returning with the captives and the booty, he asked Abraham to give him the prisoners that he might send them to their own homes, but would let Abraham keep all the spoils. Abraham, however, refused, saying he would not keep anything for himself.

God spoke to Abraham and praised him for what he had done, A I,183 saying, "You shall not, however, lose the rewards which your goodness deserves."

Then Abraham answered, "And what good will these re-wards be to me, if I have no one after me to enjoy them?" Abraham was still childless.

But God promised he would give him a son, and his descen-dants would become as numerous as the stars. Abraham offered a sacrifice, as God had commanded him to do: he took a heifer, a she-goat, and a ram—all three years old—as well as a turtle dove and a pigeon, and he cut them into sections, except for the birds. And when he built his altar and burnt these sacrifices, he heard a voice telling him that his descendants would live for 400 years in the land of Egypt and be treated cruelly there, but that afterward they would return victoriously to possess the land of Canaan.

Several years passed, however, and still Abraham and Sarah had no children. By God's command, Sarah brought one of her Egyptian handmaidens named Hagar to Abraham's bed, that he might have children by her. When she became pregnant, she insolently abused Sarah and acted presumptuously. Abraham gave her to Sarah to be punished, but Hagar fled into the wilder-ness, where she almost died. An angel of God persuaded her to return, and shortly afterward she gave birth to Ishmael.

Now the people of Sodom had been growing insolent to men and impious to the Divinity. Angry at this arrogance, God resolved to obliterate them.

One day Abraham sat at the door of his courtyard by the Oak of A I,196 Mamre and saw three strangers approaching. He rose and greeted them, asking them to stop and share his hospitality. When they agreed, he killed a calf, roasted it, and served it to them. While they were eating, they asked Abraham where his wife Sarah was. When he replied that she was in the tent, they told him they would return one day and find that she had become a mother. Sarah smiled and said that childbearing was impossible, since she was 90 years old and her husband 100. Then the strangers told Abraham that they were not men but angels of God, and that one of them was sent to inform him about the child, and the other two to destroy the Sodomites. When Abraham heard this, he prayed that God would spare the city of Sodom for the sake of the few good people living there. But God told him that there were not any good Sodomites, for if there were only ten, He would spare everyone. So Abraham held his peace.

When the angels came to the city of the Sodomites, Lot invited them to be his guests, for he had learned hospitality from Abraham. The Sodomites, however, lusted after the handsome young men, but Lot told them to restrain their passions and not dishonor his guests. God blinded the Sodomite wretches so they could not find the entrance to the house, and warned Lot to flee the destruction of Sodom. When he had fled from the city with his wife and two virgin daughters, God cast a thunderbolt upon the city and burned it to the ground, along with its inhabitants and the surrounding countryside. But Lot's wife, who was continually turning around to observe the city's fate, despite God's warning not to do so, was turned into a pillar of salt. I have seen this pillar, which remains to this day.

Lot and his daughters escaped to Zoar, a tiny spot where they eked out a miserable existence, hungry and isolated from mankind. Believing that all humanity had been destroyed, Lot's maiden daughters had intercourse with their father, to prevent the extinction of the race. They gave birth to Moab and Amman, the progenitors of the Moabites and Ammonites.

[Josephus records the Abimelech episode of Genesis 20 at this point.]

Isaac

A I,213   Not long after this, Abraham and Sarah had a son, as God had foretold, and named him Isaac, which means "laughter," for Sarah had smiled when God said that she would give birth. Eight days later, they circumcised him, and from then on this has been the Jewish practice. Arabs defer the rite until the thirteenth year, when Ishmael, son of Hagar, was circumcised.

Afraid that Ishmael, as the elder son, might harm her Isaac after Abraham died, Sarah urged her husband to dismiss Hagar and her son. Seeing that Sarah's request was also sanctioned by God, Abraham yielded and sent them off. When their provisions ran out, an angel and some shepherds sustained the outcasts. Later, Ishmael married an Egyptian woman, by whom he had twelve sons, and their descendants became the Arabian nation.

As Isaac grew up, he endeared himself to Abraham as his only A I,222 son and because of his many virtues. He was zealous in the worship of God, and loved and honored his parents. Abraham's happiness focused on Isaac as his successor.

To test his obedience, however, God appeared to Abraham. After reminding him of all the blessings He had lavished on him—Isaac was only one of His many gifts—He required that Abraham take his child to Mount Moriah, build an altar, and sacrifice Isaac on it as a burnt offering.

Abraham never thought of disobedience, for he knew that God's will must be done. He did not tell Sarah or any of their household about God's command, for he was afraid that they might try to dissuade him from obeying God. He had Isaac and two servants load a donkey with requisites for sacrifice, and they set out for Mount Moriah. They traveled for two days, and on the third, the mountain came into view. Abraham left the servants in the plain and continued with his son to the mount, on which King David would later erect the temple.*

While building the altar, Isaac, now age 25, asked his father what victim they would offer. God would provide the victim, his father replied. But when the altar was finished, Abraham laid the split wood on it and all was ready, and then he said to Isaac, "My son, through many prayers I implored God for your birth. And when you came into the world, I lavished everything on your upbringing, and my highest happiness would have been to see you grow to manhood and become heir to my dominion when I died. But since it is now God's will that I resign you to Him, bear this consecration valiantly. Depart this life not by the common road, but sped on your way to God by your own father through the rites of sacrifice."

Isaac received these words with gladness. He exclaimed that if he were to reject the decision of God and of his father, he would deserve never to have been born at all. Indeed, if this were his father's decision alone, it would have been impious to disobey. With that, he rushed to the fateful altar.

And the deed would have been done had not God interposed. Forbidding him to kill the lad, God said that He did not desire human sacrifice but had only wanted to test Abraham's obedience. Since He was now sure of it, God was glad that He had bestowed so many blessings upon him, and would continue to watch over him and his race. Isaac would live a long life and have numerous descendants, who would become wealthy, inherit the land of Canaan, and be envied by all men.

---

* Solomon would erect it on property purchased on Mt. Moriah by his father David.

After God had spoken, He produced a ram for the sacrifice. Then father and son, greatly rejoicing, embraced one another and returned home to Sarah after the sacrifice, and they lived in bliss.

Not long afterward, Sarah died at 127 years of age. Abraham buried her in Hebron, where he and his descendants built their own tombs.

Rebekah

A I,242   When Isaac was 40 years old, Abraham decided to obtain a wife for him, a girl named Rebekah, the granddaughter of his brother Nahor. He chose his oldest servant and entrusted to him a number of presents which he was to give to Abraham's friends in Mesopotamia. After traveling many days, the servant approached the town of Haran and saw a number of girls coming out of the town to fill their pitchers with water at the well. He prayed that Rebekah might be among these girls, if it were God's will that she should marry Isaac, and that she would be the only one to offer him a drink of water.

When the girls were at the well, he went up to them and asked for some water. But while the others refused, claiming that they wanted to carry it all home and could spare none for him, one of them rebuked the others for their rude behavior to this stranger. She turned to him, graciously offering him water. In order to be certain, the servant praised her for her generosity in sharing water which had cost so much effort to draw. He asked who her parents were that he might congratulate them on such a daughter.

"I am called Rebekah," she replied, "and my father was Bethuel, but he is now dead, and I live with my mother and my brother Laban, who directs our affairs."

The servant was delighted, for now he plainly saw that God had directed his journey and answered his prayer. He took out a necklace and some other jewelry and gave them to her. He added that from her kindness he might guess how good and hospitable her mother and brother were, who had raised her, and perhaps they might welcome him to their home. He said he would not be a burden, but would pay for his accommodations. She replied that he was right about her relatives, for they were generous people, but complained that he had considered their accepting money for their hospitality. He must come as a guest.

Having obtained permission from Laban, she invited the stranger inside, while his camels were taken care of by the servants. He himself was brought to supper with Laban. After dinner, Abraham's servant told Laban and Rebekah's mother who he was, and why he had come. He explained that Abraham was a wealthy and good man, and that Isaac was his heir. Abraham, he said, could have chosen any of the wealthy women who lived in his neighborhood as a wife for his son, but he preferred a girl of his own tribe. And this also seemed to be the will of God, who had answered his prayer when he asked that Rebekah should be pointed out to him. Abraham's servant urged them to give their consent to the marriage.

Laban and Rebekah's mother saw that the will of God had directed everything, and freely gave their consent. Abraham's servant brought Rebekah back with him, and she was married to Isaac, now master of his father's estate.

Shortly after this, Abraham died, supreme in every virtue. He lived to be 175, and was buried by Isaac and Ishmael in Hebron beside his wife Sarah.

The Cave of Machpelah, where Abraham, Isaac, Jacob, and Joseph are buried, lies in Hebron under the crenelated structure at the center of the photograph, whose impressive walls were constructed by Herod the Great and are magnificently preserved.

Jacob and Esau

A I,257   Isaac's young wife conceived and became alarmingly large with child. But God told Isaac that Rebekah would bear twins. They would also both be the founders of great nations and the younger would excel the older. When they were born, the elder was called Esau, which means "hairy," because he was born with hair all over his body. Esau was favored by his father, but Jacob, the younger, was his mother's darling.

When his sons were grown, Isaac had become old, feeble, and blind. He told Esau that he was anxious that he become his successor, so he asked Esau to go out hunting and then prepare him a supper, after which Isaac would pray to God for him. Esau left, but Rebekah, anxious that Jacob receive God's favor, had him kill some young goats and prepare a supper. Jacob obeyed, and when the supper was ready, he took a goat's skin and laid it on his arm, so that his blind father, feeling the hair of the goat, would mistake him for his brother Esau. When he brought the meal in, Isaac recognized his voice as Jacob's, and had him approach. But when he took hold of Jacob's hand, which was covered with the goat skin, he said, "Your voice is Jacob's, yet because of the thickness of your hair, you must be Esau."

Suspecting no deceit, Isaac ate the supper, and then poured out his prayers to God, saying, "O Lord of all ages, and Creator of all substance, inasmuch as You bestowed upon my father an abundance of good things, and have graciously lavished on me all that I have, and have promised to support my family, now, therefore, confirm these promises, and do not overlook me because of my present infirmity. Be gracious to this, my son, and keep him from all evil. Give him a happy life, and the possession of as many good things as Your power can bestow. Make him terrible to his enemies, and beloved to his friends."

This was Isaac's prayer, and he had just finished when Esau came in from hunting. Esau asked his father to give him the same blessing that he had given to Jacob. But Isaac, realizing the mistake, could not remedy it, because all his prayers had been exhausted on Jacob. However, when Esau burst out weeping, his father tried to comfort him, and predicted that he would excel in hunting and strength of body and bravery. Esau would obtain glory forever because of this, both he and his descendants after him. Nevertheless, he would always serve his brother.

Jacob Flees to Mesopotamia

A I,276   Rebekah was afraid that Esau might punish Jacob because of this deceit, so she persuaded Isaac to choose a wife for Jacob from among her own relatives in Mesopotamia. Esau had already married Ishmael's daughter, Mahalath. Isaac consented that Jacob wed Rachel, the daughter of Rebekah's brother Laban, and sent Jacob to Mesopotamia to marry her.

On his journey through Canaan, where the inhabitants were idolaters, Jacob refused to lodge with any of them. He preferred to sleep in the open air, with a pile of stones serving as a pillow. One night he had a vision while sleeping: he saw a ladder that reached from earth to heaven on which were descending beings of grander nature than that of mortals, and at last God Himself stood above it and was plainly visible. God, calling Jacob by name, told him that because he was the descendant of such a good father and grandfather, He would guard and bless him. The marriage which he contemplated would be a happy one, and he would have a great multitude of descendants, to whom the land of Canaan would be given. "Fear no danger, therefore," said God, "and don't be dismayed at the many hardships you must experience, for I will watch over you and direct all you do both now and hereafter."

Jacob rose from his sleep refreshed and strengthened. Because of the great promise that had been made to him there, he poured oil on the stones, promising that if he lived and returned safely, he would offer sacrifice upon them, and would give a tenth of all his acquisitions to God. So he named the spot "Bethel," which means "God's hearthstone."

Continuing on his journey, he finally arrived at Haran. Meeting a number of shepherds in the suburbs of the town, he asked them whether they knew a man named Laban, and whether he were still alive. They answered that they knew him well, for he was an important man in the town, and that his daughter Rachel fed his flock together with the shepherds. They wondered why she had not yet arrived, but even as they spoke, the girl approached, and the shepherds introduced Jacob as a stranger who came to inquire about her father. Pleased with his appearance, Rachel asked him who he was and what he wanted, hoping to be able to meet his needs.

Jacob was surprised at the girl's beauty and grace, which few women of those days could equal. He told her that he was the son of Isaac and Rebekah, and the nephew of her father Laban. "And now," he continued, "I have come to greet you and your family, and to renew those friendly feelings which already exist between us."

She gladly embraced him, and led the way to her father's house. She assured him that his visit would greatly please Laban, for he was always thinking of Rebekah and talking about her.

When Laban heard who Jacob was, he welcomed him into the house. After they had conversed for some time, he asked Jacob why he had left his aged father and mother to come on so long a journey, assuring him that if he needed anything, he would gladly give it to him. Then Jacob explained that he had left home because Esau sought to kill him.

Laban promised he would treat Jacob with kindness, and make him overseer of his flocks. When he wanted to return to his parents he would send him back loaded with presents. Jacob replied that he would gladly work for his uncle, but as a reward for his labors he asked only for the hand of Rachel. Laban was pleased with this arrangement, and said he would give her to Jacob provided he agreed to remain with him for some time, for he would not send his daughter among the Canaanites. Jacob consented to stay for seven years.

AI,300　　But when the seven years had ended, Laban gave him his elder daughter, Leah, instead of Rachel. Leah was devoid of beauty, but Jacob, deluded by wine and the darkness of his bedroom, had union with her, thinking she was Rachel. When daylight came, he accused Laban of treachery. It was not malice, but an overpowering motive that compelled him, Laban explained [Gen. 29:26: "To give the younger before the firstborn is not done."] However, he told Jacob that if he would work another seven years he could have Rachel also as his wife. So Jacob submitted and worked seven more years for him, and at the end of that time he won Rachel. Both of his wives bore him sons and daughters.

Finally, after tending the flocks of his father-in-law for twenty years, Jacob resolved to take his wives and go home. However, since Laban would not permit this, he decided to go secretly. When he learned that his wives were willing to go, Jacob and his entire household escaped, along with half of the cattle.

But the next day Laban discovered Jacob's departure and was furious. Pursuing him with a band of men, he overtook the fugitives on the seventh day as they were camped on a hill. It was evening, and Laban decided to wait until the next morning. But during the night, God appeared to Laban in a dream and warned him to act peacefully to his son-in-law and daughters. He was not to do anything rashly or in anger, but to make a covenant with Jacob. But if Laban despised their small number and attacked them, God would Himself assist them.

The next day, Laban met with Jacob and asked why he had gone away secretly, taking his daughters with him. Jacob replied that it was because Laban would not let him go in any other way. "I am not," said Jacob, "the only person to whom God has given a love for his own country. He has made it natural for all men, and it was only reasonable that after so many years I would desire to return. As to your daughters, I did not force them to come away with me, but they were willing to come out of love for me. Indeed, they are not following for my sake as much as for their own children."

Laban made a promise, and bound it by oaths, that he would not harm Jacob for what had happened, and Jacob made the same promise. He also swore to love and cherish Laban's daughters. In memory of these promises they raised a slab in the form of an altar on the mountain where they were standing. That place is called Mount Gilead [meaning "cairn of witness"], and the land is known as Gilead to this day. They feasted after the oath-taking, and Laban returned home.

Jacob and Esau Meet

As Jacob was traveling home, he was afraid that Esau had not A I,325 forgiven him. Desiring to know what his brother's intentions were, he sent some servants ahead. They were to go to Esau with this message: "Your brother Jacob is returning, and he is bringing his wives and children along with all his possessions. He would be very happy to share with you what God has bestowed on him."

When they delivered this message, Esau was very glad, and went to meet his brother with 400 men. But Jacob, hearing that he was coming with so large a force, was very afraid. Yet he committed himself into the hands of God, while preparing to defend himself and his family as best he could. He divided his company into parts: some he sent on ahead, and others to the rear, to follow. Then if the first group were overpowered, it could retreat to those who followed.

Next, he sent his brother presents of cattle and other four-footed animals, some of which were rare and valuable. He dispatched them by separate droves in order to appear more numerous, hoping that these presents would pacify Esau, if he were still angry.

It took Jacob a whole day to make these arrangements. Then, as night fell, he sent his company across a torrent called Jabbok while he remained behind. Later, a phantom appeared, who wrestled with him. Then it informed Jacob that he had defeated an angel of God, and this victory meant that the race of which he was to be the founder would be great and victorious. The angel also told Jacob to take the name of Israel, which means in Hebrew, "contender with an angel of God." Then he disappeared. During the struggle Jacob had hurt his thigh, and for this reason he never ate that part of an animal, and his descendants have never eaten it either.

The next day, Esau and his men came into sight, and Jacob prostrated himself before his brother. Esau raised him up and embraced him. After they had spoken, Esau offered to go with Jacob to their father, Isaac, but Jacob thanked him, and said that his wives and children were tired from their long journey and needed rest. So Esau left him and returned to his own country of Seir, while Jacob went on to Succoth and Shechem. [Josephus includes here the rape of Jacob's daughter Dinah and her brothers' revenge (Genesis 34).]

A I,337   Jacob continued his journey to Bethel, where he had seen the vision of the angels and the ladder on his way to Mesopotamia, and he offered sacrifices there. Then he came to Ephratha [near Bethlehem], where Rachel died in childbirth. He buried her

The traditional tomb of Rachel just north of Bethlehem.

there, the only member of his family not interred at Hebron. Mourning deeply, he called the child Benjamin. In all, Jacob had twelve sons and one daughter.

At last he arrived at Hebron, in the land of Canaan, where his father Isaac, although very old, was still living. But only a few years after Jacob's return Isaac himself died, at age 185. Esau and Jacob buried their father beside his wife in their ancestral tomb at Hebron.

Joseph and His Brothers

After the death of Isaac, his sons divided the land between A II,1 them. Esau left Hebron to his brother, and ruled over Idumea, naming the country after himself, for he had the surname Adom, being Hebrew for "red." He became the father of five children.

Jacob grew rich and more prosperous, and in time he came to be looked upon as the most highly blessed of all the men in that country. His children were strong and bright, and Jacob was especially fond of Joseph, who was not only handsome but also virtuous and wise. However, this preference aroused the envy and hatred of Joseph's brothers, as did two of Joseph's dreams.

In his first dream, Joseph thought that at harvest time, as he and his brothers were binding up sheaves of grain, his sheaf stood still where he set it, but their sheaves ran to bow down to it, as servants bow down to their masters. The brothers were angry when they heard the dream, because it seemed to mean that Joseph would have power over them. Yet they did not let Joseph know what they thought, but instead prayed in secret that what they feared might not come to pass.

The second dream was even more wonderful than the first. It seemed to Joseph that the sun, the moon, and the stars came down from heaven and bowed down to him. He told this vision to his father in the presence of his brothers, and begged him to interpret it. Jacob was delighted with this dream, for it seemed to promise great things for his son. He surmised its meaning: the sun and moon signified the father and mother of Joseph, and the eleven stars were his brothers. The time would come when Joseph, by God's blessing, would be considered worthy of veneration by his parents and his brothers. The second dream made the brothers even angrier than the first.

A short time after the harvest, they went to Shechem, which A II,18 was famous for its pastures, and tended their flocks. But since they had not told their father they were leaving, Jacob grew worried and sent Joseph to see if he could find out anything about them. The brothers rejoiced when they saw Joseph approaching, for they had resolved to kill him. But Reuben, who was the oldest, objected, claiming that it was a great crime to kill a brother, even if he had done a serious wrong, and Joseph had done no wrong. But when they were not persuaded, he begged them at least not to kill their brother with their own hands, but to throw Joseph into a pit that was nearby, where he could die without defiling their hands with his blood. The young men agreed. Reuben took Joseph, tied a cord around him, and let him down gently into the pit, which was dry. Then he left to look for pastures suitable for the flocks.

After he was gone, Judah, another brother, saw a company of Ishmaelites, who were carrying spices and Syrian goods out of the land of Gilead to sell to the Egyptians. He convinced the others to pull Joseph out of the pit and sell him to these merchants, and thus be rid of him without the guilt of murder. They all agreed, and Joseph was lifted out of the pit and sold to the merchants for twenty pieces of silver.

At night, Reuben came back to the pit with the intention of secretly saving Joseph. When he called to him and received no answer, he was distressed, fearing his brothers had killed him after he had gone. When he went to them and complained, they told him what they had done, and Reuben was satisfied.

The brothers then wondered what they should tell their father. They had taken away from Joseph the tunic which he was wearing when he came to them, so they decided to tear it to pieces, and dip it into goat's blood. Then they would show it to Jacob, leading him to believe Joseph had been killed by wild animals. They came to the old man, and he recognized Joseph's tunic and, believing that he had been killed, was overcome with grief, and could not be comforted.

3
THE HEBREWS IN EGYPT

Joseph had been taken and sold by the merchants to Potiphar, A II,39 an Egyptian and chief of King Pharaoh's cooks. Potiphar found Joseph to be so trustworthy that he placed him in charge of his whole house, and taught him the liberal arts.

Potiphar's wife, however, fell in love with Joseph. Twice she proposed an illicit union, the second time feigning illness to avoid a public festival and be alone with him. But Joseph rejected her overtures, and when she tried to restrain him physically, he fled, leaving his cloak behind. When her husband returned, she said, "May you die, my husband, or else punish this wicked slave who tried to defile your bed." She went on, in tears, to accuse Joseph of attempted rape and produced the cloak as proof that Joseph had tried to violate her. Prouder than ever of his wife, Potiphar threw Joseph into the malefactors' prison.

Even in prison, however, God showed His providence. The keeper of the prison found that Joseph was careful and faithful in everything that he asked him to do, so he allowed Joseph better food than was given to the rest.

Often after working hard all day, the prisoners asked one another why they had been sentenced. Among them was the king's cupbearer, who told Joseph of a dream, since he had a high opinion of Joseph's wisdom, and asked him to interpret it. He saw in his sleep a vine with three branches, and on each branch was a cluster of grapes, large and ripe. He squeezed the juice of these grapes into a cup and gave this cup to the king to drink, and the king received it graciously. Then Joseph told the cupbearer to be happy, because the three branches in his dream meant three days, and within three days Pharaoh would release him from prison, and he would wait on the king as he had before. Joseph told the cupbearer to remember him when this good fortune arrived, and to speak to the king on his behalf, for he had been unjustly put into prison.

Another slave, once chief of the king's bakers, was also in prison, and asked Joseph to interpret his dream. "I thought," he said, "that I was carrying three baskets on my head, one on top of the other. Two were full of loaves, and the third contained pastry and other dainties, such as are prepared for kings. But birds came and ate them all up, though I tried to drive them away." When Joseph heard this dream he felt sorry for his friend. He told him that the baskets meant three days, and that on the third day he would be crucified and devoured by birds, being unable to defend himself.

It happened exactly as Joseph had foretold. On the third day after this conversation, the king freed the butler and restored him to his former position. But he had the chief baker taken out and crucified.

For another two years Joseph remained in prison, since the butler forgot all about him, until finally he was reminded about Joseph in the following way. One night Pharaoh had two dreams which greatly troubled him. When all the wisest men of the country failed to interpret them, he was even more distressed. Then the cupbearer remembered Joseph and his skill in dreams. He went to the king and reported that when he and the chief baker were in prison together, they each had a dream, and their dreams were interpreted by a young man in prison, and what he told them came true.

Then the king commanded that Joseph be removed from prison and brought to him. When he appeared, Pharaoh told him that he had heard of his skill in interpreting dreams, and that he had two dreams whose meaning he wished to know. "I thought," said the king, "that as I stood by the river, seven cows came up out of the water. They were large and fat, and they went into the marshes nearby. And seven other cows, who were lean and scrawny, met them at the marshes. They ate the fat cows, yet remained as lean and scrawny as before. Then I awoke. But I fell asleep again, and had another dream, more extraordinary than the first, which disturbed me even more. I saw seven ears of grain growing out of one root, all ripe and filled with wheat. And near these I saw seven other ears of grain which were spoiled and bad with no good wheat in them. And the seven bad ears ate up the seven good ones."

Then Joseph told the king that both his dreams meant the same thing. The seven fat cows and the seven good ears meant seven years of plenty. They symbolized fruitfulness for Egypt, while the seven lean cows and the seven bad ears meant seven years of famine and distress.

Joseph advised Pharaoh to prepare for this famine. He told him that during the seven good years he should see that the Egyptians were not wasteful of the grain, but were made to reserve what they would have spent in luxury for the time of want. He should take the grain away from the farmers as soon as it was ripe, and allow them only what would be sufficient for their needs.

Since Joseph had shown so much wisdom in explaining his dreams and in advising him, the king entrusted him with the duty of storing up the grain, and gave him power to do what he thought best for the benefit of Egypt. Joseph was clothed with purple, and he drove his chariot through all the land, taking grain from the farmers, allowing them only what was necessary for food and for seed. But he did not tell any of them the reason why.

Joseph Tests His Brothers

When Joseph was 30 years of age, the king, who held him in A II,91 high honor, provided a wife for him. She was a virgin named Asenath, who was the daughter of one of the priests of Heliopolis. Later, two sons were born to Joseph, Manasseh and Ephraim.

After Egypt had happily enjoyed seven years of prosperity, the famine arrived as Joseph had foretold. When the people came running to the king's gates, crying for bread, he summoned Joseph, who sold them grain. Nor did he limit this market for the people of Egypt only, but Joseph gave permission to strangers to buy also, believing that all men should have assistance from those who lived in prosperity.

Now Canaan had also suffered terribly from the famine. When Jacob learned of the open markets in Egypt, he sent all his sons there to purchase grain except for Benjamin. He was his child by Rachel, born of the same mother as Joseph.

The brothers came to Joseph to buy grain from him. Joseph recognized them at once, but they did not know him, for he was a boy of seventeen when they had sold him into slavery. He now appeared as an older man of exalted rank, and he proceeded to test them. He said it was impossible that a private man could bring up ten sons to be so distinguished, when even kings found it hard to do the same. He accused them of being spies, claiming that they really came from various countries and joined themselves together, only pretending to be related. Joseph said this to learn about his father and Benjamin, fearing that they might have gotten rid of his brother also.

The brothers were very distressed, assuming that they were in great danger. But Reuben, the eldest, spoke up and assured

Joseph that they were true and faithful men, not spies, and that they really were all brothers. "Our father's name," he said, "is Jacob, a Hebrew, and we, his twelve sons, were born to him by four wives. While we were all alive, we were a happy family, but when Joseph—one of our brothers—died, everything changed for the worse. Our father mourned him many years, and now we are afflicted, both on account of our brother's death and the sorrow of our aged father. We have now come to buy grain, having entrusted the care of our father to Benjamin, our youngest brother. If you send to our house, you may judge if we are guilty of any falsehood in what we say."

But Joseph put them in prison as if to question them at leisure. On the third day he released them, and told them that in order to satisfy him that what they said was true, they must bring their youngest brother with them the next time they came to Egypt. And as a pledge that they would do this, one of them was to remain behind until they returned.

Greatly troubled, the brothers wept, and told one another that God was now punishing them for their wickedness to Joseph.

The great pyramids and sphinx at Gizeh, near Cairo, which were already more than 1000 years old at the time of the Hebrew exodus.

Reuben, however, urged them to bear patiently the just punishment of God. They talked to each other in their own language, not knowing that Joseph understood them. But Joseph, seeing their distress, had to leave so that they would not see him weep. Soon he returned, and took Simeon as a hostage to insure that the others would return. Then he told them to take the grain they had bought and go their way. He also told his steward to put back secretly into each of their sacks the money they had paid.

Returning to Canaan, they told their father what had happened. He was very disturbed, and refused to let Benjamin return with them. When they opened the sacks of grain and found their money, they were even more perplexed. But in time, the grain they had bought was used up, and Jacob was forced to allow Benjamin to go with his brothers to Egypt to buy more grain. The old man and his sons wept bitterly at their departure. A II,111

As soon as they arrived in Egypt, they were brought before Joseph. Afraid that they would be accused of having cheated Joseph regarding the grain money, they made a long apology to Joseph's steward. They told him that when they arrived home they found the money in their sacks, and now they had brought it back with them. He said he did not know what they meant, and they were relieved.

Then Simeon was released and allowed to join them, and when Joseph arrived, the brothers offered him the presents of myrrh and honey which their father had sent. He asked how their father was, and they replied that he was well. Pointing to Benjamin, Joseph asked if he were the youngest brother they had spoken of, and they told him that he was. But when Joseph began to weep, he left, unwilling to betray himself to his brothers. Then he invited them to supper, and they were placed in the same order as at their father's table. Although Joseph treated them all kindly, he sent Benjamin double helpings of food.

After supper, when they had gone to bed, Joseph commanded his steward to give them their measures of grain, and again to hide the purchase money in their sacks. Joseph also had him put his favorite silver drinking cup into Benjamin's sack. He did this to test his brothers: would they stand by Benjamin and be arrested for theft, or abandon him, depending on their own innocence, and return to their father without him?

Early the next morning, the brothers started on their journey back to Canaan. They rejoiced at their good fortune, having been treated so kindly, and that they were returning with both Simeon and Benjamin. But suddenly they were surrounded by a troop of horsemen, including the steward who had placed the cup in Benjamin's sack. They asked, in surprise, the reason for this sudden attack, when just a little earlier their master had given them an honorable reception. The pursuers called them wicked wretches who had forgotten Joseph's kind hospitality, and had stolen their master's favorite cup. The brothers protested that they were innocent, asking that a search be made, and that if the cup were found, they should all be punished. But the steward answered that only the one who was guilty of the theft would be punished, and the rest should not be blamed. The troop searched until the cup was found in Benjamin's sack, and the brothers lamented, tearing their clothes, and weeping for the punishment which Benjamin was to undergo. Then they all returned with him to Joseph.

When they came before him, Joseph scolded them, saying, "Why, vile wretches, do you return evil for my kindness to you?" Yet he would let them return to their father in safety, he said, and punish only Benjamin.

The brothers were speechless in consternation until Judah spoke up. He said Benjamin was their father's most loved son, and none of them would go home without him. He begged that Joseph punish him instead of Benjamin. All the brothers threw themselves at Joseph's feet and offered themselves to save Benjamin.

Joseph could not contain himself any longer. Sending all the servants out of the room, he revealed his identity to his brothers. He told them that he had only tested their love for Benjamin, and found them better men than he had expected. "So," he continued, "I believe that all has happened according to God's will, and instead of bearing you a grudge, I return you my thanks."

Joseph then embraced his brothers, who were all in tears, and there was great feasting and rejoicing. Pharaoh heard of Joseph's good fortune in finding his brothers, and he sent them wagons full of grain, gold, and silver as presents for their father. Joseph also gave them many valuable gifts (to Benjamin in particular) and they went on their way.

A II,168   When Jacob learned that Joseph was not dead, but living in great splendor in Egypt, he immediately set out to visit his son. At Beersheba, he offered sacrifice to God. He was afraid that the prosperity in Egypt might tempt his children and their descendants to settle there rather than return to the land of Canaan, whose possession God had promised them. He also feared that if this departure to Egypt were made without God's sanction, his family might be destroyed there.

Tormented by these doubts, he fell asleep. But God appeared to him in a dream and assured him that the journey was in accordance with His wishes. "I come now," God said, "as your guide for this journey, and foretell that you will die in the arms of Joseph, and your descendants will long remain in authority and glory, and I will settle them in the land which I have promised.''

Encouraged by this dream, Jacob set out more cheerfully toward Egypt, along with the 70 in his family. When Joseph learned that his father was approaching, he went out to welcome him, and they met at a place called Heroopolis. Jacob almost fainted at this unexpected joy, and Joseph was also delighted. He advised his father to continue his journey slowly, while he hurried ahead with five of his brothers to let the king know that his family had arrived. Pharaoh rejoiced to hear this, and asked Joseph what sort of life they lived, so that he might allow them to follow the same trade. Learning that they were good shepherds, Pharaoh said they should be employed in this way in Egypt also.

When Jacob was brought before the king and saluted him, Pharaoh asked Jacob how old he was, and marveled greatly when told that he was 130 years old. He permitted Jacob to live with his children in Heliopolis, for near that city the king's shepherds pastured their flocks.

After Jacob had lived seventeen years in Egypt, he became ill and died. On his deathbed he prayed for his sons, and foretold that their descendants would possess the land of Canaan. He commanded his sons to admit Ephraim and Manasseh, the sons of Joseph, into their number and let them share in the division of Canaan.

Joseph, with the king's permission, carried his father's body to Hebron, and buried it there at great expense. His brothers were at first afraid to return to Egypt, fearing that after their father's death, for whose sake he had been so merciful, Joseph might be tempted to punish them for their former wickedness. But Joseph persuaded them not to be afraid. He brought them back with him, giving them great possessions, and never stopped holding them in highest favor.

At last, when Joseph was 110 years of age, he died, a man of admirable virtue. After living happily in Egypt, his brothers also died, and their descendants later buried them at Hebron.

4

MOSES AND THE EXODUS

After the death of Joseph and his brothers, the Israelites, as A II,201 their descendants were now called, flourished in Egypt. Meanwhile, the Egyptians, forgetful of the benefits they had received from Joseph, began to envy the prosperity and happiness of the children of Israel. The kingdom had passed to another dynasty, and they became very cruel to the Israelites, forcing them to cut numerous canals from the river, build walls around their cities, and erect pyramid after pyramid.

They spent 400 years enduring these afflictions. Eventually, they suffered a still greater cruelty. One of the Egyptian wise men, who was able to foretell the future, told Pharaoh that a child would be born to the Israelites. If he were allowed to live, he would diminish the Egyptian dominion and raise the Israelites. He would excel all men in virtue, and would obtain everlasting fame. Alarmed, the king commanded that every male child born to the Israelites be thrown into the river, and that if any parents should try to save their offspring, they and their families would be killed. This calamity was terrible, a plan sure to extinguish their race.

Amram, a Hebrew of noble birth, was greatly troubled be- A II,210 cause of this law, and he prayed to God. Appearing to him in his sleep, God reminded him of what He had done for the Israelites in the past, and told him He would continue His favor in the future. "Know, therefore," He continued, "that I will provide for your common welfare, and particularly for your own fame. For that child, whose birth has caused such dread that the Egyptians have doomed the Israelite children to destruction, shall be your child. He will be concealed from those who seek to destroy him. He will deliver the Hebrew nation from their bondage in Egypt, and his memory will live as long as the universe, not only among the Hebrews, but among other nations also."

After the vision, Amram awoke and told it to Jochebed, his wife. Shortly thereafter, she had an easy delivery, which was kept secret from the Egyptians. They nourished the child privately for three months, but after that, Amram, fearing it might be discovered and killed, decided to entrust the care of the infant to God. He and his wife made a basket of papyrus reeds, in the form of a cradle, and covered it with pitch to keep out the water. Putting the infant inside, they set it afloat on the river, commending it to God. But Miriam, the child's sister, kept pace with it along the river bank to see where the basket would go.

Pharaoh had a daughter named Thermuthis, who was playing by the river bank. Seeing the basket carried along by the current, she sent out some of her swimmers to bring it to her. When they returned with the basket, she was delighted with the size and

Moses Island in the Nile River near Cairo, the traditional site of his rescue by Pharaoh's daughter.

beauty of the little child. Thermuthis then ordered a woman to suckle the infant, but he spurned her breast, as well as those of several other women. Miriam then appeared and asked if she could go and call a Hebrew woman to nurse the child. The princess told her to do so. She went, and returned with her mother—no one there knew her—and the infant gleefully fastened on her breast. So, the princess had entrusted the nursing of the child to its own mother!

Thermuthis named him Moses, which means, in Egyptian, "saved from the water." His growth in understanding surpassed his stature, and his charm captivated passers-by as he was carried along the highway. She adopted him as her son, since she had no offspring of her own.

One day, Thermuthis brought Moses to her father and said, "I am bringing up a beautiful, well-behaved child. Since I received him from the bounty of the river, I thought best to adopt him as my son and heir of your kingdom." With that, she put the infant into his hands. He took him and kissed him, and playfully put his crown upon the child's head. But Moses threw it down to the ground and trod upon it with his feet in mere childishness. But when the sacred scribe saw this (he was the one who had foretold that a child would be born to the Hebrews who would reduce the dominion of Egypt) he made a violent attempt to kill him. He cried out, "This, O King, is that child we must kill to calm our terror! He shows it by treading upon your crown. Kill him, and deliver us from our fear and thus deprive the Hebrews of the hope he inspires!"

But Thermuthis stopped him, snatching the child away. The king hesitated to kill him, and Moses was educated with great care. The Hebrews, therefore, hoped that he would do great things, while the Egyptians were suspicious of him. Yet because there was no one else that would rule more wisely over Egypt, they refrained from killing him.

The Bravery of Moses*

When Moses had grown to be a man, war broke out between A II,238 the Egyptians and their neighbors the Ethiopians. They fought a great battle in which the Ethiopians were victorious, and they determined to conquer all of Egypt. Their armies invaded as far as Memphis and the sea. Overtaken by this calamity, the Egyptians turned to oracles and divinations. They were urged to seek the assistance of Moses and make him their general, so Pharaoh commanded his daughter to produce him. She made her father swear he would not harm him, and then brought Moses. But she reproached the priests who had previously advised to kill him, and were now not ashamed to ask his help.

---

* The story in this section is not contained in the Bible, and Josephus derived it from traditional sources.

Moses went out leading a great army, and he surprised the enemy before they knew he was coming. They expected that he would attack them by water, since the interior was difficult to traverse due to the vast number of poisonous snakes that infested it. But Moses devised a marvelous strategy. He took baskets full of ibises, a bird that devours serpents and is their greatest enemy. As soon as he reached the infested region, he released the ibises, and drove the serpents away. Moses then achieved his march and defeated the Ethiopians in a surprise attack. They fled Egypt, and were pursued by Moses into their own country and defeated again, to the extent that they were in danger of being reduced to slavery.

In the end they retired to Saba, the capital of Ethiopia. It was very difficult to besiege, as it was built on an island in the river Nile and surrounded by a great wall. Moses was impatient at having to stay idle, for it seemed mad to attempt an attack. However, the daughter of the king of the Ethiopians, Tharbis, saw Moses below the ramparts and fell madly in love with him because of his bravery. She sent him the most faithful of her servants to propose marriage. He accepted, provided she would surrender the city to him. No sooner was the agreement made than it took effect. When Moses had punished the Ethiopians, he gave thanks to God and celebrated his marriage. Then he led the Egyptians back to their own land.

Moses Flees to Midian

A II,254 Instead of being grateful to Moses for his success, the Egyptians hated him even more, partly because they were envious and partly because they were afraid. They thought he might take advantage of his good fortune and try to subvert their government. The king was also afraid of him, and prepared to assist in the murder of Moses. Learning that there were plots against him, Moses secretly escaped across the desert, since the roads were patrolled.

When he came to a city called Midian, near the Red Sea, he sat down by a well and rested after his long journey. Now water was very scarce there, and this well had been seized by some shepherds, who would not let any one else use it, fearing there would not be enough water left for their own flocks. While Moses was resting, seven sisters, who were daughters of a priest named Jethro, came and drew water, but the shepherds appeared and attacked them. Moses rose and beat them off, and then helped the girls. The sisters went home and told their father how the stranger had helped them, and asked that he not let this generous action go unrewarded. The father was pleased with his daughters' gratitude, and had them bring Moses to him. He thanked Moses for his kindness, and adopted him as his son. He also gave him one of his daughters in marriage, and appointed him as the guardian and master of his flocks.

One day, Moses led Jethro's flocks to graze on a mountain called Sinai. This was the highest of all the mountains there, and the best for pasture. But the shepherds were afraid to ascend it, believing that God dwelt there. And here Moses witnessed a wonderful prodigy: a fire sprang up out of a bramble bush, yet its green leaves and flowers were not consumed by it. Moses was terrified at this strange sight, and even more so when a voice out of the fire called to him by name. This voice, however, predicted the glory Moses would win under God's direction, and instructed him to return to Egypt where he would be made the commander and leader of the Hebrews. "For," said the voice, "they will live in the land which your forefather Abraham inhabited, and enjoy all its blessings. And it is you who will guide them there with your wisdom."

Astonished, Moses asked, "How will I, a private man of no abilities, persuade my countrymen to leave Egypt and follow me? And even if they might be persuaded, how can I force Pharaoh to let them go?"

But God urged him to be courageous, promising to help him speak when he needed to persuade men, and assist him when he was to perform miracles. He told him to throw his staff on the ground. It became a serpent and rolled itself around in its coils, rearing its head as if to dart at anyone that might attack. Then it became a staff again. Next, God had Moses put his right hand to his chest, and when he took it out, it was as white as chalk, but later returned to its natural color. Then Moses, at God's command, took some of the water that was near him and poured it on the ground, and it turned the color of blood. After this, God told him to use these wonders to convince all men that he was sent by God and that he did everything at His command. He also revealed His sacred name to Moses, which until then no human had heard, and of which I am forbidden to speak.

Moses, accordingly, returned to Jethro, and got permission to A II,277 go to Egypt to help his own people. He took with him Zipporah, his wife, and when he approached the borders of Egypt, his brother Aaron met him. He told Aaron about the amazing encounter on the mountain, and of God's commands. As they went on, they were met by the most distinguished of the Hebrews, and Moses also told them about these commands. When they doubted, he showed them the signs that God had taught him. Seeing these wonders, they took courage and believed that their day of deliverance had come.

Now the Pharaoh, from whom Moses had fled, had died, and a new king reigned. Moses went at once to his palace, and reminded him of what he had done for the Egyptians in their war against the Ethiopians, and how he had not received any reward for it. He also told the king what had happened to him on Mount Sinai, and when the king mocked, he showed him the signs. The king became angry, and called him a criminal who had escaped from his Egyptian slavery, and now was returning with fraudulent tricks and magical arts to deceive him. He then commanded the priests to display the same spectacles, proving that the Egyptians were skillful in magic also. The priests threw down their rods, and they became pythons.

But Moses was undaunted and said, "O King, I do not despise Egyptian cunning, but what I do is as much superior to what these do by magic tricks, as divine power exceeds that of humans. And I will show that my miracles are not done by craft or deceit, but by the power of God." With that, he dropped his staff on the ground, and commanded it to turn into a serpent. It obeyed, and went around devouring the python-like rods of the Egyptians until it had eaten them all. Then it reverted to its own form, and Moses picked up the staff.

However, the king was no more impressed than before, and becoming very angry, told Moses that he would gain nothing by

Like the Hebrews, Egyptians still make bricks in the Delta area from the red clay of the region.

this cunning and shrewdness at Egyptian expense. He commanded the chief taskmaster over the Hebrews to give them no rest from their work, but to subject them to even greater oppression than before. And although he had previously given them straw to make their bricks, he now made them work hard at brick-making during the day, and gathering straw at night.

When their labor was now doubled, the Hebrews blamed Moses. Yet he did not lose courage at the king's threats, nor did he yield to the Hebrews' complaints, but devoted all his efforts to liberating his countrymen. He again went to the king, and urged him to let the Hebrews go to Mount Sinai and sacrifice to God. Moses warned him not to oppose God's plan, or he would bring down terrible punishment on himself and his people. In any case, they would see the Israelites leave Egypt.

The Ten Plagues

But the king despised the words of Moses, and horrible A II,293 plagues came upon the Egyptians, unlike those of any nation before. First the river ran with bloody water, and the Egyptians who risked drinking it were overcome with great pain and torment. There was no other source of water, but to the Israelites the river was sweet, drinkable, and perfectly normal. Then the king, fearful and perplexed, gave the Israelites permission to go. But when the plague ended, he changed his mind.

God saw that he was ungrateful and unwise, so He sent a second plague on the Egyptians. A huge number of frogs spread over the land, and the river also was full of them. The frogs crept into their houses, ruining everything inside. They turned up in their food and drink, and swarmed across their beds. Again Pharaoh was afraid, and ordered Moses to take the Israelites and be gone, after which the frogs vanished. But as soon as Pharaoh saw the land free of the plague, he stopped the Israelites' departure.

The Deity punished him with a third plague. Innumerable quantities of lice appeared on the bodies of the Egyptians, and no lotion or salve would destroy the vermin. Pharaoh gave them permission to go, but when the plague stopped, he said they must leave their wives and children behind as pledges that they would return. God was provoked and sent another plague, filling the country with wild beasts of every species that had never been seen before. But Pharaoh refused to yield to this plague. He would only allow the Israelites and their wives to go if they left their children behind. So the Deity punished the land with even worse calamities. The bodies of the Egyptians broke out into terrible sores, and a great number of them died. Then

Two of the four colossal statues of Rameses II which stand at Abu-Simbel along the Upper Nile. Some scholars suggest that he may have been the Pharaoh of the Oppression.

hail descended in the spring, larger than had ever been seen, and beat down their crops. After this, a horde of locusts ate whatever seed had not been ruined by the hail, so that all hope of harvest was lost.

Still Pharaoh contested with God, and ordered Moses to take the Israelites away with their wives and children but to leave their cattle behind. So a thick darkness covered the land of the Egyptians, blinding their sight and hindering their breathing. This lasted three days and nights.

Then God told Moses that with one more plague He would compel the Egyptians to let the Israelites go. Moses told his people to get ready for the journey. In every household he commanded that a lamb should be killed as a sacrifice, and its blood sprinkled on the door-post. Then the lamb should be roasted and eaten, and whatever portion of it was left should be burned.

That night God went through the land of Egypt, and the first-born in every Egyptian house died. But He passed over every house that was marked with bloodstains, so that none of the Israelites died. In commemoration of this event, the children of Israel have celebrated a yearly feast called Passover, because God passed over their households while visiting the plague on the Egyptians.

Multitudes of those in homes surrounding the palace now went to Pharaoh and begged him to let the Israelites go. He himself was now anxious to be rid of them, so he summoned Moses and ordered him to depart. The Egyptians even gave them gifts, some to speed their departure, and others out of friendship for old acquaintances.

The Crossing of the Red Sea

Thus the Israelites departed from Egypt. Their total number, A II,315 including women and children, is not known with certainty, but those of military age numbered 600,000. They left Egypt 215 years after Jacob had moved there with his sons*, and in Moses' eightieth year.

The Egyptians, however, soon regretted having allowed the Israelites to go. Pharaoh was also mortified, and gathered together his soldiers, his horses, and 600 chariots, in order to pursue the fugitives.

Moses was avoiding the direct route to Canaan and was instead taking the difficult journey through Sinai. He wanted to evade the Philistines, and also fulfill God's directive to sacrifice

---

* This is inconsistent with Josephus' earlier claim that the Hebrews endured a 400–year oppression in Egypt.

Pharaoh Rameses II at Abu-Simbel.

at Mount Sinai. The Egyptian army caught sight of them just as they reached the banks of the Red Sea. The Israelites were unarmed, and could not fight. They were trapped between mountain cliffs and the Red Sea in front of them, so they could not flee. In despair, the Hebrews considered surrendering to the Egyptians and stoning Moses, for their women and children were wailing in the face of death. But Moses, assuring them that God would not forsake them in their trouble, led the Israelites to the sea. Having prayed to God, he struck the sea with his staff. The waters parted and rolled back on each side, leaving the sea bed dry. He walked down on the dry ground, and the Israelites followed him.

Now when the Egyptians saw the Israelites descend into the sea, they thought at first they were mad and were rashly going to certain death. But when they saw that they had gone a great distance without any harm, they hurried to pursue them. By the time they had armed themselves and reached the shore of the sea, the Israelites had safely crossed over to the other side. The Egyptians marched down into the sea in pursuit, but were not aware that this was a road reserved for the Hebrews. It was not a public highway, but was intended to save those in danger, not their attackers. As soon as the whole army was in the sea, the waters came together again and covered them. Torrents of rain also fell from the sky with dreadful thunder and lightning. All these men perished and not one was left to tell the rest of the Egyptians what had happened.

The Hebrews were unable to contain their joy at the miraculous deliverance and the destruction of their enemies. All night long they celebrated in song and mirth. Moses also composed a song to God in hexameter verse, praising and thanking Him for His kindness.

No one should doubt this astonishing narrative. Whether by the will of God or by accident, the armies of Alexander, king of Macedon, saw the Pamphylian Sea retreat before them and offer a passage through itself.*

The next day, the tide was fanned by a west wind, and deposited Egyptian arms at the Hebrews' camp. Moses, surmising that this was also due to God's providence, collected them and armed his men. Then he led them on to Mount Sinai.

Manna Falls

It was not long before the Hebrews' rejoicing again turned into A III,1 moaning and sorrow. The country into which they had come was a desert, and there was nothing to eat or drink. They had brought some water along, but this was soon depleted, and they were forced to dig wells with great effort, due to the hard ground. The little water they found was bitter and not fit for drinking.

One evening they came to a place called Marah, because of the vile nature of its water, for *mar* means "bitterness." Here was the only well in the region, yet its water was bitter, and not fit for man or beast. Moses grieved to see his people in distress, for they ran to him begging: the men for the women, and the women for the infants and children. He prayed, therefore, that God would change the water. When God had granted him that favor, he took a stick that lay at his feet, split it, and threw it into the well. He told the Hebrews that God had heard his prayer and would sweeten the water if they followed his orders. When they asked what they were to do, he directed the strongest men among them to stand in a circle and draw up water. After most of it was taken out, the remainder would be fit to drink. So they worked at it until the water came up sweet and pure.

---

* See Arrian, I, 26, and Strabo, XIV, 666 ff.

Elim, the oasis which refreshed the Israelites with its twelve springs and 70 palms, is very likely this site in the Sinai desert, not far from the Red Sea.

They journeyed on and came to Elim. This place looked pleasant from a distance, for there was a grove of 70 palm trees there. But when they arrived, the palms were found to be dwarfed and feeble for lack of moisture. Having exhausted their provisions on the thirtieth day of the march, the people complained bitterly, and blamed Moses. But he came among them even as they accused him and had stones in their hands to kill him. Reminding them of the wonderful ways God had helped them in the past, he promised that He would assist them also in the future. This pacified the people and restrained them from stoning him.

Then he went up a hill to pray for help, and God promised to supply their needs. Soon, a vast flock of quail—of a species abundant in the Arabian Gulf—fell down on the Hebrews, who ate them and were satisfied. Moses thanked God for this assistance.

Following this first supply of food, He sent them a second. As Moses was lifting up his hands in prayer, a white dew descended. When he found it sticking to his hands, he guessed that this also was food sent by God. He tasted it and found it delicious. Since the people thought it had snowed, he told them this dew was not as they supposed, but was sent them for food.

They tasted it and were pleased, for it was like honey in sweetness and pleasant flavor, but like coriander seed in size. They were very eager to gather it up, but were told to collect only as much as was necessary for one day, because every day there would be more. Some distrusted this promise and gathered up more than was necessary, but the next day they found it spoiled and wormy. The Hebrews called it *"manna,"* which means, "What is this?"

They continued their journey and came to Rephidim, where again they thirsted, and again vented their anger against Moses. He avoided the multitude's fury, and asked God to give them drink. God promised Moses He would procure for them a spring and plenty of water, from where they would least expect. He commanded Moses to strike a rock with his staff. When he did so, water gushed out in abundance, and it was very sweet and pure. They were all astonished at this wonderful provision and offered sacrifice to God.

The probable location of Rephidim in the Sinai, where Moses struck the rock in order to provide water for the thirsty Israelites.

Victory Over the Amalekites

A III,39 Now the Amalekites, the most warlike people in that region, heard of the coming of the Hebrews and determined to fight them. Moses encouraged his people to be brave and to resist these enemies. There was a good, courageous man among them, named Joshua, of the tribe of Ephraim, whom Moses chose to be their commander. When the Amalekites arrived, the battle broke out and both sides fought long and bravely. Moses, his brother Aaron, and another man named Hur had gone up a mountain to pray for their people. As long as Moses stretched out his hands toward heaven, the Hebrews defeated the Amalekites. But when he became tired and lowered them, the Amalekites prevailed. Therefore Aaron and Hur stood on each side of him and held up his hands. This enabled the Hebrews to conquer the Amalekites, and they would have killed them all if darkness had not intervened to stop the bloodshed.

This was a strategic victory, for it so terrified their enemies that they dared not attack them. Moreover, a great deal of silver and gold was left in the enemy's camp, as well as brass vessels and other items of practical use. The Hebrews now began to pride themselves on their courage and strength, and believed that they could achieve anything if they worked hard enough.

The next day, Moses stripped the dead bodies of the enemy and collected the armor of those who had fled and left it behind. He also gave rewards to those who had distinguished themselves in battle, and he highly commended Joshua, whom all the army praised. He also foretold that the Amalekites would be utterly destroyed, because they had fought the Israelites when they were in distress in the wilderness. He then refreshed the army with festivity and allowed them to rest a few days. Finally, advancing in short stages, they reached Mount Sinai, three months after leaving Egypt.

5
SINAI

Now Jethro, his father-in-law, had heard of his success, and A III,63 warmly welcomed Moses and Zipporah with their children. Moses had a great feast for him, near the place where he had seen the vision of the burning bush, and all the multitude shared in the festivity. Then they sang hymns of thankfulness, and Jethro made a speech praising the people, especially their leader, Moses.

The next day, Jethro saw Moses in the midst of a great crowd, settling their disputes, for whenever they differed about anything they came to Moses. They believed that he would give them justice, and so they kept him very busy. After the day's work, Jethro took him aside and counseled him to leave the lesser disputes to others. He should judge only the greater ones, for others could be found who were fit to decide disputes, but only Moses could care for the safety of the people by interceding with God.

"Review the army," Jethro advised, "and appoint chiefs over units of 10,000 men, divided into thousands, then into groups of 500, and again into hundreds, and into fifties. Let each group have its own officer, to be approved by the whole multitude as a good and righteous man. These officers should decide the controversies for people under them, but let them refer any serious problem to the higher officials. Then if it is too hard for even their determination, let them send it up to you. In this way, two advantages will be gained: the Hebrews will have justice done them and you will be able to attend constantly on God."

Moses gladly accepted his advice. Nor did he hide the origin of this method, but informed the multitude who devised it.

Jebel Safsafa, the northern face of Mt. Sinai, according to ancient tradition, before which the Israelites encamped in what is today a vast and sagebrush-dotted plain, while Moses ascended to receive the Decalogue. Centuries later, the prophet Elijah would also spend some time here.

Moses even named Jethro in the books he wrote as the person who invented this system, which indicates the integrity of Moses.

Moses Ascends Mount Sinai

Now Moses called the people together and told them that he A III,75 was going to Mount Sinai to talk with God. He directed them to pitch their tents near the mountain while he went up Mount Sinai, which is very difficult to climb due to its height and precipices. It was also an awesome place because of the belief that God lived there. The Hebrews moved their tents, as Moses had ordered, and occupied the foot of the mountain. They were glad that Moses would return from God with promises of blessings, so they feasted and put on their best clothing, celebrating for two days.

But on the third day before sunrise, a cloud spread itself over the whole camp of the Hebrews. They had not seen any like it before, and it enveloped the place where they had pitched their tents. And while the rest of the sky was clear, strong winds brought torrents of rain, along with lightning and thunder. These sights and sounds terrified the Hebrews, for they were extraordinary, and the rumor that God frequented the mountain alarmed them even more. So they quivered inside their tents, fearing that Moses had been destroyed by divine wrath and expecting a similar fate for themselves.

While tormented by these fears, they suddenly saw Moses coming down the mountain, his face joyful and exalted. The air also became clear and pure as the storm passed. Then Moses called together all the people, and stood on a platform so that all could hear him.

"Hebrews," he said, "God has received me graciously as before, and has dictated rules for a happy life and an orderly government. And He is now present in the camp. I therefore charge you, do not scorn what I am going to say, because the commands do not come from me, Moses, the son of Amram and Jochebed, but from Him who caused the Nile to run bloody for your sakes, and tamed the haughtiness of the Egyptians by various plagues; who opened a path through the sea; who sent us food from heaven when we were hungry, and made the water to gush out of a rock when thirsty; by whose means Adam enjoyed the fruits of the land and the sea, and Noah escaped the deluge, and our forefather Abraham settled in Canaan; by whom Isaac was born of aged parents, and Jacob was graced with twelve virtuous sons; by whom Joseph became lord over the Egyptians' might—it is He who conveys these instructions to you through me as His interpreter. Hold them in great respect, for if you will follow them, you will lead a happy life. The land will be fruitful, and the sea calm. You will also be invincible to your enemies. For I have been admitted into the presence of God, I have listened to His immortal voice—so great is His concern for our race and its perpetuation.''

Then he brought the people, with their wives and children, near the mountain that they might hear God Himself speaking. And they all heard a voice that came from above and spoke ten commandments, which Moses has left inscribed on two tables.

A III,91   The first commandment teaches us that there is but one God, and that we ought to worship Him only. The second commands us not to make the image of any living creature for adoration. The third, that we must not swear by God in any frivolous matter. The fourth, that we must keep the seventh day, by resting from all work. The fifth, that we must honor our parents. The sixth, that we must refrain from murder. The seventh, that we must not commit adultery. The eighth, that we must not steal. The ninth, that we must not bear false witness. The tenth, that we must not covet anything that belongs to another.

When the multitude had heard God Himself giving these precepts, they rejoiced in these commandments, and the congregation was dissolved. But on the following days they came to Moses' tent and asked him to bring them other laws from God, and he did so.

Again Moses went up Mount Sinai, but stayed there so long—40 days—that fear seized the Hebrews. Nothing horrified them more than the thought that Moses had died. Some said that he had fallen among wild beasts, and others that he had gone to God. But the camp dared not move, because Moses had ordered them to stay there.

Finally, after 40 days and nights, Moses came down, having tasted no food during that time. His appearance filled the army with joy, and he revealed how much God cared for them, and what sort of government would promote their happiness. He also said that God wanted a tabernacle made, into which He could descend whenever He came among them. They were to carry it about with them, and would no longer need to ascend Sinai. Then Moses showed them two tables with the ten commandments engraved on them, five on each table; and the writing was by the hand of God.*

---

* Josephus omits the episode of the golden calf (Exodus 32) because it would have been embarrassing to Judaism before a Greco-Roman readership, and would have assisted the malicious rumor at that time that Jews worshiped an ass.

The Tabernacle

The people rejoiced at what Moses told them, and they A III,102 brought him silver and gold, brass and wood of all kinds, so that he might build the tabernacle. He appointed architects, and gave them the plans for the building, which he had drawn from directions given by God Himself.

The tabernacle, a large tent, was nothing less than a portable, traveling temple. It was 30 cubits long, 10 wide, and was divided into two rooms. In the first, the priests were admitted to perform their duties, but the second—the "Holy of Holies"—no one could enter except the high priest. In the Holy of Holies was placed the Ark of the Covenant. This was a chest made of stout wood and covered over with gold. On its top were the figures of two winged cherubs, and inside were placed the two tables of the ten commandments. The tabernacle stood in a large court, which was surrounded by a wall made of poles and curtains. At the entrance of the court was a large altar on which animals were burned as sacrifices. Between this altar and the entrance to the tabernacle was the laver, made of brass, where the priests washed.

[At this point, Josephus devotes many pages to describing the vestments of the priests, a roster of festivals, and detail about Hebrew ceremonial law.]

The tribe of Levi, to which Moses and Aaron belonged, was set apart to furnish priests for all the Hebrews. Aaron was appointed high priest, for God had so commanded. Beautiful garments were made for him, which he was to wear when performing his sacred duties.

The Spies

They broke camp at Mount Sinai and came to a place called A III,295 Hazeroth. Here, suffering again from thirst, they became rebellious and complained, blaming Moses for taking them out of Egypt with false promises. They also wanted meat, and Moses promised he would obtain for them a great quantity for many days. They were not willing to believe this, so Moses replied, "Although we hear many complaints from you, neither God nor I will abandon our labors for you." And indeed, he had barely finished speaking when the whole camp was filled with great numbers of quail, and the people gathered them. But shortly afterward, God punished the Hebrews for their disrespect, and many of them died.

From Hazeroth Moses led them to Paran, which was near the borders of Canaan. He gathered the people together, and said: "Two things God promised to grant us: liberty and the possession of a happy land. The first you now enjoy, and the other you will quickly obtain. For now we are near the borders of Canaan, which no human strength can prevent our taking. Let us then prepare ourselves for the task, for the Canaanites will not give up their land without fighting. We must first send spies to view the richness of the land and the strength of its defenders. But above all, let us be of one mind and honor God, who is our helper and ally.''

Twelve scouts were chosen, one from each tribe, who traversed Canaan for 40 days, and then returned. They brought with them some of the fruit that grew in the land, and reported

Grapes and pomegranates today in the Valley of Eschol, from which Joshua and Caleb brought back sample fruit to Moses and the Israelites.

many good things about the country. The multitude was pleased, and wanted to go to war at once. But the spies went on to warn them of the great difficulty in obtaining the land: rivers so large and deep that they could not be crossed, and cities fortified by walls and ramparts.

Now convinced that it was impossible to get possession of the country, the people moaned, as if God had made false promises. Again they blamed Moses and also his brother Aaron, the high priest, and spent that night murmuring. The next morning they rushed together, intending to stone Moses and Aaron, and then return to Egypt.

But two of the spies, Joshua and Caleb, went into the middle A III,308 of the crowd and restrained them, challenging them to be courageous and not believe those who had frightened them. They assured them that neither mountains nor rivers could deter men of true courage, especially when God would assist them.

Meanwhile, Moses and Aaron fell to the ground and prayed to God. They did not ask for their own deliverance, but that He would settle the people's minds, which were disordered by passion. The cloud then appeared and stood over the tabernacle, demonstrating to them the presence of God.

Moses now boldly informed the people that God was disgusted at their insolence, and would punish them, not as they deserved, but as fathers correct their children. "For," he said, "when I was in the tabernacle in tears, God recalled the things He had done for you, and yet how ungrateful you had been, thinking the words of spies truer than His own promise to you. Therefore, He will not destroy you all, nor utterly exterminate your race, which He esteemed above all mankind. Yet He will not permit you to take possession of the land of Canaan or enjoy its happiness. Instead, He will make you wander in the wilderness and live without home or city for 40 years, as a punishment for your transgression. He has promised, however, to give that land to your children. He will make them masters of those good things which, by your ungoverned passions, you have deprived yourselves of."

The people were overcome with grief, and pleaded with Moses to intercede for them with God to spare them this wandering in the wilderness and give them cities. Moses answered that he could not do this; that God had not determined lightly or rashly, but had deliberately passed sentence on them.

Murmuring Against Moses

The life which the Hebrews led in the wilderness was so hard A IV,1 and disagreeable that, although God had forbidden them to meddle with the Canaanites, they attacked them anyway, believing they could defeat them even without Moses' support. They claimed that God watched over them not because of Moses, but on account of their forefathers, and because of their own virtue He had obtained their liberty. And even if Moses should alienate God from them, it was best for them to be their own masters and no longer endure the tyranny of Moses.

Having decided that this was the best course, they marched to battle against their enemies. But the enemy was not dismayed either by the attack itself, or the multitude that made it, and fought courageously. Many of the Hebrews were killed, and the rest of the army, very confused, fled and were pursued to their camp. Filled with despair, they now understood that this affliction came from the wrath of God, because they rashly went to war without His consent.

Moses was afraid that the enemy might grow insolent at this victory and attack them, so he decided to withdraw the army away from the Canaanites into the desert. The people once again submitted to his leadership.

A IV,11   Great armies, especially after reverses, are often ungovernable, which was the case with the Jews. Because the 600,000 were hardly subordinate even in success, due to their vast numbers, the present distress made them unusually angry, both with each other and with their leader. A sedition broke out, through which they were all in danger of being destroyed.

A man named Korah, distinguished both by birth and wealth, was of the same tribe as Moses and also related to him. This made him all the more jealous, because he thought that, being his equal in birth and of far greater wealth, it was not fair that Moses should be his superior. But he was especially angry because Aaron, the brother of Moses, had been appointed high priest rather than himself. So, gathering around him 250 of his friends, he raised a great clamor against Moses. They said he should not have conferred the priesthood on his own brother, when there were so many others better suited for the office. Korah was able to speak well and was very persuasive, so others also conspired with him who provoked the people to rebel. They denounced Moses, saying that God never chose Aaron for the priesthood, because He would not have passed over so many superior persons for one who was inferior. Or, even if He did choose Aaron, He meant the honor to be bestowed on him by the people and not by his own brother.

Moses was not afraid of these calumnies, for he knew that he had always acted correctly. He shouted to Korah at daybreak that he and all others who wished to be appointed to the office of high priest should come to the tabernacle, carrying a censer full of burning incense. Aaron would do the same, and the Lord would decide which man He chose to be high priest.

The multitude was pleased with this, and the next day they gathered together at the tabernacle in order to be present at the sacrifice. But Abiram and Dathan, two of the men who had desired the priesthood, refused to be present at the decision, although Moses sent for them to come. Then Moses himself went out to their tents, inviting the leaders of the people to follow. There he prayed in a loud voice, asking God to give a sign of His displeasure. Suddenly, the ground heaved in a motion like that which the wind produces in the waves of the sea. The people were terrified. Then the earth underneath those tents gave way with a great boom, and the victims and all their possessions sank into it and were swallowed up and totally obliterated. The ground that had opened under them closed again and became as it was before.

Now Moses called for those who aspired to the priesthood, that he whose sacrifice best pleased God might be selected. A group of 250 men gathered, all of whom were honored by the people. Aaron and Korah also arrived, and they all offered incense in their censers before the tabernacle. Instantly, a great fire blazed down, a brilliant flame with fierce heat such as is kindled at the command of God alone. It destroyed the entire company, including Korah himself, so completely that no trace was left of their bodies. Aaron alone was preserved, because it was God who sent the fire.

But the people were still not satisfied, and continued to complain about the priesthood. Moses therefore called the multitude together and patiently heard what they had to say. Then he asked that the heads of the tribes should each bring a staff to him, inscribed with the name of the tribe to which each belonged. He whose staff God marked should receive the priesthood. This was approved. So they brought their staffs, as did Aaron. Aaron had written upon his staff "Levi," the tribe to which he belonged. Moses placed these staffs in the tabernacle of God. The next day he brought them out before the multitude. While those of the others were the same as before, Aaron's staff had sprouted with buds and ripe almonds, the staff having been cut from an almond tree. The people were so amazed at this strange sight that they abandoned their hatred of Moses and Aaron. They accepted the favorable judgment of God, and permitted Aaron to enjoy the priesthood honorably, and also his children after him.

Now the tribe of Levi was exempted from military service in order to devote itself to the service of God. Moses supported their sacred ministry by commanding the Hebrews to assign 48 cities to the Levites, as well as the surrounding land, after they conquered Canaan. The people were also to pay a tithe of the annual produce for their support.

Moses then set out with his whole army and came to the borders of Idumea. Sending envoys to their king, he asked for passage through their country, but was refused. Since God had not authorized battle, Moses withdrew.

Shortly after this, Miriam, the sister of Moses and Aaron, died. In the same year, the Israelites came to a place called Petra, in Arabia. Aaron, having been warned by Moses that the time had come for him to die, went up a high mountain in the sight of them all. He took off his priestly garments and delivered them to Eleazar, one of his sons, to whom the high priesthood belonged because he was the eldest. Then, while the multitude was watching, he died.

The Defeat of King Sihon and Og

A IV,85   The people mourned 30 days for Aaron, after which Moses moved the army on to the river Arnon, which plunges into Lake Asphaltitis [the Dead Sea]. On the other side of this river lay the land of the Amorites, a fruitful region capable of supporting a host of men. Moses sent messengers to Sihon, the king of this country, asking if he would grant his army passage. He promised not to harm the country or its inhabitants. But Sihon refused, put his army in battle array, and prepared to stop the Israelites from crossing the river.

Moses then asked God if He would give him permission to fight. God answered yes, and that He would give him the victory, so they joyfully put on their armor and went to meet the enemy. Although brave enough before the battle, the foe proved cowardly, fleeing even before the first attack. The Hebrews pursued them with a great slaughter. Sihon, their king, was also killed, and the Hebrews took possession of their land, which was full of abundance. Thus the Amorites were destroyed, being neither wise in council nor brave in action.

Meanwhile, Og, the king of Gilead and Gaulanitis, attacked the Israelites. He was a friend of King Sihon, and had quickly gathered an army to come to his assistance. Finding him already dead, Og determined to avenge him by defeating the Hebrews. But after a great battle, he was himself defeated and killed. Og was a huge and handsome king, and he had ruled over 60 cities, all of which fell into the hands of the Israelites. He was a giant, his iron bedstead measuring four cubits in width, and nine in length.

The Prophet Balaam

The Israelites journeyed on and came to the land of the Moa- A IV,102
bites. Their king, named Balak, saw how great the Israelites
were growing and became very concerned. He did not know that
the Hebrews would not meddle with any other country, but
were to be content with the possession of the land of Canaan, as
God had ordained. Not judging it prudent to fight them after
they had met with such great successes, Balak sent ambassadors
to the neighboring country of the Midianites to consult with
them.

Now these Midianites knew that there was a great prophet
named Balaam who lived on the Euphrates River. They sent
some of their notables along with the ambassadors of Balak to
urge the prophet to come and curse the Israelites. Balaam received the ambassadors very kindly, and told them that he was
willing to comply with their request, but that God was opposed
to it, because He favored the army which they asked Balaam to
curse. Balaam therefore advised them to go home and renounce
their hatred of the Israelites.

But the Midianites, at the urgent insistence of Balak, sent
another group to Balaam, and at last he consented. He saddled
his ass and started on the journey. But an angel of God met him
on the road at a narrow passage which was hedged in with a wall
on both sides. Balaam could not see the angel, but the ass did,
and backed against one of the walls, ignoring the blows which
Balaam gave her as he was crushed against the wall. But when
the angel continued to distress the ass, and Balaam redoubled
his blows, she fell down. Then, by the will of God, the ass spoke
in a human voice, complaining of Balaam's injustice in whip-
ping her when she was hindered in proceeding by God Himself.
While he was startled at hearing his ass speak, the angel became
visible to Balaam, and blamed him for his cruelty, telling him
that the beast was not at fault but he himself. Terrified, Balaam
would have turned back, but God told him to go on, and instead
to speak only what He suggested to Balaam's mind.

Balak received the prophet joyfully. When he had been entertained in a magnificent manner, he was asked to go up one of the
mountains to view the camp of the Hebrews. Balak and his
attendants went up the mountain with him. At the top, Balaam
ordered seven altars built, and as many bulls and rams delivered, and the king did so. Balaam offered sacrifice and began to
prophesy, declaring that the Israelites were a happy people
because God was with them. They would excel all nations in
virtue and take possession of the land which God had desig-

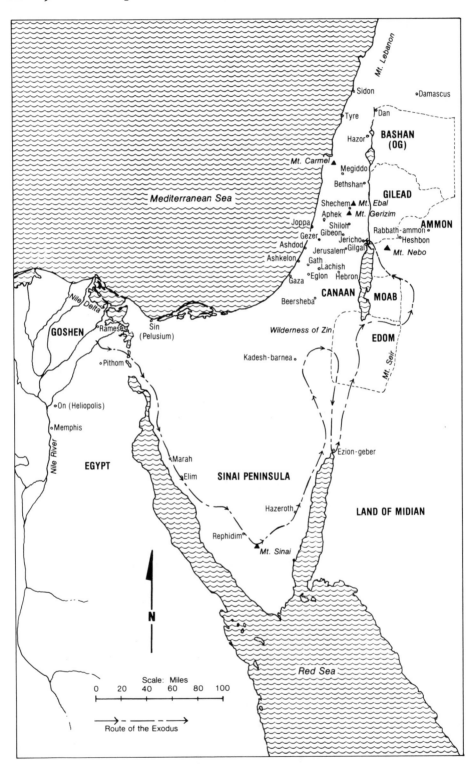

THE ROUTE OF THE EXODUS

nated for them. They would be numerous enough to supply every region of the world with inhabitants from their race.

Balak was furious, and accused Balaam of breaking his contract with him, because instead of cursing his enemies he had blessed them. But Balaam answered that he could not help it, for God put His words in the mouths of the prophets. "But now," he continued, "let me oblige you and offer the sacrifices again, and see whether I can persuade God to permit me to bind these men with curses."

When Balak agreed, God again prevented Balaam from cursing the Israelites. Then Balaam fell on his face and foretold the calamities that would afflict the great cities of the earth. Balak was fuming, and sent the prophet away without any of the gifts he had promised him. Balaam, however, did tell Balak and the Midianites of a plan by which they could destroy the Hebrews. He advised that the Midianite girls should make the young Israelites fall in love with them and then make the Hebrew youths abandon the Lord for Midianite gods. Following this advice, the Midianites lured many distinguished Hebrews into apostasy. Then God was angry, and sent a great plague, which destroyed 14,000 transgressors.

Because of what the Midianites had done, Moses sent an army A IV,159 of 12,000 to destroy them. The Midianites were defeated in a great battle, in which their five kings were killed. The Hebrew army returned rejoicing, with a great number of oxen, sheep, and asses which they had captured, as well as quantities of gold and silver for use in their homes.

About this time the tribes of Gad and Reuben, as well as half the tribe of Manasseh, came to Moses and asked that they be given the land of Gilead, which had been captured from the Amorites, since it was excellent for pasturing flocks. Moses at first was angry, believing that they wanted to stay there because they were afraid of fighting the Canaanites. He said to them, "Will you rest here while your brothers go to war?" But they answered that once they had built cities to defend their wives and children and possessions, they would rejoin the army. Moses was satisfied, and called for Eleazar, the high priest, and for Joshua and the heads of the other tribes. They granted the Amorite land to these tribes on condition that they would fight alongside their brothers until the general settlement.

The Death of Moses

The 40 years of wandering had almost come to an end, and A IV,176 only 30 days were left. Moses felt—on God's prompting—that it was time for him to die.* So he appointed Joshua to be his successor, both as commander of the armies and as prophet to receive the messages of God. God had indicated to Moses that this was the man of His choice. Then Moses called together an assembly near the Jordan at Abile [Abel-Shittim] and delivered many words of wisdom to them, as well as laws for their government. [Here Josephus provides a detailed summary of Mosaic laws cited in the Pentateuch, particularly Deuteronomy.]

On one of the following days, he recited a poem he had composed in hexameter that contained predictions of future events, which happened, or are happening, as Moses predicted. He delivered all the books which he had written to the priests, as well as the tabernacle and the ark, which contained the ten commandments written on two tables. He also exhorted the Israelites that when they had conquered the land of Canaan they were to destroy all the people and not forget the insolence of the Amalekites, but take vengeance for what they had done to them while in the wilderness. The tribes were also to pronounce blessings on those who were diligent in the worship of God, but curses on those who would transgress His laws. He wrote down these blessings and curses that they might never be forgotten, and also inscribed them on each side of the altar. These ordinances of Moses are observed by the Hebrew nation to this day.

A IV,309   The next day, he again called the people together, all the men, women, and children, and even the slaves. They were all to swear to observe the laws which he had given them and to take vengeance on those who disobeyed. The people took the oath. He also warned them that if they broke this vow they would experience great misfortune. "Your lands," he said, "will be overrun by your enemies, and your cities and temples overthrown. You will be sold as slaves to hard masters and your repentance will be too late."

Finally, Moses said the time had come for him to join his forefathers, as this was the day appointed for his death. He said farewell, blessed them again, and commended them to God. The multitude broke into tears, the women beating their breasts and the children crying. Moses knew that he should not be sad at the approach of death, yet what the people did overcame him and he also wept.

As he went on to where he would disappear, they all followed after him weeping. But Moses signaled with his hand to those

---

* According to Deuteronomy 32:15, Moses was condemned to die before the Israelites entered Canaan because he broke faith with God in the wilderness of Zin. As a great admirer of Moses, however, Josephus omits this embarrassing detail.

that were far off to be quiet, and he urged those near him not to make his departure so sorrowful. So they sobbed in silence, and let him depart as he desired. Only the tribal elders, with Eleazar and Joshua, followed him. But then he came to the mountain called Abarim, which is opposite the city of Jericho, and provides those on its summit a wide view of the land of Canaan. There he dismissed the elders. As he said farewell to Eleazar and Joshua, and was still talking with them, a cloud suddenly descended on him, and he disappeared in a ravine.

Moses was 120 years old at his death, having ruled over the Hebrews for 40 years. The people mourned for 30 days, and no grief ever affected them as deeply as this.

THE 6
CONQUEST OF CANAAN

When the mourning for Moses was over, Joshua commanded A V,1
the people to prepare for a military campaign. He sent spies to
Jericho, to discover what forces it had. Meanwhile, he reviewed
his army, intending to cross the Jordan soon. The rulers of the
tribes of Reuben, Gad, and Manasseh, who had been allowed to
settle in the country of the Amorites, were called before Joshua.
He reminded them of their promises to Moses, and told them to
prepare themselves quickly. Thus 50,000 of them accompanied
him, and he marched from Abile toward the Jordan.

After he had pitched his camp, the spies returned, full of
intelligence about the Canaanites. They had been able to survey
all of Jericho without being detected. They noted where the
walls were strong, or insecure, and which of the gates were
weak enough to allow the army to enter. At first those they met
ignored them, thinking they were merely strangers. But at night
they retired to an inn near the wall, which was kept by a woman
named Rahab. They ate supper there, and were planning their
escape. But information was given to the king that some had
come from the Hebrews' camp to spy on the city, and that they
were at Rahab's inn. The king sent men to arrest them, so that he
could torture them and learn why they had come. But Rahab hid
the spies under some bundles of flax drying on her roof. She told
the king's messengers that some strangers had eaten with her a
little before sunset, and had just left, but might easily be caught.
The messengers ran off at once down the road they thought the
spies had taken, but found no trace of them.

After the commotion, Rahab brought the men down and asked
that when they had overcome the land, to remember the risk she
had taken for their sakes. And she made them swear to save her

and her family. The spies thanked her for what she had done, and swore to return her kindness. When she saw that the city was about to be taken, they said, she should lock her possessions and family inside the inn. Then she was to hang out red pennants, so that the commander of the Hebrews might not harm her. After this, the men let themselves down the wall by a rope and escaped. Joshua told the high priest Eleazar and the council of elders what the spies had sworn to Rahab, and they confirmed the oath.

Now since the army was afraid to cross the Jordan, for there were no bridges or boats, God promised to reduce its volume. Three days later, Joshua had the priests go down to the river first, with the ark on their shoulders. Then the Levites went, carrying the tabernacle and the sacred vessels used in the sacrifices. After them, the entire throng followed according to their tribes, protecting their wives and children in the center. When the priests entered the river, they found it fordable and shallow, and they stood in the middle until the whole multitude had

The Jordan River bending toward the southeast, at approximately the place where Joshua led the Israelites across it into the Promised Land on the right bank. The mountains of Nebo are in the background.

crossed. Then they emerged also, and the river swelled and A V,16 flowed as before.

The Israelites pitched their camp at a distance of ten stades from Jericho. The heads of the tribes had each been commanded by Joshua to take a large stone from the bed of the river while they were crossing it. He now took these stones and built an altar as a memorial to the stopping of the river. They also celebrated the feast of the Passover there, and harvested the ripe grain of the Canaanites. Now they were amply supplied with all they had lacked before. It was then that the manna, which for 40 years had sustained them, ceased to fall.

Since the Canaanites remained inside the walls of Jericho, Joshua decided to besiege them. On the first day of the feast, the priests marched around the walls of the city, carrying the ark on their shoulders. Seven priests blew their trumpets, with the council of elders following them. They did this for six days. On the seventh, Joshua gathered the troops and all the people together. He told them that the city would now be captured, for God would make the walls collapse spontaneously, and he commanded them to kill everyone in the city, even the women and children. They were also to destroy all the animals, but not to take anything for themselves. All the gold and silver was to be collected and consecrated to God. But he reminded them to spare Rahab as well as her family and their possessions.

He led his army against the city, and they all marched around its walls, following the priests with the ark and the trumpeters. When they had gone around it seven times, and had stopped for a while, the walls fell down. Yet no siege engine or other force had been used on them by the Hebrews.

They rushed into Jericho, killing all the men while they were still stunned at the miraculous overthrow of the walls and were unable to defend themselves. And not only the men, but the women and children were killed also, and the city was filled with corpses. Rahab and her family alone were saved, and when she was brought to Joshua he thanked her for what she had done. He also gave her land to live on, and showed her every consideration.

An immense quantity of gold, silver, and brass was gathered A V,32 before they burned Jericho, riches which Joshua gave to the priests. But Achan, of the tribe of Judah, found a royal garment woven entirely of gold, and a large piece of gold. He thought it was cruel to have to surrender these to God, who did not need what he had won at such great risk, so he dug a ditch inside his own tent and buried his treasure.

A few days after the capture of Jericho, Joshua sent 3,000

Ruins of ancient Jericho. A stone watchtower has been excavated at the lower center, while the Mount of Temptation looms upward in the background, the traditional location of Jesus' confrontation with Satan.

troops to take Ai, a city situated above Jericho. But they were defeated, and driven back, with a loss of 36 men. Now the Israelites were greatly distressed, not so much about the casualties, but from fear that God had forgotten His promises. Joshua then cried out to the Lord. He answered Joshua, saying that this defeat was due to pollution among them: one of them had stolen things that were consecrated to Him, and they must search out and punish the offender.

Joshua summoned Eleazar the high priest, and other men in authority. He cast lots, tribe by tribe and man by man, until at last the lot fell on Achan. He confessed his theft and produced the stolen goods, but was immediately put to death and buried at night as a condemned criminal.

When Joshua had finished purifying his army, he led them against Ai. After posting ambushes around the town, he encountered the enemy at dawn. Bold from their former victory, the enemy marched out against them. Joshua feigned a retreat, drawing their army away from the city. Then suddenly he ordered his forces to turn around and attack the enemy, at the same time giving a prearranged signal to the men hiding in ambush. Those men rushed into the city through open gates and killed everyone they encountered. Joshua, meanwhile, broke the lines of his adversaries, who retreated to find safety in Ai. But when they saw it in flames, they scattered across the country, now unable to defend themselves. Joshua plundered the city of cattle and money, for this was a wealthy region, and distributed the booty to his soldiers.

Gibeon

The Gibeonites, who lived near Jerusalem, saw the destruc- A V,49 tion of Jericho and Ai. Fearing similar miseries for themselves, they sent ambassadors to Joshua to make a treaty of friendship with him. However, they thought it would be dangerous to admit that they were Canaanites, since Joshua had been commanded to destroy that entire race. They had therefore put on old and torn garments, and told Joshua they had come a long distance to see him, as their clothes witnessed, which were new when they had started out. They said they were sent by the people of Gibeon, who lived far from the land of Canaan, to make a treaty of friendship with the Hebrews. The Gibeonites had rejoiced to hear that by God's favor the Israelites were to possess the land of Canaan, and they wanted to become their fellow citizens.

Believing that these men were not Canaanite, Joshua made a treaty with them, and the envoys returned to their own people. But when he marched his army to the foothills of Canaan, Joshua learned that the Gibeonites lived nearby, and were indeed of Canaanite stock, so he sent for their magistrates and reproached them for the fraud. They replied that they feared for their lives, and saw no other way to save themselves. After some debate, Joshua made them public slaves to avoid violating his oath.

But the king of Jerusalem was angry that the Gibeonites had A V,58 gone over to Joshua, and he called the kings of the neighboring nations to join him in war against the traitors. The Gibeonites then appealed to Joshua, who hurried to assist them. With his whole army, he attacked the enemy, completely dispersing them, and pursued them down the slopes. Indeed, God lengthened the day to prevent darkness from hindering the Hebrews' ardor. Joshua captured the allied kings as they were hiding in a cave, and punished their armies.

News of the Hebrews' valor frightened their neighbors, so a number of Canaanite kings, joined by the Philistines, gathered into one great army. They numbered 300,000 infantry, 10,000 cavalry, and 20,000 chariots. Because of these vast numbers, Joshua and the Israelites were terrified and hopeless of any success. But God rebuked them for their cowardice and promised them victory over their enemies. Joshua regained his courage, and after five days' march he confronted the enemy. It was a fierce clash, in which most of the Canaanites were slaughtered. When they fled, Joshua pursued them, and even their kings were killed, along with their chariots and horses. The Israelites could now pass through all their country without any opposition. No one dared meet them in battle, and they besieged the cities and massacred their inhabitants.

Five years had now passed, and Joshua moved his camp into the hill country, setting up the tabernacle at Shiloh. Later, he gathered all the people at Shechem, where he erected an altar. Dividing his army so that half were posted on Mount Gerizim and half on Mount Ebal, they pronounced the blessings and cursings prescribed by Moses.

A V,71   Joshua had now grown old, and felt that the Canaanites would no longer try to besiege the Israelite strongholds. He gathered his people at Shiloh, and asked them to choose a man from each tribe who was skillful at surveying. These were sent out across the land of Canaan to measure it and to estimate the fertility of its different parts. After they had been gone seven months, they returned to Shiloh, where Joshua made an equal division of the land, according to their assessment. He cast lots among the nine tribes and the half tribe of Manasseh which had not yet received any land. The territories and towns were distributed to each tribe, according to lot.

The tribes of Reuben and Gad and the other half tribe of Manasseh had already settled in the land of the Amorites beyond the Jordan. Joshua therefore gathered the 50,000 men from those tribes who had followed him during his wars, and told them to go home to their wives and children. But above all, he commanded them to respect the laws of Moses, to love and serve God, and to remember their kinship with the other tribes of Israel.

A V,100   These men said farewell to the other tribes, and they all shed many tears. When they had crossed the river Jordan, they built an altar on its banks, as a monument to future generations, to remind them of their relationship with those who lived on the other side. But when Joshua's armies heard about this altar, they thought it was built because their brothers worshiped strange gods, so they armed themselves for war against them. But Joshua, Eleazar the high priest, and the council of elders restrained them, suggesting that messengers first be sent to their brothers to discern their intentions in erecting that altar. Phineas, Eleazar's son, and ten other men who were held in high esteem crossed the river and questioned the other tribes.

Their leaders stressed that they had not abandoned their God, but still intended to come to the tabernacle and offer their sacrifices with the rest of the Hebrews. The new altar had not been built for worship, but to serve as a memorial of their tribal relationship.

Phineas commended them, and, returning to Joshua, reported their answer to the people. Joshua, rejoicing that war with relatives had been avoided, offered sacrifices of thanksgiving to God.

Twenty years later, when he was very old, Joshua assembled A V,115 the magistrates and as many of the common people as possible. He reminded them of all the benefits God had bestowed on them—how from a low position He had raised them to glory and affluence—and he warned them that only through piety would the Deity continue to be their friend.

Then Joshua died, when he was 120 years old, and in his twenty-fifth year as commander-in-chief. About the same time, Eleazar the high priest died, leaving the high priesthood to his son Phineas.

The Destruction of the Benjamites

Phineas declared to the people that the tribe of Judah, in A V,120 accordance with God's will, should be given command for the destruction of the Canaanites. But the Canaanites, under King Adonibezek, thought that with Joshua dead, they could easily defeat the Israelites, and went to war. The Hebrews, however, cut down over 10,000 of them, and in pursuit they captured Adonibezek and cut off his fingers and toes. Adonibezek acknowledged that this was an appropriate judgment of God, for he had done the same to 72 kings whom he had conquered. He was then taken to Jerusalem, where he died.

The Israelites continued conquering the Canaanites, as God had commanded, and took much of their land. They laid siege to Jerusalem, but failed to conquer it, so they went on to Hebron and took the town, massacring its inhabitants. Cities in the hill

country and on the plain and seaboard fell to them, as did
Bethel.

But they failed to persevere until they had conquered all the
land, and allowed many Canaanites to live in peace, on condition that they pay them tribute. Tired of fighting, the Israelites
turned to cultivating the land, and derived wealth and luxury
from it. God told them that the Canaanites they had spared
would cause them great trouble in the future. And although the
Israelites were distressed at what God told them, they were still
unwilling to go to war, preferring a life of peace and prosperity.
Because of this extreme laziness, they fell into civil war.

AV,136   A certain Levite was traveling with his wife through the land
which belonged to the Benjamites, and stopped to rest overnight
at Gibeah. Some of the young men of that town had seen the wife
of the Levite in the marketplace. They were so struck by her
beauty that they took her from the house where she and her
husband were resting, and they spent the night raping her. At
dawn, she staggered back to the house and died. Horrified, her
husband laid his dead wife on his beast and returned to his
home in Ephraim. There he divided her body, limb from limb,
into twelve pieces. He sent one to each tribe through a messenger, who denounced the debauchery of the tribe of Benjamin.

Greatly angered, the Israelites gathered in large numbers at
Shiloh and decided to take up arms against the citizens of
Gibeah if the murderers were not turned over to them. Ambassadors arrived in Gibeah with this ultimatum, but the Benjamites refused, and said they would go to war first.

The people of the other tribes were even angrier, and took an
oath that none of them would ever give his daughter in marriage
to a Benjamite. They would fight with greater fury against that
tribe than their forefathers had fought the Canaanites, and they
sent out an army of 400,000 against Gibeah. Now the army of the
Benjamites numbered only 25,600, but included 500 excellent
left-handed slingers. With their help, the Benjamites defeated
the Israelites when they first joined battle. The Israelites lost
22,000, and the Benjamites returned to the city rejoicing.

On the next day, they were again victorious, and 18,000
Israelites were killed. The rest deserted their camp, fearing a
great slaughter. At Bethel, a city near their camp, the Israelites
implored God, through Phineas the high priest, asking that He
be satisfied with these two defeats and give them the victory
over their enemies. God promised that He would do so.

The Israelites then divided the army into two parts. Half of
them hid in ambush at night around the city of Gibeah, the other
half attacked the Benjamites and then retreated, to draw the men
out of the city. And indeed, even the old and young men, who

had been left in town as too weak to fight, joined in pursuit. But then the Israelites turned back to fight them, and those in ambush attacked from behind. The Benjamites saw that they had been deceived, and were driven into a valley, where they were shot down by Hebrew arrows. All were destroyed except 600, who fled to the surrounding mountains. The Israelites burned Gibeah, disposed of the women and the males that were under age, and did the same to the other Benjamite cities.

Later, however, they felt sorry for the Benjamites. Although A V,166 they still believed they had suffered justly for their sins, they recalled those 600 Benjamites who had escaped, and found these men on a rock called Rimmon, in the wilderness. The Israelites lamented their mutual disaster, and urged them not to let their tribe die out. "We give you the whole land of Benjamin," said the Israelites, "and as much booty as you can carry off."

They also gave them 400 virgins of Jabesh-Gilead for wives, leaving 200 Benjamites who would still have no wives. The Israelites deliberated the problem: they had sworn that no one would give his daughter to marry any of that tribe, and the oath could not be broken. While they were debating, someone suggested a solution. "Three times a year," he said, "when we meet at Shiloh, we have our wives and children with us. Let the Benjamites capture and marry some maidens, while we neither encourage nor stop them. And if any of the parents demand punishment, we will tell them that they ought to have guarded their daughters more closely."

The assembly concurred with this plan of marriage by capture, so, when the festival was about to begin, these 200 Benjamites scattered themselves along the roads near the city of Shiloh. They hid by twos and threes in the vineyards and other places, waiting for the maidens to arrive. As the girls walked along playfully, unguarded and unsuspecting, the men rushed out, carried them off, and married them. In this way, the tribe of Benjamin, in danger of total extinction, was saved through the shrewdness of the Israelites. They flourished and soon increased to be a multitude, and so ended the war.

Deborah and Barak

The tribe of Dan also suffered. Now that the Israelites had A V,175 turned to agriculture, the Canaanites restored their armies and forced the Danites to flee from the plain to the hills. They migrated north to one of the sources of the Jordan and founded the city of Dan.

The Israelites, however, continued to be slothful, and neglected God while contaminating themselves with the vices of the Canaanites. God therefore was angry with them, and their prosperity failed. Cushan, the king of the Assyrians, conquered them.

After eight years of servitude, a man of the tribe of Judah named Othniel felt that the time had now come to deliver the Israelites from bondage. With a few other brave men, he massacred one of the Assyrian garrisons. When the Israelites saw that he had been successful in his first attempt, they rallied around him in great numbers. They soon defeated all the Assyrian armies, and forced them to recross the Euphrates. Othniel was then chosen as ruler of the people—as their judge—and he ruled them for 40 years.

But after his death, the Israelites again fell into disorder. They neither paid God the honor that was due Him nor obeyed His laws, so they were conquered again by Eglon, king of the Moabites. He built himself a royal palace at Jericho, and oppressed the people for eighteen years, reducing them to poverty. Again the Israelites appealed to God, who arranged their liberation.

A V,188   Ehud, a young Benjamite, lived in Jericho, and had won the favor of Eglon and his attendants. One noon, Ehud went to the palace, carrying presents for the king, as he had often done before. Eglon told the servants who attended him to leave so he could talk with Ehud in private. The king was sitting on a chair, and Ehud feared that he might miss his thrust and not kill him. So he claimed he had a dream from God to reveal to the king, and when Eglon stood up from his chair to hear it, Ehud plunged the dagger into his heart. Leaving it there, he went out and locked the door behind him.

Now the attendants of Eglon, hearing no sound, thought he was sleeping, and dared not disturb him. But toward evening, fearing something was wrong, they entered the room. When they found the king dead, they were stunned and panicked. Before Eglon's garrison could be assembled, Ehud and an army of Israelites attacked the palace. Many Moabites were killed, and the rest escaped across the Jordan. Thus freed from their oppressors, the Israelites appointed Ehud their judge. When he died, Shamgar succeeded him, but ruled only a short time.

A V,198   Again the Israelites sinned, and so were conquered by Jabin, the king of the Canaanites, who attacked them from Hazor with 300,000 troops, 10,000 horse, and 3,000 chariots, under the command of his general, Sisera. For twenty years they endured hardship until they learned obedience to the divine laws, and went to a prophetess named Deborah, imploring her to pray to God to take pity on them. God told them to choose—as their general—Barak, of the tribe of Naphtali.

Deborah sent for Barak and directed him to select 10,000 young men to march against the enemy, for God had said that this number was sufficient to achieve victory. But Barak said he would not take command unless Deborah would share it as co-general. She replied in anger, "You, Barak, confer that authority which God has given you to a woman! But I do not reject it."

They mustered 10,000 and pitched their camp on Mount Tabor, but when Sisera came to meet them, the number in his army so alarmed the Israelites and Barak that they were ready to

Mount Tabor in Galilee, where Deborah and Barak defeated the king of Hazor about 1125 B.C. During the Jewish War in A.D. 67, the Roman general Placidus defeated the Jews who had erected a wall around the summit of Tabor.

withdraw. But Deborah restrained them, and commanded them to fight that very day, for God had assured them victory.

Thus the battle began, but a great storm of rain and hail arose, and the wind blew the rain in the faces of the Canaanites, so blinding them that their bows and slings proved useless, and their infantry found it difficult to use their swords in the cold. But the storm hampered the Israelites less, since it blew at their backs, and they took courage in this help from God and fought more bravely. After a great number of the Canaanites had been killed or crushed to death beneath the chariots, Sisera leaped from his chariot and fled until he reached the house of a woman named Jael. He asked her to conceal him, and she let him come inside. When Sisera asked for something to drink, she gave him sour milk, which he drank so immoderately that he fell asleep. While he was sleeping, Jael took an iron nail and hammered it through his mouth and jaw into the floor. When Barak's company arrived shortly afterward, she showed them Sisera, nailed to the floor. And so this victory was credited to a woman, as Deborah had predicted [Judges 4:9].

Barak now marched on Hazor, killed Jabin in battle, and razed the city. Then, as judge, he ruled the Israelites for 40 years.

Gideon

A V,210　Barak and Deborah died about the same time. After their deaths, the Midianites called to their aid the Amalekites and the Arabians, and made war against the Israelites. They defeated the Hebrews, and drove them from the plains into the hills, where the Israelites lived in caves and cried to God for help.

Gideon, of the tribe of Manasseh, was secretly threshing some wheat in his wine press, for he was too afraid of the enemy to do this openly on the threshing floor. An apparition in the form of a young man confronted him, telling Gideon that he was blessed and loved by God.

Gideon responded: "Is this an indication of God's favor, that I am forced to use this wine press instead of a threshing floor?" But the visitor urged him to take courage and try to regain liberty for his people. That was impossible, Gideon replied, because his tribe was small, and he was too young for such great exploits. God, however, promised to supply his needs and grant the Israelites victory under his guidance. Gideon reported this to other young men, who believed him, and immediately an army of 10,000 gathered, ready to fight.

At night, as Gideon slept, God appeared to him and said that He wanted the Israelites to acknowledge that victory came from Him and not from the size of their army, so He told Gideon to bring his army to the river during the heat of noon. Those men that bent down on their knees and drank calmly he should regard as brave men, while those who hurriedly scooped up the water in their hands he should deem cowards and terrified of their enemies. Gideon did as God commanded, and 300 men hurriedly drank water with their hands. God told him to choose this cowardly group for the attack.

Since Gideon was numb with fear, God wanted to reassure

The spring of Harod near the hill of Moreh, where Gideon diminished the numbers in his army according to their mode of drinking the water.

him, so He told him to take one of his soldiers and go near the tents of the Midianites at night. He obeyed, taking his servant Purah with him, and approached one of the tents. He found that those inside were awake, and that one of them was recounting a dream to his companion, which Gideon could hear clearly. The dream was this: he thought he saw a barley cake, too revolting to eat, come rolling through the camp. It smashed the royal tent and those of all the troops. Now the other soldier interpreted this to mean the destruction of the army. "For," he said, "*barley* is the foulest kind of seed, and the Israelites are the foulest of all the people of Asia. Since you saw the cake destroying our tents, I'm afraid that God has granted the victory to Gideon.''

Now inspired with hope and courage, Gideon commanded his soldiers to arm themselves. He reported this vision to them, and they were encouraged. He divided his army into three sections of 100 men each, and they each carried torches inside empty pitchers to conceal them, as well as a ram's horn in their right hand, to be used as a trumpet. About 3 A.M., they crept into the enemy's camp, and at a given signal sounded the rams' horns, broke their pitchers to reveal their lamps, and shouted, ''Victory to Gideon with God's help!'' Panic and confusion seized the sleeping Midianites, so that few of them were actually killed by the Hebrews and far more by their allies: because of the diversity of languages, they killed everyone they met, thinking them to be enemies also.

As the report of Gideon's victory reached the other Israelites, they grabbed their weapons, pursued the enemy, and overtook them in a valley surrounded by deep ravines. There they killed them all, including their kings. Gideon was made judge over Israel, and ruled 40 years.

Abimelech and Other Judges

A V,233   Gideon had 70 sons by many wives, and also one bastard, named Abimelech, by a concubine. After his father's death, Abimelech went to his mother's family at Shechem, and with money from them, [hired a band of thugs] who followed him to his father's house and killed all his brothers except Jotham, who was lucky enough to escape. Abimelech then converted the government into a tyranny and did what he pleased in defiance of the laws.

After Abimelech had governed for three years, the Shechemites expelled him both from their city and their tribe. But he gathered an army, defeated the Shechemites, and razed their city to the ground, sowing salt over its ruins. Some, however, escaped to a strong rock where they settled and prepared to build a wall for their protection. When Abimelech heard about their plans, he attacked them with his forces and heaped dry wood around the rock until it was entirely surrounded. The blaze he ignited was so immense that it engulfed the rock, and everyone died: the women, children, and 1,500 men.

After destroying Shechem, Abimelech marched against Thebez and took the city, but its inhabitants had taken refuge in a great tower there. While Abimelech was laying siege to the tower, a woman threw down a piece of millstone, which struck him on the head and knocked him to the ground. Dying, Abimelech did not want it said that he had been killed by a woman, so he told his armorbearer to kill him, and he did.

Leadership of the Israelites was then assumed by Jair, of the A V,254 tribe of Manasseh, who was blessed in many ways. He had 30 sons who were excellent horsemen, and he ruled for 22 years.

After the death of Jair, however, the people began *again* to despise God and His laws. Then the Ammonites and the Philistines ravaged their country, and the Israelites called once again to God, who would assist them. When the Ammonites invaded Gilead, the people gathered in the hills, but they lacked a commander.

Now a man among them named Jephthah was a valiant and powerful man, who had been disinherited by his brothers. When the people asked him to assume command, he declined because they had not assisted him in the family dispute. But when the Hebrews pleaded with him and promised him the government for his entire lifetime, he finally consented, and camped his army at a place called Mizpah. Here he prayed for victory, and vowed, if he came home safely, to sacrifice the first living creature that met him on his return. Then he joined battle with the enemy and defeated them in a great slaughter, after which he pursued them into their own land. He destroyed many of the cities of the Ammonites, freeing his countrymen from an oppression of eighteen years.

But a great sorrow overcame him, for the first living thing he met on his return was his only daughter, who was still a virgin. Crying in anguish, Jephthah told his daughter that he had dedicated her to God. But she told him that she was willing to die in return for her father's victory and the liberation of her fellow citizens. She only asked for two months to mourn her youth with her friends, and she would then fulfill his vow. When that time was up, he sacrificed his daughter as a burnt offering, a sacrifice which was neither conformable to the law nor acceptable to God.

After a war with the tribe of Ephraim in which he killed 42,000, Jephthah died. He had ruled for six years, and was buried in his native Gilead. Three judges, named Ibzan, Helon, and Abdon, ruled after him in succession, but nothing remarkable happened in these years.

7

SAMSON AND SAMUEL

After the death of Abdon, the Philistines conquered the Isra-
 elites and exacted tribute from them for 40 years. A distin-
 guished Danite named Manoah had a remarkably beautiful wife, <br /> but they were without any children, though they frequently <br /> prayed to God for them. One day an angel of God appeared to the <br /> wife as she was alone and brought her the good news that she <br /> would bear a son. He would be very strong, and when he had <br /> grown up, would punish the Philistines. He was to abstain from <br /> all other drink except water, and his hair should never be cut.
 Then the angel disappeared.

A V,275

The woman told Manoah about the angel's visit and message.
 But he became jealous and would not believe it, so his wife <br /> asked God to send the angel again, that her husband might also <br /> see him. When the angel appeared to her again, she called
 Manoah, and although he saw the angel, he was still suspicious.
 He asked him who he was, so that when the child was born they <br /> might return the angel thanks and give him a present. The angel <br /> replied that he needed nothing, but at the urging of Manoah he <br /> agreed to stay long enough to let them provide a token of <br /> hospitality. Manoah then killed a young goat and had his wife <br /> cook it. When the meal was ready, the angel told them to set the <br /> bread and meat upon a rock. Touching them with a rod he held, <br /> a flame blazed out and consumed them, while the angel as-
 cended to heaven by means of the smoke, as on a chariot.
 Manoah was afraid that some danger would come to them from <br /> this vision of God, but his wife told him to be encouraged, since
 God had appeared to them for their benefit.

When the child was born, they called him Samson, which <br /> means "strong." As the child grew, his frugal diet and long, <br /> flowing locks showed that he would be a prophet.

When Samson was a young man, he went with his parents to Timnah, a city of the Philistines, where there was a festival. He fell in love with a girl there, and asked his parents to let him marry her. But they were against it, because she was not of their race. God, however, was arranging this marriage for the good of the Hebrews, and so Samson won permission to court the girl.

A V,287   Once, as he was going to Timnah, Samson met a lion, and, though unarmed, he wrestled with the animal and strangled it with his hands. Later, on another visit to the girl, a swarm of bees had made a hive inside the carcass of the lion at the side of the road. He removed three honeycombs and gave them to the girl, along with other gifts.

At their wedding feast in Timnah, 30 sturdy, young Philistine stalwarts were given to Samson under the pretense of being his companions. In reality, they were to keep him in check. During the celebration, Samson said to his companions, "Come now, I will tell you a riddle. If you can solve it within seven days, I will give you fine linen clothing as a reward for your wisdom." They asked him to tell it. Then Samson said, "An omnivorous devourer produced pleasant food from its grossly unpleasant self."

When his companions were unable to solve the riddle in three days, they came to Samson's wife and asked her to find out the answer from her husband and let them know it, threatening to burn her if she refused. She asked Samson to tell her, and when he refused she cried, complaining that he did not love her, until finally he told her how he had killed a lion and had brought honey away from its carcass. She then reported this to the Philistine youths.

On the seventh day they came to Samson and said, "Nothing is more unpleasant than to meet a lion, and nothing more pleasant to taste than honey."

But Samson added, "And nothing is more deceitful than a woman who betrays secrets!"

Then Samson went out, and encountering some Philistines from Ashkelon, he took their clothing and gave it to his companions, as he had promised. But he renounced his wedding, and the girl, despising his anger, soon married the Philistine youth who had been Samson's best man.

At this, Samson grew still angrier, and he decided to punish all the Philistines as well as her. Summer had come, and the crops were almost ready for harvesting. Samson caught 300 foxes, and tying lit torches to their tails, he let them loose in the fields of the Philistines, so that their crops burned up. When the Philistines learned that this was Samson's doing, and why he had done it, they sent their rulers to Timnah. They burned alive the girl who had been his wife and her kin, for being the cause of their misfortunes.

After killing many Philistines in the plain, Samson went to live on top of a rock called Etam. Some of the Israelites came and told Samson that the Philistines would treat them cruelly as long as they allowed him to remain in their area. Therefore they, along with 3,000 troops, wanted to deliver him to the Philistines, and asked that he come peacefully. He made them swear they would do no more than deliver him to the enemy. When they had sworn, he came down from the rock, and they bound him with two ropes and took him to the camp of the Philistines, who shouted for joy when they saw him. But as they approached, Samson broke the ropes, grabbed the jawbone of an ass that lay at his feet, and attacked his enemies. With this weapon he killed 1,000 of them, and routed the rest.

Samson was too proud of this victory, claiming that it did not A V,301 come with God's help, but from his own strength. But a great thirst seized him, and he cried to God for help. Moved by his prayer, God caused water to spring out of a rock.

After this encounter, Samson had so little fear of the Philistines that he went to Gaza and lodged at one of the inns. When the magistrates of Gaza heard that he had come, they set guards at the gates to stop him from leaving. But Samson got up in the middle of the night, hurled himself against the gates, hoisted them—posts, doors, and all—upon his shoulders, and carried them to the mountain above Hebron.

Samson now kept company with a Philistine harlot named Delilah, and the rulers of the Philistines promised her much if she would find out from Samson the secret of his strength. So she asked him how he could be so extraordinarily strong. He replied, "If I am bound with seven supple vines, I will be as weak as other men."

Later, when Samson was asleep [or drunk], some soldiers arrived, and she bound him tightly with the vines. Then she awoke him, crying that some men had come to attack him. Samson broke the vines apart and defended himself.

Again she pressed him to tell her the secret of his strength, complaining that he did not trust her. Again Samson deceived her and said, "If I am bound with seven cords, I will lose my strength."

But when Delilah had tried this too with no success, the third time he told her to braid his hair in a special weave. But when this attempt also hid the truth, Samson finally yielded to Delilah and said, "God ordered me not to cut my hair, for my strength is equal to its growth and preservation."

Learning the secret, she cut off his hair and betrayed him to

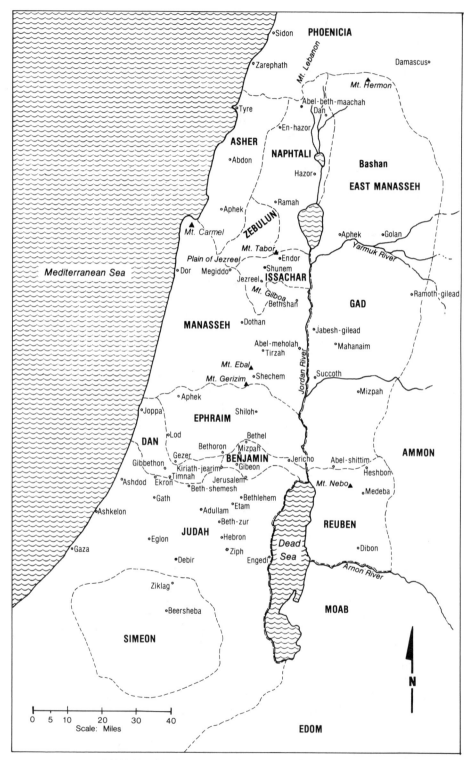

CANAAN, AS DIVIDED AMONG THE TWELVE TRIBES

his enemies. Since he was no longer able to resist them, they bound him, put out his eyes, and threw him into prison.

Some time later, the Philistines held a festival at Gaza, and their lords and notables were feasting in a great hall. They ordered Samson brought there so they could mock him. Now Samson's hair had grown long again, and to deceive them, he pretended to be weak. He asked the youth who led him by the hand to let him rest on the two central columns that supported the roof. When the boy had done this, Samson butted all his weight against them, overturned the columns, and brought down the hall, crushing more than 3,000, all of whom died, including Samson himself.

The Story of Ruth

After the death of Samson, Eli the high priest ruled over A V,318 Israel, and a famine engulfed the land. Elimelech of Bethlehem, a city of the tribe of Judah, was unable to obtain food, and so he took his wife Naomi and their two sons to the land of Moab. Elimelech prospered there, and married his sons to Moabite women. After ten years he died, and his sons soon after him, so a grieving Naomi decided to return to her own country, which was prosperous again. Her daughters-in-law wanted to go with her, but Naomi told them they had better remain, and she prayed that they might be happier in their second marriages than in their first. One of her daughters-in-law, Orpha, stayed behind, but the other, Ruth, would not leave her.

When they arrived in Bethlehem, any who called Naomi by name would receive the response: ''Do not call me Naomi, for that means 'happiness,' but rather Mara, which means 'grief.''' Now Boaz, a relative of Naomi's husband Elimelech, owned an estate on which Ruth went out to glean. Seeing her, Boaz asked his steward about the girl and learned who she was. He then welcomed Ruth, appreciating her kindness to Naomi, and told his steward that she should not glean but rather reap and carry away all she could. He was also to give her lunch and drink when he fed the harvesters. When she came home, she told Naomi what had happened, and Naomi informed her that Boaz was a relative who might well take care of them.

Some time later, Boaz was sleeping on his threshing floor, and Naomi schemed to get him involved with Ruth by sending her inside to sleep at his feet. When he awoke and learned who was lying beside him, he suggested that she gather up all the barley she could and take it to Naomi. Then he added, ''He who is a closer relative to you than I must be asked if he wants to marry you. If he does, you must follow him. But if he declines, I will take you for my lawful bride.''

Ruth returned to Naomi and they rejoiced, for now they knew he would take them under his care. Boaz went down to the city at noon, and had Ruth come before an assembly of the elders. He also summoned the nearest relative of Ruth's dead husband and asked him, "Do you possess the heritage of Elimelech and his sons?"

"Yes," he answered, "I possess it, for the law grants it to me as nearest of kin."

"Then," continued Boaz, "it is not sufficient to perform only half of the law, for the wife of Mahlon is here, whom you must marry, according to the laws, if you want to keep those lands."

The man answered that since he was already married and had children, he would forego his right, and give up the widow and the inheritance to Boaz. Boaz accepted the offer, and Ruth loosened the man's shoe and spit in his face, as the law required. Then Boaz married Ruth, and a year later they had a son, Obed. Of Obed was born Jesse, and of him David, who became king. God, then, can easily promote even ordinary people to illustrious rank.

The Boy Samuel

A V,338   When Eli the high priest ruled in Israel, a Levite named Elkanah went from Ramah, where he lived, to offer sacrifice before the tabernacle at Shiloh. Hannah, one of his two wives, grieved at not having any children. She came to the tabernacle and prayed, vowing that if God would give her a son she would consecrate him to His service. Because she lingered long in prayer, Eli, who was sitting at the entrance of the tabernacle, thought she had drunk too much and told her to leave. "No," said Hannah, "I have drunk only water, but I grieve at having no children, and I was asking God to give me one." Then Eli urged her to be cheerful, because God would grant her children.

And indeed she bore a son and called him Samuel, which means, "Asked of God." True to her vow, she brought him to Eli to be raised up in the sanctuary. She also had other sons and daughters.

Eli had two sons, Hophni and Phinehas, who were very wicked, stealing some of the offerings and molesting women who came to worship. Eli mourned over their wickedness, and feared that some punishment would be inflicted on them by God.

One night, Samuel, who was then twelve years old, heard God calling him by name as he slept. He woke up and ran to Eli, thinking it was he who had called him. But Eli replied that he had not called him. God did this three times. Then Eli said,

"No, Samuel, I was silent now as before. It is God who is calling you. Say to Him, 'Here I am.'"

The voice did call him again, and Samuel answered as directed. God told him that the Israelites would suffer a great disaster, and Eli's two sons would be killed because Eli loved them more than worshiping God. Samuel hesitated to report this to Eli, but Eli obliged him. And Samuel's fame began to spread, since whatever he prophesied came true.

Shortly afterward, the Philistines attacked the Israelites and defeated them in a great battle at Aphek, where 4,000 were killed. The Hebrews thought that if they sent for the ark, they would be victorious, so the ark was brought to the camp, and Hophni and Phinehas accompanied it, because their father was too old to come. The arrival of the ark brought great joy to the Israelites, and the Philistines were afraid when they learned of it. But both sides would find that they were mistaken, one in its joy and the other in its fear. For the Philistines conquered again, and killed 30,000 Israelites, among whom were the sons of Eli, and the ark itself was carried off by the enemy.

A young Benjamite, who had survived the battle, brought to Shiloh the news of the defeat and the loss of the ark. Eli, who was sitting on a high seat at one of the gates, heard lamenting and summoned the messenger. He was not surprised at the news, because God had prepared him to expect these things. But when he was told of the loss of the ark, he fell off his seat and died, having lived 98 years and having ruled 40.

The Return of the Ark

The Philistines took the ark in triumph to their city of Ashdod A VI,1 and put it in the temple of their god, Dagon, as a trophy. Early the next morning, when they came to worship Dagon, they found him doing the same to the ark, for their idol had fallen off its pedestal and lay prostrate. Alarmed, they put it back in place, but again and again they found it toppled. God also sent a loathsome dysentery upon the people of Ashdod, and many of them died. Then a horde of mice ate up all the fruits and plants, until the townspeople concluded that the ark was the cause of their troubles. So they decided to send it to Ashkelon, whose inhabitants were willing to receive it. But the plagues visited this city also, and when the ark was sent elsewhere—it made the round of all five Philistine cities—the same suffering followed.

The magistrates of the principal cities met together to decide what to do. Since they did not all agree that their troubles derived from the ark, some wise men proposed a plan to discern if this were so. They told the Philistines to build a new cart for transporting the ark. They were to yoke to it two cows that had young calves, and drive it to a place where three roads met, and then abandon it. "And if," they said, "the cows do not return to their calves, but of their own accord choose the route that leads to the Hebrews, we shall know that the ark has been the cause of all our evils. But if they take another road, then we will know our troubles have come to us by chance."

With the Philistines following at a distance to observe, the cows headed straight to a village of the tribe of Judah called Beth-shemesh, where they stopped, even though a lush and grassy plain lay ahead. The people were harvesting their wheat when they saw the ark, and were overcome with joy. Lifting the ark off the cart onto a rock, they made a burnt offering of the cows and cart.

Despite their joy, however, God caused 70 of them to die for daring to approach the ark, for since they were not priests, they were forbidden to touch it. Realizing that they were not worthy to have the ark in their midst, the villagers informed the Hebrew state that the ark had been returned by the Philistines. It was then taken to Kirjath-jearim, where it was placed in the house of a righteous man named Abinadab, who was a Levite. There it remained for twenty years, after having spent four months among the Philistines.

A VI,19   Since the people showed great zeal in serving God during this period, the prophet Samuel exhorted them to recover their liberty from the Philistines. Urging them to rely on God for victory and turn from wickedness, he promised them blessings not attainable by arms alone.

The people loudly approved his words, fasting and offering up public prayer. The Philistines, however, learned of this gathering, and attacked them with a large army, thinking they would surprise them. But suddenly the earth began to tremble and shake under their feet, then it yawned open to engulf the Philistines, while thunder deafened and lightning blinded them, striking the weapons from their hands. As the attackers fled in confusion, Samuel and his people massacred many. After that they gained other victories, and Samuel finally recovered from the Philistines all the towns they had lost, humbling the Philistines' pride.

A VI,31   Serving also as itinerant judge, Samuel adjudicated disputes among the people by making an annual circuit of the cities where trials took place, dispensing perfect justice. When he grew old, he assigned the direction of the nation to his two sons, Joel and Abijah. But they had none of their father's virtues. They took bribes in judging disputes and wallowed in luxury, defying God and His prophet, their own father.

The people came to Samuel at Ramah, and told him he was now too old to govern. And since his sons were so lawless, they begged him to choose a king from among them to rule and take vengeance on the Philistines. Samuel was greatly distressed at this, since he hated monarchy and favored aristocracy as divinely ordained.

While these thoughts churned through his mind at night, the Deity appeared to console him, and said, "It is not you they are spurning, Samuel, but Me, for they no longer want Me to reign alone. They will soon be sorry, when it is too late. But I command you to give them as their king whomever I name, although first you must point out to them all the evils attending kingship."

Samuel called the people together, and told them that the king they wished for would become a cruel master to them. He would take their money and possessions to maintain his grandeur, as well as making their children his soldiers and servants. But they insisted, "Forget the future! We want a king *now*, like the other nations, to lead us in battle against our enemies!"

Then Samuel dismissed the assembly, telling them that when the time came, he would announce to them whom God had chosen as their king.

8
SAUL

There was a man of the tribe of Benjamin whose name was Kish, and he had a son called Saul, who was a tall and gifted youth. One day, some of the asses that belonged to Kish strayed away from his pastures, and he told Saul to go in search of them. Saul and his servant wandered about the country for some time without finding the asses, and decided to return home lest his father worry. When they came near Ramah, Saul's servant advised him to go to Samuel the prophet, who perhaps could tell them where to look. Arriving at Ramah, they asked the way to the prophet's house. Some girls pointed it out to them, adding that they must hurry, for the prophet was just about to sit down to a great feast. Now the reason so many were attending Samuel's feast was this: the day before, when he was praying, God had told Samuel that on the next day, at that very hour, He would send to him the man who was to be king of Israel. Samuel was now expecting the visitor, for the hour had almost arrived.

When Saul appeared, Samuel invited him in to the feast, assuring him that the asses he was searching for were safe. He made him and his servant sit down above the 70 other guests and gave orders that royal portions were to be set before Saul. At bedtime, the others left, but Saul and his attendant slept at the prophet's house.

Early the next morning, Samuel woke Saul and escorted him out of town. He asked Saul to send his servant on ahead, for he had something to say to him privately. Samuel then took out a small vial of oil, and, pouring it on Saul's head, he kissed him and said, "God has appointed you king over His people to avenge them against the Philistines. And as a sign that what I say is true, you will meet three men on the road who are going to worship God at Bethel. One will carry three loaves, the second a kid, and the third a wineskin. After that you will come to a place called 'Rachel's Tomb,' where someone will tell you that your asses are safe. And when you come to Gibeah, you will meet a company of prophets, and, divinely inspired, you will begin to prophesy with them.'' Everything happened exactly as Samuel had said.

Samuel now called all the tribes together at Mizpah, and informed them that since they had rejected God and decided to have a king instead, they must throw lots to choose one. The first lot fell on the tribe of Benjamin, the next on the family of Matri, and finally on the person of Saul himself. But Saul was not at the assembly, for he left when the lot fell on him, since he did not want to appear anxious to be king. Messengers found him hiding, and when he arrived Samuel presented him to the people. When they saw how tall and regal he was, they cried out, "God save the king!" But Samuel wrote down in a book all that would take place, and he placed the book in the tabernacle of God.

The Defeat of the Ammonites and Philistines

A VI,68 A month later, war broke out with the Ammonites. Nahash, their king, had attacked those tribes which lived beyond the Jordan and had taken many of their cities. To make it impossible for them to regain their liberty, he put out the right eye of every Israelite who fell into his hands. This rendered the men useless in war, since their left eyes were obstructed by their shields.

Nahash then marched into the land of Gilead and camped before the city of Jabesh. He sent ambassadors to the people, commanding them to surrender and let their right eyes be plucked out, or else to endure a siege and have their city entirely destroyed. The citizens of Jabesh were so terrified that they could not decide. They asked Nahash to give them seven days to seek help from the rest of the Israelites, saying they would fight if they received it, but would surrender if not. Nahash was so contemptuous of the Gileadites that he permitted them to find any allies they could.

When the messengers reached Saul, he was seized with a divine fury, and promised them he would gather his army and be with them on the third day, when he would defeat the enemy before sunrise. He did as he said, and on the third day, before the sun was up, he attacked the Ammonites from three directions. They were taken by surprise and totally defeated, and King Nahash himself was slain. Saul pursued them to their own country, destroyed it, and took much booty, returning to his own land in glory.

After Samuel had, for the second time, confirmed him as king A VI,95 at Gilgal, Saul selected a guard of 3,000 men. He kept 2,000 of these as a royal bodyguard; the other 1,000 he placed under the command of his son Jonathan and sent him to Gibeah. Now the Israelites there were still dominated by the Philistines, who had deprived the people of all iron weapons. Jonathan attacked the Philistine soldiers garrisoned near Geba* and defeated them. The Philistines then sent a vast army into the area. Saul went to Gilgal and called upon the inhabitants to arm themselves, but they were so terrified at the numbers of the enemy that they hid themselves in caves or crossed the Jordan into Gilead.

Excavations at Gibeah, where the ravishing took place which almost led to the extermination of the tribe of Benjamin. Gibeah was also the home of King Saul and the location of his royal palace.

Saul now sent word to Samuel to come and advise him, and Samuel replied that he would arrive at the end of seven days, when they would offer up sacrifices together. But since Samuel did not come until the evening of the seventh day, Saul grew impatient and offered up the sacrifices alone. As soon as he had done so, Samuel appeared and Saul went out to meet him. The prophet criticized Saul for what he had done—he would accept

---

* This location is to be distinguished from Gibeah. Compare I Samuel 13:3.

no excuses—and told him that God would have granted him a long reign had he not disobeyed. Then Samuel returned home.

Saul and Jonathan had only 600 troops at Gibeah, and most of these had no arms, because the Philistines had deprived them of weapons. From a high hill, they watched the devastation of their land with intense anguish. The Philistines were camped near them on a steep precipice, and since they did not believe anyone could climb up, they failed to guard it. Jonathan then proposed to his armorbearer that they try to create confusion in the Philistine camp. They crept out near dawn, and were seen by the enemy, who sneered, "Here come the Hebrews out of their dens and caves. Come on up and receive what you deserve for your insolence!" This was precisely the sign of victory Jonathan had envisioned. Scaling the precipice by a different route, they attacked the enemy while they slept and killed twenty men. Then the whole camp awoke in great disorder, and because there were many different tribes in the army, they did not know one another in the darkness. Each thought the other was the enemy and so fought against one another. Many were killed in this way, while others trying to get away fell down the precipice.

A VI,115 Saul was informed by his spies that there was a strange commotion in the enemy's camp, so he and his men attacked the Philistines in their confusion and mutual massacre. Moreover, the Israelites who had fled to tunnels and caves, hearing that Saul was gaining a great victory, now came rushing out to join him. He soon found himself leading an army of 10,000, while the Philistines were scattered all over the countryside. Saul set out in pursuit, but first he invoked a curse on the Hebrews if any of them stopped to eat anything until night intervened to halt their slaughter of the enemy.

Jonathan, however, knew nothing about this curse. While pursuing the enemy, he came to a thicket of oaks swarming with bees, and breaking off a piece of honeycomb, he ate part of it. Then he learned of his father's curse and stopped eating, but he said that his father was wrong, since they would have had more strength for pursuit had they eaten.

At evening, Saul asked the high priest Achitob to offer sacrifice and learn from God whether they should plunder the enemy camp. But the priest told him he could not receive an answer. "Surely," said Saul, "there is a reason for God's silence: some secret sin against Him in our ranks. Now I swear that even if he who committed this sin turns out to be my own son Jonathan, I will kill him, and appease the anger of God against us."

The multitude applauded his decision. Lots were cast, and the lot fell on Jonathan. Saul asked him what he had done wrong. "Nothing, father," he replied, "except yesterday, when I knew nothing of your oath, I tasted a honeycomb while pursuing the enemy."

When Saul then swore to kill him, Jonathan declared that he would die happily if his father so willed, gladdened by their great victory over the Philistines. But all the people were so grief-stricken and so grateful to the initiator of their victory, that they swore not to let Jonathan be put to death. So they saved him from his father's curse and prayed that God would forgive his sin.

Saul's Disobedience

After destroying some 60,000 of the enemy, Saul subdued the A VI, 129 Moabites, the Ammonites, the Idumeans, and the king of Soba, making the Hebrews more powerful than the other nations. Then Samuel came to Saul and told him that God remembered how the Amalekites had attacked the Hebrews while they were passing through the wilderness, and that the time had now come for vengeance against them. God therefore commanded Saul to attack and kill them all, sparing neither women nor infants, cattle nor asses.

In obedience to this order, Saul marched against the Amalekites, defeated them in battle, took their cities, and killed the men, women, and children. But when he had captured Agag, their king, Saul admired his tall, handsome figure and decided to spare him. His soldiers also disregarded the commands of God and kept the best of the cattle and wealth for themselves.

God told Samuel that He now repented of having made Saul king. The next morning, Samuel went to Gilgal, and when Saul saw him, he ran out to meet him and said, "I give thanks to God, who has given me the victory, and I have performed everything He has commanded."

"How is it, then," Samuel replied, "that I hear the lowing of cattle, and beasts of burden in the camp?"

"The people," said Saul, "have reserved these for sacrifices, but the Amalekites are all destroyed. Not one of them remains alive except their king, and I have brought him with me in order that I may consult with you about his fate."

But the prophet said that God was not pleased with sacrifices made in disobedience to His commands, and because Saul had offended God, his kingdom would be taken away from him. Saul admitted that he had acted wrongly, but said that it was from fear of his troops that he had not curbed their plundering of the spoils. He asked for mercy and pardon, promising not to offend in the future, and wanted the prophet to offer sacrifices to God.

But Samuel, knowing that God would not be reconciled, turned to go home. Then Saul hastily grabbed hold of the prophet's mantle to stop him, and the cloak tore in his hands. "Even so," said Samuel, "your kingdom will be torn from you and given to another who is virtuous and just."

Saul again confessed that he had sinned, and asked that the prophet at least stay and worship God with him in the presence of the people. Samuel granted him that request and went with him to worship God. Then he ordered that King Agag be brought before him. When Agag lamented that death was very bitter, Samuel replied, "Because you have made many Hebrew mothers mourn their children, so shall your mother mourn over you." Then, having commanded that Agag be put to death, Samuel returned to Ramah.*

A VI,156   Saul realized that God was now his enemy, and he went up to his royal palace at Gibeah and stayed away from Samuel. When Samuel mourned for him, God told him to quit mourning and take the sacred oil and go to the city of Bethlehem, to a man named Jesse. There he was to anoint one of his sons whom God would designate as future king.

At Bethlehem, Samuel prepared a sacrifice and invited Jesse and his sons to attend the sacred feast that followed. Jesse came with his eldest son, who was so well-grown and attractive that the prophet felt sure this must be the chosen one. But God told him no, that He did not view the exterior but rather the heart and soul. Samuel asked Jesse to bring his other sons. Five others came, all as handsome and strong as the first, but none of these was selected. Samuel then asked Jesse if he had any other sons.

"Only one more," answered Jesse, "but he is a shepherd who is tending our flocks. His name is David."

"Summon him quickly," said the prophet, "for we cannot feast without him."

When David arrived, a rosy-cheeked boy with piercing eyes, Samuel knew he was the chosen one, and made the youth sit down next to him. Then he took the oil and anointed him, explaining that God had chosen him as king, and exhorted him to follow all of God's commandments. The divine spirit now left Saul for David.

Meanwhile, strange disorders and evil spirits harassed Saul, and his physicians advised him to look for some musician who could play the harp to charm away the evil spirits and soothe his torment. Someone told him that in the city of Bethlehem he had seen a son of Jesse, a mere boy in years, who was skilled in the harp and in singing songs, and also a fine soldier. Saul con-

---

* Josephus omits the brutal details of 1 Samuel 15:33: "And Samuel hewed Agag in pieces before the Lord at Gilgal."

tacted Jesse, asking that David come to the palace, so Jesse sent his son and also gave him presents for the king. Saul was delighted with the lad, and made him his armorbearer. And when David played on his harp, the evil spirits left the king and he was restored to health.

David and Goliath

Another war broke out between the Israelites and the Phil- A VI,170
istines, and their two armies camped on adjacent hills with a

The Valley of Elah, where the Hebrews faced the taunts of the Philistine giant Goliath, until David selected five stones from the brook which runs through the center of the valley and used them to kill Goliath.

valley between them. A giant named Goliath then emerged from the Philistine camp. His height was four cubits and a span [c. 7 or 8 ft.], his armor had to be carried by many, and his spear was so heavy he had to shoulder it. Standing between opposing forces, he shouted to Saul and the Hebrews in a mighty voice, ''I will liberate you from battle and its dangers! Send one of your men to fight with me, and let the war be decided by the single victor. To the nation of the victor the other side will be slaves.

Risk one man's life rather than all!'' Then he returned to his own camp. The next day he came out with the same words, repeating the performance for 40 days and leaving Saul and his army totally demoralized.

Three of Jesse's sons were in Saul's army, and David now came and brought them provisions from their father. Hearing the taunts of Goliath, he grew furious and told his brothers that he was ready to fight the giant in single combat. But his eldest brother scolded him for talking foolishly, and told David to return to the flocks. David did not answer his brother, out of respect, but he told some of the soldiers that he was willing to fight the challenger. When Saul learned what the boy had said, he sent for him.

"Do not fear, O King," said David, "for I will humble this insolent giant, and your army will have more glory if he is killed, not by a grown man prepared for war, but by someone apparently no older than a boy."

Saul admired the courage of the youth, but told him that he was too young for such a feat. "No," said David, "for God is with me. Once He helped me kill a lion that had stolen a lamb from my flock, and also a bear that attacked me. And now God will deliver this Philistine beast into my hands."

Saul said to David, "Go to battle, then, and may God go with you."

Saul gave David his own armor to wear, but when he had put it on, he found it too heavy, and laid it aside. Taking a staff in one hand and a sling in the other, he chose five stones from the brook, which he put into his shepherd's sack, and went out to meet Goliath.

When the giant saw him coming in this manner, he jeered at him, "Do you take me for a dog, that you come at me with stones?"

"No," said David, "for something less than a dog!"

Goliath grew furious and cursed David, telling him he would give his flesh to be torn apart by the beasts and the birds.

"You come against me with sword, spear, and breastplate," said David, "but I have God for my armor, who will destroy both you and your host by my hands, and I will this day cut off your head and throw the rest of your body to the dogs!"

Now the Philistine lumbered toward David in his heavy armor, confident of an effortless kill. Then David fitted one of the stones into his sling, and he ran forward and shot it at Goliath, hitting him in the forehead. The stone penetrated into his brain, and he fell on his face, stunned. Running forward, David stood over him and cut off his head with the giant's own sword.

At the fall of Goliath, the Philistines fled, while Saul and the Hebrews pursued them to the borders of Gath and the gates of

Ashkelon. They killed 30,000 Philistines, and wounded twice as many. As the army returned in triumph, the women came out to meet them with songs and dances, rejoicing in their victory. A VI,193 "Saul has killed his thousands," sang the older women, "but David his *ten* thousands!" the girls responded. The king was angry at these songs, and now grew jealous and afraid of David. Removing him from his post as armorbearer, he made him captain over 1,000 men and sent him on the most dangerous campaigns, in the hope that he would be killed.

But David always returned safely, and his great bravery won him the applause of all. [Michal], the king's daughter, fell in love with him, and Saul used that love for further plots against David. He told David that if he brought him the heads of 600 Philistines, he would give him his daughter in marriage.* (He hoped David would be killed himself before he could kill so many.) But David went out and killed a great number of Philistines and brought 600 of their heads to Saul. The king was obliged to give David his daughter Michal as his wife.

But Saul hated and feared him more than ever, and resolved to have David slain by commanding his son Jonathan and his most trusted servants to kill him. Now Jonathan loved David, and was shocked at what his father commanded, so instead of obeying, he told David of the secret mission that had been given him, and advised him to be absent the next day. Jonathan hoped to find his father in a better mood and then dissuade him.

The next day, Saul was in much better humor, so Jonathan told him that it would be a great crime to kill David, who had been so valiant in avenging them against their enemies, and it would wrong Michal. Saul agreed with Jonathan, and he welcomed David back into his presence.

Saul Attacks David

Again David was sent against the Philistines and he returned A VI,213 victorious, and again Saul was angry and jealous. When the evil spirit returned to torment him, Saul called David to his bedside to sing and play for him on his harp. While he was playing, Saul threw a javelin at him with all his might, but David saw it coming and dodged out of the way. Then he fled to his own house and remained there all day.

But at night the king sent officers to guard the house against his escape, for he intended to bring David to trial and have him put to death. Michal learned of her father's intentions and came

---

* According to 1 Samuel 18:25, it was "a hundred foreskins of the Philistines."

in great distress to her husband, and said, "Don't let the sun find you here, for if it does, it will never look on you again. Escape while night permits, for if my father finds you, you are a dead man!" She let him down by a cord out of the window, and he escaped. Then she arranged the bed to make it look as if a sick man were lying in it, and put a goat's liver under the covers.

At daybreak, when Saul's men knocked at the door, Michal told them that David had been sick during the night. The liver, which was still quivering, shook the bedclothes, and convinced them that David was gasping for breath. They returned to the king with this story, but Saul ordered that David be brought just as he was. When they returned and lifted up the covers, they discovered the trick and told Saul, who rebuked his daughter.

A VI,220   David fled to the prophet Samuel at Ramah, and told him all that Saul had done. Samuel took him to a place called Naioth, where they lived together for some time. Later, David went to Jonathan and complained that although he had done nothing wrong, Saul was still anxious to have him killed. But Jonathan told him he was mistaken, since his father, who always consulted him, had said nothing about desiring David's death.

But David swore to him that it was true, and said, "Tomorrow, if the king asks why I am absent, tell him that you gave me permission to go to Bethlehem to feast with my own tribe. If he says, 'It is well,' then you will know that he bears no hostility to me. But if he answers otherwise, that will be a sure sign of his plans against me. Then let me know what the king's response was."

Jonathan promised he would do as David requested, and swore an oath of lasting friendship with him. He would let David know his father's attitude by going into the plain where he regularly exercised. "After I throw three darts at the target," he said, "I will order my lad to bring them back to me since they fell short—that will show you have nothing to fear from my father. But if I say the opposite, then look for the opposite from the king."

When Saul sat down on the second day of the feast and saw that David's seat was again empty, he asked Jonathan why the son of Jesse was not present. Jonathan replied, "I gave him permission to go to Bethlehem to celebrate a festival with his own tribe."

Then it was that Jonathan learned the depth of his father's hatred for David. Saul could not contain his anger, and heaped abuses on Jonathan, calling him a traitor and an offspring of deserters. He ordered him to get David, that he might be punished.

"For what crime would you punish him?" asked Jonathan.

Livid and beyond words, Saul snatched up his spear, leaped at Jonathan, and would have killed him had he not been prevented by his friends.

The king's son rushed away from the table, too grieved to be able to eat anything. All that night he wept, because he knew now that David was doomed. At daybreak, he went to the plain, gave the prearranged signal, and then sent the boy attending him back to the city, so that David could come out of hiding and speak with him. David fell at Jonathan's feet to do homage, but Jonathan lifted him up. They embraced each other and wept, then bade each other farewell, and parted.

David Flees From Saul

David fled first to the city of Nob, where the high priest A VI,242 Achimelech sheltered him, and then to the land of the Philistines. When he came to Gath, he was recognized by the servants of King Achish, who said, "This is the David who has killed myriads of Philistines," and they brought him before the king. But David, fearing he would be executed, pretended to be raging mad, foaming at the mouth and acting so strangely that Achish said, "You see the man is mad! Why did you bring him to me?" So they let him go.

David then fled to a cave near the city of Adullam, and he lived there. He sent word to his brothers, and they came with relatives and others who were discontented with the way Saul governed, until David had 400 men around him. Encouraged by this force, he went to the Moabites, and asked their king to let his parents live in Moab until he knew his destiny. The king granted him this request.

A prophet now told David to go and live in the land of Judah, so he went to the city of Hareth and remained there. When Saul heard that David had been seen with a large following, he was worried, and accused his officers and bodyguards of supporting David, as Jonathan did. None of them responded until Doeg, his mule keeper, said that he had seen David in the city of Nob, where he was provisioned by the high priest Achimelech, and given the sword of Goliath. Saul sent for the high priest and all his family and asked him, "Have I ever done you any wrong that you have received the son of Jesse, and given him food and weapons when he is plotting against my rule?"

The high priest replied that he did not know that David was an enemy of the king, for was he not his son-in-law, a captain in his army, and his friend?

Saul would not believe him. He commanded his guards to kill the high priest and his relatives. But they dared not, fearing the

Deity more than the king. Saul then turned to Doeg and told him to murder them. Collecting others as wicked as himself, Doeg slew Achimelech and his relatives, 305 in all. Saul also sent men to Nob, where they slaughtered all the inhabitants, sparing neither women, children, nor the aged, and burned the town. The only person to escape was Abiathar, a son of Achimelech, who went to David and told him what Saul had done. David blamed himself for having brought this misfortune upon the high priest and his family, and urged Abiathar to remain in safety with him.

The Cave at Engedi

A VI,271   At this time David heard that the Philistines had invaded the countryside around Keilah, and he attacked and defeated them. He and his companions stayed with the people of Keilah until they had harvested their grain and fruits. The news of this exploit reached Saul, who was delighted to learn that David was at Keilah. "At last, God has put him into my hands," he said, "forcing him inside a city with walls, gates, and bars." He commanded his army to besiege Keilah, take it, and kill David. But God revealed to David that if he remained in that city, the people of Keilah would surrender him to Saul, so he took his 400 men and withdrew into the desert above Engedi. When Saul heard that David had fled, he abandoned his campaign against Keilah.

From the desert David went to the land of the Ziphites, where he lived in the woods. Jonathan came to see him there, and encouraged him. Again they made a solemn covenant of friendship, promising never to harm each other, after which Jonathan returned home. To please Saul, however, the men of Ziph informed the king that David was there and promised to help Saul capture him. But David learned of their evil plans, and fled to a great rock which was in the wilderness near Maon, after which he moved to the narrow passes of Engedi.

A VI,283   Saul took 3,000 men and went to Engedi in pursuit. Near there he came to a deep cave, where, by chance, David and his 400 men were hidden. To answer nature's call, Saul went inside the cave alone. One of David's companions spotted him, and told David he had a God-given opportunity for vengeance against his enemy and should cut off his head. David refused, saying, "Even though he assaults me, I will not assault him," and he merely cut off the fringe of Saul's mantle. When Saul rose and left the cave, David followed and called out to him. As Saul turned around, David prostrated himself and asked Saul why he

Engedi, near the western shore of the Dead Sea, has caves in the rift to the right center of the photograph, in one of which David confronted Saul.

had listened to the fabricators who told lies about him, claiming that it was his desire to kill the king. "Had I wanted to kill you," David said, "I could easily have done so just now. For when I cut off the fringe of your mantle, I could just as readily have done the same to your head." David then held up the piece of cloth he had cut.

Saul was so amazed at his extraordinary escape and so touched by David's generosity that he wept. "You have brought me only good," he said, "while I have brought you distress. Now I know that God is reserving the kingdom for you. Swear to me, then, that you will not destroy my posterity but will save and preserve my family." David gave this oath, and Saul returned to his own kingdom.

About this time, the prophet Samuel died. Many came to Ramah to see him buried, and they mourned him for many days.

Nabal and Abigail

A VI,295   David and his men returned to Maon, where a rich man named Nabal had great flocks of sheep and goats. David and his followers had protected Nabal's flocks against all theft and danger, so at shearing time, David sent Nabal ten of his men, who, reminding him of the good care they had taken of Nabal's sheep, asked him for some provisions in return. But Nabal was a foolish and bad-natured cynic, and he asked, "Who is David?" When they answered that he was the son of Jesse, Nabal sneered, "So, then, runaway slaves now think highly of themselves and boast about forsaking their masters!" David was furious when these words were reported, and he swore that he would that night destroy Nabal's house and all his possessions. By this time he had 600 men under his command, 400 of which armed themselves and followed him.

Nabal had a very wise, virtuous, and lovely wife, whose name was Abigail. She had learned of her husband's abusive insults, and, while he lay in drunken slumber, she saddled her asses, loaded them with presents, and went in search of David. She met him as he was coming up a hill at the head of his men, and she fell to the ground and bowed down before him. She pleaded with him to ignore the words of Nabal, for the man was simply like his name—*nabal* in Hebrew means "folly"—and she implored mercy from one who was destined to be king. David's anger vanished, and, accepting her presents, he reassured her and dismissed her.

When Nabal was finally sober, Abigail told him everything, at which he collapsed, dying ten days later. When David learned that Nabal was dead, he said that he had received his proper punishment, while he himself had clean hands.

David loved Abigail, and invited her to come live with him and be his wife. She replied to his messengers that she was not worthy even to touch his feet, but she would do as David said, and she came with all her servants. David already had a wife from the city of Jezreel, and as for Michal, Saul's daughter, who was his former wife, her father had given her in marriage to Phalti of Gallim.

David Again Spares Saul

Learning from some of the Ziphites that David was in the wilderness of Maon, Saul [who had again turned hostile to David] took 3,000 men and went in search of him. David heard of his coming and sent out spies, who told him that Saul had camped at Hachilah. David took with him his nephew Abishai and Achimelech the Hittite, and at night they stole into Saul's camp while all were asleep. Abner, the commander, and his men were sleeping in a circle around the king, whose place David recognized by the spear stuck in the ground at his side. Abishai would have killed the king, but David prevented him. He merely took the spear and the water flask that lay next to Saul, and then they slipped silently out of the camp without having been seen or heard by anyone.

A VI,310

When David had reached the top of a neighboring hill, he called out in a loud voice and woke up the troops. Abner, the commander, asked who was calling. "I," said David, "the son of Jesse, your fugutive! But why are you, the commander, so negligent in guarding your master that you prefer sleep to safety? Look for the king's spear and his water flask, and you will learn how close you were to disaster without knowing it!"

When Saul recognized David's voice and understood what had happened, he thanked him for again having acted nobly despite the way he had treated him. David could go home in safety, he promised, and fear no further injury. When day broke, Saul led his army back to the palace.

The Witch of Endor

David was still afraid of Saul, so he decided to go and live in the land of the Philistines. With his band of 600, he went to Achish, the king of Gath, who welcomed him and his men. David settled in Gath with his two wives, Ahinoam and Abigail. Later, David asked the king if he and his men could move out of Gath to avoid being a burden, and Achish gave them Ziklag.

A VI,319

With this village as base, David and his men made clandestine raids on neighbors of the Philistines.

War broke out again between the Philistines and the Israelites, and Achish asked David to go with him to battle and bring his men. David promised to do so.

The Philistines made their camp near a city called Shunem, while Saul and his army made theirs on Mount Gilboa. Saul was dismayed at the numbers of the Philistines, and he inquired of God by the prophets about how the battle would go, but God gave him no answer. Now terrified, Saul determined to consult a woman who could raise the spirits of the dead and make them foretell the future. Previously, he had banished from the country all witches, diviners, and practitioners of such arts, except the prophets. Now, one of his servants informed him that there was such a woman at Endor.

Stripping off his royal robes and disguising himself, Saul paid this woman a secret, nocturnal visit accompanied by only two trusted aides. He told her she must raise up the spirit of whomever he would name, but she refused to obey him until he swore that he would tell no one of her divination, and that she would be in no danger. Having persuaded her, Saul asked her to raise the spirit of Samuel. Unaware of who Samuel was, she summoned him from Hades. But when he appeared as a venerable, godlike man who disclosed the identity of her visitor, she turned to Saul and cried in terror, "Are you not King Saul?"

"I am," he replied, and then asked her to describe the apparition that frightened her.

"He is advanced in age," she said, "with distinguished features, and wearing a priestly mantle."

Saul then knew it was Samuel and he fell to the ground in obedience. The spirit of Samuel asked him, "Why have you disturbed me and brought me up?"

Saul replied, "I am forsaken by God in the face of the enemy, and cannot obtain any knowledge of the future, either by prophets or by dreams. You must provide it."

"It is useless to seek me when God has abandoned you. But know this: David is chosen king and will be victor in this war, but you will lose both your dominion and your life, because you did not keep the commandments of God. Your people will be defeated tomorrow by the Philistines, and both you and your sons will fall in battle, and you will be with me."

When Saul had heard this, he collapsed onto the floor in grief and shock. The witch raised him up and insisted that he eat something. Slaughtering her only calf, she prepared the meat and set it before her three visitors, after which they returned to their camp.

The Death of Saul

Meanwhile, David and his 600 followed Achish into the Phil- A VI,351
istine camp. The commanders asked Achish to explain why
David, who had slaughtered so many Philistines, would now be
fighting on their side. Achish replied that David was both
repaying him for providing refuge and anxious to avenge himself on Saul. But the commanders advised Achish not to let
David join in the battle, for he might turn against them and help
the forces of his own nation. Achish then told David that while
he fully trusted him, the other chiefs did not, and so it would be
best for him to take his men back to Ziklag and guard Gath
against any attack while they were gone. "That too is the role of
an ally," he said, and David did as he was told.

While he was away, the Amalekites had fallen on the defenseless town of Ziklag and burned it. They also carried away much
booty, as well as the wives and children of David and his men.
Upon their return, they tore their clothes and wept aloud. Blaming him for their misfortunes, his comrades were so angry with
David that they talked of stoning him. But he took counsel from
God, and led his 600 in pursuit of the enemy. Soon they came
upon a man who had wandered in the desert three days without
nourishment, and they gave him food. He told them he was an
Egyptian, and that his Amalekite master had abandoned him
when he fell sick. David used the man to guide them to the
enemy.

The Amalekites were feasting and drinking, wallowing in
their booty, or lying on the ground in drunken slumber. They
were easy prey for David's attack, and were massacred at their
tables—all but 400, who mounted swift camels and escaped.
David and his men recovered their wives and children, as well
as the spoil the Amalekites had taken.

The Philistines, meanwhile, had joined battle with the Israelites [at Mount Gilboa] and won a great victory. Saul and his
sons fought bravely, knowing that they had nothing to hope for
except an honorable death. Attracting to themselves the front
line of the enemy, Saul's three sons were surrounded and killed,
including Jonathan. When they fell, the Hebrews fled in disorder, confusion, and slaughter. Saul himself was forced to flee
with a strong body of troops around him, but most of these were
caught by Philistine arrows and javelins. Saul turned and fought
magnificently, but he received so many wounds that he was too
weak to kill himself, and he told his armorbearer to run his
sword through him before the enemy could take him alive. But
since he refused, Saul fixed his own sword and flung himself on
it. When it failed to penetrate, he begged a young Amalekite

After the Battle of Mt. Gilboa (background), the bodies of King Saul and his son Jonathan were hung on the walls of Bethshan (ruins in the foreground).

to force the sword in. This he did, and after taking the royal crown from Saul's head and a gold bracelet from his arm, he fled. When the armorbearer saw that Saul was dead, he killed himself.

The next day, when the Philistines came to strip the bodies of the slain, they found those of Saul and his sons, and they cut off their heads and impaled their bodies on the walls of Bethshan. But when the Israelites of Jabesh-Gilead learned about this mutilation, the bravest of them marched all night to Bethshan, removed the bodies of Saul and his sons, and carried them to Jabesh, where they buried them. The enemy was either not able or not bold enough to stop them, because of their great courage.

Saul came to this end, as Samuel had predicted, because of his disobedience regarding the Amalekites and his destruction of the high priest and his family. He reigned eighteen years during the lifetime of Samuel, and 22 more after his death.

9
KING DAVID

David had just returned to Ziklag on the same day as the Philistine victory. On the third day after the fight, the man who killed Saul at his bidding arrived at Ziklag, his clothes torn and ashes on his head. He told David that the Hebrews were defeated and tens of thousands of them killed, including Saul and his sons. To prove that, he produced the crown and the bracelet and gave them to David. David tore his garments, weeping and lamenting all that day. His grief was increased by the memory of Jonathan, his dearest friend who had saved his life. He told the man who killed Saul that he had accused himself, and when he learned that he was an Amalekite, he ordered him put to death. David also composed eulogies for the funeral of Saul and Jonathan, which have survived.

When he had paid these honors to the king, David inquired of God by the prophet where he should live. When God answered that he was to go to Hebron, in the land of Judah, David left Ziklag with his followers, and the people of Judah proclaimed him king.

At this news, however, Abner, Saul's commander-in-chief, hurried to the camp. He took with him a fourth son of Saul, named Ishbosheth, and crossed over the Jordan to the people beyond. There he proclaimed him king over all the Israelites except the tribe of Judah. Angry with Judah for choosing David king, he declared war against them. Meanwhile, David appointed Joab, his nephew, as commander-in-chief and sent him out to fight Abner.

The two armies met near the city of Gibeon and prepared for battle. Abner proposed that twelve of the bravest men should be selected from each side and meet in combat to determine the outcome. This done, the 24 threw their spears and then drew their swords, fighting so desperately that all of them were killed. Then the two armies also clashed, and after a stubborn fight, Abner's men were beaten.

From this time on, there was civil war among the Hebrews, which lasted a long while. The followers of David grew stronger, while Saul's son and his subjects grew weaker by the day. Abner contacted David at Hebron, asking him to pledge friendship if he persuaded the people to revolt from Saul's son and declare him king. David agreed, but asked Abner, as proof of his good faith, to recover for him the bride that had cost him 600 Philistine heads. Accordingly, Abner took Michal away from her husband and sent her to David. Then he persuaded the officers and the people that God, through Samuel, had chosen David as king, and they all agreed.

Abner went to Hebron to plan the transfer of power, and David gave him a splendid reception. Joab, however, became jealous, fearing that he would be replaced as commander-in-chief, and he treacherously assassinated Abner while he was returning from Hebron. David swore before God that he had no part in the murder, and called down terrible curses on the murderer and his house. Then he led the people in profound mourning for Abner, and gave him a magnificent funeral at Hebron.

Ishbosheth, crushed by Abner's death, did not survive him for very long. Two Benjamite officers of his thought that if they killed him they would receive large rewards from David and be made commanders. They slipped into Ishbosheth's house one hot day at noon and found him alone and asleep, with no guards around him. They killed him, cut off his head, and brought it to David at Hebron. But David cried, "Vile wretches, you will receive instant rewards!" and ordered them put to death, while the head of Ishbosheth he buried in Abner's grave with great honor.

A VII,53   The Hebrew leaders then came to David in Hebron and acknowledged him as king. At last, then, David ruled over all the tribes of Israel. He called a meeting of all fighting men, and they came to Hebron in martial array, together proclaiming David king. When they had feasted for three days at Hebron, David marched them all against Jerusalem.

The Conquest of Jerusalem

The Jebusites, of the Canaanite race, lived in the city, and shut their gates against David. On the ramparts they stationed their maimed and blind to mock the king. Their walls were so strong, they claimed, that these cripples would stop him from entering.

Angry at their insults, David laid siege to Jerusalem and soon conquered the lower city. Because the citadel would be difficult to take, he offered a reward to his soldiers: the first to climb from the gullies below to capture the citadel would command the entire army. All eagerly rushed forward to climb the walls, but Joab was ahead of the rest. As soon as he reached the top of the citadel, he shouted to the king and claimed the chief command.

When David had driven the Jebusites out of the citadel, he c.1003 B.C. rebuilt Jerusalem, calling it the City of David, and lived there his entire reign. Hiram, king of Tyre, made an alliance of friendship with David, and sent him cedar wood and skilled carpenters to build a royal palace in Jerusalem. David enclosed the lower city and joined it to the citadel to form one unit. He surrounded it with a wall, appointing Joab keeper of the walls. Although Joshua had previously alloted this city to the Hebrews, they were not able to expel the Canaanites until David's siege 515 years later.

At Hebron, David had fathered six sons by six wives. Now, in Jerusalem, he married still more wives and concubines, who bore him eleven sons and one daughter.

When the Philistines learned that David had been chosen king of the Hebrews, they marched against Jerusalem, camping at the so-called Valley of the Giants not far away. After the high priest had prophesied a decisive victory, David marshaled his forces and attacked from the rear, killing and scattering them. Later, the Philistines returned with an army three times as large, but David routed them too, and pursued them as far as Gezer on their border.

The Ark Comes to Jerusalem

David decided to bring the ark of God to Jerusalem to keep it A VII,78 there and offer before it sacrifices pleasing to God. He called together the priests, Levites, captains, elders, and chief citizens, and they went in solemn procession to Kirjath-Jearim. The priests carried the ark out of the house of Abinadab and laid it on a new cart pulled by oxen. In front of it went the king, playing on his harp. The singing multitude followed, accompanied by trumpets and cymbals and other musical instruments—all of them escorting the ark to Jerusalem.

On the way, the oxen tilted the ark forward, and someone named Uzzah stretched out his hand to steady it. Because he was not a priest and had touched the ark, God caused his death. David was afraid that if he brought the ark into his house he might also die, so he left it instead at the house of a righteous

The Ark of the Covenant being transported on a wheeled vehicle, according to a stone relief discovered at Capernaum in Galilee.

man named Obededom, who was a Levite. The ark remained here for three months, and Obededom prospered during that time. Although he had been poor, he became very wealthy and envied by all. David then assumed it was safe to move the ark to his house. The priests carried the ark from the house of Obededom, preceded by seven choirs. David played his harp and sang and danced with the multitude. Then, when they had brought the ark into the city and placed it under a tent, David offered expensive sacrifices and feasted the people.

Michal, David's wife, pronounced blessings on him, but also criticized his dancing as inappropriate for a king. He replied that he was not ashamed to do what was pleasing to God, and would dance and play in the future without caring whether it seemed disgraceful to her and her maidservants. David had no children by Michal.

When the king looked around his palace and saw how beautifully furnished it was, he decided it was not right to keep the ark in a tent. He consulted the prophet Nathan to learn if he could build a temple to God, as Moses had envisioned. Nathan at first told him he could do as he chose, but at night, God appeared to the prophet. He had him tell David not to build the temple, because he had fought many wars and was stained with the blood of his enemies. But after his death, a temple would be built by Solomon, his son and successor. David rejoiced to learn that he would have a son, and gave thanks to God in front of the ark.

Shortly afterward, he marched against the Philistines and annexed much of their territory. He did the same to the Moabites, destroying two-thirds of their army. At the Euphrates, he won victories over neighboring monarchs, including the king of Damascus, and stationed garrisons in Syria and Idumea, where he collected tribute. The king of Hamath made an alliance with him, sending him gifts, which David dedicated to God. When the Ammonites insulted David's envoys, shaving off half of their beards, both he and Joab triumphed over them and their Mesopotamian allies.

David also remembered his friendship with Jonathan, and searched for any surviving members of his family. When he learned that he had left a crippled son, Mephibosheth, David allowed him to inherit all of Saul's and Jonathan's estates, and to share the king's table daily.

David and Bathsheba

One evening, David went for a walk on the roof of the palace, _{A VII,130} as was his custom. He noticed a very beautiful woman bathing at her house with cold water. Her name was Bathsheba. Captivated by her beauty and unable to restrain his desire, he sent for the woman and slept with her. When she became pregnant, Bathsheba asked the king to find some way of concealing her sin, because according to the laws, she deserved death for adultery.

David summoned her husband Uriah, who was Joab's armorbearer. He came from their siege of the Ammonite capital, Rabath, and David asked him about the campaign. Then he gave him some of his supper and ordered him to go home to his wife and rest with her. Uriah, however, slept with the other armorbearers instead. David asked him why he had not gone home after such a long absence. He replied that it was not right for him to rest with his wife when his colleagues were sleeping on the ground in enemy territory. That night, the king invited him to supper and toasted him repeatedly until Uriah was drunk. But again he slept in front of the king's door, and felt no desire for his wife. Finally, David wrote a sealed letter to Joab that Uriah

deserved punishment. He suggested that he be placed opposite
the strongest part of the enemy line, and that his comrades
should withdraw when the battle began.

Joab, accordingly, placed Uriah in front. The Ammonites
suddenly burst through their gates and he had to fight alone,
since everyone else was retreating. He cut down some of the
enemy before he himself and a few of his comrades were surrounded and killed.

*To conceal his adultery with Bathsheba, King David arranged for the death of her husband Uriah at
the battle for Rabath-Ammon, the later Philadelphia, where this Roman theater was built. Today the
city is Amman, the capital of Jordan.*

When David learned of the assault, he was angry that it had
been directed against the city walls, until he heard that Uriah
had been killed. Bathsheba mourned her husband's death many
days, but when she had finished grieving, David married her.
God, however, was angry at what David had done, and sent
A VII,147 Nathan the prophet to confront him. He came and said, "O king,
I want to ask your opinion about something. There were two
men living in the same city, one of whom was rich, the other
poor. The wealthy man had many herds of cattle and sheep, but
the poor man had only one ewe lamb. He raised it with his

children and let it eat food with them, and loved it as if it were one of his daughters. Once, a guest came to visit the wealthy man. But instead of killing one of his own flock to feast him, he sent for the poor man's lamb and prepared it for his guest."

David was very angry and said, "That man is a villain! He must repay for the lamb fourfold and then be executed!"

Nathan answered, "You are that man! And you have condemned yourself for a terrible crime. God has made you king over Israel, and given you lawful wives, yet you took another man's wife and caused his death. Know, then, that God will punish your wickedness: one of your sons will violate your wives and plot against you, and your baby will die soon after birth."

David bowed his head and confessed in tears that he had sinned. God took pity on him, and, now that he had repented, promised to preserve his life and his kingdom.

The infant Bathsheba bore to David became very sick. David was so troubled that he wore black, refused to eat for seven days, and lay on the floor, pleading with God to spare the baby's life. On the seventh day it died, and the servants were afraid to tell David. But when David saw them whispering, he knew what had happened. Having confirmed the death, David rose, washed, put on a white garment, and went to the tent of God, after which he ate. His servants were surprised that he had grieved so much while his child was sick, but not now that he was dead. David explained that while the child was alive he had shown appropriate grief, hoping God would be gracious. But after he died, further grief would be useless. They commended the king's wisdom. Then David slept with his wife Bathsheba, and she conceived and bore a son. By the direction of Nathan, he was named Solomon.

Meanwhile, Joab's siege of the Ammonite capital was starving the city into submission, and he invited David to make the final assault. Taking his men, the king victoriously stormed the city, killed its inhabitants, and allowed his soldiers to plunder the spoils.

Amnon and Tamar

After David returned to Jerusalem, however, a great scandal A VII,162 developed in his house. His daughter Tamar was still a virgin and strikingly beautiful. Amnon, David's oldest son, fell in love with her, and in his frustration became pale and ill. He told a friend of his lovesickness, and then followed the plan suggested by him. Pretending to be ill, Amnon went to his bed and begged his father to send his sister in to look after him. Dismissing his servants, he watched Tamar prepare some baked goods for him. He asked that she serve the meal in his inner bedroom, and she agreed. There he grabbed her, trying to seduce her, but she cried out, "No! Don't force me to do this, my brother, and bring shame on yourself and on our house!" She suggested he ask their father, who would consent to their marriage. But she was only playing for time, in order to blunt his lust.

Burning with desire, Amnon ignored her protests and violated his half sister. No sooner had he ravished her, however, than loathing overcame him and he became abusive, ordering her to leave. She thought it was outrageous for him to send her out in broad daylight to parade her shame, but he told his servant to throw her out.

Tamar tore her tunic in rage, poured ashes over her head, and walked through the middle of Jerusalem, crying loudly about the violence against her. Her brother Absalom met her—they had the same mother—and learned what had happened. He urged her to calm down, and then took her to his house.

When David found out, he was grief-stricken. But since he deeply loved Amnon, who was also his firstborn, he was compelled not to punish him. But Absalom hated him fiercely, and two years later arranged Amnon's murder at a feast where he had too much to drink. Absalom then fled from David to his maternal grandfather at Geshur, where he stayed for three years.

Joab finally helped to reconcile father and son, and happily brought Absalom back to Jerusalem. He was still remarkably handsome, and his hair was so thick he could hardly trim it every week. But *still* David refused to welcome Absalom, and told him to live in his own house.

The Rebellion of Absalom

A VII,190   For two years Absalom lived in Jerusalem without seeing his father. One day he sent for Joab, asking him to intercede with his father, but Joab ignored him. Then Absalom had his servants set fire to a field adjacent to Joab's. Joab was angry, and came to Absalom to ask why he had ordered the fire. Absalom replied, "To get your attention. Now that you are here, I beg you to pacify my father. My return is worse than my exile if my father's anger continues."

Joab was touched, and agreed to try to reconcile them. David was persuaded and sent for Absalom, who fell on the ground and begged for forgiveness. The king lifted him up and promised to forget what he had done.

Shortly afterward, Absalom obtained a large number of horses and chariots, and had 50 armed men around him. Early each morning, he would go to the palace and console those who had lost their cases at his father's tribunal. He claimed that he would have judged differently, and won favor with the people. Four years later, he decided the time had come for rebellion. He asked his father's permission to go to Hebron and offer sacrifice to God, for he had vowed it while in exile. When Absalom reached Hebron, a multitude of his followers declared him king. Among them was Ahitophel, David's counselor.

David was shocked and alarmed when he heard of Absalom's rebellion, and decided to escape to the lands beyond Jordan. Many were eager to accompany him, including his 600 stalwarts from Saul's era. The priests and Levites would have followed too with the ark, but David advised them to stay behind, saying that God would deliver him. As David ascended the Mount of Olives, barefoot and in tears, news arrived that Ahitophel had gone over to Absalom. This distressed him even more, for he knew that Ahitophel's wisdom would benefit Absalom, so he asked God to make Absalom distrust the counselor. At the top of the mountain, David looked back on the city in tears. A faithful friend of his, named Hushai, wanted to come with him, but David urged him to remain in Jerusalem as a spy. He was to pretend loyalty to Absalom, but contradict the counsel of Ahitophel.

A little further on, he was met by Ziba, who gave the king provisions. He was a servant whom David had sent to Mephibosheth, son of Jonathan. When asked about Mephibosheth, Ziba replied, "He waits to be chosen king during the present confusion, in return for all that Saul did for the people." David was furious, and instantly conferred on Ziba all he had previously granted Mephibosheth.

Farther down the road, a relative of Saul named Shimei came A VII,207 out and threw stones at David, cursing him as a criminal, stained with blood, who was now being punished as he deserved. David's nephew, Abishai, would have cut him down but David stopped him, saying, "I feel no shame from this cur's barking, for it is God who is behind his frenzy." So he continued on, ignoring Shimei, who ran along with them down the other side of the mountain, cursing him all the way.

Meanwhile, Absalom had come to Jerusalem with his counselor, Ahitophel, and all his followers. David's friend, Hushai, went to Absalom and offered his services. Absalom was suspicious at first, but Hushai explained that he now supported Absalom because God did, and further because the kingship was remaining with the same family. Convinced of his loyalty, Absalom deliberated strategy with Ahitophel, who advised him to sleep with his father's concubines and so cause an irreparable breach with him; for the people were hesitant to fight David in view of a possible future reconciliation between father and son, Ahitophel warned. Absalom had a tent pitched on the roof of the palace. In public view, he went and lay with his father's concubines—fulfilling Nathan's prophecy.

Next, he asked Ahitophel's advice about the war against his father. Ahitophel said that if he would let him have 10,000 men, he would march against David, kill him, and bring the soldiers back safely. Absalom liked this plan, but he sent for Hushai to ask his opinion also. Now Hushai feared that if Ahitophel's strategy were followed, David *would* be killed. Therefore, he advised Absalom to wait until he could raise a large army, and then he would safely defeat the king if he personally took command. God made Absalom prefer Hushai's advice to Ahitophel's.

Then Hushai went to the high priests, who supported David, and told them what had been decided. They sent David some messengers, who had to hide in a well for a while to elude pursuers before reaching the king.

When Ahitophel heard that his advice had been rejected, he saddled his donkey and rode away to his native city. Calling his family together, he told them that since Absalom would not follow his advice, he would surely be defeated by David. Therefore, he said, it was better to leave the world as a free man than surrender to David, who would certainly punish him for helping Absalom. Then he took a rope and hanged himself.

The Death of Absalom

A VII,230   David crossed the Jordan in his flight and came to Mahanaim, a fine, strong city. All the chief men received him cordially and supplied him and his exhausted followers with plenty of provisions.

By this time, Absalom had gathered a large army, and he led them against his father. David counted his own men—there were 4,000—and he set captains over them. He himself would have led them into battle, but his friends would not let him, for if they were defeated under him, all hope would be lost. But as long as he lived, he could inspire recovery from any defeat. Thus David remained in the city and sent out his commanders to meet Absalom. He urged them to be brave and loyal, but implored them to spare his son Absalom.

David's army, though small, was stronger and more skillful. After a very hard fight they were victorious and pursued the enemy, killing many thousands. They chased Absalom, his height clearly visible, but he mounted his royal mule and fled.

The mule galloped under the thick branches of a rugged tree, which entangled Absalom's long hair, yanking him off the back of the mule, which ran on without him.

One of David's troops told Joab that Absalom was swinging from a tree. Joab answered, "If you had killed him, I would have given you 50 shekels."

"I would not have killed my master's son for 1,000," the soldier replied. "We all heard the king plead that the young man be spared."

Joab asked him where he had seen Absalom, and soon found him, still hanging from the tree. Joab shot an arrow into his heart and killed him. Then his aides pulled down the corpse, cast it into a deep pit, and threw stones over it. Meanwhile, Joab trumpeted a cease-fire, sparing his people from further fighting.

Ahimaaz, one of the high priest's sons, came to Joab and asked permission to go and tell David about the victory. But Joab replied, "You have always been a messenger of good news, and it would not be right for you to tell the king his son is dead." Joab called a Cushite servant and told him to run to the king and tell him. But again Ahimaaz asked Joab to let him go, promising to talk only about the victory. Joab let him, and Ahimaaz arrived first.

David was sitting at the gates of the city, waiting for news of the battle. When Ahimaaz had come near enough, the watchman recognized him. He told David, who was very glad, saying, "He is a messenger of good news!"

Ahimaaz appeared at the gate and announced the happy news of victory. Then David asked him what had become of Absalom. Ahimaaz replied that he had heard the shouts of those who were chasing Absalom, but could learn nothing more. When the Cushite arrived, David asked him how Absalom had fared, and he replied, "May all your enemies come to the same end as Absalom!"

Overcome with sorrow, David went up to a chamber above the gate and wept, beating his breast, tearing his hair, and crying, "Oh, Absalom, my son, I wish I had died with you!"

When the army and Joab learned how deeply the king mourned for his son, they were ashamed to enter the city as conquerors, arriving instead with heads drooped as if they had been beaten. Joab, however, went to David and comforted him, saying, "O Master, you seem to hate those who love you and risk their lives for you, but love those who are your worst enemies. For if Absalom had won, none of us would have been left alive. Everyone, beginning with you and your children, would have died miserably. Stop your unreasonable grief, then, and go to your soldiers and thank them for victory." David made himself presentable and sat by the gates of the city, where all the people ran to greet him.

David Returns to His Kingdom

A VII,258   The Hebrews who had supported Absalom now regretted it, and sent envoys to invite David back to his kingdom. When he reached the river Jordan, some Israelite leaders came out to meet him. They set up a bridge of boats across the river so that the king and his men could cross more easily. Among them was Shimei, who fell at David's feet on the bridge and pleaded for forgiveness. Then Abishai, Joab's brother, said, "Shouldn't you die for cursing the king whom God placed over us?" But David answered that he did not intend to punish the rebels, and told Shimei to be encouraged, for he would not be executed.

Saul's grandson, Mephibosheth, also met him there, wearing a soiled garment with hair unkempt from grief. He claimed his steward Ziba had lied about him to David. When the king asked why he had not, then, gone into exile with him, he replied, "If I had healthy feet and had been able to use them to escape, I would not have been far behind you." David forgave him, and ordered that half his property be restored to him, to which he exclaimed, "Let Ziba have it all! It is enough for me that you have recovered your kingdom."

Later a certain rabble-rouser named Sheba, of the tribe of Benjamin, refused to submit to David and stirred up a sedition. David appointed Amasa as commander to put it down, but when he delayed raising an army, he dispatched Joab. But at Gibeon, Joab found Amasa and his army. As the two met, Joab took Amasa by the beard as if to kiss him, but instead thrust his sword into his belly and killed him. This impious deed stemmed from Joab's envy that Amasa had been honored with a rank equal to his own. Both forces then followed Joab to a fortified city named Abel-Beth-maachah, where Sheba had taken refuge, and besieged it.

A wise old woman appeared on the walls and called for Joab. When he appeared, she said, "God ordained kings and commanders to expel the enemies of the Hebrews, but you are determined to destroy an Israelite city which has done nothing wrong." Joab answered that he did not want to kill any of the people or destroy the city. If they surrendered Sheba, who had rebelled against the king, he would withdraw his army. Then the woman went down to the citizens, and asked, "Do you want to die miserably for the sake of a worthless fellow nobody knows? And do you want him for your king instead of David, who has been your benefactor?" Thus she persuaded them to cut off Sheba's head and throw it to Joab's army. The king's commander then sounded a retreat and lifted the siege.

After further battles with the Philistines, in which David was victorious, he finally enjoyed prolonged peace. He composed songs and hymns to God, and designed musical instruments of strings and brass. He was surrounded by many brave men, 38 of whom were especially famous.

The Census and the Plague

King David was anxious to know the size of his population, A VII,318 and told Joab to go out and count the people. Joab, who claimed there was no need for it, took with him the heads of the tribes and the scribes and went across the country to tabulate the census. After nine months and twenty days, he returned to the king, reporting that, except for Levi and Benjamin, the tribes numbered 900,000 men who were able to fight, including 400,000 from Judah alone.

There was a law given by Moses that if a census were taken, a half-shekel should be paid to God for every person.* David failed to comply with this law, and the prophets told him that God was angry with him. David begged God for mercy and forgiveness. Then God sent the prophet Gad to tell David he could choose one of three punishments: a seven-year famine, a three-month defeat by his enemies, or a three-day plague. David was distressfully perplexed, but finally he chose the last, saying that it was better to fall into the hands of God than into those of his enemies.

God then sent an angel that brought a great plague upon the Hebrews—pain, suffocation, consumption, blindness—and in one morning 70,000 of them died. David put on sackcloth and lay on the ground, praying that the plague might now stop, and that God would be satisfied with those who had already died. Looking up into the sky he saw the angel floating over Jerusalem with his sword drawn, and implored God to punish him alone and spare his people.

God heard him, and stopped the plague. He sent the prophet Gad, who commanded David to go up at once to the threshing floor of Araunah the Jebusite and build an altar there to offer sacrifice. Araunah was threshing his wheat when David and his attendants appeared. He ran out to the king, bowed, and asked what he desired. David said that he had come to buy his threshing floor, so that he could build an altar there and offer sacrifice to God.

---

* Exodus 30:12 ff.

Araunah said he would offer the threshing floor as a gift, and would also provide his oxen for a burnt offering. David thanked him, but asked to pay for everything, since it was not proper to offer a sacrifice that cost nothing. So he bought the threshing floor for 50 shekels, built the altar, and offered sacrifice. God was appeased and became gracious again. Now this was the same place where Abraham had formerly sacrificed a ram instead of his son Isaac. When David saw that God was pleased with his sacrifice, he called that entire area the altar of all the people, and he chose it as the place where the temple would be built.

The Death of David

A VII,335 David began to prepare stone, cedar, bronze, and iron for the building of the temple, assigning 80,000 masons to cut the stones, and importing huge cedar trees from Tyre and Sidon.

To prepare for the building of the temple, David imported cedar timbers from Lebanon. Today, the last forest of these cedars stands in a special preserve at the highest point in Lebanon, where snow caps the mountains in winter.

Since his son Solomon was young and inexperienced, David said, he would prepare for him the materials to build the temple.

He called Solomon, and told him that God had chosen him as his successor to the kingdom, and had foretold that he would build the temple. David cited the preparations he had made for this purpose, and informed Solomon that he had reserved a great deal of gold and silver in his treasury to pay for materials and labor.

David was now very old and his body so numb and cold that not even many clothes could keep him warm. His doctors suggested that a beautiful virgin be chosen to sleep with the king to warm him. They found a woman of surpassing loveliness named Abishag, who merely kept the king warm in the same bed, for he was too weak to have intercourse with her.

But the fourth son of David, Adonijah, aspired to be king instead, and was supported by Joab and the high priest Abiathar. He prepared a great dinner outside the city in the royal garden for all his supporters, who were jesting, applauding, and wishing him a long reign. The prophet Nathan, however, alerted Bathsheba, and they both came to David and asked him if he had just declared Adonijah king in view of the festivities in progress. David decided to make Solomon king at once. He ordered his aides to saddle the royal mule and place Solomon on it, and take him to the spring named Gihon, where they were to anoint him king. Then they were to blow trumpets and shout aloud, "Long live King Solomon!" so that all the people would know he had been declared king by his father. _{A VII,345}

After this was done, Solomon went to the royal palace and sat on the throne, while the people came, shouting and rejoicing with dancing and singing. Adonijah and his guests were still sitting at their feast when they heard the sound of trumpets and rejoicing, and a messenger arrived to tell them of the anointing of Solomon. All the guests jumped up and fled to their homes, while Adonijah, in fear and contrition, prayed to God. But when Solomon was told that Adonijah was gripping the horns of the altar in humility and feared for his life, he had Adonijah brought before him. With great moderation, he told him not to be afraid, but to behave well in the future.

David divided the chiefs', priests' and Levite families, giving them specific duties. He also regulated the army and treasury, and then summoned all the Hebrew leaders in order to commend Solomon to them as designated by God to be his successor. He also told them about the temple which he had desired to build, but was prevented from doing so, and how Solomon had been appointed to the task instead.

Then David, in the sight of them all, gave the plans of the building to Solomon. He asked the Levites to help Solomon in the work, because of his youth, explaining that the work would be easy because of the preparations he had made and the large sums of money reserved for this purpose. When David had finished speaking, many of the priests and Levites came forward and promised to help Solomon, and to give him quantities of gold and silver, iron and jewels. David ordered that solemn sacrifices be offered, and then a great festival was celebrated, at which he himself feasted with the multitude.

A little later David became ill, and on his deathbed gave last instructions to Solomon, urging his obedience to God, and then he added: "Remember the crime of Joab, who through envy killed two brave generals. Avenge their deaths in whatever way you think best, since Joab, being more powerful than I, has so far escaped punishment. And as for Shimei, who cursed me but received a pledge for the time being that he would not be harmed, find a reasonable excuse to punish him."

971 B.C.   With these instructions, David died at age 70, having ruled seven years in Hebron over the tribe of Judah, and 33 years in Jerusalem over the whole nation. Solomon buried him in Jerusalem with great splendor and a vast amount of wealth.

SOLOMON 10
AND HIS SUCCESSORS

At the beginning of the king's reign, the whole multitude A VIII,1 hailed him joyfully and prayed that he might end his rule at a happy old age. His brother Adonijah, however, went to the king's mother, Bathsheba, asking her to request of Solomon that he be given Abishag in marriage, since his father had not had intercourse with her and she remained a virgin. Bathsheba did so, but Solomon rejected the request. He claimed that Adonijah was aiming at kingship for himself, with such powerful friends as Joab and Abiathar the high priest. He sent for Banaias, the chief of his bodyguard, and ordered him to kill Adonijah. He also stripped Abiathar of the high priesthood, and transferred it to the family of Sadok.

When Joab, the commander, heard that Adonijah had been executed, he fled to the altar for refuge and would not leave it to appear before Solomon to make his defense. Solomon ordered Banaias to cut off his head there, judging himself blameless for Joab's death, and appointed Banaias his successor as commander of the army.

As for Shimei, Solomon ordered him to remain in Jerusalem and pledge, under oath, never to leave the city. Shimei did so, but after three years passed, two of his slaves escaped to Gath and he set out after them. When he returned with them, the king learned of it and had Banaias put Shimei to death.

Having punished his enemies, Solomon married the daughter of the king of Egypt and strengthened the walls of Jerusalem, governing the state in perfect peace. He went to Hebron and sacrificed to God on the bronze altar built by Moses, offering up 1,000 victims as a burnt offering. God was pleased with his piety, and appeared to the king in his sleep, offering him anything he desired. Solomon did not ask for gold or silver or other wealth, as a young man might have done. Instead he said, "Give me, O Lord, a sound mind and good understanding, so that I can judge the people in truth and righteousness."

God was pleased with this answer. He promised to give him unparalleled wisdom, as well as those things which Solomon had not asked for, such as wealth, glory, and victory over his enemies. He also promised to preserve the kingdom for Solomon's descendants if he continued to be righteous and imitated the virtues of his father.

A VIII,26   One example of Solomon's wisdom is the case of two harlots who came before him. One of them said to him, "O king, this other woman and I live together in the same room. We each had a little son, and this woman accidentally smothered her child by sleeping on it. But while I was sleeping, she put her dead child in my arms, and took my child from me and laid it at her side. And in the morning when I wanted to feed the baby, I found in its place this dead body, and she refused to give my baby back to me."

Solomon then turned to the other woman and asked what she had to say. She denied having done this, insisting that the living child was hers, and the dead one was her opponent's. Everyone present was puzzled as to which of the women to believe. Then the king had them bring in both the dead and the living child, and he sent for one of his guards. He ordered him to draw his sword and cut both children in half, that each of the women might have half the living and half the dead child. All in attendance laughed secretly at the king, thinking he was but a boy. But the true mother of the living child cried out that he should not do this. Rather, he should give the living child to the other woman as if it were hers, and she would be content merely to look at it. The other woman was willing to see the child divided.

Then the king knew which was the true mother, and he gave the child to the one who had cried out to save it. He condemned the other as a wicked woman, who had not only killed her own son, but was willing to see her friend's child killed also. The people looked upon this judgment as a sign of great wisdom, and they regarded the king as one who had divine intelligence.

Enjoying the benefits of peace, the Hebrews turned to husbandry and cultivation, and were rewarded with abundance. Solomon, who ruled from the Euphrates river to Egypt, collected much tribute, and had so many chariots that there were 40,000 stalls for his horses and 12,000 horsemen. He also composed

Ruins of the traditional "Solomon's Stables", including stone mangers, at Megiddo, which guarded the pass from the seacoast highway into the interior Plain of Jezreel in Galilee.

odes, songs, parables, incantations, and exorcisms, and he learned the properties of nature.

Building the Temple

In the fourth year of his reign—592 years after the exodus from Egypt—Solomon began to build the temple, after gathering the timber, stone, and iron. Hiram, king of Tyre, who had been David's friend, made a treaty of friendship with Solomon also. He let Solomon have cedar and cypress timber and many of his most skillful workmen. Solomon, in return, sent Hiram annually 20,000 kors* of grain, oil, and wine. Hiram's men and Solomon's servants cut down the cedar trees on Mount Lebanon, and split them into beams. Others cut large stones from quarries, and both timber and stone were transported to Jerusalem.

A VIII,50

---

* The kor was equivalent to c. 11 bushels or 370 liters.

The foundations of the temple were made of great stones, buried deep in the ground. The body of the building was white marble, 60 cubits long and 20 wide, and it stood two stories tall. In front was a porch, and surrounding it were 30 smaller rooms that were interconnected. The roof was made of cedar, and the walls were also adorned at intervals with boards of cedar covered with gold.

The interior of the temple was divided into two chambers. The innermost of these, the Sanctum, was for the ark. Across the doorways between the two chambers hung a veil of blue, purple, and scarlet, made of the brightest and softest linen. Two cherubim of solid gold, five cubits in height, stood in the Sanctum with their wings extended. The wing of one touched the southern wall, and the wing of the other the northern wall, and the other wings touched each other so as to cover the ark, which was placed between them.

In the outer chamber stood the golden altar [of incense], and 10,000 candlesticks, one of which was always kept lit. There were also many tables in this room, one of which was made of gold. On this were set the loaves dedicated to God, while the others were smaller and contained vessels of gold and silver, many thousands in number.

In the court before the temple stood the bronze altar on which sacrifices were offered. There was a great basin here, so large that it was called "the bronze sea," which rested on the backs of twelve calves, three facing in each direction. This was to hold water for the priests to wash their hands and feet before offering sacrifices. There were ten lavers also, which were set on wheels, and these were used for washing the animals prepared for sacrifice.

At the entrance to the temple stood two tall pillars of bronze, with cast metal lilies as capitals. One of these pillars was called Jachin, and the other Boaz. In addition to pitchers, bowls, censers, and priestly vestments of precious materials, Solomon ordered 200,000 trumpets and 40,000 stringed instruments. He also surrounded the temple with various magnificent courts on all sides, with parapets, quadrangles, and porticoes. Some of these rested on chasms which Solomon had filled in with an immense amount of material to bring them level with the temple mount. He finally completed the temple after seven years.

A VIII,100 When it was finished, Solomon ordered all the Hebrews to gather at Jerusalem to see the temple and join in moving the ark into it. They came and celebrated in song and dance as the priests lifted the ark and carried it into the temple, placing it in the Sanctum between the two cherubim. (The ark held nothing but the two stone tablets with the ten commandments inscribed.) When the priests had finished placing the other tables, altars, and vessels, a cloud streamed into the temple. Everyone sensed that God had descended into the structure and that He was pleased.

Then Solomon stood and prayed: "We know that you, O Lord, have your eternal dwelling in the heaven and air and earth and sea which you have created, and yet you are not contained by them. But I have built this temple so that from it we may send up our prayers to you, and may always be convinced that you are present to all people, even when dwelling here." Then Solomon turned to the multitude and reminded them of how perfectly God had fulfilled his prophecies to David by this temple, for which they should praise Him and never lose hope in His promises.

Solomon threw himself on the ground in humility, and then rose to heap sacrifices on the altar. A fire rushed down upon the altar in everyone's sight and consumed the victims laid on it. The people rejoiced, knowing that God had accepted the sacrifices.

The king offered up other sacrifices also, slaughtering 12,000 calves and 120,000 sheep. He celebrated the Feast of Tabernacles at the same time, which lasted fourteen days, and all the people feasted with the king. After this they went home in joy, thankful to the king and asking God to give him a long reign.

God appeared to Solomon in his sleep and told him that He had heard his prayers and would dwell in the temple forever if the people were righteous. And if Solomon would obey Him, he would have a long life and his descendants would reign after him. But if he abandoned the true God and worshiped idols, then He would cut him off. And if the people fell away, they would be thrown out of the land which He had given to their fathers, and be scattered over strange lands. Their temple would be burned down and sacked by the enemy, and their city smashed to the ground.

The Queen of Sheba

After the temple had been built and dedicated, Solomon A VIII,130 began erecting a palace for himself, and took thirteen years to complete it. Constructed of white marble, cedar, gold, and silver, it contained several great halls lined with columns. One was for public trials and judgments, and another for the king and his immense ivory throne. Another hall was designated for the queen, and yet another for feasts and banquets, in which all the utensils were made of gold. There were also many smaller rooms, all expensively decorated.

Solomon constructed towers into the walls around Jerusalem to fortify it. He also built or rebuilt a number of powerful cities—Hazor, Megiddo, and Gezer—and founded others, including Tadmor [Palmyra], which boasted springs and wells in the desert of Upper Syria. He also subjugated all unconquered Canaanites and built a fleet of ships in the gulf of the Red Sea at Ezion-geber. Some of them sailed as far as Ophir, near India.

A VIII,165   The queen of Egypt and Ethiopia was a great lover of wisdom. Having heard so much about Solomon, she decided to come to Jerusalem to talk with him and test his wisdom. She arrived with great splendor, bringing camels carrying gold, precious stones, and spices.

Solomon gladly received her, and effortlessly solved the problems she posed. She was astonished with his wise answers. The magnificence of the royal palace, the food lavished on the table, the dress and skill of the servants, and the daily sacrifices that were offered up by the priests and Levites also impressed her. She confessed that she had not believed the reports about the power and glory of Solomon, but now she saw that they fell far short of the truth. And she gave gifts to Solomon of the things she had brought with her, including twenty talents of gold and a great quantity of spices and gems. In return, he gave expensive presents to her, some of which she selected. Then the queen returned to her own country.

The ships from Ophir brought Solomon 666 talents of gold as well as exotic wood and gems. Surrounding kings sent him valuable gifts, which he used to decorate the palace and his cavalry. He also paved the roads leading to Jerusalem with black stone. He especially loved to mount his chariot, dressed in white, and go for a ride to a delightful spot called Etan,* which had many parks and flowing streams.

Solomon's Decline

A VIII,190   Although God had blessed Solomon in so many ways, and made him one of the wisest and wealthiest kings, he did not persevere, but abandoned his fathers' customs. Falling madly in love with women and going to excesses in passion, he was not satisfied with Hebrew women. He married those from Tyre, Sidon, the Ammonites, and the Idumeans, although Moses had forbidden marriage with other races. He also began to worship his wives' gods to humor them. He married 700 women of royalty or nobility, and 300 concubines. Old and weak, he turned from God to their idols. He also sinned by placing images

---

* The modern Ain Atan, c. five miles southwest of Bethlehem.

of bronze bulls beneath "the Sea" at the temple, as well as the lions carved around his throne. God warned him in a dream twice, and then sent a prophet, who told him that because of his wickedness his kingdom would be divided, and his sons would rule over only two tribes.

A young Israelite named Jeroboam had supervised the strengthening of Jerusalem's walls for Solomon. One day, a prophet came and greeted him. Taking him aside in privacy, he tore his cloak into twelve pieces and told Jeroboam to take ten of them. "For this is the will of God," the prophet said. "He will divide the kingdom of Solomon: only two of the tribes will be left to his son because of his promise to David, and He will give ten tribes to you, because Solomon has sinned against Him." When Solomon learned that Jeroboam planned revolt, he tried to kill him, but the young man fled from the country and sought the protection of Shishak, king of Egypt, remaining with him until Solomon's death.

Soon afterward, Solomon died at age 94, having ruled 80 931 B.C. years, and was buried at Jerusalem. He surpased all other monarchs in wealth and wisdom, except that he was seduced by his wives into illegalities as he neared old age.

The Folly of Rehoboam

Solomon's son Rehoboam succeeded him, but the leaders of A VIII,212 the common people sent for Jeroboam to return from Egypt. He was to meet them at Shechem, where they would proclaim the next king. When Rehoboam arrived there, Jeroboam and the leaders asked him whether he intended to rule more leniently than his father, whose yoke had been very heavy. Rehoboam told them he would give them an answer in three days.

He then went to his father's old counselors, who told him to speak kindly to the people and assure them that he would be a mild and just king. But Rehoboam rejected their advice, and consulted with his young friends instead. They gave him the exact words to use in an arrogant response. When the multitude had reassembled, Rehoboam told them: "My little finger is thicker than my father's hips, and if you thought my father was harsh, expect even rougher treatment from me. He punished you with whips, but I will use scorpions!"

The people were furious, and yelled that they would not have Rehoboam as their king. They even stoned to death an emissary he had sent to pacify them, so he mounted his chariot and fled for his life to Jerusalem. Ten of the tribes chose Jeroboam to rule over them, but the tribes of Judah and Benjamin remained faithful to Rehoboam. Rehoboam was preparing a large army to attack Jeroboam and his people, but God sent a prophet to forbid it, and so he abandoned the plan.

Jeroboam

　Jeroboam built himself a palace in Shechem and lived there. To prevent his subjects from worshiping in Jerusalem, fearing that they might be tempted to return to Rehoboam, he made two golden heifers and built shrines for them, one at Bethel, and the other at Dan. As the Feast of the Tabernacles approached, he called the people together and told them it would no longer be necessary to go to Jerusalem, the enemy's city, to worship God. "For I have made two golden heifers," Jeroboam declared, "one at Bethel, the other at Dan. You may go to whichever city is most convenient, and worship God there. And I will appoint for you priests and Levites from among you so that you will not need the sons of Aaron."

Jeroboam ordained himself high priest, and prepared to offer sacrifices at the shrine in Bethel. Just as he ascended the steps of the altar in sight of all the people, the prophet Jadon came to him from Jerusalem. He spoke to the altar: "God bids me tell you that a successor of David named Josiah will sacrifice on you the false priests living in his time. He will also burn the bones of those that are dead, because they are deceivers of the people, imposters, and unbelievers. And to prove that this will happen, I will give the people a sign: this altar will be broken to pieces, and all the fat of the sacrifices will be spilled on the ground."

In fury, Jeroboam stretched out his hand to order his arrest, but the hand was instantly paralyzed. It hung there, numb and dead, and he could not pull it back. The altar shattered, and everything on it fell to the ground. Then Jeroboam begged the prophet to ask God to restore life to his right hand. The prophet did so, and his hand was cured. Jeroboam invited Jadon to eat with him, but he said, "God has forbidden me to taste bread or water from this city. He has also told me to return on a different road from that on which I came."

Now a wicked old man, who was a false prophet, also lived there. When his sons told him what the prophet from Judah had done, he was afraid that the stranger would replace him as Jeroboam's prophet, so he ordered his sons to saddle his donkey, and he pursued Jadon. Finding him resting under a large tree, he complained that Jadon had not come to his house and eaten with him. Jadon replied that God had forbidden him to eat or drink in the city of Bethel. "Surely God did not forbid you to eat and drink with *me*," said the old man, "for I am a prophet like you and we worship God in the same way. He sent me to bring you back to my house as my guest."

Jadon believed these lies and returned with him. But as they were eating lunch and conversing, God appeared to Jadon and told him he would be punished for transgressing His commands. On the way home, a lion would kill him, and he would not be buried in the tomb of his fathers.

Everything happened as predicted. Some travelers told the false prophet that they had seen Jadon's body lying by the road, while a lion stood beside it. The old man sent his sons to bring the body to Bethel, where he gave it an expensive burial. And he said to his sons, "When I am dead, bury me in the same tomb with this genuine prophet."

Then he went to Jeroboam and said, "Why are you bothered by the words of this silly fellow?" Jeroboam described the miracles Jadon had performed. But the old man said, "Your hand was numbed by carrying the sacrifices, and a little rest restored it. And since the altar was new, it could not bear the weight of so many sacrifices, and fell apart." He also told Jeroboam of the prophet's death, proving that his prophecies were false. The king was persuaded, and continued to outrage the Deity with his wickedness.

Rehoboam

Rehoboam, king of the two tribes, built large cities in Judah A VIII,246 and Benjamin, with regiments in each. Priests, Levites, and righteous people from the other tribes came to worship God in Jerusalem, refusing to venerate the golden heifers of Jeroboam.

Rehoboam had 18 legal wives and 30 concubines, and he fathered 28 sons and 60 daughters. But as his prosperity increased, he also showed disrespect for God and was guilty of blasphemy. Many of the people followed his example, until God showed his anger at them. He punished them by sending Shishak, king of Egypt, to march against them with an immense army and conquer their cities. When he advanced on Jerusalem, the prophet Shemaiah said God would abandon them just as they had abandoned their worship of Him. King Shishak took the city without a fight. He sacked the temple, and carried off great quantities of gold and silver from its treasuries and the palace.

After Shishak returned to Egypt, Rehoboam ruled in fear and 913 B.C. died at age 57 after ruling 17 years. He was buried at Jerusalem in the tombs of the kings, and was succeeded by his son Abijah.

THE KINGDOMS OF ISRAEL AND JUDAH

Jeroboam's Punishment

Meanwhile, Jeroboam had also invited on himself God's pun- A VIII,266
ishment. When his son became sick, Jeroboam told his wife to
disguise herself in the dress of a common woman, and go to the
prophet Ahijah at
Shiloh. This was the
prophet who had
foretold that Jer-
oboam would be
king. "Speak to him
as a stranger," said
Jeroboam, "and ask
him if our son will
recover."

When Jeroboam's
wife was near the
prophet's house,
God appeared to
Ahijah, informing
him who she was
and what answer to
give her. So the
prophet called out
to her, "Come in,
wife of Jeroboam!
Why do you dis-
guise yourself? God
knows you have
come here, and has
told me what to tell
you. Return to your
husband, and repeat
to him these words
from God: 'I made
you great when you
were a little man,
and conferred on
you the kingdom of
David. But because
you have forgotten

*"Gods of molten metal" included this golden statuette of Baal
(Oriental Institute, U. of Chicago).*

this and have forsaken me to worship gods of molten metal, I
will diminish you again. All your family will be destroyed, and
they will be food for dogs and birds. Your people will share in
punishment by being exiled from their good land to the country
beyond the Euphrates.' And you, woman, hurry back to your
husband, and when you reach the city, your son will be dead."

Returning to her husband in tears, she found the child dead, and told the king everything.

Their Successors

A VIII,274   When Abijah succeeded his father Rehoboam, Jeroboam attacked him with a huge army. Although Abijah's forces were much smaller, he gained a wonderful victory through God, killing 500,000 of the enemy. Then he stormed their strongest cities, including Bethel, and plundered them.

Abijah had ruled only three years when he died, leaving fourteen wives. He was succeeded by his son Asa, under whom there was a decade of peace. Jeroboam also died, after he had been king for 22 years. He was succeeded by his son Nadab, in the second year of Asa's reign.

Nadab took after his wicked father. When he had ruled for two years, a friend of his named Baasha plotted against him. He killed Nadab and made himself king. Baasha put all of Jeroboam's family to death, and the words of the prophet Ahijah came true, for their bodies were devoured by dogs and birds.

Asa, King of Judah

A VIII,290   Asa, the king of Jerusalem, was admirable and righteous in all his actions. He looked to the Deity for guidance, and he purified his kingdom of wicked practices. In the tenth year of Asa's reign, Zerah, king of Ethiopia, marched against him with an army of 900,000 men and 100,000 cavalry. Asa met him at Mareshah, a city of Judah. When he saw the size of the enemy, he cried to God for victory, since only He could make the few triumph over the many. God indicated that he would be victorious. Asa then joyfully met the enemy, defeated them, and plundered their camp.

When Asa and his army were returning to Jerusalem, they met the prophet Azariah on the road. He told them: "You have obtained this victory from God because you have followed His will. And if you continue to do so, He will always give you victory over your enemies. But if you abandon Him, the time will come when no true prophet will be left among your people. Your cities will then be overthrown, and your nation scattered over the whole earth as aliens and wanderers."

From Baasha to Ahab

A VIII,298   I will return to Israel and their king Baasha, who killed Jeroboam's son and seized power. He reigned 24 years at Tirzah, but grew even more wicked and blasphemous than Jeroboam. God, therefore, sent the prophet Jehu to warn him of the destruction awaiting such conduct, but he completely disregarded the admonitions of the prophet. He attacked and captured Ramah, only 40 stades from Jerusalem, intending to use it as a base from which to ravage Asa's kingdom. But Asa made an alliance with the king of Damascus, who invaded Baasha's northern cities, including Dan, and caused him to withdraw from Ramah.

Shortly afterward, Baasha died, and his son, Elah, succeeded him. After reigning only two years, Elah was treacherously killed by Zimri, his cavalry commander, while alone at dinner. Zimri made himself king and destroyed Baasha's entire family, fulfilling the prophecy of Jehu. At that time, the army was besieging Gibbethon, a Philistine city. Declaring their commander Omri as king, the soldiers lifted their siege and attacked Tirzah instead. Zimri fled into his inner palace, set it on fire, and burned himself to death after ruling only seven days.

Omri reigned for twelve years, six at Tirzah, and the rest at Samaria, a city he built on a mountain purchased from a man named Shemer. Even worse than his predecessors, Omri died in Samaria and was succeeded by his son Ahab. The Deity, then, keeps a close watch on human affairs: the kings of Israel had only brief reigns and their families were destroyed, due to their iniquity. But Asa, king of Jerusalem and the two tribes, died happily after a reign of 41 years, and was succeeded by his son 870 B.C. Jehoshaphat.

[*A complete listing of the kings of Judah and Israel, as well as their dates, is provided on pages 388 and 389. The next three chapters, like their biblical counterparts, offer much dynastic detail, and the more casual reader may wish to scan them.*]

11
THE PROPHET ELIJAH

Ahab, king of Israel, ruled for 22 years at Samaria, and outdid A VIII,316 the previous kings in extraordinary wickedness and lawlessness. He worshiped the heifers which Jeroboam had made, as well as the native gods of his wife Jezebel, who was the daughter of the king of Tyre. This bold woman built a great temple to Baal, the Tyrian god, and appointed priests and false prophets to this deity.

There was a prophet of God from Tishbi [Elijah] who came to Ahab and told him that God would not send any more rain or dew in the land until he returned. With that, he departed and lived by a stream, where ravens brought his food each day. But when the drought dried up the stream, he went to the town of Zarephath, between Sidon and Tyre. God had said he would find a widow there who would provide him with food.

Close to the city he met a woman laborer gathering wood. God identified her as the widow, and Elijah greeted her and asked for some water to drink. As she was going to get it, he called her back and asked her to bring a loaf of bread too. But the woman said she had only a handful of flour and a little oil. She was now gathering a few sticks to make a fire and bake bread for herself and her son, after which they would starve to death. Elijah replied, "Have courage and hope, but first prepare a little food. For I promise you that your bowl will never be empty of flour, nor your jar of oil, until God sends rain."

The woman did as he directed, and neither she, her son, nor the prophet lacked anything to eat until the drought ended. This arid period is also cited by Menander in his work on the king of Tyre.

One day the widow's son became sick and died. Weeping and beating her breast, she accused Elijah of having come to punish her sins by causing the death of her son. But he carried the body into his own room, laid it on the bed, and cried to God, asking that his life be restored. God took pity on the mother, and beyond all expectation, brought the child back to life. The mother thanked the prophet, saying she was now sure that the Deity spoke with him.

The Test on Mount Carmel

A VIII,328 Now the famine grew so severe that not only men, but horses and other animals found little to eat. King Ahab told Obadiah, his steward, to go to the springs and streams to cut any grasses that grew near them and bring them to feed his livestock. He also told Obadiah to join him in a search for Elijah.

Statue of Elijah killing the prophets of Baal, atop Mt. Carmel, where Elijah watched for rain clouds to form.

Obadiah took one road and the king another. When Obadiah was alone, Elijah met him and told him to go to the king and inform him that he was coming. But Obadiah replied, "What have I done to you, that now you want to see me killed? Don't you know that Ahab has searched everywhere, trying to kill you?" He went on to report what he had done for Elijah's colleagues when Jezebel had ordered that all the prophets be killed: he had saved 100 of them by hiding them in caves, where he had fed them with bread and water.

Elijah told him to go to the king without any fear. Obadiah did, and when Ahab met Elijah, he asked, "Are you the man who has brought famine and trouble to the Hebrews?"

"No," Elijah answered, "you and your family have, by introducing foreign gods and abandoning the true One." He told Ahab to assemble all the people on Mount Carmel and to bring the prophets of Baal, about 400 in number.

When they had all gathered there, Elijah asked them: "How long will you waver between two opinions? If the Lord is the only true God, follow Him. But if you wish to serve the foreign gods, then follow them!'' When the people failed to respond, Elijah asked that a test be made between the foreign gods and his own. He, the only prophet of God, would take an ox and kill it as a sacrifice. He would lay it on pieces of wood without starting any fire, and the 400 prophets of the foreign gods would do the same. He would pray to God, and they to their gods, to set the wood on fire. They would then see who was the true God.

His proposal accepted, Elijah had the prophets select an ox and sacrifice first. But when no fire came in answer to their prayers, Elijah mocked them. He told them to call louder, for perhaps their gods were asleep, or on a journey. They prayed all morning, cutting themselves with lances and knives, according to their custom, but still no answer came.

Then Elijah told the prophets to leave, but asked the people to come near and watch that he did not secretly set the wood on fire. He took twelve stones and built an altar, then dug a deep trench around it. After placing sticks and the ox on the altar, he ordered the people to fill four barrels with water. He had them pour it over the altar, so that the water soaked down and filled the trench. Then Elijah prayed to God, asking Him to show His power to a people that had remained in error for so long. Suddenly, fire fell from heaven and consumed the altar. Even the water was evaporated, and the place was completely dry.

When the Israelites saw this, they fell down and worshiped the one God, acknowledging Him the only true God, while the others were merely invented names. Then, at Elijah's direction, they grabbed their prophets and killed them.

Elijah told the king that he could go home for lunch, since rain was coming. He himself went up to the summit of Mount Carmel and sat on the ground, leaning his head on his knees. The sky was still entirely clear, and Elijah told a servant to go look toward the sea and let him know if he saw a cloud rising. The man went six times but saw nothing. But on the seventh, he said he saw a small black object in the sky not any bigger than a man's footprint. When Elijah heard this, he sent to Ahab, telling him to hurry to the city before the rain poured down, and so Ahab departed for Jezreel. Soon the sky was covered with clouds, a violent wind arose, and rain came in torrents. Elijah, filled with the spirit of God, ran beside the king's chariot all the way to Jezreel.

When Jezebel, Ahab's wife, heard about the miracles Elijah A VIII,347 had performed, and how he had killed her prophets, she was furious. She sent messengers to him, threatening to kill him. Frightened, Elijah fled to the city of Beersheba. Leaving his servant there, he went into the desert. After praying that he might die, he lay down to sleep under a tree. On awakening, he found food and water next to him. Refreshed, he went on to Mount Sinai, where he found a cave and lived in it for some time. One day a voice asked, "Why have you left the city and come here?"

"The king's wife wants to punish me," Elijah answered, "because I killed the prophets of the false gods and persuaded the people that the One they had worshiped from the beginning was the only true God."

The voice told him to come out into the open air the next day and learn what he was to do. When Elijah emerged, he saw a bright fiery light and heard the earth rumble. But when all was quiet, a divine voice ordered him not to be afraid, but to return home. He was to appoint Jehu king of Israel and Hazael king of Damascus, two kings who would punish the unrighteous people. He was also to ordain as prophet in his place Elisha, of Abel-meholah.

Elijah left Sinai, and on his way home he met Elisha, who was plowing the fields. Elijah threw his mantle over Elisha, who at once stopped plowing and began to prophesy. After receiving permission to say farewell to his parents, Elisha followed Elijah, and became his disciple and servant for the rest of his life.

Naboth's Vineyard

A VIII,355   Now a certain Naboth of Jezreel had a field adjacent to those of the king. Ahab asked to purchase the field at any price so that he could add it to his own property. But Naboth refused all his offers, saying that the land had been passed down to him from his fathers.

Ahab was so perturbed that he refused to bathe or eat. When Jezebel asked why, he told her he felt insulted by Naboth. She urged him to stop sulking, for she would arrange Naboth's punishment. She sent word to the magistrates of Jezreel, commanding them to call an assembly. There three unscrupulous men would accuse Naboth of having blasphemed God and the king, after which they were to stone him to death. They obeyed the queen, and she then presented Naboth's vineyard to the king. Ahab leaped out of bed in delight and went to see the vineyard. But God was angry and sent Elijah to meet him there. "What have you done?" asked the prophet. Accusing him of murder and theft, Elijah said that in the very place where Naboth's body had been devoured by dogs, Ahab's own blood and that of his wife would be shed, and his whole family would be destroyed. Ahab repented in sackcloth, and God told the prophet he would delay the punishment during Ahab's lifetime.

Ben-hadad of Syria Battles Ahab

Ben-hadad, the king of Damascus and Syria, marched against A VIII,363
Ahab in alliance with 32 kings. Ahab retreated into the city of
Samaria, which the Syrian surrounded and besieged. Ben-
hadad then sent messengers to Ahab, who said that Ahab's
wealth, children, and wives now belonged to him. If Ahab
allowed him to take what he wanted, he would lift the siege and
withdraw, so Ahab agreed.

Ben-hadad informed Ahab that he must receive Ben-hadad's
servants, who would be sent to search through his palace and
the houses of his friends to select whatever they liked. Then
Ahab gathered the people and told them what Ben-hadad had
said, but they insisted that Ahab should not give in to these
demands and instead prepare for war.

When the messengers returned with this answer, Ben-hadad
sent word to Ahab that he would besiege the city. He said his
army was so large that if every man took a handful of earth, they
would raise earthworks higher than the walls of Samaria. Ahab
replied that he should not boast until he had won the victory.
Ben-hadad was feasting with the 32 kings when this answer
reached him, and he immediately ordered his men to build
earthworks around the city.

Ahab, meanwhile, was terrified, but a certain prophet told the
king not to fear, for he would be victorious. While Ben-hadad
and his army were getting drunk in their tents, Ahab and the
Israelites attacked them victoriously, and sent them running.
Ben-hadad himself barely escaped on horseback.

The prophet warned Ahab that Ben-hadad would return the A VIII,379
following year, so he kept prepared. In spring, the Syrian again
invaded with a large army, and although Ahab's was very small,
God gave him the victory again. More than 100,000 were killed
in this battle, and the rest of the enemy fled to Aphek. But just as
they reached it, the walls of the city collapsed on them, killing
27,000 more.

Ben-hadad, with some of his faithful servants, hid in a cellar.
There they assured him that the kings of Israel were merciful,
and that if they pleaded with Ahab, he would spare his life. Ben-
hadad approved their plan. Wearing sackcloth and with ropes
around their necks—the Syrian costume for suppliants—they
were well received by Ahab, who told them to bring Ben-hadad.
When he appeared, Ahab took him into his chariot and embraced him. After they made a treaty of friendship, Ahab sent
him back into his own kingdom with gifts, in return for his
promise to give back some Israelite cities.

But a prophet named Micaiah came to one of the Israelites and
said, "Strike me on the head, for this is God's will." When he

refused, Micaiah foretold that, because he had disobeyed God, he would meet a lion and be killed. And this happened. Then Micaiah came to another Israelite and repeated his command, but this one struck him and cracked his skull. Micaiah bound up his head, and went to Ahab. He told him that he was a soldier who had allowed a prisoner assigned him to escape and now was afraid his officer would kill him. When Ahab replied that he deserved the death penalty, Micaiah took off his bandage, and Ahab recognized him. Micaiah then said, "And so God will punish you for letting Ben-hadad escape, who has blasphemed Him. You will die at his hands, and your people at the hands of his army." Enraged at the prophet, Ahab ordered that he be locked up and put under guard.

The Death of Ahab

A VIII,399   Because Ben-hadad had not given up Ramoth in Gilead, one of the cities conquered from the Israelites, Ahab planned to attack him. Jehoshaphat was king of Jerusalem at this time, and his son had married Ahab's daughter. When Jehoshaphat and his army were being lavishly honored in Samaria with much grain, wine, and meat, Ahab invited him to join in a campaign against the Syrians. Jehoshaphat was a righteous man who feared God, so he asked Ahab to inquire of the prophets whether they should fight when there had been three years of peace between Ahab and the Syrian. Ahab gathered his [false] prophets, and asked them if he would be victorious against Ben-hadad. They replied that he would defeat the king of Syria as before.

But Jehoshaphat asked, "Is there not some other prophet of God who can tell us more precisely what will happen?"

Ahab admitted, "There is one named Micaiah, but I hate him, for he prophesied that I would be defeated and killed by the king of Syria. So I have thrown him into prison."

"Bring him to us," said Jehoshaphat.

When he appeared, and Ahab demanded the truth, Micaiah replied, "God has shown me the Israelites fleeing from the Syrians, as a flock of sheep is dispersed without a shepherd. This means that the Israelites shall return to their homes, and only the king will fall in battle."

But Zedekiah, one of the false prophets, urged Ahab not to listen to Micaiah. "For Elijah," he said, "is a greater prophet than Micaiah. And Elijah predicted that the blood of the king would be licked up by dogs near Jezreel, whereas Micaiah claims you will be killed [at Ramoth]. And if you need a further sign that he is no true prophet, I will strike him. Let him then wither my hands as the prophet Jadon once did Jeroboam's."

When Zedekiah struck Micaiah and was not harmed, Ahab was encouraged. He led his army against the Syrians, along with Jehoshaphat. The king of Syria marched to oppose them, and camped near Ramoth.

To prevent the prophecy of Micaiah from being fulfilled, Ahab dressed himself as a common soldier, giving his robe to Jehoshaphat so that the enemy would confuse them. Before the battle, Ben-hadad had told his troops to kill only Ahab, so when they saw Jehoshaphat ahead of the lines, they all rushed at him. But when they approached and saw that it was not Ahab, they retreated. Yet one of Ben-hadad's pages, in shooting arrows at the enemy, struck Ahab in the lung through his armor. Ahab told his charioteer to drive off the battlefield, for he did not want his men to see him dying and lose courage. Although he was in great pain, he remained upright in his chariot until sunset, when he died from loss of blood.

When a herald announced Ahab's death, the Israelites returned to their own country to bury him in Samaria. As his driver stopped at the spring of Jezreel to wash the blood off his chariot, the dogs came and licked up the blood of Ahab, as Elijah had prophesied. Yet he died at Ramoth, as Micaiah had foretold. His son Ahaziah succeeded him. 852 B.C.

Jehoshaphat, King of Judah

When Jehoshaphat returned to Jerusalem from the battle with A IX,1 Ben-hadad, he was met by the prophet Jehu, who rebuked him for having allied with so impious a king as Ahab. Jehu said God was displeased, but would nevertheless deliver him from his enemies because of his piety. The king gave thanks and sacrificed to God.

Jehoshaphat then toured his kingdom to teach the people God's laws through Moses. He also appointed judges in each city, and told them to fear God. They were to see that justice was done in cases of appeal, especially at Jerusalem.

The Moabites and the Ammonites now marched against Jehoshaphat, camping at Engedi on Lake Asphaltitis. Jehoshaphat prayed to God at the temple in Jerusalem and the whole multitude joined him. Then a prophet stood up and told them that God had heard their prayers. The king was to take his army against the enemy the next day, though not to fight them. They were to stand still and see how the Deity would destroy the enemy.

The next morning, they all went into the wilderness below Tekoah, and Jehoshaphat placed priestly trumpeters and Levite singers on the front line. God now struck the enemy with such terror and confusion that they fought one another, and not one man of that vast army escaped. When Jehoshaphat looked down that valley and saw it full of dead bodies, he gave thanks to God, and let his army strip the corpses. After this, foreign nations feared to attack Jehoshaphat, and he lived in peace and splendor.

Ahaziah, King of Israel

A IX,18   Ahaziah, the son of Ahab, was as wicked as his father, and led the people astray. One day, while descending from his roof, he fell down and was badly hurt. He sent messengers to the Fly-god of Ekron [Baal-Zebub] to ask if he would recover. But God sent Elijah to intercept the messengers en route. He asked them, "Don't the people of Israel have a God of their own? Why does your king consult foreign gods? Return and tell the king he will not recover."

The king learned, from the messenger's description—"a hairy man with a leather belt"—that it was Elijah who had met them. He sent an officer with 50 soldiers to bring the prophet to the palace.

The officer found Elijah sitting on a hill. He commanded him to come with him, by force, if necessary. Elijah answered, "To prove that I am a true prophet, I will pray down fire from heaven to destroy you and your men." A whirlwind of fire descended and consumed them all. Then the king sent another officer with 50 men, who made the same demand of the prophet. He received the same response, and suffered the same fate.

Finally, the king sent out a third officer with 50 men. This captain was prudent, and spoke diplomatically to Elijah. He claimed that he had been sent by the king, and had not come of his own accord, and therefore begged for compassion. Elijah was pleased with his courtesy, and he came down from the mountain and followed the officer. When he stood before the king, he said, "Because you have scorned the true God, and consulted the god of Ekron, you will surely die."

Ahaziah died shortly thereafter. Since he was childless, he was succeeded by his brother Jehoram, who was also wicked. It was in the reign of Jehoram that Elijah disappeared from among men, and to this day no one knows what happened to him.* A disciple named Elisha succeeded him. But in reference to Elijah and Enoch, the sacred books state that they became invisible, and no one knows how they died.

---

* According to 2 Kings 2, Elijah was taken up into heaven.

12

THE PROPHET ELISHA

Jehoram, king of Israel, decided to attack the Moabite king, A IX,29
Mesha, who had risen in revolt. He asked Jehoshaphat, the king
of Judah, to join the campaign. He agreed, bringing along the
king of Idumea. The three kings merged forces and set out
together. Because they traveled for seven days via a circuitous
desert route, intending to surprise the enemy, they exhausted
their water supply. When Jehoram lost hope, Jehoshaphat encouraged him, and told him to see if any prophet of God had
come along with the army. One of the soldiers said he had seen
Elisha, Elijah's disciple. The three kings then went to Elisha's
tent and asked him, "What will happen to the army?"

Elisha saw Jehoram and said, "Why come to me? Go to your
parents' prophets, since you claim they are the true prophets."
But Jehoram begged him to prophesy and save them. Elisha
swore he would not respond were it not for Jehoshaphat, who
was a holy and righteous man. Then he asked for someone who
could play the harp.

A musician came, and as he began to play, the prophet was
inspired. He told the kings to dig many ditches in the dry river
bed. "For even if no cloud or wind or downpour occurs," he
said, "you will see this stream bed full of water, and your army
and animals will be saved by drinking it. God will also enable
you to conquer your enemies."

The next morning, a heavy rain, which had fallen a distance
away in Idumea, flooded the stream bed and filled the ditches.
When the Moabites learned that the three kings were marching
against them, they gathered their army to meet the Israelites.
The sun had just risen, and its rays made the water in the ditches
look red, like blood. They thought that their enemies had been

fighting with each another, and that this was their blood, so the Moabites rushed in disorder toward the camp to gather the loot. Instead, they were surrounded by their enemy, who killed many and scattered the rest. The three kings pursued them into Moab, took their cities, demolished their walls, and plugged up their springs. They besieged the king of Moab in his royal city, and when he saw that he could not escape, he took his eldest son, who was to succeed him, lifted him up on the wall where he would be visible to all the Israelites, and offered him up as a burnt sacrifice to his god. When the kings saw this, they were so overcome with pity that they lifted the siege, and everyone returned from the campaign.

Jehoshaphat died soon afterwards at age 60, having reigned 25 years. His eldest son Jehoram had the same name as his wife's brother, the king of Israel. He succeeded Jehoshaphat as king of Judah.

The Miracles of Elisha

A IX,46 Jehoram, king of Israel, returned from Moab to Samaria. He had Elisha the prophet with him, who did many glorious things recorded in the sacred books. The story is related about the widow of Obadiah, Ahab's steward, who told Elisha that her husband had fallen into debt in order to support the 100 prophets he had hidden from Jezebel. And when he died, the widow and her children were being consigned to slavery by the creditors, so she needed help. When he asked what she had in the house, she replied, "Nothing but a little oil in a juglet."

The prophet told her to go and borrow many empty containers from her neighbors. She was then to shut her door and pour oil into all of them, for God would fill them. She did so, and all the containers were filled from the little juglet of oil. The prophet told her to sell the oil, using part of the proceeds to pay off her debts, and keeping the rest for herself and her children. In this way, the woman was delivered from her creditors.

[When Ben-hadad, king of Syria, declared war on Jehoram of Israel, he ordered his soldiers to capture Jehoram while he was hunting].* But Elisha warned the king to avoid that area. Ben-hadad thought that his own men had betrayed his plot to capture Jehoram, and threatened them with death. But one of those present told him that it was Elisha who had alerted the king. Ben-hadad asked where Elisha was living, and when he learned it was Dothan, he sent a large force of horses and chariots there,

---

* A hiatus in Josephus' text at this point omits biblical material extending from II Kings 4:8 to 6:8.

and surrounded the city by night. At dawn, Elisha's servant came running to inform him. The prophet asked God to blind the eyes of the enemy so that they would be unable to see him. God did so, and Elisha walked into the middle of the enemy and asked them whom they were searching for. They replied, "The prophet Elisha." Elisha said, "If you follow me, I will take you to him."

He led them to Samaria, where he ordered King Jehoram to shut the gates and surround the Syrians with his army. Then he asked God to clear the eyes of the Syrians. When they saw themselves surrounded by their enemies, they were shocked and helpless. Jehoram would have killed them all, but Elisha made him spare them and provide hospitality and food. Thus the king entertained the Syrians lavishly and sent them back to Ben-hadad.

When the men reported their experience, Ben-hadad gave up A IX,60 secret assassination attempts on Jehoram and decided to trust the superior strength of his army to attack openly. He laid siege to Samaria, and soon famine in the city was so terrible that the head of an ass sold for 80 pieces of silver, while a measure of dove's dung, used for salt, cost five.

One day, a woman cried to Jehoram, "Have pity on me, O king!" Then she told him how she and another woman with whom she lived, in their dire hunger, had both agreed to kill and eat their sons. "So I killed my son first," continued the woman, "and we both ate him yesterday. But today, the other woman broke her agreement and will not give up her son, but has hidden him." Jehoram tore his clothes and thundered in anger against Elisha because he had not asked God to relieve them. Instantly, he sent a man to cut off his head.

Elisha was sitting in his house with his disciples, and he told them that Jehoram had sent someone to decapitate him. "But when he arrives," Elisha continued, "don't let him in, but push against the door, because the king himself will soon arrive, having changed his mind."

When precisely this happened, Elisha told Jehoram that the very next day they would have plenty of barley and fine flour. The king and his company rejoiced, but one of his commanders, on whom the king was leaning, was skeptical. "That's unbelievable, prophet," he said, "because it isn't possible for God to rain torrents of barley and fine flour into this town." To which the prophet replied, "Nevertheless, you will see it happen, but you will not have any share in them."

Now four lepers were sitting by the gate of Samaria—no one afflicted with leprosy was allowed by law inside the walls of the city—and they realized that if they stayed there they would die of hunger. Yet even if they could get inside they would die of famine there too, so they decided to give themselves up to the enemy and die by the sword rather than starvation.

Meanwhile, God had begun to frighten the Syrians. He caused the noise of chariots and horses to resound in their ears, so that they assumed a great army was approaching. They rushed out of their tents to Ben-hadad, declaring that Jehoram had hired the king of Egypt and the king of the Islands [Hittites] as allies, for they could hear the noise of their approach. Ben-hadad, too, was convinced by the same noise, and he and his army left everything and fled for their lives.

When the lepers arrived at the enemy camp, no one was there. They cautiously crept from one tent to another and found them all deserted. So they ate, drank, and plundered them before shouting to the watchmen on the walls of Samaria what they had seen. The king thought at first that the Syrians were laying a trap for them and had hidden themselves. He envisioned that when the Israelites plundered the camp the Syrians would attack and kill them. Therefore he sent out scouts to search for any Syrian ambush. But they went as far as the Jordan, and found only weapons and provisions that the Syrians had hurriedly discarded on the road.

The king now turned the people loose to raid the camp, and they found a large amount of gold, silver, and cattle, together with huge quantities of wheat and barley. The king sent the officer who had doubted Elisha to control traffic at the gate, but the crowd trampled him to death.

A IX,87   Ben-hadad had fled to Damascus. When he learned that it was the Deity who had confused his army and not the enemy, he was troubled and became sick. About this time, Elisha came to Damascus, and Ben-hadad sent Hazael, his most trusted servant, to meet him with many expensive gifts and to ask whether the king would recover from his illness.

The prophet told Hazael not to tell the king, but he would die. Then Elisha began to cry, and Hazael asked why. Elisha replied, "I cry out of pity for the people of Israel, and the terrible miseries they will suffer at your hands. For you will kill their best men, burn their strongest cities, destroy their children by dashing them against the rocks, and rip up their pregnant women."

Hazael asked, "How can it be that I will have the power to do these things?"

"God has informed me that you will be king of Syria," Elisha answered.

Then Hazael returned to Ben-hadad and reassured him about his illness. But the next day he spread a thick, wet, cloth over the king's face, suffocating him. Hazael then assumed the royal power himself.

Jehoram, King of Judah

The other Jehoram had just acceded to the throne of Judah A IX,95 when he killed his brothers and his father's friends. This was only the beginning of his wickedness. His instructor in iniquity was his wife, Athaliah, the daughter of Ahab. She taught him to worship foreign gods, and he forced the people of Judah to abandon their national God for idols. A letter reached him from Elijah,* the prophet, promising that God would punish him for his wickedness and murders. His wives and children would die, and a loathsome and mortal intestinal disease would cause Jehoram's death, the letter foretold.

Not long after this, an army of Philistines and Arabians invaded Jerusalem, and plundered the palace. They killed Jehoram's sons and wives, and only his son Ahaziah escaped. The king was struck with a long and tormenting illness, which ended when he watched as his intestines fell out. He died at age 40, having ruled eight years. The people refused to put him in the tombs of his fathers, and buried him as a commoner. His son Ahaziah was appointed king in his place.

Jehu Kills Jehoram of Israel

After the death of Ben-hadad, Jehoram, king of Israel, be- A IX,105 sieged the city of Ramoth and captured it from the Syrians. While the siege was in progress, however, he was wounded by an arrow and returned to Jezreel to have the wound healed, leaving the army in charge of Jehu, his commander. Elisha then sent one of his disciples to Ramoth. He took Jehu into a private chamber, anointed him with sacred oil, and said, "God has chosen you king to destroy the house of Ahab and avenge the blood of the prophets killed by Jezebel." Then he slipped away, unseen. When Jehu came out, the officers, who had seen him go in with the disciple, asked him why that young man had come to him, for he looked like a madman.

"True enough," answered Jehu, "the words he spoke were those of a madman."

When they begged him to reveal his words, Jehu said, "God has chosen me king of Israel."

---

* Either a prophetic letter from Elijah's time, or, more likely, a copyist's error for Elisha.

Then the officers took off their cloaks and spread them under Jehu's feet. They blew the trumpets, and shouted, "Jehu is king of Israel!"

Jehu marched the army toward Jezreel. Then, at a distance from the city, he rode forward in his chariot, accompanied by his best horsemen.

Ahaziah, the king of Judah, had come to Jezreel to visit Jehoram, who was his maternal uncle. A watchman reported that a troop of cavalry was approaching the city. Jehoram ordered that a horseman be sent out to intercept them and learn their identity. But when the horseman met Jehu and questioned him, Jehu told him to spare the effort and follow him. The watchman reported to Jehoram that the horseman had joined the approaching company. When the king sent a second messenger, Jehu issued the same directive, and he also joined him.

Jehoram finally mounted his chariot himself, along with Ahaziah, and drove out to meet the approaching group. They confronted Jehu at the field of Naboth. Jehoram asked, "Are all things well in the camp?" But Jehu reviled him, calling his mother a witch and a whore. Jehoram turned his chariot and fled, shouting to Ahaziah, "We've been led into a trap!"

But Jehu drew his bow and shot an arrow that pierced Jehoram's heart and killed him. Ahaziah turned his chariot onto another road, but Jehu pursued him until he shot and wounded him. Abandoning his chariot for a horse, Ahaziah fled to Megiddo, where he died from his wound a few days later. He was buried in Jerusalem, after reigning only one year.

841 B.C.   As Jehu entered Jezreel, Jezebel adorned herself and stood on a tower. She shouted, "A fine servant *you* are, killing your own master!" He asked who she was, and commanded her to come down to him. When she refused, he ordered his eunuchs to throw her off the tower. The wall was spattered with her blood as she fell; her body was trampled by the horses, and she died. Later, as Jehu and his friends sat down to dinner at the palace, he told his servants to bury Jezebel out of respect for her royal descent. But they found only her limbs, since the rest of her body had been eaten by dogs. Jehu marveled at this fulfillment of Elijah's prophecy.

Ahab had 70 sons who were being raised in Samaria. Jehu sent letters to their tutors and the magistrates of the city, ordering them to cut off their heads and send them to him. They did so, putting the heads in woven baskets and sending them to Jezreel. Jehu had them deposited in two heaps on either side of his gate. He told onlookers that he had not killed these youths, but that all this had happened to Ahab's family in fulfillment of Elijah's prophecy.

The western gate of Samaria, capital of the northern Kingdom of Israel. Herod the Great beautified and further fortified the city, and his masonry appears here and at the towers in the background.

Jehu next went to Samaria and lured all the priests of Baal inside their god's temple, under the pretext of offering sacrifice to him. When they had all gathered, he had them massacred and the temple burned down, thus purging Samaria of foreign rites. He did, however, continue to permit the Israelites to bow down before their golden heifers.

Hazael, king of Syria, now ravaged Israel east of the Jordan. Jehu failed to oppose him, since he had grown contemptuous of the Deity and His laws. He died after ruling the Israelites for 27 years and was buried at Samaria, leaving his son Jehoahaz as his successor.

Jehoash Is Made King of Judah

Athaliah, the wife of Jehoram, king of Judah, learned about A IX,140 the death of her brother Jehoram, the king of Israel. She was also informed that her son Ahaziah, as well as the whole royal family of Ahab, was killed. She was then determined to put an end to the family of David also, and carried out her bloody resolution. But one son of Ahaziah, Jehoash, was preserved. Ahaziah had a sister, Jehosheba, who was married to the high priest Jehoiada. When Jehosheba entered the palace after the royal slaughter, she found Jehoash alive, only a year old, lying among the dead. After hiding him in a bedroom, she and Jehoiada raised him secretly in the temple.

Athaliah made herself queen of Judah, and ruled for six years. But then Jehoiada showed the boy he had raised to the priests, Levites, and tribal leaders he had gathered, and they decided to make him king. The temple armory contained spears and shields of King David, which the priests now distributed. While the Levites kept guard around the temple, Jehoiada put the boy Jehoash in their midst. Having anointed him with oil, he placed the crown on his head. All the people rejoiced and applauded, shouting, "Long live the king!"

Athaliah heard the shouts and hurried to the temple with her guards. The Levites allowed her to enter, but they excluded her guards. When she saw the child standing on the dais with the crown on his head, she tore her garments and cried out that Jehoiada be killed. But he commanded his captains to take Athaliah to the Kedron valley and put her to death.

Then Jehoiada made the people swear loyalty to Jehoash, while he, in turn, swore that he would observe the laws of Moses. The people then ran to the temple of Baal, which Athaliah had built, and demolished it, killing its priest. Jehoiada took Jehoash out of the temple into the palace, and when he had put him on the throne, the people shouted for joy and feasted for many days.

A IX,161   Jehoash was seven years old when he took the kingship. During his youth and his entire lifetime, he was careful to observe the commandments of God. Anxious to repair and rebuild the temple, he had the high priest put a wooden chest with a hole in the lid beside the altar. The people put into the chest whatever they wished to give toward the repair of the temple. When a large amount had been collected, the king and Jehoiada the high priest put carpenters and masons to work and thus restored the temple.

But when Jehoiada died, the king turned away from God and the prophets who warned him. Zechariah, the son of Jehoiada, denounced the king and the people for their apostasy, and prophesied that God would punish them. Jehoash ordered Zechariah to be stoned to death inside the temple.

It was not long before the priest was avenged. Hazael, king of Syria, invaded the country and would have taken Jerusalem, but Jehoash sent him everything in the palace and temple treasuries, buying him off. Later, Jehoash suffered a severe illness and was killed in bed by some of Zechariah's friends. He was succeeded, at age 47, by his son Amaziah.

The Death of Elisha

Meanwhile, the king of Syria had turned his victorious armies A IX,173 against Israel, which was now governed by Jehoahaz, son of Jehu. Typically impious, Jehoahaz saw his cities fall according to the schedule predicted by Elisha. He turned in desperation to God, who restored peace and prosperity.

Jehoahaz died and was succeeded by his son Jehoash. He had the same name as the king of Jerusalem, but this Jehoash was a good man, unlike his father. Old Elisha now became ill, and the king came to his bedside in tears. He cried, "Father!" and "Armor!" because he was leaving him unarmed before the Syrians.

But Elisha comforted him, and asked for a bow and some arrows. The prophet touched his hands and told him to let them fly. The king shot three arrows and stopped. Elisha said, "If you had shot more arrows, you would have destroyed the kingdom of Syria. But since you were satisfied with three, you will defeat the Syrians three times and only recover the territory they took from your father."

When Elisha died, he was buried magnificently. Shortly afterward, some robbers killed a man and threw his body into Elisha's grave, and the man's corpse came back to life.

Jehoash attacked Ben-hadad,* the king of Syria, who had succeeded his father Hazael. He defeated him in three battles, restoring all the territory taken from Israel, as Elisha had prophesied. He also defeated Amaziah, king of Judah, as will be related. Having done these things, he died, leaving the throne of 782 B.C. Israel to his son Jeroboam.

---

* Ben-hadad II, regarded by some scholars as Ben-hadad III.

CONQUEST, DESTRUCTION, AND CAPTIVITY **13**

A IX,186

Amaziah, the son of the Judean Jehoash, executed his father's murderers. He then gathered an army of 300,000 to war against the Amalekites, Edomites, and Gebalites. He also hired 100,000 from the king of Israel for 100 talents of silver, but a prophet warned him that he should dismiss the Israelites. They were impious, he said, and God predicted defeat if he used them. Although Amaziah was reluctant to discharge the Israelites after paying for them, he obeyed the prophet. Then he marched his own army against the enemy and triumphed.

Elated in victory, Amaziah forgot that God had caused it, and actually started worshiping the idols he had brought from the Amalekites. When a prophet scolded him, Amaziah angrily told him to be quiet. The prophet replied that he would, but God would not overlook his innovations. In his presumption, Amaziah wrote an arrogant letter to Jehoash, king of Israel. He demanded that he and his people submit to him, as they had formerly submitted to David and Solomon, his ancestors. The alternative, he warned, was war.

Jehoash wrote back as follows:

> There was once a tall cypress tree on Mount Lebanon, and a thistle that grew beside it. The thistle spoke to the cypress, asking that the daughter of the cypress be given in marriage to the son of the thistle. But while the thistle was speaking, a wild beast came by and trampled it down. Let this, then, be a lesson to you not to be so ambitious. Don't be proud because you were lucky in battle against the Amalekites, or you will endanger yourself and your kingdom.

When Amaziah read this letter, he was indignant and marched out against Jehoash. But just as the men of Judah were about to join battle, a sudden terror from God overcame them, causing them to flee, and leaving Amaziah alone. The Israelites took him captive, and Jehoash threatened to kill him unless he persuaded the people of Jerusalem to open their gates and receive him and his army into the city. Afraid for his life, Amaziah did as he was told. Jehoash demolished part of the wall, and, driving his chariot through the breach, became master of Jerusalem. He took all the treasure in the temple and palace and returned to Samaria, having released Amaziah. Later some of his friends conspired against Amaziah and killed him. He had lived 54 years, reigned 29, and was succeeded by his son Uzziah.

The port of Joppa on the Mediterranean, from which Jonah set sail in his attempted escape from responsiblity.

The Prophet Jonah

A IX,205   Jeroboam, son of Jehoash, was a very arrogant, lawless king of Israel, yet he brought much benefit to his people. A certain Jonah prophesied that the king would defeat the Syrians and extend his realm from Hamath in the north to Lake Asphaltitis in the south. Jeroboam did as Jonah had predicted.

God also told Jonah that he should go to Nineveh and warn the city that it would lose its power. But out of fear he fled instead to the city of Joppa. There he embarked on a ship bound for Tarsus.* On the passage a terrible storm arose, and the ship was in danger of sinking. The captain and his men began to pray, but Jonah did not join them. The tempest increased, and the sailors began to think that one of the passengers was the cause of the storm. They drew lots to determine who it was, and the lot fell on Jonah. They asked him about his home and occupation. He replied, "I am a Hebrew and a prophet of the Most High God. If you want to escape this danger, throw me overboard, for I am the cause of this storm."

At first they did not dare to do it, but finally, with the ship almost sinking, they threw him overboard. The sea became calm, and word has it that a whale swallowed Jonah. After three days and nights he was ejected on the shore of the Euxine [Black] Sea, alive and unharmed. Asking God to forgive his sins, Jonah then went to Nineveh and announced to its people that they would soon lose their rule over Asia.

After ruling for 40 years, Jeroboam died, and was buried at Samaria. His son Zechariah succeeded to the throne.

Uzziah, King of Judah

Uzziah was sixteen years old when he was made king of Judah A IX,215 in place of his murdered father, Amaziah. He was very energetic, defeating the Philistines, Arabs, and Ammonites. Then he repaired the walls of Jerusalem, dug canals, and strengthened the army. But this success made him proud, and he forgot that it was God who enabled him.

One day, during a public festival, he put on the priestly garment and went into the temple to offer sacrifice to God on the golden altar. The priests tried to prevent him, saying it was not lawful for anyone except the descendants of Aaron to offer sacrifice. The king became angry and threatened to kill them unless they were quiet. While he spoke, however, the earth began to shake, and the temple split open. A bright shaft of sunlight shone through the opening and fell on the king's face, which instantly became leprous. As soon as the priests saw the

---

* Josephus refers to the city in Cilicia, although the O.T. destination is "Tarshish," which was probably Tartessus in Spain. The Bible also does not identify where Jonah was disgorged, but Josephus assumed the Black Sea, as nearest Assyria.

leprosy, they told the king to leave the city as an unclean person. In horror and shame, he did as he was told, and lived outside the walls as a private citizen. His son Jotham took over the government, and Uzziah died in despondent grief at age 68, having reigned 52 years.

From Zechariah to Pekah

A IX,228 Zechariah, the son of Jeroboam, reigned over Israel only six months. He was treacherously assassinated by one of his friends, named Shallum, who proclaimed himself king. But Menahem, the general, heard what Shallum had done, so he brought his army to Samaria, killed Shallum in battle, and made himself king. Menahem ruled for ten cruel years, killing all subjects who opposed him. But he bribed Pul [Tiglath-Pileser III] of Assyria with 1,000 talents of silver to call off his war with Israel.

When Menahem died, his son Pekahiah succeeded him, and was as cruel as his father. But after a reign of two years he was treacherously killed at a banquet by one of his captains, named Pekah. Pekah made himself king, and reigned for twenty years in a lawless and impious manner. Again Tiglath-Pileser of Assyria attacked the Israelites, conquering all of Gilead, Galilee, Kedesh, and Hazor, transporting the inhabitants to his own kingdom.

Ahaz, King of Judah

A IX,236 Meanwhile, Jotham, Uzziah's son, had been ruling with wisdom and justice in Judah. He made the necessary repairs to the temple and in the city. A certain prophet at that time, named Nahum, foretold the overthrow of Assyria and Nineveh. He used phrases like: "all the people, disturbed and agitated, shall flee . . . their eyes will be darkened with fear . . . God says to you, Nineveh, 'I will blot you out.'" And all these things came to pass 115 years later.

After ruling sixteen years, Jotham died at age 41, and the kingdom went to his son Ahaz. Ahaz impiously imitated the kings of Israel and raised altars in Jerusalem to idols. He even sacrificed his own son as a burnt offering, as the Canaanites did.

While Ahaz was acting like a madman, Pekah, king of Israel, made an alliance with Rezin, the king of Syria and Damascus. They joined forces to invade Judah. The Syrian king took several cities, killing their inhabitants and resettling them with his own subjects, and then returned to Syria. Ahaz, who was besieged inside Jerusalem, learned that the Syrians had departed. He believed he would be more than a match for the Israelites, and pursued them with his army. But the Judeans were terribly slaughtered, losing 120,000. The Israelites plundered the country, taking the women and children of the tribe of Benjamin before returning to Samaria.

Obed, who was a prophet in Samaria, met the army by the city walls. He loudly declared that their victory had not come by their own power, but because God was angry at King Ahaz. And not satisfied with this success, they had dared to capture their own relatives. "Therefore let these captives return home, and do not harm them," he said, "for otherwise God will punish you!" The people deliberated, and finally decided to return the captives. Giving them supplies, they escorted them as far as Jericho.

Later on, King Ahaz asked Tiglath-Pileser of Assyria for assistance against the Israelites and Syrians, promising him large sums of money. He agreed and attacked the Syrians, conquering Damascus and killing Rezin before invading Israel and taking many captives. Ahaz took all the gold and silver that was in his treasury and in the temple of God and gave it to the king of Assyria. A IX,252

Ahaz had been stupid enough to worship the Syrian gods even when he was at war with them! Now he began to honor the gods of the Assyrians, for he was always ready to revere any god rather than the one true God, whose wrath was the cause of his defeats. Ahaz even shut up the temple and forbade the priests to offer sacrifices in it.

Hezekiah

When Ahaz died at age 36, his son Hezekiah succeeded to the kingdom. He was an upright, good-natured, and righteous man, whose first priority was to restore the worship of God. So he gathered the people, the priests, and the Levites, and addressed them as follows: "Because my father violated the worship of God and corrupted you in worshiping false gods, you have suffered greatly. But now that you have learned how horrible impiety is, purify yourselves, and let the priests and Levites open the temple and cleanse it with the customary sacrifices. Then God might set aside His anger toward us." A IX,260

When the king had finished speaking, the priests opened the temple and prepared the vessels of God. Discarding what was impure, they offered the sacrifices of the law.

Hezekiah also sent out messengers to all his people, and to the Israelites. He told them that the worship of God had been restored in Jerusalem, asking them to come and celebrate the feast of Unleavened Bread, which had lapsed for a long time under the lawless kings. But the Israelites laughed at the envoys as fools. When their prophets predicted that they would suffer if they refused this opportunity to return to God, they grabbed the prophets and killed them. However, many in the tribes of Manasseh, Zebulon, and Issachar listened to the prophets and flocked to Jerusalem to worship God.

When they arrived, Hezekiah, the rulers, and all the people went up to the temple and offered solemn sacrifices. Then, at the festival of Unleavened Bread, they offered additional sacrifices for seven days, with thanksgiving. After the festival ended, the people went throughout the country and destroyed all pollution from idols. The king also ordered that daily sacrifices be made according to the law and at his own expense. Tithes of all that the ground produced were to support the priests and Levites. Thus they once again returned to their ancient religion.

The king of Assyria now threatened to conquer Hezekiah's realm unless he resumed the tribute his father had paid. But Hezekiah ignored these threats, confident in God and the prophet Isaiah, who provided accurate predictions.

The End of the Kingdom of Israel

A IX,277   After Pekah, king of Israel, had ruled for twenty years, he was killed through a conspiracy organized by one of his friends named Hosea, who made himself king. Hosea secretly allied with So, the king of Egypt, against the Assyrians. When Shalmaneser, king of Assyria, heard this, he besieged Samaria for three years until he captured it. Then he completely destroyed the government of Israel, transporting all its people, including Hosea, to Media and Persia. He gave their country to the 722 B.C.   Cutheans, who settled in Samaria.*

Thus, the ten tribes of Israel left the land 947 years after the exodus, and 247 years after their revolt against Rehoboam. The Israelites came to such an end because they violated the laws and disregarded the prophets who had warned them that this would happen.

A IX,288   When the Cutheans first came into Samaria, each of their five tribes reverenced its own god. But God sent an epidemic on them, and many died. When they could not cure their miseries, a prophet told them that if they worshiped the Most High God they would be relieved. Thus they sent emissaries to the king of Assyria, asking him to send them some of the Israelite priests he

---

* Shalmaneser V of Assyria died at the time Samaria was being captured in 722 B.C., and it was his successor, Sargon II, who deported the population.

had taken captive. The priests came and taught the Samaritans the worship of God, and the plague stopped immediately. These same rites have continued to this day among those who are called *Cuthim* in Hebrew, and Samaritans in Greek. They vary in their attitude to the Jews, calling them relatives when they are prospering, but aliens when they are in trouble.

The Destruction of Sennacherib's Army

In the fourteenth year of the reign of Hezekiah, king of Judah, A X,1 Sennacherib, the king of Assyria, conquered all the cities of Judah and Benjamin. When he planned to march on Jerusalem as well, Hezekiah sent him envoys promising to pay whatever tribute he stipulated if he withdrew. Sennacherib accepted 300 talents of silver and 30 of gold, but then treacherously refused to leave. He himself left to fight the Egyptians, but his general, Rabshakeh, was ordered to sack Jerusalem with his large army.

Rabshakeh and his officers met with three of Hezekiah's representatives near the walls of Jerusalem. He pointed out their weakness and demanded surrender. The Judeans asked them to speak in Aramaic rather than Hebrew, afraid that their people would be discouraged. The Assyrians responded by issuing their threats in much louder Hebrew!

Hezekiah took off his royal garments, put on sackcloth, and fell on his face, imploring God's help. He also sent priests to the prophet Isaiah, asking for his intercession. Isaiah foretold that God would destroy the enemy without a battle; Sennacherib would also fail against Egypt, and would die by the sword when he returned home.

The hexagonal clay prism of Sennacherib, in which he gives his version of the Assyrian campaign against King Hezekiah, claiming to have shut him inside Jerusalem "like a caged bird" (Oriental Institute, U. of Chicago).

Indeed, Sennacherib quickly retreated from Egypt, having learned that the army of Ethiopia was coming to its assistance, and then joined Rabshakeh at Jerusalem. He discovered that on the first night of the siege, God had sent a terrible plague on the Assyrians, and 185,000 had died.* In great anxiety, he fled with what remained of his forces back to Nineveh, where Sennacherib was treacherously killed by his two older sons.

After offering thanks to God for this extraordinary deliverance, Hezekiah soon became so ill that his doctors gave up all hope of his recovery. Compounding his grief was the realization that he was still childless, and no son would succeed him on the throne. Hearing his plea to live a little longer, God sent the prophet Isaiah, who informed him that within three days he would recover, and would live another fifteen years and have sons. Freed from his illness, Hezekiah went up to the temple to pray.

Berodach-baladan, the king of Babylon, sent Hezekiah envoys with gifts, suggesting an alliance. Hezekiah received them enthusiastically, and showed them his treasures and arms before sending them back with gifts. Isaiah, however, told him, "In a short time, that wealth will be taken to Babylon, and your offspring will be made eunuchs to the king of Babylon." Isaiah had marvelous knowledge of the truth, never speaking falsely, and he wrote down his prophecies in books for future generations.

686 B.C.   Hezekiah died peacefully at age 54, having reigned 29 years, and was succeeded by his son Manasseh.

Manasseh and Amon, Kings of Judah

A X,36   Instead of following in the footsteps of Hezekiah, Manasseh pursued the wicked practices of the Israelites and even slaughtered the prophets. Therefore, God incited the king of Babylon and Chaldea to invade Judea and ravage the country. Manasseh himself was taken captive, but he repented and turned to God. He heard his prayer, and made the enemy merciful enough to release Manasseh and let him return to Jerusalem.

His repentance was sincere, for he sanctified the temple and reestablished the sacrifices according to the law of Moses. Thus he lived a blessed and enviable life until his death at age 67, having reigned 55 years. But his son Amon, who succeeded him, imitated only the youthful wickedness of his father. He

---

* 2 Kings 19:35 has this number killed by "the angel of the Lord." In documenting Sennacherib's reverses in Egypt, Josephus cites Herodotus' *History* (ii,141) that the Assyrians abandoned the siege of Pelusium because a horde of mice ate through their weapons in one night, reading "Assyrians" for "Arabs" in that context.

ruled only two years when he was killed at age 24 by a conspiracy of his own servants.

Josiah, King of Judah

The people punished Amon's murderers and gave the king- A X,48
dom to his son Josiah, who was eight years old. He had a wise
and excellent character, for at age twelve, he urged the people to
reject their idols and return to the God of their fathers. The boy-
king also traveled the country and demolished all the altars and
groves devoted to foreign gods. He then collected funds, on a
freewill basis, to repair the temple.

In the eighteenth year of his reign, the high priest Hilkiah
came across the sacred books of Moses that had been stored in
the temple and forgotten. He gave them to a scribe, who read
them to the king. When he heard what was written about those
who transgressed the law, he tore his clothes and sent messengers to the prophetess, Huldah, imploring her to pray to God
and appease His anger. Because their forefathers had sinned,
Josiah feared that his people would be driven out of their own
country and exiled to a foreign land.

Huldah sent back word that the Deity had already passed
sentence against them, and no supplications would be effective.
Because of the virtue of Josiah, however, He would postpone the
disasters until after his death.

The king then ordered the people to gather in Jerusalem.
Josiah read the holy books and asked them all to swear that they
would worship God and keep the laws of Moses. They all
eagerly did so, and went on to sacrifice and sing and pray.

Next, Josiah killed all the false priests who remained. He also
went into the country where the Israelites had lived, and there
burned the bones of the false prophets on the altar built by
Jeroboam. This fulfilled [Jadon's] prophecies, after 361 years.
He also urged those Israelites who had escaped the Assyrians to
return to God. When all the land had been purged, he called the
people together to celebrate the feast of the Passover. This was
the greatest such observance since the time of Samuel.

Necho, the king of Egypt, marched against the Medes and
Babylonians, but was intercepted at Megiddo by Josiah. Necho
sent a messenger to him, explaining that he only wanted free
passage on his way to the Euphrates. But Josiah ignored the
request and prepared for battle. When an Egyptian archer shot
him, Josiah sounded a retreat and later died of his wound in
Jerusalem. He had reigned 31 of his 39 years, and was mourned
greatly. The prophet Jeremiah composed a lament for his fu- 609 B.C.
neral, which has survived to this day. He also wrote predictions

about the misfortunes and capture of Jerusalem, as did the prophet Ezekiel.

When Josiah died, his son Jehoahaz succeeded to the kingdom. But Necho of Egypt, returning from battle, took him prisoner. He caused a brother of his, whose name he changed from Eliakim to Jehoiakim, to be installed as king in his place. Then Necho returned to Egypt with Jehoahaz, who died soon afterwards.

Nebuchadnezzar Destroys Jerusalem

A X,84   In the fourth year of Jehoiakim, Nebuchadnezzar, the king of Babylon, marched against Necho. He conquered him, took Syria from him, and held all the land up to Pelusium with the exception of Judea. Then he advanced on the Jews and threatened to destroy the country unless Jehoiakim paid him tribute. Alarmed, Jehoiakim purchased peace for three years. But then he heard that Nebuchadnezzar was about to fight the Egyptians, so he did not pay his tribute, hoping the Egyptians would be victorious.

The prophet Jeremiah repeatedly warned him against putting any trust in the Egyptians, but it was in vain. Jeremiah foretold that Jerusalem would be overthrown by the king of Babylon, who would take Jehoiakim captive.

Jeremiah then wrote down all his prophecies in a book and read them to the people in the temple. The leaders took the book and brought it to the king. He was so angry that he tore it up and threw it into the fire.

Soon, Nebuchadnezzar appeared at Jerusalem with his army, and Jehoiakim received him, assuming he would suffer no harm, since he had not battled or excluded him. After entering the city, however, the Babylonian king did not keep his pledge. Instead he killed the Judean leaders, including King Jehoiakim, and made his son Jehoiachin king in his place. Later, Nebuchadnezzar feared that Jehoiachin would try to avenge his father's death, so he replaced him with his uncle Zedekiah, having first made Zedekiah promise that he would always be faithful to him. Meanwhile, Nebuchadnezzar had deported to Babylon thousands of Judean leaders. These included the prophet Ezekiel, who was then a boy, the ex-king Jehoiachin and his family, and thousands of young people and craftsmen.

Zedekiah, Jehoiakim's brother, allowed his entourage and subjects to act as outrageously as they pleased. Jeremiah warned him to stop his transgressions, while Ezekiel, writing from Babylon, also predicted the disasters that would overwhelm the people. But Zedekiah did not believe these prophets, because while they agreed on all other points, they had a discrepancy. Jeremiah claimed that Zedekiah "would be carried captive to Babylon," while Ezekiel said that "he would not see Babylon."

After Zedekiah had been king eight years, he broke his pledge to Nebuchadnezzar and allied with the king of Egypt, who was fighting against Babylon. Nebuchadnezzar gathered his army, and, having defeated the Egyptians, marched against Jerusalem and besieged it. A X,108

The prophet Jeremiah had been thrown into prison by his enemies. Yet he urged the people to open their gates to the king of Babylon and save themselves; otherwise they would be destroyed by famine or sword. But the leaders angrily denounced him to Zedekiah, accusing the prophet of undermining the people's morale, and they persuaded the king to turn Jeremiah over to them. Taking him from prison, they let him down by ropes into a pit, full of mud. There, they assumed, he would suffocate and die by his own hand, so to speak. Jeremiah remained up to his neck in mud until one of the king's servants reported the prophet's predicament to the king, pleading on his behalf. Regretting his original decision, the king ordered Jeremiah rescued and brought to the palace, where he asked his advice. Again the prophet urged Zedekiah to surrender to the Babylonians, or else see the temple burned and the city destroyed.

For eighteen months months Nebuchadnezzar besieged Jerusalem. He constructed huge earthworks surrounding the city, towers, and engines. Finally, the defenders were no longer able to hold out against the Babylonians, who stormed the city about midnight. When Zedekiah saw that all was lost, he took his wives and children, officers and friends, and fled out of Jerusalem by night.

At daybreak, however, the Babylonians overtook the fugitives near Jericho. They brought Zedekiah and his family before Nebuchadnezzar. He denounced Zedekiah as a violator of treaties and an irreverent, ungrateful wretch for having broken his pledge given when Nebuchadnezzar had made him king. He ordered Zedekiah's sons to be executed while he watched, and then his eyes were put out and he was bound and taken to Babylon. Thus the prophecies of both Jeremiah and Ezekiel were fulfilled, since the king of Judea was brought captive to Babylon, yet he did not see that city.

Nebuzaradan, the general of Nebuchadnezzar's army, was ordered to plunder the temple and the palace, then to set fire to both. He was also to raze the city to the ground and transplant its people to Babylonia. And so the temple was burned 470 years after it was built, while the people of Jerusalem were transported 586 B.C. to Babylonia. The gold, silver, and all the treasures of the temple and the palace were taken to Babylon, and Nebuchadnezzar dedicated the holy vessels to his own gods.

Thus David's line ended, which included 21 kings who had reigned 514 years in total, after Saul had ruled 20.

The Murder of Gedaliah

A X,155   Nebuzaradan appointed Gedaliah governor over the poor, the deserters, and the farmers left behind in the country. He also took Jeremiah out of prison, and invited him to return with him to Babylon. The king had ordered Nebuzaradan to provide Jeremiah with everything he needed, but the prophet preferred to live among the ruins of his country at Mizpah.

Now, some of the Jews had fled from Jerusalem during the siege. When they heard that the Babylonians had gone, they returned to their land and submitted to the rule of Gedaliah. But among them was a scoundrel named Ishmael, who was of the royal line, and he plotted to take the government from Gedaliah. He came with ten men to Mizpah, where Gedaliah hosted them at a banquet. Now, the governor had been warned about Ishmael's plot, but in his good nature discounted it, so he drank with his guests until he was drunk and asleep. Ishmael and his colleagues then murdered Gedaliah, as well as all the citizens and Babylonian soldiers in town.

The Jews were angry at Ishmael, being afraid that the king of Babylon would avenge the death of his governor. In their distress they came to Jeremiah, and asked him what they should do. Jeremiah promised that they would be safe if they remained in Judea. But they would not accept his advice, and they all moved to Egypt, taking Jeremiah and his disciple Baruch with them. There, God revealed to Jeremiah that the Babylonian king would conquer Egypt and kill some of his Jewish colleagues and deport others to Babylon. And so it happened, five years after the sacking of Jerusalem. But the king did not settle any other people in Judea and Jerusalem, which remained deserted for 70 years.

THE 14
RETURN TO JERUSALEM

Nebuchadnezzar, king of Babylon, chose from among the captive Jews a number of young men of noble birth who were strong, handsome, and intelligent. He put them under the care of tutors, who instructed them in Babylonian culture. Among these youths were four members of the house of Zedekiah, whose names were Daniel, Hananiah, Mishael, and Azariah, but Nebuchadnezzar changed their names to Belteshazzar, Shadrach, Meshach, and Abednego, respectively. And he cherished them for their zeal in learning.

Daniel and his relatives preferred a strict diet of fruit and vegetables. They asked the eunuch in charge of them to take for himself the meat dishes that were sent them from the king's table, and to leave the non-animal food for them. But the eunuch was afraid that they would become thin and pale, and the king would discover what he had done and be angry with him. They suggested a ten-day trial, promising to return to their former diet if they became thinner.

The servant agreed. At the end of ten days, the four youths looked healthier than the rest of the young men who were fed from the king's table, so he continued the arrangement. They mastered Hebrew and Chaldean learning, and Daniel was especially favored in that God revealed to him the interpretation of dreams.

Daniel

One night, King Nebuchadnezzar had a remarkable dream, and while he was sleeping God explained it to him. But when he awoke he forgot both the dream and its interpretation. Thus he sent for the wise men and the soothsayers from among the Chaldeans, and asked them to tell him his dream and its interpretation. The magi told him this was impossible, but if he would tell them the dream they would give him the interpretation. But Nebuchadnezzar threatened them all with death unless they could tell him the dream and its meaning.

When Daniel heard this, and that he and his relatives were in danger, he asked the king to put off the slaughter of the wise men for one night. Daniel hoped within that time to learn from God both the dream and its meaning. When the king consented, Daniel returned to his house with his relatives and prayed all that night. God took pity on those in danger and revealed to him the dream and its interpretation.

Early the next morning, Daniel told the king: "You seemed to see a large standing statue, whose head was of gold, the shoulders and arms of silver, its belly and thighs of brass, but the legs and the feet of iron. Then a stone broke off a mountain and fell on this statue, knocking it down and breaking it to pieces. The gold, silver, iron, and the brass were ground into powder, and the wind blew them away. But the stone grew so large that the whole earth seemed to be filled with it. That was the dream, and here is the interpretation: The head of gold denotes you and the kings of Babylon before you. The two hands and shoulders signify that your kingdom will be conquered by two kings. But their empire will be destroyed by another king from the west, armed with brass. And still another power like iron will end the rule of the western king. It will have dominion forever through its iron nature, which is stronger than gold, silver, or brass."

Daniel also revealed to the king the significance of the stone, but I think it is inappropriate to relate this, since I must write of what is past, not future. If anyone, however, wants to learn about the hidden things that are to come, let him read the Book of Daniel among the sacred writings.*

When Nebuchadnezzar heard this—it was indeed his dream—he was astonished, and fell on his face before Daniel as if he were a god. He appointed Daniel and his relatives to be governors of his kingdom.

A X,212   Later, however, Daniel's colleagues incurred the anger of Nebuchadnezzar. The king made a huge statue of gold and set it up on the great plain of Babylon, and he called all the rulers in his empire to bow down and worship the statue at the sound of a

---

* Josephus evades an explanation of the stone, because in his day Jews interpreted it as a symbol of the Messianic kingdom or Messiah, who would terminate the iron kingdom, i.e., the Roman Empire. This also explains his failure to include the additional division of iron and clay feet (Daniel 2), to avoid offending Roman readers.

trumpet. Those who refused would be thrown into a fiery furnace. When the trumpet sounded, everyone worshiped the statue except Shadrach, Meshach, and Abednego, who refused to violate the laws of their fathers. They were convicted and thrown into the fire. But they were miraculously rescued by divine providence, for the fire did not touch them. This proved to the king that they were righteous and favored by God, and he continued to regard them very highly.

A little later, Nebuchadnezzar had another dream: he would fall from power and pass seven years in the desert with wild beasts, after which he would resume his rule. None of the magi could explain the dream except Daniel, and his interpretation came true.

After Nebuchadnezzar had reigned for 43 years, he died. 562 B.C. [Here Josephus adds detail on Nebuchadnezzar's improvements at Babylon from Berosus' *History of Chaldaea*.] He was succeeded by Evil-Merodach, his son, who released Jehoiachin from his chains. He also lavished many gifts on him, because his father, Nebuchadnezzar, had not kept faith with Jehoiachin when he had surrendered himself and his family to spare Jerusalem.

Belshazzar's Feast

One of the successors of Evil-Merodach was named Belshaz- A X,232 zar. After Belshazzar had ruled for seventeen years, Cyrus, the king of Persia, and Darius, the king of Media, attacked and besieged him in Babylon. During a feast in his palace with his concubines and friends, Belshazzar ordered that the vessels of God which Nebuchadnezzar had taken as spoil from Jerusalem be used at their table. While he was drinking and blaspheming God, he saw a hand coming out of the wall, and it wrote certain syllables there. Disturbed by the vision, the king summoned the magi and Chaldeans to interpret the writing, but they could not. Belshazzar then proclaimed throughout the country that if anyone could read the writing on the wall and explain its meaning, he would receive a necklace of gold and purple clothing, as well as a third of his realm. Many magi were tempted, but when they came and saw the writing they could not decipher it.

The king's grandmother saw how despondent he was, and told him that there was a man among the Jews, named Daniel, who had explained to Nebuchadnezzar many things known to no one else. Belshazzar called Daniel and repeated his promises to him if he would interpret the writing on the wall. But Daniel

Ruins of the Ishtar Gate at Nebuchadnezzar's Babylon. The Procession Street ran through the Gate in this city of the sixth century B.C. The modern ground level is indicated by the top of the embankment in the background.

begged him to keep his gifts, and said he would explain the writing.

"*Mane,*" Daniel explained, "means 'number,' and it signifies that the number of years God has appointed for your life and reign have nearly expired. *Thekel* means 'weight,' for God has weighed your kingship and finds it declining. *Phares* means 'a fragment,' for God will break your kingdom into pieces and divide it among the Medes and Persians."

Although he was full of dread at this revelation, Belshazzar did not withhold the gifts he had promised Daniel. But soon afterwards, both he and Babylon were captured by Cyrus of Persia, and this was the end of Nebuchadnezzar's descendants.

Daniel in the Lions' Den

Now Darius the Mede was the son of Astyages, who ended A X,249 Babylonian rule along with his relative, Cyrus. He took Daniel to his own palace in Media and honored him as one of the three principal satraps in the land. But the other rulers were jealous of Daniel, and determined to get rid of him. Noting that he prayed to God three times a day, they told Darius that his satraps and governors had decided to give the people a thirty-day moratorium. During this time, they were not to offer a petition or prayer either to the king or to the gods, and whoever disobeyed the decree would be thrown into a den of lions.

Suspecting nothing, the king approved the decree. Everyone obeyed except Daniel, who continued his daily prayers in the sight of all. Then the satraps went to Darius and accused Daniel of having transgressed the law, and demanded that he be thrown into the lions' den.

Darius, hoping the Deity would save Daniel, told him to endure his fate courageously. With Daniel inside, he sealed the stone that served as door to the lions' den. After leaving, he was so distressed that he could not eat or sleep. Early the next morning, Darius rose and went to the den, where he found the stone in place and the seal unbroken. Opening it, he shouted to Daniel, asking if he were safe. Daniel answered that he had not been harmed, and the king ordered him to be removed.

Daniel's enemies, however, refused to believe that he had been saved by the Deity. They claimed that some one had stuffed the lions with food, which explained why Daniel had not been touched. The king then ordered a large quantity of meat to be thrown to the lions. When they had eaten their fill, he had Daniel's enemies thrown into the den to see if the lions would avoid them because they were full. But the lions tore them to pieces as if they were famished. Accordingly, it was evident to

Darius that it was God who had saved Daniel, and he praised Him throughout the country.

Daniel was now held in greater honor than ever, and he built a fortress at Ecbatana in Media which was magnificently constructed, and stands to this day. He also wrote books, still read, in which he predicted the future, and they convince us that Daniel spoke with God, because whatever he predicted came to pass. [Here Josephus details the visions in Daniel 7 ff.]

The Return From Babylon

A XI,1   In the first year of Cyrus' reign, which was the seventieth year since the Jewish migration to Babylon, God took pity on the captive people. Jeremiah the prophet had predicted that after they had been held in bondage for 70 years they would again be restored to the land of their fathers and rebuild the temple. Now God induced Cyrus to write throughout Asia: "Thus says King Cyrus: Since the Most High God has appointed me king of the habitable world, I am convinced that He is the God whom the Israelites worship. He foretold my name through the prophets, and that I was to build His temple in Jerusalem."

Cyrus knew this from reading Isaiah's prophecies given 210 years earlier. He marveled at the divine power, and he was controlled by a desire to fulfill what was written. Gathering the most distinguished Jews in Babylon, Cyrus told them that he would permit them to return to their native land and rebuild Jerusalem and their temple. He would be their ally and would write his satraps and governors near Judea to contribute gold and silver for the building of the temple.

538 B.C.   The leaders of the tribes of Judah and Benjamin, the priests, and the Levites set out for Jerusalem. Yet many remained in Babylon, unwilling to leave their property. On their arrival, Cyrus' friends contributed much to the construction of the temple. Cyrus returned to them the holy vessels which Nebuchadnezzar had taken out of the temple and carried to Babylon. He gave a specific list of these to the satraps of Syria. The number of those who returned from captivity to Jerusalem was 42,462.

A XI,19   While they were laying the foundations of the temple, the Cutheans who settled in Samaria urged the satraps to obstruct the Jews from rebuilding the city and temple. And when Cyrus died, shortly afterwards, the Samaritans and most neighboring states wrote his son Cambyses that the Jews were a proud and rebellious race. And if they became powerful again, the letter said, the Jews would not submit to the rule of the Persians or pay them tribute, but would attempt to overthrow them. Cambyses believed them and ordered the Jews to stop rebuilding the city and the temple. After ruling six years, during which he conquered Egypt, Cambyses died. Some months later, Darius, son of Hystaspes, was appointed king.

Darius of Persia and Zerubbabel

In the first year of his reign, Darius gave a great feast, to which A XI,31 all the satraps and governors of his kingdom were invited. After they had stuffed themselves, the king went to bed. But, unable to sleep, he started conversing with his three bodyguards. He proposed a contest: whoever gave the most intelligent response to his question would receive these prizes: purple garments, gold drinking cups, a golden bed, a chariot with a gold bridle, a fine linen headdress, a gold necklace, and first rank after the king. And his question was this: which of the following is the strongest—wine, kings, women, or truth? With that, he went to sleep.

In the morning he gathered the nobles, satraps, and rulers of Persia and Media. They sat down in his judgment hall to hear each bodyguard give his opinion.

The first said that wine was the strongest of all, because it could reduce the mightiest king and elevate the lowest slave. It could make the poor rich, the sorrowful happy, and friends enemies. And when sober the next morning, people forget what they have done while drunk, so wine had most power.

The second guard said that kings were the mightiest of all, for they rule over men. And men are the most powerful of all living beings, compelling the earth and the sea to produce for them. But men, in turn, are forced to obey the commands of their kings, even in the ultimate dangers of war. Kings, therefore, are the mightiest.

Now the third guard, whose name was Zerubbabel, said that wine and kings were mighty indeed, but women were mightier. For women bring kings into the world, as well as those who plant vines that produce wine. A beautiful woman could make one give up his wealth and forget his parents and friends. Moreover, the greatest kings were ruled by their wives and would do anything to please them.

"But, mighty as women are," continued Zerubbabel, "both women and kings are weaker than truth. For although the earth is large, and the heaven high, and the sun swift, yet all these move according to the will of God. And since He is true and just, truth must also be the strongest thing. All else is mortal and temporal, but truth is immortal and eternal."

The assembly acclaimed Zerubbabel as the best, and the king was so pleased that he told him to ask for something beyond what he had promised. Zerubbabel then reminded him of a vow he had made if he should ever possess the kingdom: to rebuild Jerusalem and restore the temple of God.

Darius was pleased with this, and arose to embrace him. Then he wrote to his satraps and toparchs to accompany Zerubbabel and those who went with him to rebuild the temple. He also sent letters to the governors of Syria and Phoenicia, ordering them to cut cedar wood from Lebanon and send it to Jerusalem. Moreover, he made the Samaritans and neighboring nations return the villages they had taken from the Jews and contribute to building the temple. Thus, all that Cyrus intended to do for the restoration of the temple Darius now decreed.

A XI,64   Zerubbabel joyfully left the palace for Babylon, where he brought the good news to his countrymen. In thanksgiving, they selected those who would return, and 48,462 men, as well as 40,742 women and children went to Jerusalem. The work on the temple resumed and progressed quickly. Even the Samaritans came to Zerubbabel and asked to help in rebuilding the temple, but he replied that they could not be partners in the reconstruction. But when it was finished, Zerubbabel said, they would have the same privilege as all other people to come and worship there if they wished.

The Samaritans were angry and protested to the Persians, warning that the temple looked more like a fortress. The Jews were concerned that Darius would change his mind, but the prophets Haggai and Zechariah encouraged them. Then Darius read a document in the archives at Ecbatana which detailed Cyrus' authorization that the temple be rebuilt. It warned that anyone opposing it should be crucified. Darius sent a copy to his governor of Syria, endorsing it, and ordered him to help the Jews, which he did.

At the end of seven years, the temple was completed, and sacrifices were offered on the altars. It was time to celebrate the feast of the Passover, and the Jews came in great crowds to Jerusalem from all their villages and cities. They celebrated the feast for seven days with great joy. Their form of government was now aristocratic and oligarchic, with the high priests in charge. When the Samaritans continued harassing them, they sent a delegation of five, including Zerubbabel, to Darius. He sent a letter of warning to the Samaritans.

Ezra

A XI,120   When Darius died, his son Xerxes took over the kingdom, and he continued to esteem the Jews highly. Ezra, the chief priest of

Two contemporary Samaritans holding their most sacred treasure, the scroll of the Samaritan Pentateuch. Mount Ebal, the "Mount of Cursing," is in the background.

the Jews remaining in Babylon, was very knowledgeable about the laws of Moses. He decided to go to Jerusalem with another group of Jews from Babylon. Having obtained a letter of authorization from King Xerxes, they set out and reached Jerusalem four months later, bringing many gold and silver vessels to the temple treasury, and offering sacrifices.

Later on, certain men told Ezra that some of the people, including the priests and Levites, had broken the law by marrying foreign women. They asked Ezra to enforce the laws, thinking God might become angry and punish them.

Ezra tore his clothes and his hair at this, and threw himself on the ground. He was afraid that if he told the men to divorce their heathen wives they would not do it. All moderate Jews came to Ezra and grieved with him. Then he rose, stretched out his arms to heaven, and said that he was ashamed to look up at it because of the sins the people had committed. Yet he implored God, who had saved a remnant of His people out of captivity in Babylon and restored them to Jerusalem, to take pity on them and forgive them.

When Ezra finished praying, Shecaniah, a leader in Jerusalem, said that they had sinned in marrying foreign women. He urged Ezra to order that these wives be divorced along with their children, and to punish those who disobeyed. Following this advice, Ezra made the priests, Levites, and people swear to send away those wives and children. Next, he summoned all the rest of the people to come to Jerusalem within three days, or have their property confiscated. When they had assembled, Ezra told them they had sinned in taking foreign wives, but God would be pleased if they divorced them. They did so, and then brought sacrifices to appease God.

Later, at the festival of Tabernacles, the people gathered at the court of the temple and asked Ezra to read to them the laws of Moses. He stood up among the multitude and read from early morning until noon. As they listened, the people recalled how often they had broken those laws, and they wept. But Ezra told them to hold their tears, for it was a festival and it was not lawful to lament. Instead, they were to feast and rejoice, for their repentance would prevent their lapsing back into sin.

Ezra lived to a good old age before he died, and was given a magnificent funeral in Jerusalem.

Nehemiah

A XI,159   One of the Jewish captives, named Nehemiah, was wine steward to King Xerxes. While walking one day below the walls of Susa, the Persian capital, he overheard some travelers speaking

Hebrew as they entered the city after a long journey. He asked where they came from, and they replied, "Judea." Then he asked how the people and the city were faring.

"They are in trouble," they replied. "The walls have been torn down, neighbors are plundering the country, Jews are taken captive, and the roads are full of corpses."

Nehemiah burst into tears out of pity for his countrymen. Looking up to heaven, he asked, "How long, O Lord, will you look away while our nation suffers such misery?"

While he was lamenting at the gate, someone informed him that the king was ready to recline for dinner, so he hurried and went as he was, without washing himself, to serve the king as wine steward. But after dinner, the king was more cheerful than usual, and when he saw Nehemiah's gloomy look, he asked him why he was sad. Nehemiah prayed for persuasive words and said, "How can I, O King, appear other than sad when I hear that the walls of Jerusalem, where the graves and monuments of my forefathers are, have been demolished and its gates consumed by fire? But graciously permit me to go and erect its walls, and to finish building the temple."

The king granted his request, and let him carry letters to the satraps, instructing them to pay Nehemiah due honor and provide whatever he needed. In joy, Nehemiah worshiped God, and thanked the king for his promise. The next day, the king gave him a letter to the eparch of Syria, Phoenicia, and Samaria, ordering him to honor Nehemiah and provide building supplies.

Nehemiah went to Babylon and took with him many of his A XI,168 countrymen. He set out for Jerusalem, reaching it in the twenty-fifth year of the reign of Xerxes. Summoning all the people to the city, he stood in the temple court and told them that he had come with the permission of the king of Persia to rebuild their wall and complete the temple. Relying on God, and working day and night, they would succeed, he assured them. Then he told the officers to measure the wall and divide the work among the people by villages and cities. Thus the Jews prepared for the 445 B.C. work. This name [Jews], by which they have been called since their return from Babylon, is derived from the tribe of Judah.

But when the Ammonites, Moabites, Samaritans, and all who lived in Coele-Syria heard that the walls were going up again, they tried to interfere with the builders. They killed many of them, and hired foreigners to assassinate Nehemiah himself. But Nehemiah surrounded himself with bodyguards and was not deterred. Not that he feared death, but he knew that if he were killed, the walls of the city would never rise. He also gave orders that the builders should have arms when they worked, and so the masons had swords and shields nearby. Trumpeters were stationed at intervals of 500 feet to signal if the enemy approached, so the builders would be ready for them. Despite all hardships, the work went on, and in 28 months the walls were finished.

Nehemiah and the people celebrated with sacrifices to God and an eight-day feast. Because Jerusalem had a small population, Nehemiah urged the priests and Levites to move from the country into the city, where he constructed houses for them at his own expense. In this way, Jerusalem's population expanded. Then, after providing many other admirable public services, Nehemiah died at an advanced age, and he left the walls of Jerusalem as his eternal monument.

Footnote for page 193.

* Josephus follows the Septuagint in this identification, but many scholars today think that Xerxes is intended.

FROM ESTHER 15 TO THE PTOLEMIES

After the death of Xerxes, the Persian empire passed to his son A XI,184 Ahasuerus, whom the Greeks call Artaxerxes*. In the third year of his reign, Artaxerxes entertained his friends and governors at a lavish feast that lasted 180 days. After this, he gave another seven-day feast at Susa for the other nations and their ambassadors. At the banquet, Artaxerxes pitched a huge pavilion on pillars of gold and silver. Linen and purple cloth were spread over them so that myriads could dine. The serving bowls were gold adorned with precious stones. The king also ordered his servants to supply wine as desired without forcing it on guests, which was the Persian custom.

Vashti, the queen, also had a feast in the palace for the women. But the king wanted to display her to his guests, since her beauty exceeded that of all other women, and commanded her to appear at his banquet. Because the laws of Persia forbid their women to be seen by strangers, she refused repeated summons from the king. Artaxerxes was so angry that he broke up the banquet and called the Seven Persians, who interpret their laws. Accusing the queen of disobedience, he asked how she should be punished. One of them replied that her insult affected all Persians, "for wives will no longer respect their husbands when they hear about the queen's arrogance to you, who have power over all." The king decided to dismiss Vashti, although he was deeply in love with her, and take another queen in her place.

The Story of Esther

Artaxerxes ordered some of his men to select the most beautiful virgins in the kingdom and bring them to him. Among the many who came was a Jewess from Babylon named Esther, an orphan who was being brought up by her uncle Mordecai. He was of the tribe of Benjamin and one of the principal men among the Jews. Now Esther surpassed all women in beauty, and she joined the 400 virgins who were pampered for six months before they were considered ready for the king's bed. The eunuch in charge of them then sent one of them each day to the king, who had intercourse with her and then sent her back to the eunuch. But when Esther came to him, he fell in love with her and made her his lawful wife. After a month-long celebration, the king placed a diadem on her head, and she came to live at the royal palace. Mordecai then moved from Babylon to Susa, and each day he inquired about Esther at the palace, for he loved her as his own daughter.

A XI,207   Some time later, two of the king's eunuchs plotted to kill Artaxerxes, but Mordecai discovered the plot, and revealed it to the king through Queen Esther. The king crucified the eunuchs, and while he gave no reward to Mordecai at the time, he told the scribes to enter his name in the archives, and let him stay at the palace.

A man named Haman, of Amalekite descent, was greatly favored by the king. Both Persians and foreigners prostrated themselves before him, but Mordecai would not. When Haman noticed this, he asked about his background. Learning he was a Jew, Haman was seething and said to himself that while free-born Persians prostrated themselves in his presence, this slave refused to do so. Since his own race, the Amalekites, had been destroyed by the Jews, he decided to obliterate Mordecai's entire nation rather than take revenge on him alone. Accordingly, he went to Artaxerxes and warned him of a certain wicked, unfriendly, and unsocial nation scattered throughout his kingdom, which observed a different religion and law. "It is the enemy of your people and of all mankind," he said, recommending total annihilation of the Jews.

The king told Haman he could do what he wished to the Jews. So he sent out a decree that all Jews in the Persian empire should be put to death, with their wives and children, on a specified day. Artaxerxes' governors prepared to carry it out, and everywhere the Jews were anxious and distressed. Mordecai also mourned, but he told Queen Esther about the danger that threatened their nation, and asked her to intercede with the king.

Now there was a law that no one could come into the king's presence unless he were summoned, and men with axes stood around his throne to punish those who approached. But the king held a golden scepter, and if he wished to spare someone, he held it out, and whoever touched it was free from danger.

Esther prayed to God for assistance, and fasted for three days. Then she adorned herself as became a queen, and, taking two of her maids with her, she came into the presence of the king. But when she saw him sitting on his throne in splendor and frowning at her in anger, she fainted from fear and fell unconscious at the feet of her attendants. But the king, by God's will, changed his mood, and he sprang from the throne to lift her up. Placing the scepter in her hand, he reassured her.

Reviving, she explained her fainting in such a weak voice that the king was even more alarmed. He told her to ask any favor of him, even up to half of his kingdom. Esther asked that he and his friend Haman come to a banquet which she had prepared for him. He consented, and they came. While he was drinking, Artaxerxes asked Esther what she desired, but she put off telling him until the next day, if she could again entertain them.

Haman was elated, because he alone had been considered worthy of dining with the king at Esther's banquet. But as he left, he saw Mordecai in the courtyard. He again refused to honor Haman, who angrily reported it to his wife and friends. Haman's wife advised him to have a gallows constructed, 60 cubits high, and in the morning he should ask the king for permission to crucify Mordecai. Haman ordered his servants to prepare the gallows in his own courtyard.

That night God would not let the king sleep. Since he wished to use his time profitably, he had his scribe read from the records of the kings before him and those of his own administration. As he was reading about various awards accorded people, he came to the conspiracy which had been discovered by Mordecai. The king stopped him, and asked, "Isn't it written that Mordecai received a reward?" The scribe said there was no such reference.

The king told him to stop reading, and because it was nearly day, he asked if any of his friends had arrived at the court. It so happened that Haman was there, for he had come earlier than usual to petition the king to have Mordecai put to death. The king at once summoned Haman and said to him, "Because you are my only loyal friend, please advise me. How should I honor someone I cherish in a manner worthy of my magnanimity?"

Haman, thinking the king had him in mind, said, "If you want to honor this man, let him ride on horseback wearing royal dress and a gold necklace. And have one of your close friends go before him and proclaim throughout the whole city that this is the way the king honors his favorites."

Pleased with this answer, the king told Haman to take the robe, the golden chain, and the horse, and do for Mordecai the Jew what he had suggested. "And since you are my close friend," he continued "you precede him, for he saved my life."

Haman was confounded and helpless, but he went to Mordecai as the king directed. At first Mordecai thought Haman was mocking him, but then he put on the purple robe, mounted the horse, and was led through the city by Haman. Disgraced and in tears, Haman went home and told his wife and friends what had happened.

Just then Esther's eunuchs summoned Haman to her banquet. While they were feasting, Artaxerxes asked the queen what her request was. She then confessed that she was a Jewess, and that she and her nation were marked for destruction; she begged him to help them avoid this disaster.

The king asked, "Who desires to destroy your people?"

"Haman," Esther answered.

Confused and angry, the king rushed out of the banquet hall into the garden, while Haman fell on the queen's couch and pleaded for his life. But when the king returned and saw him there he was only angrier, shouting, "O worst-of-all-men, are you now trying to violate my wife?" While Haman was speechless, the eunuch Harbonah reported that he had seen a cross at Haman's house, 60 cubits high, prepared for Mordecai. At once the king ordered that Haman be hanged on the very cross he had prepared for Mordecai.

Then the king told Esther to write letters in his name and under his seal. These letters were sent to the governors of the 127 satrapies from India to Ethiopia, exposing Haman's plot. They were ordered to protect the Jews, who were permitted to arm themselves and take revenge on their enemies. Horsemen were sent all over the kingdom with these letters, and on the appointed day, the Jews killed 75,000 of their enemies. On the following days they feasted, and Jews ever since have held them to be holy days, called Purim.

Mordecai became a great and illustrious person in the king's estimation, assisting him in the government. He also enjoyed the companionship of the queen, and through them the status of the Jews was better than they could have hoped for.

Bagoses Defiles the Temple

A XI,297   In the reign of Artaxerxes II, Johanan became high priest [in Jerusalem]. He had a brother named Jesus, who was a friend of Bagoses, the general of the Persian army. Bagoses had promised to obtain the priesthood for Jesus, but when Johanan and Jesus argued in the temple, Johanan killed Jesus in anger.

The Deity, however, did not overlook this crime, for when Bagoses heard about it, he angrily asked the Jews, "Have you dared to commit murder in your own temple?" When he tried to enter the temple, they stopped him. But Bagoses replied, "Am I not purer than the dead body inside?" So he went inside the temple, defiling the sanctuary. He also imposed tribute on the Jews, ordering them to pay 50 drachmas out of the public treasury for every lamb that was offered in sacrifice during the next seven years.

Manasseh

When Johanan died, his son Jaddua succeeded to the high A XI,302 priesthood, and he had a brother named Manasseh. Now Sanballat had been sent by Darius [III], the last king of Persia, as satrap of Samaria. He was a Cuthean by birth—the Samaritans also came from the same stock—and he was anxious to live on friendly terms with the Jews, so he gladly gave his daughter in marriage to Manasseh.

But when Jaddua became high priest, the elders of Jerusalem were disturbed that Manasseh, who was married to a foreigner, participated with him in priestly duties. They were concerned that this marriage would encourage others to transgress the law against taking foreign wives. Thus they commanded Manasseh either to divorce his wife or not approach the altar. The high priest himself joined with the people in their anger against his brother, and kept him from the altar.

Manasseh went to his father-in-law, Sanballat, and told him that although he loved his daughter, he would be forced to give her up. But Sanballat told him that he could keep his wife, and not only be a priest but governor and high priest. For with Darius' consent, Sanballat would build another temple on Mount Gerizim, the tallest mountain near Samaria.

Elated, Manasseh stayed with Sanballat. Many other priests and people who had married foreign women deserted to Manasseh and Sanballat, who settled them in Samaria.

Alexander the Great

About this time, Alexander, king of Macedon, crossed the A XI,313 Hellespont. He defeated Darius' satraps at the battle of Granicus, and was advancing further into Asia. Darius awaited him at Issus, in Cilicia, and everyone in Asia thought that Darius would easily defeat the invaders. This included Sanballat, who promised Manasseh that when Darius returned from his victory he would fulfill his promises. But Darius was defeated in a great slaughter, and fled back into Persia. Alexander marched into Syria, taking Damascus and Sidon, and then besieged Tyre.

Mount Gerizim, the "Mount of Blessing" and center of Samaritan worship, overlooks the excavations of ancient Shechem in the foreground.

From there he sent a letter to the high priest of the Jews, asking him for supplies, and requesting that he transfer his allegiance and tribute from Darius to Alexander. The high priest answered that he had promised Darius not to bear arms against him, and that he would keep his oath as long as Darius lived.

Alexander was very angry, and threatened that as soon as he had taken Tyre he would march against the Jewish high priest. His example would teach all men to whom they must keep their oaths.

When Sanballat heard that Darius had been defeated, he decided to join Alexander with 8,000 Samaritans. The kind reception that Alexander gave him encouraged Sanballat to ask permission to divide the Jews by building a temple in Samaria, and permission was granted. So the new temple was built, and Manasseh was made high priest. But before it was finished, Sanballat died.

332 B.C.   Meanwhile, Alexander had conquered Tyre, following a seven-month siege. After two more months he had taken the city of Gaza also. Then he hurried to go up to Jerusalem.

When Jaddua, the high priest, heard that Alexander was coming, he was terrified, and ordered his people to join him in sacrifice and prayer to God. Appearing to him in a dream, God told him to take courage and decorate the city with wreaths. The people were to clothe themselves in white and the priests with the robes of their order. Then they were to march out of the gates to meet the Macedonians, for they would not be harmed.

Jaddua awoke rejoicing, and announced the revelation to all. When he learned that Alexander was not far from the city, he went out in procession with the priests and the people. A XI,331 Alexander saw the procession coming toward him: the priests were clothed in linen and the high priest in a robe of blue and gold. On his head was a miter with the golden plate on which God's name was inscribed. Approaching alone, Alexander prostrated himself before the Name and greeted the high priest. As the Jews welcomed Alexander with one voice and encircled him, his officers wondered if he had suddenly become insane. One of them, Parmenio, went up to Alexander and asked him to explain. He replied, "When I was at Dium in Macedonia, considering how I could become master of Asia, I saw this very person in my sleep, dressed as he is now. He urged me not to delay, but to cross over confidently and take dominion over the Persians."

Sculpture of Alexander the Great (Archaeological Museum, Istanbul).

Alexander was escorted into Jerusalem by the high priest and his attendants. He went up into the temple, where he sacrificed to God according to the high priest's directions. And when the book of Daniel was shown to him, which predicted that one of the Greeks would destroy the Persian empire, he thought himself to be the one so designated. When he offered the Jews whatever they desired, the high priest asked that they might observe their own laws and be exempt from the tribute every seventh year. Alexander granted these requests. They further asked that the Jews in Babylon and Media be allowed their own laws, and he also agreed. Finally he told the people that if any of them wanted to enlist in his army, he would allow them to continue their own customs, and many joined his army.*

Alexander now left Jerusalem. The Samaritans of Shechem, which was beside Mount Gerizim and was inhabited by Jewish apostates, saw how Alexander had honored the Jews. They now also claimed that they were Jews and asked Alexander to visit their temple and to grant them the seventh-year exemption from tribute. He promised to consider it in the future, and took Samaritan troops with him to Egypt.

When Alexander died [nine years later, after conquering Persia], his empire was divided among his succeeding generals.

323 B.C.

Ptolemy Soter

A XII,1   Egypt came under the rule of one of Alexander's generals named Ptolemy, who was called Soter. Determined to take all of Syria, Ptolemy advanced against Jerusalem and seized it by cunning and deceit: he entered the city on the Sabbath as if to sacrifice, but then conquered it. The Jews failed to resist him, not suspecting his hostile intentions, and enjoying their day of ease and rest. Ptolemy took back with him many captives from Judea and Samaria, and settled them in Egypt. They proved so reliable there that he gave them equal civil rights with Macedonians in Alexandria. Many other Jews came to Egypt on their own, attracted by Ptolemy's liberality and the excellence of the land.

Ptolemy Philadelphus

A XII,11   After Ptolemy Soter had ruled for 41 years, Philadelphus took over Egypt for the next 39. Demetrius of Phalerum, who was in charge of the king's library, wanted to collect all the books in the world, if possible. Ptolemy once asked him how many thousands of books he had gathered. He replied, "About 200,000, but shortly I should have some 500,000."

Demetrius went on to say that there were many books of law among the Jews, which were worth studying and adding to the king's library. But they were written in the Jewish language, he said, and ought to be translated into Greek for the library. The king was pleased with Demetrius' proposal and wrote to the high priest of the Jews about the matter.

---

* The historicity of Alexander's contact with the Jews on this occasion is quite doubtful. No surviving non-Jewish source mentions this episode, although rabbinical traditions contain a similar story (*Megillath Ta'anith*).

Meanwhile, Ptolemy followed the advice of one of his wise and just friends named Aristaeus and freed the Jews who had been brought captive into Egypt by Ptolemy Soter, who now numbered 120,000. He also had Demetrius draw up a formal memorial of his decree regarding the translation of the Hebrew writings.

The king then ordered gold and precious stones as gifts for the high priest at Jerusalem. He sent a letter with these telling the priest that he had set free all his countrymen who had been in bondage. The letter continued:

> I have decided to have your Law translated into Greek and deposited in my library. You will do well, therefore, to select from each tribe six men of good character. They should be mature, knowledgeable about the laws, and able to make an accurate translation.

Eleazar, the high priest at this time, was delighted with the A XII,51 king's letter and his gifts. He gladly selected and sent him 70* educated men out of the twelve tribes, who carried with them to Alexandria the sacred books of the Jews. When the king heard that the elders had reached the city, he dismissed all other visitors and ordered that the 70 be brought into his presence at once. As the old men came in, he treated them with great respect, and asked them many questions about their books. He also marvelled at the way in which they were written, for they were in letters of gold on leather skins. These were joined together so perfectly that no one could tell where one membrane ended and the other began. He then expressed his thanks to them for coming, and more so to him who sent them, and, above all, to God whose laws these were. The elders then shouted as one to wish all happiness to the king, at which he was so moved that he wept for joy. He invited them to dine with him at a long feast, during which they discussed philosophy, and arranged that they be given the best lodgings near the citadel.

The elders worked on their translation in a house that Demetrius had prepared for them. It was on an island near the seashore, a quiet place where they could write and talk together without being interrupted. When the Law had been translated after 72 days, Demetrius called together all the Jews and read the translation aloud in the presence of the elders. They expressed their approval and desired copies.

---

* Josephus does not explain the numerical problem: six each from twelve tribes should be 72, not 70, but from the latter number is derived the familiar name for this translation, the *Septuagint*.

The king was delighted when the laws were read to him, and was astonished at their depth and wisdom. He asked Demetrius why such admirable laws had never been mentioned by the poets or historians. Demetrius explained that no one dared to describe these laws because of their divine nature, and that some who attempted it had been afflicted by God. Theopompus, for example, had intended to write about these laws, but became mentally disturbed for 30 days. He tried to appease God during sane intervals, learning in a dream that his madness was because he had been too curious about divine matters. When he gave up the attempt his reason returned. Demetrius also told about the tragic poet Theodectes. He intended to mention items contained in the sacred book in one of his dramas, but was afflicted with cataracts until he appeased God.

The king ordered that great care should be taken of the sacred books, so that nothing might ever be changed from what was written in them. He then allowed the translators to return home, loaded with generous gifts, and invited them to return frequently.

The Seleucids

A XII,119   The Jews were also honored by [Alexander's successor] kings of Asia when they served them in war. Seleucus Nicator, for example, granted them citizenship in the cities he founded and in Antioch, his capital. They have equal privileges with the Greeks there until this day.

When Antiochus [III] the Great ruled Asia, however, the Jews underwent many hardships because of his war with the Ptolemies. After he annexed Judea, the people of Jerusalem supported Antiochus, and he rewarded them by ordering his governors to assist them in completing the temple. Antiochus finally made a treaty of friendship with Ptolemy [V Epiphanes], giving him his daughter in marriage, along with Coele-Syria, Samaria, Judea, and Phoenicia as dowry.

Ptolemy Epiphanes and Joseph

A XII,158   The high priest in Judea at this time was Onias. A great lover of money, he withheld the twenty silver talents which the king of Egypt received every year as tribute. Ptolemy was angry, and sent an ambassador to Jerusalem to warn Onias. If the tribute were not paid, the king would seize their land and send his soldiers to settle it. But Onias was unmoved, so great was his greed.

Onias had a young nephew, named Joseph, who was highly respected in Jerusalem for his wisdom. He went to Onias and accused him of bringing the nation into danger. If he were so passionately fond of money, Joseph said, he ought at least to go to the king and ask him to remit either all or part of the sum demanded. But Onias answered that he did not care about going to the king, and was ready to give up the priesthood. Then Joseph asked whether he could go as envoy to Ptolemy instead, and Onias consented. Joseph went into the temple and called the people together. He told them not to be disturbed about his uncle's neglect because he himself would go to the king in their behalf.

After they thanked him, Joseph entertained Ptolemy's envoy lavishly. Giving him valuable gifts, he sent him back to the king to herald his mission. Pleased with Joseph's openness and generosity, the envoy promised that he would assist him in every way. In Egypt, he praised the young man so highly that both the king and queen felt well disposed to him even before his arrival.

Meanwhile, Joseph borrowed money for his journey from his wealthy friends in Samaria, and set out for Alexandria. Now at the same time, the magistrates in Syria and Phoenicia were coming there to bid for the tax-farming concessions. When they saw Joseph on the road, they laughed at his poverty and humble clothing.

Arriving at Alexandria, Joseph learned that Ptolemy was at Memphis. He went there and met the king, who happened to be in a chariot with his wife and his friend Athenion, the envoy who had been sent to Jerusalem. Athenion at once recognized Joseph and introduced him to the king. Ptolemy invited him to come up into his chariot, and when he was seated, began to complain about Onias' conduct. "Forgive him because of his age," Joseph replied, "for you know that old people and infants often have the same intellect. But from us who are young, you will receive everything, and have no cause to complain."

Ptolemy was pleased with the young man's wit and charm, and invited him to live at the palace and dine at his table. When they returned to Alexandria, the Syrian tax-farmers were disagreeably surprised to see Joseph seated at Ptolemy's side.

On the day in which the rights to farm taxes were to be sold, the bids from Coele-Syria, Phoenicia, Judea, and Samaria totaled 8,000 talents. But Joseph stepped forward and said that this group had rigged their bids at too low a price, and that he would provide twice as much. The king was delighted, and said he would sell the rights to Joseph, but he asked him if he had any guarantors.

"Yes," he replied, "persons of the highest character whom you will *not* distrust."

"Who are they?" asked the king.

"You yourself, O King, and your wife, each to guarantee the other's share."

Ptolemy laughed and granted him the tax-farming concessions without guarantors. The other embarrassed bidders returned to Syria.

Joseph took with him 2,000 of the king's foot soldiers and returned to collect the taxes. Arriving in Ashkelon, he demanded the tribute from its citizens, but they refused and even

Ashkelon, on the Mediterranean, was one of the cities in the Philistine pentapolis, the place where Joseph executed twenty tax-evaders, and the birthplace of Herod the Great. Its ruins are being excavated.

insulted him. Joseph therefore seized twenty of their principal men, put them to death, and sent their property to the king, informing him of what he had done. Ptolemy commended his actions and gave him permission to do as he wished. When the other cities heard what had happened in Ashkelon, they readily received Joseph and paid their tribute.

Hyrcanus, Son of Joseph

For 22 years Joseph continued to collect the taxes. Since the A XII,186 amount he gathered every year was larger than what he paid to the king of Egypt, he grew very wealthy. He married and had seven sons by one wife, and an eighth, Hyrcanus, by his brother's daughter, whom he married under the following circumstances.

When he was dining with the king in Alexandria, he became infatuated with a beautiful dancing girl who entertained them. But since Jews were forbidden to have intercourse with a foreign woman, he asked his brother to help him arrange the sin and conceal it too. His brother agreed, but instead beautified his own daughter and brought her by night to sleep with him. Befuddled by too much drink, Joseph failed to recognize his own niece, and after repeated intercourse, fell violently in love with her. Later, he learned that his brother had chosen to dishonor his own daughter rather than see Joseph fall into disgrace. Grateful for this brotherly love, Joseph married the girl and she bore him Hyrcanus.

Joseph sent all his sons to prominent teachers, but only Hyrcanus profited. The others were too dull and lazy to learn anything. To test Hyrcanus' cleverness as a thirteen-year-old, Joseph once sent him with 300 yoke of oxen into the wilderness to sow the land there. But when Hyrcanus came to the place he was to plough, he found he had no harnesses—they had been hidden by his father. Yet rather than waste time retrieving them, as his men advised, he slaughtered ten yoke of oxen and gave the meat to his men to eat. Then he cut up their hides into harnesses and sowed the land. His father was delighted.

About this time, Joseph learned that a new son had been born A XII,196 to King Ptolemy, and the leaders of Syria were going to Alexandria to celebrate the child's birthday. Too old to make the journey himself, Joseph asked his sons if any of them wished to go. They excused themselves, saying they were uneducated, and suggested that Hyrcanus be sent. When he agreed, Joseph wanted to send many beautiful presents for the king along with him, but Hyrcanus thought it would be better to wait until he reached Alexandria and buy the gifts there. Joseph agreed, and gave him a letter of credit to one of his stewards, named Arion, who lived in Alexandria. Now, Hyrcanus' brothers were all envious of him. After he left, they wrote to the friends of the king, asking them to kill Hyrcanus.

When he arrived in Alexandria, Hyrcanus presented his father's letter to Arion and asked for 1,000 talents. Expecting he would ask for only ten, Arion refused. Hyrcanus then had him thrown in prison, but Arion's wife was a friend of Cleopatra, Ptolemy's wife. She informed the queen, who told the king.

Ptolemy asked for an explanation, and Hyrcanus replied that he had thrown the slave Arion into prison for disobedience. "And it makes no difference," he said, "if the master is large or small. If we don't punish such rebels, even you may be scorned by your subjects." Ptolemy laughed and admired the strong spirit of the youth. Arion, meanwhile, gave Hyrcanus the 1,000 talents, and was released from prison.

Invited to dine at the palace, Hyrcanus was placed at the foot of the table, and the other guests piled their bones in front of him. Trypho, the king's jester, said to him, "Do you see, my lord, the bones lying before Hyrcanus? They are a symbol of the way in which his father has stripped all Syria, till it is as bare as Hyrcanus has left these bones!"

The king laughed and asked Hyrcanus how he came to have so many bones before him.

"Quite naturally, my lord," he replied, "for dogs eat both meat and bones, as your guests appear to have done. But men eat the meat and throw the bones away, as I have done." The king laughed loudly and made all his guests join in applause.

The next day, Hyrcanus went to visit the king's friends, and he asked their servants privately what gifts their masters intended to give the king on his son's birthday. The highest amount given by any of them was twenty talents. Hyrcanus pretended he would be giving much less.

The day came and the others presented their gifts. Then Hyrcanus paraded in 100 boy slaves, each carrying one talent, and presented these to the king, as well as 100 virgin girl slaves, also carrying one talent each, and presented these to the queen. While all were astounded, he also distributed gifts to the very friends of the king who were supposed to kill him, and so escaped danger.

Ptolemy, in gratitude, told Hyrcanus to take any gift he wished. But Hyrcanus asked only that the king write to his father and brothers about him [and so forestall their anger]. The king sent him home with splendid gifts, and wrote to his father and brothers, as he had promised.

His brothers went out to meet Hyrcanus and kill him, and their father did not prevent them, for he was angry at the huge sum he had spent for gifts. But when the brothers attacked Hyrcanus, he defended himself so well that two of the brothers and many of their men were killed, while the rest escaped to their father in Jerusalem. Hyrcanus, however, fearing for his safety, withdrew to the land beyond the Jordan and collected tribute there.

Later, his father Joseph died, as well as the high priest, his uncle Onias. The older brothers now attacked Hyrcanus, and

Simon, the new high priest, joined them. Hyrcanus therefore gave up his intention of returning to Jerusalem and stayed in trans-Jordan near Heshbon, where he built himself a fortress of white marble. Here he ruled for seven years, but then grew afraid that he would fall into the hands of Antiochus Epiphanes, the new king of Syria. Expecting to be punished for attacking the Arabs, he took his own life, and Antiochus seized his property.

16

THE MACCABEES

In Egypt, Ptolemy Epiphanes had died, and the son who AXII,242 succeeded him, Ptolemy Philometor, was so young that Anti- WI,31* ochus [IV] Epiphanes of Syria invaded Egypt with a large force and took Memphis. But before he could besiege Alexandria, the Romans ordered him out of Egypt. Afraid of Rome, he obeyed at once and returned via Judea.

At this time, Jerusalem was in confusion, for the high priest, Onias [III], had died, leaving an infant son. The brothers of Onias then fought for the high priesthood: Jesus, a name he had changed to Jason, and Onias, who changed his name to Menelaus. Jason defeated his brother, but Menelaus and his followers fled to Antiochus. They offered Antiochus their services as guides for an invasion of Judea, and so he now marched against Jerusalem and took it without difficulty, for the friends of Menelaus opened the gates for him. Killing many in the opposition party, he plundered the city, after which he returned to Syria.

Two years later, Antiochus came back to Jerusalem with his army. Having again been admitted within its walls, he treated the inhabitants with great cruelty, sparing not even those who had let him into the city. He dismantled the walls of Jerusalem, burning the finest parts of the city, and stationed a Macedonian garrison in a citadel overlooking the temple. He carried away 167 B.C. the golden vessels and treasures of the temple, putting a stop to the sacrifices. He polluted the altar by offering up swine on it,

---

* Because Josephus begins his *Jewish War* at this point, future marginal references will be preceded by A for *Antiquities*, and W for *War*.

knowing that this was against the Law of Moses. He compelled the Jews to give up their worship of God and to stop circumcising their children. Those who persisted were mutilated, strangled, or crucified, with their children hung from their necks.

When the Samaritans saw the Jews suffering these cruelties, they sent a letter to Antiochus denying any Jewish relationship. They also asked that their "temple without a name" on Mt. Gerizim be known as that of Zeus Hellenios.

Mattathias

A XII,265
W I,36

At this time there was a Jewish priest, named Mattathias, who lived in the village of Modin. He had five sons: John who was called Gaddis, Simon called Mathes, Judas called Maccabeus, Eleazar called Auran, and Jonathan called Apphus. Some of the king's men came to Modin to compel the Jews to sacrifice as he had ordered. Because Mattathias was a leader there, they wanted him to be the first to sacrifice, knowing his fellow-citizens would follow. Mattathias refused, saying that even if all others obeyed Antiochus' commands, he and his sons never would.

But another Jew came forward and sacrificed as Antiochus had commanded. Mattathias and his sons took out broad-bladed knives and cut the man down, also killing the king's officer and his soldiers. After overturning the pagan altar, Mattathias cried out, "Whoever is zealous for the laws of our country and the worship of God, let him follow me!"

He and his sons then fled to the desert, and many others followed him, with their wives and children, and lived there in caves. Marching against them, the Syrians burned them inside their caves on the Sabbath day. Not only did the Jews not resist, they failed even to block the mouths of the caves, and about 1,000 suffered. Many, however, escaped with Mattathias, whom they appointed leader. He directed them to fight even on the Sabbath, otherwise the enemy would always choose that day to attack and they would all be destroyed.

Gathering a large force, Mattathias and his men overturned the pagan altars, killed those who had sacrificed on them, and ordered all their boys circumcised. After he had been in command for a year, however, he became ill. Urging his sons to continue the noble effort he had begun, he told them to choose their brother Simon as paternal adviser, and Maccabeus as com-

166 B.C. mander, because of his courage and strength. Then he died and was buried in Modin, greatly mourned by the people.

Judas Maccabeus

Judas Maccabeus, with his brothers and followers, drove the enemy from the country. Apollonius, the governor of Samaria, advanced against Judas, but was defeated and killed. Next, Seron, governor of Coele-Syria, met the same fate, even though his army greatly outnumbered Judas'. A XII,285 W I,38

A third army, under a general named Ptolemy, was sent against Judas by the Syrians, consisting of 40,000 infantry and 7,000 cavalry. Calling his men together, Judas urged them to be bold and put their trust in God. After dismissing the newly-married men and new property owners, he had only 3,000 men left, most of whom were poorly armed.

When Ptolemy camped at Emmaus, he decided to surprise the rebels and sent Gorgias with 6,000 troops to attack the Jews by night, using Jewish traitors as guides. When Judas learned of the plan, he decided to attack the enemy himself when they were divided. Leaving many fires burning, they marched all night to Emmaus. When Gorgias found the Jewish camp abandoned, he went on to look for the enemy in the mountains.

Near dawn, meanwhile, Judas reached Emmaus, attacked the sleeping Syrians, and pursued those who fled, killing 3,000. Rejoicing, the Jews returned to the enemy's camp to take the weapons and goods that had been left behind. When Gorgias and his men returned and saw from a distance that their camp was destroyed, they were afraid and also fled.

Lysias, who had been left in charge of Syria while Antiochus was in Persia, now invaded Judea with an army of 60,000 infantry and 5,000 cavalry and camped at Bethsura. Judas met him with 10,000, asking God to assist him, and joined battle with the enemy's advance party, killing about 5,000. Alarmed at the desperate spirit of the Jews, Lysias called back his troops and returned to Antioch, where he prepared to invade with an even larger army.

Judas then told his people that after these victories which God had given them, they ought to go up to Jerusalem and purify the temple to offer sacrifices. When they reached the city, Judas ordered some of his soldiers to continue fighting Syrian troops in the citadel. Meanwhile, he and the rest of his men purified the temple, which had become desolate, with weeds growing inside the sanctuary. Rebuilding the altar and restoring the sacred implements, they rekindled the lampstand and burned incense there, three years to the day since Antiochus defiled the temple. Judas and his men celebrated a great feast which lasted for eight days, and which we continue to observe as the festival of Lights [Hanukkah].

A XII,327   Now the nations around Jerusalem were alarmed to see the Jews regaining their power, and they attacked them. But Judas marched out, defeated them, and rebuilt the walls of Jerusalem. His brother Simon punished the invaders of Galilee, while Judas and his brother Jonathan attacked those of Gilead, as well as their enemies in Idumea, Hebron, and Ashdod.

King Antiochus, meanwhile, was in Persia. He was attempting to steal the riches from the temple of Artemis in Elam, when he was repulsed and forced back to Babylon as a fugitive. News then arrived of his reverses against the Jews, and he fell deathly ill, confessing that he was suffering for having desecrated the Jewish temple. After Antiochus [IV Epiphanes] died, Lysias appointed his son Antiochus [V] king and called him Eupator.

A XII,362   In Jerusalem, the Syrians still held the citadel. Because this
W I,41   overlooked the temple, they would frequently sally out and destroy the Jews engaged in sacrifice, so Judas pressed on rigorously with the siege of the citadel. Some of the Jewish renegades inside escaped by night and went to King Antiochus, craving his help against their own countrymen. The young king was angry and collected an army of about 100,000 infantry, 20,000 cavalry, and 32 elephants.

With this force, Antiochus and Lysias marched into Judea and faced Judas near the mountain passes at Bethzacharias.* At daybreak, their elephants marched toward the passes in single file. Eleazar, Judas' brother, saw that the tallest elephant was armed with breastplates and howdah, and assumed that the king was mounted on it. Running forward, he fought his way through the enemy to the elephant and plunged a knife into its belly. The animal fell dead, crushing Eleazar under its weight, and the rider was only a commoner.

The Jews saw this as a bad omen and withdrew to Jerusalem to prepare for Antiochus' siege. While the Jews held out bravely, the Syrian army began to suffer from lack of food. Antiochus now learned that a rebellion had broken out against him under his general Philip in Persia. Anxious to return to Syria, Antiochus offered peace to the Jews, who gladly received his proposals. Having made Antiochus swear that he would keep his promises, they allowed him to come into the temple.

But when Antiochus saw how strong the place was, he broke his oaths and ordered his soldiers to pull the walls down. Then he returned to Syria, taking with him the high priest Menelaus, for he thought that he was the cause of all his problems. He put him to death at Berea, elevating Alcimus to his place. Then Onias, the son of the previous high priest whom [his brother]

---

* Beit Skaria, 10 miles southwest of Jerusalem.

Menelaus had succeeded, saw that the priesthood had been removed from his family and that his uncle had been slain. Therefore, he fled to Egypt, where he was honored by King Ptolemy. In time, he built a temple similar to that of Jerusalem in the nome [province] of Heliopolis.

Judas' Victories

Antiochus returned home and put down the rebellion which A XII,389 had broken out, killing Philip. But a new challenge came from [his cousin] Demetrius [a hostage]. He escaped from Rome and fought successfully for the throne of Syria, killing Antiochus and Lysias.

Wicked and renegade Jews, including Alcimus, the high priest, now complained to Demetrius that Judas and his brothers were destroying the nation and killing the king's friends. Demetrius angrily sent his general, Bacchides, and a force to accompany Alcimus to Jerusalem, with orders to kill Judas and his men. The Jews were forced to submit to the high priest as long as Bacchides remained in the land. But when he returned to Syria, Alcimus was again forced to beg Demetrius for help against Judas and his attacks.

Demetrius sent another army into Judea, commanded by his friend Nicanor, who lured Judas into negotiations for peace, but gave his men the signal to kill him. Judas dashed out to escape the trap, and then fought the Syrians at Capharsalama and defeated them. Nicanor retreated to the citadel in Jerusalem, where he cursed the priests, threatening that if they did not deliver Judas into his hands, he would destroy their temple when he returned. Leaving Jerusalem, he pitched his camp at a village called Bethoron, where he was joined by another Syrian army. Judas camped at Adasa, nearby. With only 2,000 men, they encountered a fierce struggle, but won a great victory, killing Nicanor himself. Trumpets alerted villagers along the route of the fleeing enemy, and not one of the 9,000 Syrians escaped.

Alcimus the high priest died from a stroke as he was trying to pull down the old wall of the sanctuary, and the people now gave the high priesthood to Judas. Hearing about Rome's vast conquests, Judas sent ambassadors to the Romans to request an alliance. He also asked them to prevent Demetrius from attacking the Jews. The Senate acted favorably on their request, and the treaty was engraved on bronze tablets. It specified that Jews and Romans agreed to help each other in defensive wars as much as possible.

His Death

A XII,420   When Demetrius learned of the loss of Nicanor and his men, he sent Bacchides into Judea with another army of 20,000 infantry and 2,000 cavalry. Judas pitched his camp at a village called Berzetho, with only 1,000* men. But when the Jews saw the huge number of their enemies, they were afraid and all but 800 ran away. And those who remained wanted Judas to retreat and regroup before attacking the enemy. But he replied, "May the sun never see me turn my back to the enemy. I would rather die in this battle than tarnish my honor!"

Bacchides led his soldiers out of the camp and marshaled them into battle order. Then he sounded his trumpets and attacked, and both sides fought bravely until sunset. Judas noticed that Bacchides, along with his strongest forces, was fighting on the right wing of his army, so he took his bravest warriors and rushed against the right wing. He broke their ranks and forced them to flee while he pursued them. But meanwhile, the left wing of the Syrian army wheeled about to chase Judas. Coming up behind him, they surrounded Judas and his men. He stood and fought, killing many of the enemy. But then he became exhausted, fell, and died.

160 B.C.   His brothers Simon and Jonathan obtained his body under truce with the enemy. They carried it to Modin and buried him, along with much public mourning.

Jonathan

A XIII,1   After his victory, Bacchides entered Jerusalem and gathered
W I,48   all the godless transgressors among the Jews and put them in charge of the government. They turned over to Bacchides many of those who had been friends of Judas, and he tortured them to death. The companions of Judas who survived then came to Jonathan and begged him to lead them as his brother Judas had done. Jonathan gladly agreed, and gathered together those willing to join him. They made their camp in a wilderness near the marshes of the Jordan.

When he learned that Bacchides was approaching, Jonathan sent his brother John to store their equipment with friendly Nabateans. But on the way John and his men were ambushed and killed at Medeba by the sons of Jambri. Meanwhile, Bacchides attacked Jonathan on the Sabbath, thinking he would not fight, but he lost 2,000 in the battle before returning to Jerusalem.

---

* I Maccabees 9:5 cites "3,000 picked men."

Jonathan and Simon now heard that Jambri's sons would be celebrating a wedding. So on that day, they jumped out of ambush and killed everyone at the wedding, some 400, to avenge their dead brother. Bacchides, in the meantime, having garrisoned Judea, returned to the king, and the Jews had two years of peace. However, he again invaded, on the suggestion of renegade Jews. But after an unsuccessful siege against Jonathan, the two made a treaty of friendship and exchanged prisoners. Bacchides never again returned to Judea, while Jonathan went to Michmash and set up his government there.

Alexander Balas

In the 160th year*, Alexander [Balas], son of Antiochus A XIII,35 Epiphanes, invaded Syria. He had the support of many who were disgusted at Demetrius for being so reclusive. Now this attempt at the throne gave Jonathan new leverage, since both Demetrius and Alexander were anxious to gain his help, so they made him great offers. Alexander proposed a friendly alliance and sent him a purple robe, a gold crown, and appointed him high priest of Jerusalem. Demetrius also proposed an alliance, as well as remission of many different taxes. His soldiers withdrew from the towns of Judea, and Jonathan returned to Jerusalem. But the citadel in Jerusalem was still held by godless Jews and deserters, who refused to surrender.

Alexander marched against Demetrius, whose left wing was victorious. But Demetrius was in the right wing, which was defeated. Riding his horse into a swamp from which he could not extricate himself, he was killed by enemy javelins.

Alexander took over the kingdom of Syria, and wrote to A XIII,80 Ptolemy Philometor of Egypt, asking for his daughter in marriage. Ptolemy agreed, and the wedding was celebrated at Ptolemais. Alexander invited Jonathan to attend, and when he arrived he was received with highest honors. Alexander made him take off his garment, put on a purple robe, and sit with him on the dais, recording him as his First Friend.

Later, Demetrius [II] claimed his father's throne and sailed from Crete to fight against Alexander. While Alexander prepared to engage him, Apollonius, his governor of Coele-Syria, taunted Jonathan and Simon into a battle near Ashdod. But he was soundly defeated.

Ptolemy Philometor now landed in Syria with an army to help his son-in-law, Alexander, but that foolish king treacherously conspired against Ptolemy. He discovered the plot and was so

---

* Of the Seleucid era, i.e. 153/2 B.C.

angry that he retrieved his daughter and quickly allied with young Demetrius. Alexander was dethroned, and Ptolemy persuaded the Antiochenes to accept Demetrius [II] as king, rather than himself, for they had offered him the throne. Then they both fought and defeated Alexander. But in the battle, Ptolemy's horse was frightened by the trumpeting of an elephant and threw him off. Some of the enemy troops saw the accident, and rushed over to Ptolemy, inflicting severe wounds before they could be driven off by the Egyptians. Ptolemy had been mortally wounded, and died five days later. Just before his death, he received a present of the head of his enemy Alexander, which was sent to him by an Arab chief to whom the defeated monarch had fled.

Demetrius Nicator and Trypho

A XIII,120   Although he had married Ptolemy's daughter, Demetrius [II], surnamed Nicator, began to destroy the Egyptian army, which fled back to Alexandria. At this time, Jonathan besieged the citadel of Jerusalem, which was held by his godless Jewish enemies and a Macedonian garrison. Some of them escaped by night and went to Demetrius to inform him, who commanded Jonathan to come to him. Jonathan, leaving his troops to continue the siege, took with him the elders of the people, the priests, and many presents of gold and silver. He gave these to Demetrius, and pacified him. Refusing to help the renegade Jews, he confirmed Jonathan in the high priesthood and sold him three districts bordering Samaria, including Lydda and Aramathaim.

Jonathan also sent 3,000 of his soldiers to Demetrius, at his request, and they saved his life. Demetrius was very unpopular in Antioch, and its people rose in rebellion against him, laying siege to his palace. But the Jewish soldiers climbed to the roof, hurled missiles at the crowd below, and set fire to houses near the palace. Since the houses in town were built close together, the fire spread rapidly. The Jews, meanwhile, jumped from one roof to another, while the rest of the king's troops broke out against the rebellious citizens. They killed many, while others surrendered and the king forgave them.

Demetrius thanked the Jews, presented them the spoils, and sent them back to Jonathan. Later on, however, he broke his promises. He demanded the tribute that the Jews had formerly paid, threatening war otherwise. And he would have carried out his threat had it not been for Trypho.

Trypho had been a general under Alexander Balas, who took advantage of the hatred Demetrius' subjects felt for him. Placing a crown on the head of a young son of Alexander named Antiochus, he proclaimed him king. A large army soon collected around the new king, and Trypho led them against Demetrius and defeated him. Demetrius fled, and Antiochus [VI] took the throne. The young king sent letters to Jonathan, proposing an alliance and confirming him as high priest.

Jonathan listened gladly to these offers, and made a treaty with Antiochus. He helped rouse neighboring states to attack Demetrius, and, in fact, defeated Demetrius in two great battles, one near Hazor, the second at Hamath. He also sent ambassadors to the Romans, who renewed their treaty with the Jews, and to the Spartans, drawing up an alliance with them as well. Back in Jerusalem, he rebuilt the temple and city walls that had been overturned, and further fortified the city.

Demetrius, meanwhile, had crossed into Mesopotamia, hoping to make the upper satrapies there a base for war against Trypho. In fighting the Parthians, however, he lost his entire army and was himself taken prisoner. _{A XIII,184}

Trypho now plotted to kill Antiochus and usurp the throne of Syria for himself. But as Jonathan was a friend of Antiochus, Trypho thought it best to get rid of him first, so he went to meet Jonathan at Bethshan. Suspecting an attack, Jonathan had with him an army of 40,000. But Trypho persuaded Jonathan that he came only with peaceful intentions, and advised him to dismiss his army and come with personal guards to Ptolemais, which he intended to confer on him. Jonathan dismissed his army, keeping only 1,000 men as a guard, and went with Trypho into Ptolemais. But Trypho had the gates shut, killed Jonathan's men, and took him alive.

Simon

When the Jews heard what had happened to Jonathan, they were deeply distressed. They asked his brother Simon to become their leader, and he agreed. Rebuilding the walls of Jerusalem, he fortified them with very strong towers and guarded the city.

Trypho now advanced into Judea with a great army, and brought Jonathan along as prisoner. He sent word to Simon that he would release Jonathan for 100 talents of silver, providing two of Jonathan's sons were also sent as hostages, to insure that their father, when free, would not lead Judea in revolt. Simon was afraid to trust the cunning Trypho, but he also feared that if he refused his offers the people might accuse him of his brother's death, so he finally sent the money and the two sons.

Panorama of modern Jerusalem from the Mount of Olives. In the foreground is the Kedron Valley. At
spire marks the approximate location of Golgatha.

Trypho acted as Simon feared, keeping the money, the children, and Jonathan too. Trypho then intended to march against Jerusalem in order to help the wretches inside the citadel. But a heavy snow fell during the night, which made the roads impassable, especially for the horses, so he abandoned the attempt. Returning to Antioch, he killed Jonathan when they reached Gilead.

Simon had his brother's bones buried at Modin, with great mourning. He also raised a beautiful monument to his father and his brothers, of polished white marble. It was surrounded by porticoes as well as seven pyramids, which stand to this day.

In the first year of his high priesthood and in the 170th of the Seleucid era,* Simon liberated the people from Macedonian tribute and servitude. He took the citadel of Jerusalem by siege and razed it to the ground so that it might no longer serve as a

---

* 142 B.C.

ter stands the Dome of the Rock, where the temple was situated. To the left and rear of this, a   white

base for their enemies. He also put the people to work to level the hill on which it was built. Three years later, the temple alone stood on the highest spot in the city.

Meanwhile, Trypho put young Antiochus to death after he had reigned four years. Then he had the troops elect him king, since Demetrius had been taken prisoner by the Parthians. But a brother of Demetrius, named Antiochus, raised an army and attacked the usurper, for Trypho had been cruel, and his subjects were glad to rebel against him. Trypho was beaten and fled to the fortress Dora, where Antiochus besieged him. Simon, the high priest of Judea, helped him with money and supplies. Then Antiochus besieged Apamea also, where Trypho had fled, and he was finally captured and killed. A XIII,218
W I,50

However, Antiochus [VII Sidetes] soon forgot the assistance Simon had given him in his necessity, and he sent an army under one of his friends, Cendebeus, to ravage Judea and seize Simon. Simon was provoked at this injustice, and, although now very old, he set out like a young man as commander of his army. He was victorious in all his clashes with the enemy, and soon drove Cendebeus out of the country. He passed the rest of his life in peace and also made an alliance with the Romans.

But after he had ruled over Judea for eight years, Simon was assassinated at a banquet by the treachery of one of his own sons-in-law, named Ptolemy. He also captured Simon's wife and two of his sons and threw them into prison, while sending some men to kill the third son, named John Hyrcanus. But Hyrcanus escaped his intended murderers and hurried to Jerusalem. The people supported him, and refused to admit Ptolemy when he appeared at one of the gates, driving him away. Ptolemy took refuge in a fortress above Jericho called Dagon [Dok].

136 B.C.

John Hyrcanus

A XIII,230
W I,57

After Hyrcanus was proclaimed high priest, he attacked Ptolemy's stronghold. He would have taken it had not Ptolemy brought Hyrcanus' mother and brothers up on the wall and tortured them, threatening to hurl them down unless he raised the siege. Hyrcanus' mother, however, yelled out to her son not to weaken on her account, since she would rather die than have Ptolemy go unpunished. His mother's words made him press the attack, but when he saw her being beaten and torn apart, he was overcome with pity and stopped. So the siege was prolonged until the sabbatical year when the Jews are inactive, resting every seventh year as they do every seventh day. Ptolemy, being thus relieved, killed Hyrcanus' mother and brothers and fled to Philadelphia.

Meanwhile, Antiochus, angry at the reverses he had suffered from Simon, marched into Judea. He ravaged it, and besieged Hyrcanus and his followers inside Jerusalem. Since supplies were running low, they had to expel from the city all who were either too old or too young to fight. But the besiegers refused to let them pass, and they wandered miserably in the ditches below the walls of the city until the festival of Tabernacles arrived. Then Hyrcanus sent messengers to Antiochus asking for a week's truce. Antiochus not only granted his request, but sent a number of bulls with gilded horns and cups of gold and silver, filled with spices, to be used in the sacrifices. The poor Jews who were outside the walls received these, and were allowed to return with them into the city. Because of this generosity, Antiochus became known as "the Pious."

At last Hyrcanus made a treaty with Antiochus, offering 500 talents of silver and hostages, including his own brother. Antiochus then lifted the siege, leveled the walls of the city, and withdrew. Opening the tomb of David, Hyrcanus took out 3,000 talents of silver, and drew on this amount to raise the siege.

Later, Hyrcanus allied with Antiochus in a war against the Parthians. But Antiochus was defeated and killed by Arsaces, the king of Parthia. His brother Demetrius, however, had been released from captivity and again succeeded to the throne of Syria.

With Syrian cities stripped of manpower, Hyrcanus now rebelled against the Macedonians and no longer assisted them. He also attacked neighboring enemies and defeated them, including the Samaritans. Hyrcanus took Mount Gerizim, destroying the temple there, and then marched against the city of Samaria. He left the siege there under the command of his two sons Antigonus and Aristobulus. Although the inhabitants called in the assistance of the Syrians, they were finally overcome. Their city was destroyed, and they themselves were enslaved. A XIII,254 W I,62

Hyrcanus also conquered the Idumeans, sparing them on condition that they circumcise their sons and conform to Jewish custom. They did so, and from then on they continued to be Jews.

He now renewed the treaty with Rome as well, which specified that the Syrians return territories taken from the Jews. Demetrius, who had hoped to attack Hyrcanus, was unable to do so, for Alexander Zebinas seized the throne from that scoundrel, followed by Antiochus Grypus and others in the Seleucid civil wars.

The successes of Hyrcanus produced jealousy among the Jews, and the Pharisees were particularly hostile. At first, he was a disciple of theirs and was cherished by them. But he once gave a feast for them, and while they were having a good time, Hyrcanus asked them if they had any criticism of the way he governed. They replied that he was entirely virtuous, which he was delighted to hear. But one of them, named Eleazar, had a strong temper and enjoyed controversy. He said, "Since you are anxious to know the truth, if you really wish to be righteous, give up the high priesthood and be satisfied with governing the people."

When Hyrcanus asked why he should give it up, Eleazar replied, "Our elders have told us that your mother was once a captive under Antiochus Epiphanes."* This story was false, and Hyrcanus was furious with the man, as were the other Pharisees. Their teachings are opposed to the other most prominent school among the Jews, the Sadducees.

Now a certain Jonathan, a Sadducee, was a close friend of Hyrcanus. He claimed that Eleazar's slanderous statement had

---

* According to Leviticus 21:14, this would have disqualified him.

the general endorsement of all the Pharisees. This would be evident, he said, if Hyrcanus asked the Pharisees what punishment the man deserved: if severe, then they were innocent.

Hyrcanus then asked the Pharisees this question, and they replied, "Eleazar deserves to be whipped and chained, for it doesn't seem right to punish mere words with death."

Hyrcanus became angry and began to believe what Jonathan had told him, so he finally left the Pharisees to join the Sadducees. In doing this, he drew the people's hatred on himself, since they preferred the Pharisees. The Sadducees were viewed as the party of the few and the wealthy.

Still, the remainder of Hyrcanus' reign was peaceful and happy. He died after ruling the Jews for 31 years, leaving five sons. God found him worthy of three of the greatest privileges: the government of his people, the high priesthood, and the gift of prophecy. As to the last, the Deity revealed the future to him.

104 B.C. He predicted, for example, that his two older sons would not remain rulers of the state.

Aristobulus

A XIII,301   Hyrcanus had left the government of Judea to his wife, but
W I,70   Aristobulus, the eldest son, threw her into prison and let her starve to death. He also imprisoned all his brothers except Antigonus, whom he loved and considered worthy of a position like his own. Aristobulus was the first of his family to crown himself, transforming the government into a kingdom.

Now, although Aristobulus favored his brother Antigonus, the courtiers and others tried to alienate the two with malicious accusations. At first, the king would not believe them, but after a while he began to grow suspicious of his brother. At the feast of the Tabernacles, Aristobulus lay very ill in his palace. Meanwhile, Antigonus dressed royally, and, with heavily-armed officers around him, went up to the temple to offer prayers for the recovery of his brother. His enemies then went to the king and told him of the great, pompous show Antigonus had made. They claimed he had come to Jerusalem with his armed men in order to kill Aristobulus and reign in his place.

Reluctantly, Aristobulus started believing these warnings, and stationed guards in a dark underground passage leading to his castle, later called Antonia. He ordered them to kill Antigonus if he came in armor, but to let him pass if he were unarmed. He then sent word to his brother to come to him unarmed. But the queen persuaded the messenger to tell Antigonus to come in his new armor, for the king wanted to see his military gear. Suspecting nothing, Antigonus put on the armor, and when he came to the dark passage he was killed by the guards.

Aristobulus suffered remorse over his brother's murder, and became very sick in his sulking. One day he had intense pain and vomited blood. The servant who carried out the blood slipped and spilled it on the very spot where the bloodstains of the murdered Antigonus could still be seen. A cry arose among the spectators, and the king asked what had happened. At first they would not tell him, but he forced them to speak. Then he burst into tears at the story, groaning, "I can't escape the eye of God! O most shameless body, how long will you maintain a life that is owing to the spirit of a mother and a brother? How long will I offer my blood drop by drop as a libation to those murdered? Let them take it all at once!" He had barely uttered these words when he died, having reigned only one year.   103 B.C.

Alexander Janneus

The queen released Aristobulus' brothers from prison. Alexander Janneus, the eldest, took the throne and killed a younger brother who attempted to usurp it. Alexander was soon engaged in a war with Ptolemy Lathyrus. He was the king of Cyprus, the son and deadly enemy of Cleopatra of Egypt. A battle took place near the Jordan in which Ptolemy was victorious, killing 30,000 of Alexander's troops. After this, he overran some Judean villages that were full of women and children. Ptolemy ordered his men to cut their throats, chop them up, throw the pieces into boiling caldrons, and taste them. This was done to terrorize the Jews, who would regard the invaders as cannibals.

Cleopatra now came into Syria with an army to help Alexander defeat her son. Alexander then besieged and took Gadara, Amathus, Raphia, Gaza, and Anthedon. Meanwhile, Ptolemy had returned to Cyprus, and his mother Cleopatra to Egypt, while the Seleucids were torn by a series of changing thrones and fratricidal wars.

Many of the Jews hated Alexander. When he returned home and was about to sacrifice at the altar during the feast of Tabernacles, they pelted him with citrons and shouted that he was descended from captives and unfit to sacrifice. Enraged, he used foreign mercenaries to quell the riot, killing 6,000 Jews.

Again he invaded the country east of the Jordan, forced it to pay tribute, and retook Amathus. But in a battle with Obedas, king of the Arabs, Alexander was pushed into a ravine and lost his entire army. He escaped to Jerusalem, where the people soon rose in another rebellion against him. After six years of fighting them, Alexander killed 50,000 Jews. When he tried to pacify the people by asking what he should do, they cried out, "Die!"

A XIII,320
W I,85

The insurgents now called Demetrius [III] Akairos of Syria to help them. He attacked Alexander and defeated him. Alexander fled to the mountains, where he was joined by 6,000 of the rebellious Jews, who now pitied his condition. Alarmed at this desertion from his ranks, Demetrius retreated. Alexander then besieged his enemies in Bethome, took it, and marched his captives back to Jerusalem. There, while he was feasting with his concubines, he cruelly crucified 800 of his enemies, slaughtering their wives and children while they watched. This horrible act so frightened those who had opposed him that 8,000 fled from the city by night.

Alexander again engaged in foreign wars against Syria and the trans-Jordan, taking Pella, Gerasa, Golan, and Seleucia, as well as the fortress of Gamala. Returning to Jerusalem after this three-year campaign, he was cordially received because of his successes. At rest from the wars, he became ill from heavy drinking and quartan fever. He thought he could cure it by an active campaign, but he overfatigued himself. On his deathbed, he told the queen to appease the Pharisees, since they had the popular support. Then he died at age 49, having ruled 27 years. 76 B.C. She placed his corpse in the Pharisees' hands, and they eulogized him before the people and gave him a magnificent funeral.

[A dynastic chart of the Maccabees is found on page 390.]

17

THE ROMAN CONQUEST

Alexander left the kingdom to Alexandra, his wife, who was A XIII,407 W I,107 loved by the multitude, since they thought she had opposed the cruel measures of her husband. She had two sons by Alexander: Hyrcanus, the elder, whom she made high priest because he was lethargic and incompetent, and Aristobulus, whom she confined to private life because he was a hothead.

Alexandra favored the Pharisees, the Jewish sect most strict in the observance of the laws. They became the real rulers of the nation, although Alexandra managed with great wisdom, doubling the military and intimidating neighboring rulers. But if she ruled the others, the Pharisees ruled her. They urged her to kill those who had advised Alexander to crucify the 800, and they themselves began killing them one by one. The leaders who were in danger found a spokesman in Aristobulus, who persuaded his mother to spare them. Yet they had to leave Jerusalem and scatter themselves around the country.

Tigranes of Armenia now approached Judea with an army of 300,000 and was besieging Ptolemais. Alexandra sent Tigranes envoys and valuable gifts for a peace treaty, but he was suddenly recalled to Armenia by the invasion of Lucullus [of Rome].

Some time later, the queen became seriously ill, and Aristobulus seized this opportunity to strike for power. He slipped away from Jerusalem by night, gathered an army, and occupied 22 fortresses in fifteen days, conquering most of the country. Alexandra died, after a reign of nine years, leaving the kingdom 67 B.C. to Hyrcanus.

Aristobulus Versus Hyrcanus

A XIV,4 Aristobulus surpassed his brother in ability and courage. He
W I,120 met him in battle near Jericho, and many in Hyrcanus' army
deserted to Aristobulus. The rest fled, Hyrcanus with them, to
the citadel overlooking the temple, where the wife and children
of Aristobulus had been confined by his mother as hostages. The
two brothers now came to terms and agreed that Aristobulus
should become king, while Hyrcanus would possess all honors
as brother of the king, but not take part in public affairs. Their
reconciliation took place in the temple, where they embraced
each other, and then exchanged residences.

Antipater, a friend of Hyrcanus, was the son of the Antipas
whom Alexander [Janneus] had appointed governor of Idumea.
He was Idumean by birth, and a wealthy troublemaker who
gained much influence over the weak Hyrcanus. Constantly
promoting suspicions that Aristobulus was plotting to kill him,
Antipater finally persuaded Hyrcanus to flee with him to Aretas,
the king of Arabia. Aretas was prepared to help Hyrcanus because of the gifts and eloquence of Antipater, as well as Hyrcanus' promise to return twelve cities which his father had
taken from the Arabs. Aretas then marched an army of 50,000
against Aristobulus and defeated him. Many now deserted to
Hyrcanus, and Aristobulus fled to Jerusalem. Aretas besieged
him there in the temple, for only the priests now supported
Aristobulus.

A certain Onias, whose prayer for rain God once rewarded,
was asked to place a curse on Aristobulus, but he refused. When
the Jewish mob forced him, he prayed, "O God, since the men
standing here are your people, and those besieged are your
priests, I beg you not to listen to either side's curses against the
other." Some villains then stoned him to death. They also
refused to provide Passover sacrifices to Aristobulus and the
priests, even after they had paid outrageous prices for them with
money they had let down from the walls by rope. God punished
the villains immediately by destroying all their crops in a violent wind.

A XIV,29 Scaurus, an officer of Pompey, arrived in Judea after the
W I,127 Romans had taken Damascus. Both Aristobulus and Hyrcanus
sought his aid. Aristobulus offered a gift of 400 talents, which
was matched by Hyrcanus. But Scaurus decided for Aristobulus, because it would have been more difficult to dislodge
him from Jerusalem than to scatter his besiegers. Aretas, threatened with the hostility of Rome unless he raised the siege,
withdrew his forces. Aristobulus later defeated Aretas and Hyrcanus in battle.

Envoys from Syria, Egypt, and Judea now courted Pompey,
who had arrived in Damascus. Aristobulus gave him a golden

vine worth 500 talents and argued his cause against Hyrcanus and Antipater, claiming that he had to take over the government by default. Hyrcanus, in turn, replied that Aristobulus had seized the government by force in his usual violent manner. The Jews had sent a third delegation which opposed them both, claiming that their nation ought to be ruled by priests of God, not kings. Pompey promised to decide the matter when he came to Judea, and meanwhile told them to keep the peace.

Aristobulus, however, made hostile preparations. This caused an angry Pompey to march against him at Alexandrium, where he summoned Aristobulus to come out of his fortress. Aristobulus came down several times to negotiate with Pompey, who finally forced him to sign orders for the surrender of all his fortresses. Aristobulus then resentfully retired to Jerusalem and prepared for war.

Pompey immediately advanced on the capital. Aristobulus became alarmed and went out to Pompey, begging him to halt hostilities and promising to give him money and admit him into the city. But when Pompey sent Gabinius to collect the money, Aristobulus' soldiers would not allow him to enter the gates.

Pompey Takes Jerusalem

Pompey was so indignant that he arrested Aristobulus and went to Jerusalem. Inside the city, Hyrcanus' group wanted to admit the Romans, while Aristobulus' soldiers wanted to fight and liberate their king. Hyrcanus' faction, however, opened the gates for Pompey, surrendering the city and the palace to him. Aristobulus' party withdrew inside the temple, cut the bridge joining it to the city, and prepared for a siege. A XIV,57 W I,141

The temple was surrounded by a deep ravine on all sides except the north, so Pompey prepared to storm it from there. Filling in the trench with earthworks, he set up the siege engines brought from Tyre, and started battering the temple with catapults. It might never have been taken had the Romans not known that on the Sabbath the Jews abstained from all work, and would not fight except in self-defense. Therefore, Pompey ordered his soldiers not to attack on those days, but instead to fill up the ravine and move the engines closer to the walls.

At last the largest tower was battered down, leaving a breach through which the Romans poured in. Terrible carnage followed, as some 12,000 Jews fell. Some were killed by the Romans, others by fellow Jews [of Hyrcanus' party], and still others threw themselves down from the precipices. During all this slaughter, the priests were busy with the sacrifices, and contin- 63 B.C.

Marble head of Pompey, the Roman conqueror of Jerusalem (Glyptotek, Copenhagen).

ued to perform their sacred ceremonies. Sin was committed against the sanctuary when Pompey and some of his men entered it, for no one was allowed inside except the high priest. Although the golden table, lampstand, vessels, and sacred treasury of 2,000 talents were all there, Pompey did not touch any of these, out of piety. He commanded the priests to purify the temple and perform their usual sacrifices. He also restored the high priesthood to Hyrcanus.

Pompey made the state a tributary of Rome and removed from it all the cities it had formerly conquered, reducing Judea to its own borders. He gave Syria, Judea, and the countries as far as Egypt and the Euphrates to Scaurus to govern. Pompey then set out for Rome, taking with him Aristobulus and his two sons and two daughters as captives. Aristobulus' son Alexander, however, escaped during the journey, but the younger Antigonus, with his father and sisters, went to Rome in chains.

A XIV,82   Alexander now gathered a considerable force and overran
W I,160   Judea. He would soon have overthrown Hyrcanus in Jerusalem had not the Romans, under Gabinius, the successor of Scaurus, come to help him. Alexander was defeated and fled with the remainder of his forces to Alexandrium, where he was again attacked by Gabinius. One of his officers, Mark Antony, was voted the prize for bravery in that battle. Gabinius left part of his army to continue the siege, and took the rest with him. He rebuilt many of the ruined cities, after which he returned to Alexandrium. Meanwhile, Alexander's mother came to Gabinius out of concern for her family in Rome. She achieved an agreement by which Alexander was pardoned on the condition that he surrender his fortresses.

After destroying the fortresses, Gabinius entrusted the care of the temple to Hyrcanus and changed the government of Judea into an aristocracy. He divided it into five districts, each governed by a council. These were located at Jerusalem, Gadara, Amathus, Jericho, and Sepphoris.

Aristobulus, however, with his son Antigonus, escaped from Rome and gathered a following in Judea. He took Alexandrium and began to rebuild its walls, but he retreated to Machaerus when Gabinius sent troops against him. Attacked by the Romans, the Jews lost 5,000 in defeat, while Aristobulus and 1,000 escaped and attempted to fortify Machaerus. The Roman siege lasted two days, and he resisted bravely, but Aristobulus was then taken prisoner and sent to Rome a second time. His children were allowed to return to Judea, as Gabinius had promised their mother.

While Gabinius was in Egypt, however, Alexander gathered a large army and marched across the country, killing all the Romans he met. When Gabinus returned, Alexander met him with an army of 30,000 Jews near Mount Tabor, but 10,000 of them were killed and the rest were scattered by the Romans.

Crassus succeeded Gabinius in Syria. He robbed the temple of its treasures—the 2,000 talents and golden furnishings worth 8,000 more—in order to pursue a war against the Parthians. He and his whole army were destroyed, although [his officer] Cassius escaped to Syria and later attacked Tarichaeae [in Galilee], enslaving 30,000 men.

Antipater and His Sons

Julius Caesar was now master of Rome. Since Pompey and the Senate had fled, he released Aristobulus from prison. Caesar gave him two legions and sent him to conquer Syria, but before he left, supporters of Pompey poisoned him. Aristobulus' corpse was preserved in honey by Caesar's friends until Antony finally sent it back to Judea, where it was placed in the royal sepulcher. And Aristobulus' son, Alexander, was beheaded at Antioch on Pompey's orders.   A XIV,123 W I,183

When Pompey himself was killed, Antipater continued turning circumstances to his own advantage. He cultivated friendship with Caesar, as he had with Pompey. He helped Mithridates, king of Pergamum, in his march towards Egypt to aid Caesar, who was fighting [in favor of Cleopatra]. Mithridates was refused passage through Pelusium, but Antipater and his troops joined him in conquering the city. They marched on until they were stopped again by the Egyptian Jews who lived in the district of Onias. But Antipater persuaded the Jews not only to let the army pass, but also to give them supplies. After this, the Jews around Memphis also joined Mithridates.

When they passed through the Delta, they fought the Egyptians at a place called the Jews' Camp. Mithridates would have been beaten had it not been for Antipater, who led the left wing of the army. After defeating his enemies, Antipater turned and attacked the rest of the Egyptian forces that had scattered Mithridates.

Caesar commended Antipater and gave him other dangerous assignments in the war. When he had finished in Egypt and sailed to Syria, Caesar greatly honored Antipater. He awarded him Roman citizenship, freedom from taxes, and also confirmed Hyrcanus, who had taken part in the campaign, as high priest.

Bust of Julius Caesar (Uffizi, Florence).

Antigonus, the son of Aristobulus, came to Caesar at this time and accused Antipater and Hyrcanus of injustice and violence. He said that Antipater had helped Caesar not out of good will, but to gain pardon for formerly assisting Pompey. Antipater then stripped off his clothes, declaring that the wounds on his body cried out his loyalty to Caesar. He said Antigonus only wanted to obtain the government in order to stir up sedition against the Romans, like his father before him. Caesar then appointed Hyrcanus high priest and Antipater procurator of Judea, permitting them to rebuild the walls of Jerusalem which Pompey had demolished. He also instructed the consuls at Rome to record these grants in the Capitol.

After escorting Caesar out of Syria, Antipater returned to Judea, rebuilt the walls of Jerusalem, and went across the country persuading the Jews to submit to the new government. But since he found Hyrcanus to be weak and stupid, he managed the government himself. He also appointed his eldest son, Phasael, as governor of Jerusalem, and entrusted Galilee to his second son, Herod. Herod was a very bold young man, and immediately became famous by capturing and killing Ezekias and his bandits who were overrunning the borders of Syria. Phasael also distinguished himself by his management of affairs in Jerusalem. So the whole nation honored Antipater, and he remained loyal and friendly to Hyrcanus.

Some of the leading Jews, however, were jealous of Antipater and his sons. They warned Hyrcanus that these men were the real masters of Judea, and had robbed him of his authority. They also accused Herod of having broken the law by killing Ezekias and his men without trial; the mothers of these bandits daily pleaded at the temple that Herod be brought to judgment. Hyrcanus therefore summoned Herod to Jerusalem to stand trial before the Sanhedrin. But Sextus [Caesar], governor of Syria, sent word to Hyrcanus that Herod should be acquitted, and so he was set free, also because Hyrcanus loved Herod as a son. At the trial, no one dared accuse him except an upright man named Samaias. He complained that when defendants usually appeared on trial for murder, they wore black and let their hair grow. But Herod had appeared with a guard, attired in purple, and hair carefully combed. "But God is great," he concluded, "and this man whom you now release will one day punish both you and the king."

On Hyrcanus' advice, Herod fled to Sextus Caesar in Damascus, who appointed him governor of Coele-Syria and Samaria. Angry because he had been summoned to Jerusalem for trial, Herod prepared to attack Hyrcanus, but he was dissuaded by Antipater and Phasael.[At this point, Josephus lists the many favorable decrees passed by the Senate and Julius Caesar in behalf of Hyrcanus and the Jews. These announced their alliance with Rome, their tax reductions, and special privileges—including exemption from military service—which were reconfirmed after Caesar's death.]

The Death of Antipater

Civil war now raged among the Romans after the assassination of Julius Caesar by Cassius and Brutus in the Senate house. Cassius came into Syria in order to take control of the forces there, and laid a tax of 700 silver talents on the Jews. Antipater divided the job of raising this sum among his sons and acquaintances, including a powerful Jew called Malichus, who hated Antipater.

A XIV,270
W I,218
44 B.C.

Herod won Cassius' favor by being the first to bring in his share from Galilee. The Roman became so angry when some of the others delayed that he sold the officials of several cities as slaves. He would have killed Malichus had not Antipater prevented it by sending him 100 talents of his own. But when Cassius left Judea, Malichus plotted against Antipater, assuming that his death would result in Hyrcanus' rule. Yet Antipater again saved his life by dissuading Murcus, the governor of Syria, from executing him for sedition. But Malichus finally did kill Antipater by bribing Hyrcanus' butler to poison him while he was being entertained at a banquet.

Malichus claimed that he was innocent before a furious Herod and Phasael. The people were also indignant, and Malichus proceeded to gather a troop of soldiers to protect himself. Herod planned to avenge his father's death by attacking Malichus, but his brother Phasael thought it better to get at the man by deception to avoid the appearance of civil war. They therefore pretended, for the time being, to believe that Malichus was innocent. After burying their father, Herod went to Samaria and repaired the city.

Herod now wrote to Cassius and received permission to avenge the death of his father. They were in Tyre at the time, where Malichus aimed to liberate his hostage son and then strike for the kingship after his return to Judea. Herod invited both Hyrcanus and Malichus to dinner, and as they approached along the seashore, they were met by military tribunes who stabbed Malichus to death. Hyrcanus fainted, but when he was told that it had been done at the command of Cassius, he appeared pleased. He said that Cassius had saved himself and his country by destroying one who conspired against them both.

Herod and Phasael Are Made Tetrarchs

A XIV,294 When Cassius left Syria, new disturbances arose in Jerusalem.
W I,236 A certain Helix and his troops attacked Phasael to avenge the death of Malichus. Herod was at Damascus and too ill to come to the assistance of his brother, but Phasael himself overcame his enemies and rebuked Hyrcanus for supporting them.

However, Antigonus, son of Aristobulus, now came with an army to claim the throne. He advanced into Galilee and the borders of Judea, but was defeated and expelled by Herod. Herod then went to Jerusalem, and was received with great enthusiasm. He became engaged there to Mariamme, who was the daughter of Alexander, son of Aristobulus, and granddaughter of Hyrcanus. She would bear Herod three sons and two daughters.

Meanwhile, Cassius was conquered by Antony and Octavian Caesar at Philippi. After their victory, Caesar went to Italy while Antony left for Asia. When he reached Bithynia, Antony was met by ambassadors from various states. Also present were Jewish leaders who accused Herod and Phasael of depriving Hyrcanus of his sovereignty. But Herod gave large enough bribes to Antony to keep him from listening to the accusers.

Antony now came into Cilicia, where Cleopatra made him a prisoner of love. Then he arrived at Daphne [near Antioch], where 100 of the most distinguished Jews accused Herod and his brother. When he had heard both sides, Antony asked Hyrcanus who was most qualified to rule. Hyrcanus replied, "Herod and his brother." Antony then appointed Phasael and Herod as tetrarchs of Judea. When their adversaries expressed anger, Antony put fifteen of them in chains and would have executed them if Herod had not interceded. Jerusalem, in agitation, sent 1,000 more envoys to Antony at Tyre, who gathered on the beach in front of the city. Herod and Hyrcanus urged them to disperse or face destruction, but this only increased their uproar. The Romans then attacked them, killing some, wounding more. And since those who escaped would not keep quiet, Antony in fury killed those who were taken prisoner.

Antigonus and the Parthians

Two years later, the Parthians invaded Syria. They were led by Barzaphranes, a satrap, and Pacorus, the king's son. Antigonus promised the Parthians 1,000 talents and 500 women if they would replace Hyrcanus with himself and destroy Herod and his people. A XIV,330 W I,248

Many Jews flocked to Antigonus' banner, and he marched into Jerusalem with the Parthians. The battle occurred at the marketplace, where Herod and Phasael defeated the enemy and shut them up in the temple. Daily skirmishes occurred, and when the multitudes came up to celebrate Pentecost, many were armed, and clashes led to bloodshed. Antigonus then proposed to admit Pacorus into Jerusalem to act as mediator, and Phasael consented. Pacorus, as part of a plot, convinced Phasael to go to Barzaphranes, and lay their case before him. Herod, who suspected Pacorus, urged his brother not to go, but Phasael left, accompanied by Pacorus and Hyrcanus. Phasael and Hyrcanus were captured in Galilee by the Parthians, and afterwards delivered in chains to Antigonus.

Meanwhile, in Jerusalem, the Parthian royal cupbearer was trying to lure Herod outside the walls in order to seize him, but Herod had heard about his brother's capture. Instead, he and his family slipped out of Jerusalem by night and headed for Idumea. But the Parthians soon pursued him when they discovered his escape. At one point, his mother's wagon overturned and she was in danger of dying. Herod was so anguished that he drew his sword and would have killed himself if his men had not prevented him.

Fighting off the Parthians, he then encountered attacking Jews, south of Jerusalem. He would later erect a castle at this place where he defeated them, called the Herodium. Arriving at Masada, Herod was joined by his brother Joseph. He left 800 of his men to guard the women of his family inside this fortress, while he himself went on to Petra in Arabia.

Back in Jerusalem, the Parthians stole everything they could find. Then they put Antigonus on the throne, and brought him Hyrcanus and Phasael in chains. Antigonus himself bit off Hyrcanus' ears, so that he could never be high priest again, since freedom from physical defects is a qualification for that office.*
To prevent Antigonus from torturing him, Phasael, his hands shackled, dashed his own brains out against a stone. Leaving Antigonus to govern Jerusalem, the Parthians took Hyrcanus to Parthia.

In the meantime, Herod sought funds from Malchus, king of Arabia, in the hope of ransoming his brother. But Malchus had embezzled the funds Antipater had deposited with him, and now not only refused to help Herod, but ordered him out of the country. Herod then set out for Rome by way of Egypt. When he arrived in Alexandria, Cleopatra gave him a magnificent reception and wanted to make him commander of an expedition she was preparing. But he set sail for Rome, even though it was midwinter.

Antony was moved with compassion at Herod's misfortune, and remembered how hospitably he had been treated by Antipater. He considered the fact that he was fighting against Antigonus, who had called in the Parthians to help him and so made himself an enemy of Rome. Antony therefore decided to make Herod the king of Judea. Caesar [Octavian], recalling how Antipater had served his [adoptive] father in the Egyptian campaign, was also anxious to help Herod. Thus the Senate was convened and the matter discussed, and they voted that Herod should be proclaimed king of Judea. He left the Senate with Antony and Caesar on either side of him, and they recorded the decree in the Capitol. Antony then gave a banquet in Herod's honor on the first day of his reign.

40 B.C.

Herod's Return

A XIV,390
W I,286

Herod left Rome in order to relieve Masada, which was besieged by Antigonus. The fortress had plenty of supplies but little water. Joseph, Herod's brother, was just about to flee to the Arabs when God sent a rainstorm which refilled the cisterns at Masada, so they remained there.

Ventidius was the Roman general who had been sent from Syria to restrain the Parthians. He came into Judea under the

---

* Leviticus 21:17–23.

The greatest of the dozen cisterns at the fortress Masada, which could hold millions of gallons of water. Water once flowed into this one through a window to the south (top).

pretence of helping Joseph, but he really wanted to frighten Antigonus into giving him bribes. Antigonus did so, and Ventidius then withdrew most of his army. He left his lieutenant, Silo, with a small force, so it would not be too evident that he had taken bribes.

Herod, having landed in Ptolemais, gathered an army and marched toward Masada to relieve his relatives who were besieged there. Joppa stood in his way, so he took the city, and, marching onward, easily relieved Masada. Then he advanced, along with Silo's army, to the walls of Jerusalem. He shouted a general amnesty to the people, only to have Antigonus label him a half-Jewish Idumean who was unworthy of the kingship. Now, however, Silo showed that he had been bribed by Antigonus: so that Jerusalem would not be captured, he had his own soldiers demand that they be taken to winter quarters because of the scarcity of supplies around Jerusalem. Herod, however, defeated Silo's scheme by supplying him with plenty of provisions. Then he ordered the people of Samaria to bring more supplies and store them in Jericho. Antigonus heard about this and sent his men out to fight the collectors of provisions. Herod then took with him five Jewish and five Roman cohorts and marched to Jericho, which he found deserted. He stationed a garrison there, retiring the rest of his Roman army to winter quarters.

Herod, however, chose not to remain inactive, but marched into Galilee, and overran it. He expelled Antigonus' garrisons, and then assaulted the bands of robbers who infested the caves of Galilee. By letting down cages from the precipices above, armed men inside attacked the bandits and their families in the caves. They used javelins and grappling hooks or burned them alive. Herod then returned to Samaria, leaving a part of his army in Galilee. But when he had gone, rebels killed the general Herod had left in charge and plundered the country. Herod returned, suppressed the rebellion, and fined the cities 100 talents.

By this time, the Parthians had been driven from Syria, so Ventidius, by Antony's command, sent 1,000 cavalry and two legions, under the command of Machaeras, to help Herod against Antigonus. Antigonus, however, wrote to Machaeras, promising him a bribe for his assistance. Machaeras, in order to spy on Antigonus, pretended friendship and went to Jerusalem against Herod's advice. But Antigonus, who suspected his designs, excluded him from the city. The Roman general was so enraged at this that he killed every Jew he met, whether friend or foe.

Herod was furious about this, but Machaeras pacified him before the king set out to assist Antony, who was besieging Samosata. Herod helped Antony take the city, who, accordingly, lavished Herod with more honors. Antony commanded Sossius, the governor of Syria, to march into Judea with a large army to help Herod secure his kingdom.

A XIV,448 When Herod left for Samosata, he had charged his brother
W I,323 Joseph not to risk a battle with Antigonus during his absence. When Herod was a safe distance off, however, Joseph marched on Jericho with five cohorts to seize their grain. On the way, he was attacked by Antigonus, and he and his troops—all raw Roman recruits—were killed. Antigonus then cut Joseph's head off his dead body. At this victory, the Galileans rebelled, drowning Herod's supporters in the lake, and a large part of Judea also revolted.

Antigonus' Defeat

Returning from Samosata, Herod was consumed with avenging his brother's death. He collected 800 men and one Roman legion, rushed into Galilee, and defeated his enemies. Then he marched to Jericho, where he entertained the men in authority. But when the party was over, the roof collapsed, yet Herod was spared, not only in this accident but also in a javelin wound he sustained in battle the next day.

Antigonus sent an army into Samaria under Pappus, one of his generals. Many in Judea now streamed to Herod's support, and when Pappus and his army attacked, Herod was completely victorious. Taking his bath that night, Herod narrowly escaped assassination. Three armed men, who had been hiding in the house, slipped past the naked Herod and fled, happy to make a successful escape. The next day, Herod cut off Pappus' head and sent it to his brother, Pheroras, for it was Pappus who had executed their brother Joseph.

He then marched to Jerusalem, pitching his camp before the temple. He erected towers and earthworks at the same place where Pompey had assaulted the sanctuary. While this was underway, he went off to Samaria in order to marry Mariamme, to whom he was engaged. On his return, he was joined by Sossius with a large army, and together they vigorously carried on the siege. Although famine raged in Jerusalem, the city held out for five months. Herod eventually chose twenty men who finally climbed over the walls into the city, followed by Sossius' centurions. Soon the whole army poured into the city and terrible carnage followed. Infants and the aged alike were cut down, even though Herod urged restraint. Antigonus, horrified at the awful scene, came down from his castle and fell at Sossius' feet. But the Roman mocked him, applauding and calling him Antigone. But unlike a woman [with such a name], who would be left unguarded, Sossius clapped him in irons.

Having conquered his enemies, Herod now had to restrain his foreign allies from profaning the temple and looting and depopulating the city. He complained to Sossius that the Romans would leave him as king of a desert. Sovereignty over the whole world was too small a reward for the slaughter of so many citizens, Herod said. Sossius replied that it was proper to allow the soldiers this plunder as a reward for what they had suffered during the siege. Herod then promised to reward each man out of his own treasury. He gave generous gifts to every soldier and a royal bounty to Sossius, who then took Antigonus in chains to Antony.

But Herod was afraid that Antigonus would later appeal to the Roman Senate. He envisioned Antigonus pointing out that while Herod was a commoner, his own sons ought to reign because of their royal lineage, so Herod gave Antony a large 37 B.C. bribe to get rid of Antigonus. Antigonus was beheaded, and thus ended the rule of the Hasmonean line.

18

HEROD THE GREAT

As soon as Herod was established on the throne, he conferred A xv,1 honors on those in Jerusalem who had supported his cause, and punished the partisans of Antigonus. Converting his valuables into money, he sent large sums to Antony and his friends.

In Parthia, meanwhile, King Phraates had released Hyrcanus from prison, and permitted him to live in Babylon, where the Jews honored him as their high priest. But when he learned that Herod had become king, Hyrcanus returned to Judea, assuming that Herod would be in his debt for past favors, although the Jews of Babylon urged him to stay. Herod received him with due honor, but appointed an undistinguished priest from Babylon, Ananel, as high priest.

This made Herod's mother-in-law, Alexandra, mother of Mariamme and Aristobulus, furious. She thought the high priesthood should have been transferred to Aristobulus, so she wrote to Cleopatra, urging her to intercede with Antony, who was now in Egypt. Antony's friend Dellius came to Judea on business and met Mariamme and Aristobulus. He was so overcome by their beauty that he persuaded Alexandra to send portraits of the two to Antony, which she did. Antony would have liked to use them both for sexual pleasure, but since he could hardly ask Herod to send his own wife, he asked that Aristobulus come to Egypt. Herod supplied an excuse for not complying with Antony's request, and then awarded the high priesthood to Aristobulus, making peace with Alexandra.

Herod, however, placed Alexandra under such strict surveillance that she complained by letter to Cleopatra, who suggested that Alexandra flee to Egypt with her son. Alexandra concocted a plan whereby she was placed in one coffin, and Aristobulus in another, which were then taken out of the city as if for burial. But Herod was alerted, and caught them in the act. Yet he forgave them in a show of magnanimity.

At the feast of Tabernacles, the seventeen-year-old Aristobulus looked very tall and handsome as he conducted the rites, and his great popularity with the worshipers was only too obvious to Herod. Some time later, they were all being entertained by Alexandra down in Jericho. Because it was hot, Herod, Aristobulus, and their friends were at the swimming pool, and the high priest was urged to take a swim. As it was getting dark, some friends, following orders, began pushing Aristobulus under water as if in sport until he drowned. So Ananel again assumed the high priesthood.

Aristobulus was given a lavish funeral by the "grieving" Herod, while Alexandra lived only for revenge. She wrote about Herod's plot against her son to Cleopatra, who urged Antony to avenge the murder. Antony, in turn, wrote Herod to meet him at Laodicea [on the Syrian coast] to clear himself of these charges. Before leaving, Herod left his uncle Joseph in charge, with instructions to kill Mariamme if anything happened to him. He was so in love with her, Herod said, that he could not stand the thought of her in someone else's arms, especially Antony's.

While Herod was gone, Joseph began discussing with Mariamme his nephew's great love for her. He tried to prove that Herod could not live without her by revealing his secret instructions to Mariamme and Alexandra. They were impressed only with Herod's proposed cruelty, which could live on even after his death. When a false report came that Herod had been killed by Antony, the women planned to flee to the Roman garrison. However, Herod's letter then arrived, explaining his successful defense before Antony, and how Cleopatra's anger was abated by having been given Coele-Syria.

When Herod returned, his sister Salome, who was jealous of Mariamme, lied that Mariamme had had frequent intercourse with Joseph. This enraged Herod, particularly since he had heard about their plans to escape. Mariamme, however, defended herself so honestly that they both broke into tears, and, as is usual with lovers, they embraced each other intensely. But as Herod continued reassuring her, she said, "It was hardly a lover's gesture to command that if anything happened to you, I should be killed also."

At these words, Herod went into a frenzy, crying and tearing his hair. This was damning proof of Joseph's intercourse with her, he said, for Joseph would not have revealed it if they had not been intimate. He then ordered Joseph executed and Alexandra chained, as she was partially responsible.

Cleopatra, meanwhile, had poisoned her brother and had Antony kill her sister, as well as the governor of Syria, so that she could take over their possessions. She also asked him for Judea and Arabia. Now Antony was so dominated by her that it seemed it was not only their intimacy, but also drugs which influenced his behavior. However, he would not transfer Judea and Arabia to her, but instead gave her portions of both countries: a plantation of palm trees at Jericho, and several cities. When Cleopatra came into Judea, Herod leased back these places that had been torn from his kingdom by paying a yearly rent of 200 talents. She also tried to seduce Herod, whether from passion or plot is uncertain. He seriously thought of killing her, but his advisers warned him about Antony's wrath. Therefore he evaded her overtures and courted her only with gifts.

A XV,88
W I,360

Herod Defeats the Arabs

When Antony was ready to fight Caesar at Actium for the empire of the world, Herod prepared to help him. But Cleopatra persuaded Antony to send Herod against Malchus, who had stopped paying her Arabia's rent. Herod defeated the Arabians at Diospolis, and when they regrouped with larger numbers at Kanatha in Coele-Syria, Herod again attacked them victoriously. But Athenion, one of Cleopatra's generals, treacherously sent his Egyptian troops to rescue the Arabs. These troops completely routed Herod's army, which was exhausted from the first struggle. Herod could use only guerilla tactics against the Arabs after that.

An extraordinary earthquake now shook the country, destroying an enormous quantity of cattle and 30,000 lives. However, Herod's army escaped unharmed, because they were camped in the open air. Believing that most of the Jews had been killed, the Arabs assumed they could easily capture the land. And so, after killing ambassadors who had come from the Jews, they attacked Judea. Herod encouraged his dejected men by word and example, and led his army to fight against the invaders near Philadelphia. The Arabs were defeated, losing 5,000, and then were besieged in their camp. They were so short of water that in five days, 4,000 came out and voluntarily surrendered to the Jews. On the sixth day, the remaining Arabian army came to fight out of desperation, and 7,000 of them were killed. Herod so completely crushed the Arabs' spirit that they submitted to him as their protector.

Octavian Augustus and Herod

A XV,161
W I,386
Meanwhile, [Octavian] Caesar had defeated Antony at Actium. This alarmed Herod and his friends because of his close ties to Antony, and his enemies gloated. Herod wondered if he should now kill Hyrcanus to avoid revolution while he sought Octavian at Rhodes. Hyrcanus himself was not the sort to start a rebellion, but his daughter Alexandra kept urging him to write Malchus, the Arab king. She wanted him to ask for shelter for them until, at the probable failure of Herod's mission, they could reassume royal power. Hyrcanus continually refused, but finally gave in. He entrusted a letter to Malchus with Dositheus, one of his friends, who instead handed the letter to Herod. The king told him to deliver it to the Arab and bring him his reply, which was positive. Herod then confronted Hyrcanus and the Sanhedrin with the letters, and had Hyrcanus put to death, at age 81.

Bronze head of Augustus, portraying him at age 30, which was discovered near the Nile at Merowe in the Sudan (British Museum, London).

Before leaving to see Octavian, Herod put his brother Pheroras in charge and placed Cypros' mother, as well as his sister, and all his children in Masada. As for Mariamme, he put her in Alexandrium with her mother Alexandra. They were under the care of Soemus, since they did not get along with his side of the family. Herod again told Soemus to kill both women if he did not return, and preserve the kingdom for his brother Pheroras.

30 B.C.
When his ship arrived at Rhodes, Herod removed his diadem, but behaved with the dignity of a king. He manfully admitted to Caesar that he had supported Antony, and would have fought for him had the Arab war not prevented him. He did not desert Antony after the battle of Actium, Herod said, but advised him to kill Cleopatra, which would have enabled Antony to come to an understanding with Octavian. Herod now wanted Caesar to consider how faithful a friend, and not whose friend, he had been.

Impressed by Herod's manner and address, Caesar placed the diadem on his head, asking him to be no less a friend to him than he had been to Antony. Herod gave Caesar expensive presents and returned to Judea. Later, when Caesar was going through Syria to Egypt, Herod entertained him in a royal manner and supplied him during his desert crossing.

But when he returned to his kingdom, Herod found his wife Mariamme and her mother Alexandra in a hostile mood. Both had worked on Soemus during Herod's absence, and he had finally disclosed the king's instructions, which they bitterly resented. When Herod joyfully took Mariamme in his arms, she groaned at his embrace, clearly disappointed that he had been successful. Herod was now torn between loving and hating her, driven to agonizing doubts by the slanders of his mother and sister against her. Mariamme, in turn, arrogantly jeered at them both for their low birth, and hatred filled the palace.

Meanwhile, with the death of Antony and Cleopatra, Caesar had taken over Egypt, and Herod went there to discuss affairs with him as an old friend. Caesar rewarded Herod with the territories Cleopatra had taken from him, adding other cities, as well as Trachonitis and Samaria. Subsequently he appointed him procurator of all Syria.

Herod's Unhappy Domestic Life

But the more successful he was in external affairs, the greater A XV,218 he failed at home. One noon he lay down to rest and called for Mariamme, and although she came, she refused to lie down with him, despite his urging. Instead she expressed her contempt for him and bitterly accused him of the death of her grandfather Hyrcanus and brother Aristobulus. Salome, Herod's sister, then sent in the butler, who claimed that Mariamme had given him a love potion for the king. Herod, demanding to know its contents, tortured Mariamme's eunuch, upon whom she depended greatly. He only reported that Mariamme's hatred for him had grown as a result of what Soemus had told her. Herod cried out that Soemus would never have betrayed his instructions unless he had been intimate with Mariamme, so he ordered him to be killed and put Mariamme on trial.

After her daughter was condemned to death, Alexandra attempted to save herself, disgustingly accusing Mariamme of having been wicked and ungrateful to her husband. She even grabbed her by the hair, but Mariamme nobly kept her composure as she went to her death.

But when she was dead, Herod's desire for Mariamme grew even more intense, and for a while he seemed to have gone mad.

He would wander around the palace, calling for his wife and ordering the servants to bring her to him. He became very ill with inflammation and pain in the back of his head while he was in Samaria, and no remedy seemed to help.

When Alexandra heard this, she tried to take control of Jerusalem by asking for authority over the temple and citadel. The magistrates, however, informed Herod, who immediately ordered her execution. Having slowly recovered, Herod continued in an ugly mood, finding fault with everything, and even killing several of his closest friends. For example, he had appointed Costobar as governor of Idumea and given him his sister Salome in marriage. But Costobar had written Cleopatra that he was ready to transfer his loyalty to her, with Antony's approval. Antony had refused, and when Herod heard about it, he was ready to kill Costobar, but forgave him because of Salome's intercession. Later, she sent Costobar a bill of divorce, and then Herod killed him and several colleagues who were conspiring with him against Herod.

A XV,267   Herod now offended the Jews by introducing pagan games into Judea. He built a theater in Jerusalem, a hippodrome, and a large amphitheater in the plain. Here chariot races and contests of various kinds took place, including condemned men fighting wild animals. Although he removed some of the trophies with images that antagonized the Jews, ten of the Jews were still resentful, and formed a conspiracy to assassinate Herod as he entered the theater. When the plot was exposed by an informer, the men boldly showed Herod the daggers they had planned to use on him. After their execution, Jewish partisans cut the informer to pieces and threw him to the dogs.

Herod increased his security by erecting a string of fortresses across his kingdom, particularly at Samaria, which he renamed Sebaste [to honor Octavian Augustus], and at Strato's Tower, which he renamed Caesarea. But in the thirteenth year of his reign, drought and plague attacked the land. Herod relieved the people as best he could by purchasing grain from Egypt, and acted so nobly in the crisis that admiration for him replaced hatred.

Herod the Builder

A XV,318   He now erected a palace in the upper city, furnished with gold and precious stones, which contained two great wings, named after Caesar and [his colleague] Agrippa. He also learned that an Alexandrian priest named Simon had a daughter, Mariamme [II], who was the most beautiful woman in Jerusalem. Infatuated

Palace of Herod in western Jerusalem, showing the two wings within the fortified enclave named for Caesar and Agrippa. The three large towers guarding the northern end were named (l to r): Phasael, Hippicus, and Mariamme. To the upper right stand the four towers of the fortress Antonia (model of ancient Jerusalem designed by Prof. M. Avi-Yonah at the Holyland Hotel, Jerusalem).

A reconstruction of the great Temple built by Herod the Great in Jerusalem. To the upper left are the northern towers of the Palace of Herod in the western part of Jerusalem (model by M. Avi-Yonah).

with her loveliness, Herod married her after elevating her father to the high priesthood. After the wedding, Herod constructed another fortress [the Herodium] south of Jerusalem. Perched on a hill which he raised higher and formed in the shape of a breast, the fortress contained towers, royal apartments, and watered parks.

Herod's diplomacy to the surrounding cities and countries was superbly timed, and he generously underwrote building projects in them. At Caesarea he constructed a major port along a shore where there was none, enclosing a harbor larger than the Piraeus. Then he erected a whole city of white stone crowned with a temple to Rome and Augustus—all within a twelve-year period. Caesarea now also boasted a theater, an amphitheater, and a subterranean sewer system which automatically flushed itself with the sea tides.

Fallen columns in the surf at the ruins of ancient Caesarea on the Mediterranean, the port built by Herod at the site of the former Strato's Tower. The great Jewish War with Rome was ignited here.

At this point, Herod sent his sons [by Mariamme I] Alexander and Aristobulus to Rome to present themselves to Caesar, who received them with great deference. Caesar gave Herod Trachonitis, Batanea, and Auranitis, which Herod had purged of robbers with his permission. This was despite the protest of the local potentate, Zenodorus, who increased his revenues by stealing from the people. Herod also visited Agrippa in Mytilene, whom

Herod regarded as his closest friend after Caesar.

In Judea, however, Herod took steps to prevent rebellion, never allowing groups of people to gather and making them swear an oath of loyalty. His agents spied on suspects, and he himself sometimes went out at night in common dress to learn what people thought of him.

In the eighteenth year of his reign, Herod started to enlarge and reconstruct the temple at his own expense, which he knew A XV,380 W I,401 would be his greatest enterprise. After removing the old foundations, he laid new ones, and raised the structure of hard, white stones. Purple hangings covered the entrances, and a golden vine with grape clusters adorned the area below the cornice. Large porticoes with 162 Corinthian columns surrounded the temple, which was supported by walls of unparalleled size. Beyond the first court was a second, surrounded by a stone balustrade with an inscription prohibiting a foreigner from entering on penalty of death. Within this court was the sacred court which women were forbidden to enter. And still farther within was a third court where the temple stood, into which only priests could go. At the northwestern corner of the temple enclave stood the citadel, which Herod called the

Marble head of Marcus Agrippa, Augustus' greatest associate and Herod's friend, for whom the other Herodian Agrippas were named (Louvre, Paris).

Antonia to honor his friend. Here the high priest's robe was kept, which was worn only when he offered sacrifice.

The temple itself was built by the priests in a year and a half, c. 17 B.C. and was dedicated in a great celebration. It is said that during construction, no rain fell during the day, but only at night, so that there would be no interruption of the work. This story is not at all incredible if one considers the other manifestations of God's power.

More Domestic Turmoil

At this time, Herod voyaged to Italy to visit Caesar and bring home his sons, Alexander and Aristobulus, who had completed their education. When they returned to Jerusalem, they enjoyed a cordial reception from the masses. This made Salome envious, since she and those who had brought about the death of their mother Mariamme would be punished by the youths if they ever came to power. This group therefore spread rumors that the boys really despised their father for what he had done to their mother. But for now Herod let love outweigh suspicion, and he had Aristobulus marry Salome's daughter Bernice, while Alexander married Glaphyra, the daughter of the king of Cappadocia.

A XVI,12   Learning that Agrippa was in the east, Herod gave him a royal welcome in Jerusalem. Then he followed Agrippa to Asia Minor, where Herod gained confirmation from him of Jewish rights in Ionia. When Herod reported this to the people of Jerusalem, they were delighted and grateful to him.

The dissension in Herod's household, however, grew worse as Salome continued her campaign against Mariamme's two sons. For their part, the youths were less than cautious and openly vented their anger against Salome and Pheroras. Herod's brother and sister responded by spreading further rumors that the young heirs intended to avenge the death of their mother, and also reported to Herod that Mariamme's sons were plotting against him.

Herod began to suspect Alexander and Aristobulus. In order to check them, he sent for his eldest son, Antipater, born of his first wife, Doris, when Herod was still a commoner. He intended to demonstrate to the youths that the succession was not necessarily theirs. Antipater supported the plots of Salome and her brother, Pheroras. He induced Herod to bring his mother back to the palace, and carefully noted to Herod whenever the two princes mourned their mother's fate or criticized their father. Virtually grooming him for succession, Herod sent Antipater to Rome, and then went there himself, taking his two sons to accuse them before Augustus. At first they were speechless and in tears, but then Alexander answered the charges so well that Augustus urged father and sons to be reconciled, and they
c. 12 B.C. all embraced in tears. Herod gave 300 talents to Caesar in the following days, while Caesar gave Herod half the revenue from the copper mines on Cyprus. Antipater returned home with them, pretending to be glad over the reconciliation. When they reached Jerusalem, Herod assembled the people in the temple and announced the succession: Antipater would reign first, and next, Alexander and Aristobulus, his sons by Mariamme.

Ten years after its inception, Caesarea was completed, and the port was dedicated with extravagant festivities to which the emperor and his wife contributed. Herod also built the cities of Antipatris and Phasaelis as memorials to his father and brother, and awarded contributions to many cities in Syria and Greece. [Josephus goes on to list here the decrees of Augustus and Agrippa favoring the Jews in the eastern Mediterranean.]

Meanwhile, the dissension inside the palace was becoming a civil war, as Antipater continued to outmaneuver his brothers, who resented his succession. Herod's brother Pheroras rejected two of Herod's daughters in marriage because of his passion for a slave girl. When he also falsely accused Herod of being in love with Glaphyra, Alexander's wife, the king bitterly censured both Pheroras and Salome, since she was implicated in the lie. A XVI,188 W I,467

Discord now erupted in the family with greater violence than ever. Herod was kept in a constant fever of excitement by Antipater, who continued to plot the destruction of Alexander and Aristobulus. He hired the servants and even friends of the brothers to accuse them of plots against the throne. The whole court soon became a scene of suspicion, gloom, and distrust: suspects were tortured and killed, while spies were everywhere. People accused their enemies of plots so that the king would kill them, and there was a general climate of horror. Antipater finally convinced the king that Alexander wanted to kill his father, so he ordered the unhappy youth thrown into prison.

While there, Alexander, in perverse pride, refused to defend himself, and instead composed [a satire] in four books and sent it out. In these he claimed that there had indeed been a plot against Herod, but that Pheroras and the most faithful of the king's friends were assisting Alexander. Salome, moreover, had forced her way into his room one night and slept with him against his will. This only served to torment Herod further.

Alexander's father-in-law, Archelaus, king of Cappadocia, became concerned for the safety of his son-in-law and daughter and hurried to Jerusalem. He won Herod's confidence by first pretending to believe all the charges trumped up against Alexander, and by acting indignant towards him. But step-by-step, he showed Herod how improbable the charges were, and succeeded in putting the blame on the king's friends and especially Pheroras, to whom the king was already hostile. Archelaus reconciled Herod and Alexander, and he also obtained pardon for Pheroras, who confessed his guilt. Archelaus then returned to Cappadocia, with Herod's profound gratitude and gifts.

An adventurer from Sparta named Eurycles now came to Jerusalem and won the favor of the king. But when he discovered the dissensions in the royal family, he turned them to his own advantage. He wormed his way into Alexander's confi- A XVI,300 W I,513 dence by pretending to be a friend of King Archelaus. Eurycles also ingratiated himself with Antipater by spying on Alexander and reporting everything Alexander said, for which he was well rewarded. Antipater then urged Eurycles to disclose everything to Herod. Herod easily believed Eurycles' lies about Alexander's "plotting," and further rewarded him. While returning to Sparta, Eurycles got even more money from Archelaus when he claimed to have reconciled Herod and Alexander!

In fact, Herod grew even more furious when he read a forged letter, supposedly from Alexander to the commander of the fortress Alexandrium, hinting at revolution. He ordered Alexander and Aristobulus bound and thrown into prison. Enraged by further accusations, Herod wrote to Caesar, informing him of the charges against the sons of Mariamme. Caesar, who had planned to add Arabia to Herod's domain, now gave up the idea in view of his domestic discord. But he did give Herod full authority over his sons, and advised him to convene a council c. 7–6 B.C. at Berytus and take along governors and friends as assessors. Herod did not allow his sons to appear at the trial, but appeared alone before the council, which comprised 150 advisers. He seemed so eager for the death of the pair that they were condemned by a majority of the court, even though no charges were proved against them. The only evidence was letters in which they wrote of plans to flee, along with complaints about Herod's hostility to them.

When Herod came to Caesarea, all the people sympathized with the young men and waited in anxious suspense to see what would happen. Then an old soldier named Tiro, whose son was a friend of Alexander, expressed the general feeling of indignation before the king. He asked what had become of his good sense that he would put to death two youths who were paragons of virtue. Why did he instead trust Antipater, Salome, and Pheroras, whom he had so often condemned to death, and whom the silent masses and the army now hated? Herod responded by having Tiro and his son immediately arrested.

One of Herod's barbers, Trypho, then came forward to claim that Tiro had tried to bribe him to cut the king's throat when shaving him, promising that Alexander would pay him handsomely. Tiro, his son, and the barber were immediately put on the rack. Tiro endured the torture bravely, but when he was tortured even more severely, his son cried out that he would confess everything, if his father and he were spared further torment. The king agreed, and the son claimed that his father, at the persuasion of Alexander, had determined to kill Herod. Some claimed this was a lie designed to end the torture, while others maintained that it was true. Herod then indicted the military leaders implicated by Tiro, along with Tiro himself, his son, and the barber, and the crowd stoned and cudgeled them to death. Alexander and Aristobulus were subsequently taken to Sebaste and strangled to death.

The Plots of Antipater

Nine women were married to Herod [besides Mariamme I]: Doris, Mariamme II, Malthace, Cleopatra, Pallas, Phaedra, Elpis, an [unnamed] niece, and a cousin. The king now settled a colony of Babylonian Jews in Batanea to serve as a buffer zone against Trachonitis. Back in Jerusalem, Herod executed some Pharisees who refused to swear allegiance to him, and grew angrier at Pheroras because of Pheroras' scheming wife. Antipater, meanwhile, had been given more governing authority, and he plotted to take over the kingdom from his father. He had himself sent to Rome to be presented to Caesar, carrying Herod's will in which he was designated successor. But even while he was in Rome, God began punishing him for the murder of his brothers. A XVII,1
W I,552

Antipater's uncle, Pheroras, who had helped him in plotting against the young princes, became ill, and was kindly attended by Herod until he died. After the death of Pheroras, two of his freedmen told Herod that Pheroras had been poisoned by his wife. The king ordered the women servants tortured, and it was revealed that Antipater had had poison sent to Pheroras that he might kill the king with it. Pheroras' wife, who was saved from suicide, confessed the whole plot, and said that Herod's kindness to the dying Pheroras had caused him to order the poison thrown into the fire. She had destroyed most of it, but saved a little for herself. Herod's wife, Mariamme [II], daughter of Simon the high priest, was also involved in the plot, so the king divorced her. He also blotted out of his will the name of her son, Herod, whom he had appointed successor to Antipater.

In Italy, Antipater learned of Pheroras' death, but not that his plot had been discovered. He was very disturbed that his uncle had died without ending Herod's life, so he wrote his father that he planned to return. Herod urged him, in a friendly tone, to return without delay. When Antipater landed at Caesarea and proceeded to Jerusalem, he was met by averted looks or open expressions of hatred. Everyone seemed to know some secret of which he alone was ignorant. But it was now too late to run, and he could only hope nothing had been discovered. Or if it had, he thought, perhaps his cunning and nerve would again save him.

Entering the palace at Jerusalem, he was repulsed by Herod when he attempted to embrace him, and charged with being a parricide. Herod told him to prepare his defense and appear the next day before Varus, the visiting governor of Syria, and himself, as well as friends and relatives on both sides. When the council had convened, Antipater made a clever defense, couched in such touching language that he evoked compassion from Varus and all those present except Herod. Nicolas of Damascus, at the king's command, then completely refuted everything Antipater had said, supplying proofs of the culprit's guilt. The poison kept by Pheroras' wife was then given to another criminal under sentence of death, who died immediately. Varus drafted his report for Caesar and then departed, while Herod put Antipater in irons and dispatched messengers to the emperor with news of the disaster. It was later discovered that Antipater had forged letters against others in the royal household, including Salome.

Herod's Final Illness

A XVII,146 Herod's health now declined rapidly. Age and grief increased
W I,647 his ailments, for he was almost 70 years old. And he was now further distressed by an uprising against him. Judas and Matthias, two educated doctors of the law, incited a band of young men to tear down a large golden eagle which Herod had placed over the gate of the temple. This was put there in defiance of Jewish law, which forbade the image of any living thing to be introduced into the temple. The men were arrested in the act and brought before Herod, who ordered the ringleaders to be burned alive. And on the same night, there was an eclipse of the moon.*

After this, Herod grew rapidly worse and suffered horrible torments. He had a terrible craving to scratch himself, his bowels were ulcerated, and his privates gangrenous and wormy. He tried in vain to relieve his gasping and convulsions in the warm springs at Callirrhoe, and returned to Jericho. Here he assembled the men of distinction from all parts of the nation and ordered them shut inside the hippodrome. He told his sister Salome that as soon as he died, all these men were to be killed, so that there would be grief throughout the country at his death rather than joy!

While he was giving these orders, a letter arrived from Rome, in which Caesar left it up to Herod to either exile or execute his son. Herod was now suffering such terrible agony that he tried to stab himself, but was prevented by his cousin. When the

---

* March 13, 4 B.C., according to astronomers. This is the only eclipse mentioned by Josephus.

palace was filled with loud cries, Antipater thought his father had died and urged the jailor to release him, promising large rewards. The jailor went to the king and told him of Antipater's intentions. Herod cried out, beat his head, and ordered his bodyguard to kill Antipater at once and bury him at Hyrcanium. He then amended his will, appointing Archelaus, his eldest son, to succeed him; Antipas, his brother, as tetrarch of Galilee and Perea; Philip was appointed as tetrarch of Trachonitis and neighboring territories. To Caesar he left ten million pieces of silver, and to his wife Julia [Livia] and others, five million.

Herod survived his son's execution by five days. He had reigned 34 years since the execution of Antigonus, when he became master of the state, and 37 years from when he had been declared king by the Romans. 4 B.C.

Upon his death, Salome liberated the Jewish leaders whom Herod had summoned to the hippodrome. Herod's will was then read to the people, and Archelaus was declared king. He A XVII,193 W I,666

The fortress Herodium, southeast of Bethlehem, which Herod artificially heightened at the expense of a neighboring hill. Somewhere below the recently excavated citadel, Herod himself is buried.

spared no expense for his father's funeral. The bier was of gold, studded with precious stones, and the body covered with purple. A crown of gold was at his head, and a scepter at his right hand. Around the bier marched Herod's sons and his numerous relatives. They were followed by the guards, foreign troops, and the army, preceded by the commanders and officers. Five hundred servants carrying aromatic spices followed in procession to Herodium, where the burial took place.

[*A dynastic chart of the Herodian family is found on pages 392 and 393.*]

19

THE ROMAN GOVERNORS

Archelaus mourned his father for seven days, and then feasted A XVII,200 the people, according to the custom of the Jews. Addressing the W II,1 crowds from a golden throne, he thanked them for their allegiance. He said he would not take on himself the authority of king until Caesar ratified Herod's will, but after that he would be kinder to them than his father had been.

Pleased by Archelaus' speech, the people quickly put his good intentions to the test by asking for various favors. Some wanted the taxes reduced, while others begged him to release the prisoners. In order to gain the good will of the people, Archelaus promised to attend to these requests.

Toward evening, great crowds of people who had been dissatisfied under Herod's reign gathered. They mourned those whom Herod had put to death for cutting down the golden eagle from the gate of the temple. They cried out that Herod's advisers should be put to death, and that the high priest he appointed be deprived of his office. Archelaus was provoked by these clamors, but tried to quiet them in a peaceful manner. He sent an officer to pacify the mob, but they threw stones at him.

It was now the feast of the Passover, and multitudes came to Jerusalem from the country, among whom the rioters began to spread sedition. Fearing rebellion, Archelaus sent a tribune with a cohort to seize the leaders of the insurrection. But they stoned the soldiers, killing many of them, though a few escaped, including the wounded tribune. Archelaus then sent his army against them, and they killed about 3,000 of the rioters, driving the rest into the hills. Archelaus' heralds now commanded everyone to return to his own home, and they all withdrew without finishing the festival.

Archelaus, accompanied by Nicolas, set out for Rome together with many of the royal family. They went supposedly to aid Archelaus in securing the throne, but in reality to protest the massacre at the temple. His younger brother, Antipas, had also gone to Rome to claim the crown on the basis of Herod's will, in which he was made heir, rather than the codicil. Many of the relatives supported him out of hatred for Archelaus.

At Caesarea, Archelaus met Sabinus, the procurator of Syria, who had set out for Judea to take charge of Herod's property. But Varus, governor of Syria, interposed, and Sabinus agreed to remain at Caesarea and leave Archelaus in possession of the treasures and fortresses of Judea until a decision had been made at Rome. But no sooner had Varus gone to Antioch and Archelaus set sail for Rome, than Sabinus hurried to Jerusalem. He seized the palace, commanded the treasury officials to give an accounting, and tried to obtain possession of the fortresses. However, everyone remained faithful to Archelaus' instructions and refused to obey any orders unless they came from Rome.

Revolt in Jerusalem

A XVII,248 Meanwhile, Archelaus and Antipas disputed their rights to the crown before Caesar. Nicolas of Damascus supported Archelaus successfully enough to incline Caesar to confirm Archelaus' rule. Before Caesar came to a decision, however, news came that Judea was in rebellion. The feast of Pentecost had arrived, and the Jews had gathered to avenge the greed of Sabinus. Dividing themselves into three groups, they camped on the north, south, and west of the temple, and proceeded to besiege the Romans. Frightened, Sabinus sent to Varus for help, seized Phasael, the highest tower, and signaled his troops to attack the Jews. The Jews had mounted the roofs of the porticoes surrounding the temple courts, and from there hurled stones on their enemies. The Romans set fire to the porticoes, and the Jews were either burned alive or slaughtered by the enemy when they attempted to retreat. The Romans then broke into the sacred treasury, and the soldiers stole a great part of it, while Sabinus took 400 talents for himself. Maddened by this outrage, the Jews besieged Sabinus and his forces inside the palace.

Most of the royal troops deserted to join the Jewish besiegers, who offered to let Sabinus and his men leave unharmed. Sabinus would gladly have done so, but he was afraid to trust the Jews and so waited for help from Varus.

The whole country was without any government, and erupted in violence. Two thousand of Herod's army, who had been disbanded, followed his cousin Achiabus in rebellion until

Statue of Augustus as commander-in-chief (about 20 B.C.), addressing his troops. It was found at the Villa of Livia (Augustus' wife), at Prima Porta on the Via Flaminia just north of Rome. The symbols on the breastplate indicate Augustus' achievements of prosperity and peace for the Empire (Vatican Museum).

driven into the hills. Judas, son of Ezekias the bandit, plundered Galilee, while Simon, a slave of Herod, crowned himself king and burned the royal palace in Jericho until he was caught and beheaded. Athronges, a huge shepherd, also put on a diadem. With his burly brothers, he conducted a guerilla campaign, and others also spread ruin and desolation over the country.

A XVII,286   Varus, fearful for the safety of the legion besieged in Jerusa-
W II,66   lem, hurried to relieve Sabinus with two other legions, assisted by an army under Aretas, king of Arabia. Many cities were burned and sacked on the way, especially by the Arabs. When Varus approached Jerusalem, the Jewish forces besieging Sabinus quickly fled into the country and dispersed. The inhabitants of the city then declared that they were not in revolt, but instead blamed the multitudes who had come into the city to celebrate the festival. Sabinus, ashamed to look Varus in the face, stole away to the seacoast.

Varus sent his troops across the country to capture those who had been involved in the sedition, and crucified 2,000 of the ringleaders. But some 10,000 were still gathered in Idumea. Varus sent the Arabs home because he could not restrain their excesses. With his own troops, he then marched against the insurgents, who surrendered to him. He pardoned the common soldiers, but sent the officers to Rome for trial. Having settled matters, Varus left a garrison in Jerusalem and hurried back to Antioch.

Augustus Divides the Kingdom

A XVII,300   A delegation of 50 Jews arrived in Rome at this time to ask for
W II,80   the elimination of royal authority in Judea, and were supported by 8,000 of the Jews in Rome. Caesar called together a council in the temple of Apollo to hear the envoys, as well as Archelaus, Philip, his brother, and their supporters.

The emissaries spoke first, and charged their former king, Herod, with the greatest extortions and cruelties, claiming that under him the Jews had endured the worst suffering since their captivity in Babylon. Archelaus, they continued, had inaugurated his reign by slaughtering 3,000 Jews in the temple precincts to prove he was not a bastard son of Herod. Therefore, they petitioned Caesar to deliver them from kings and to annex their country to Syria and let it be ruled by Roman governors. They would show how well they could behave under moderate rulers.

Then Nicolas spoke for Archelaus and refuted the charges against the kings, declaring the Jews to be rebellious and by nature disobedient to their sovereigns. Having listened attentively to both sides, Caesar dismissed the council. A few days later, he appointed Archelaus not as king, but ethnarch of Judea, Idumea, and Samaria, promising to make him king should he prove deserving. Antipas received Galilee and Perea, while Philip obtained Batanea, Trachonitis, Auranitis, and Panias. Salome, Herod's sister, received the government and revenues of several cities, and other members of Herod's family inherited the bequests he had left them in his will. Caesar divided the thousand talents which Herod had left him among Herod's children, keeping for himself only a few items in honor of the deceased.

A young Jew later appeared in Rome, who pretended to be the prince Alexander whom Herod had ordered to be killed. He looked very much like the dead Alexander, and had been trained to act his part by a Jew who was well acquainted with affairs at the Herodian court. He completely deceived the Jews in Crete and Melos, who furnished him with money to go to Rome and claim the Jewish throne. He explained his escape from death by claiming the executioners had taken compassion on him and his brother Aristobulus, allowing them to escape after substituting corpses resembling them. As soon as this impostor arrived in Puteoli and Rome, the Jews joyously acclaimed him as the true Alexander, and provided him with all the trappings of royalty. A XVII,324 W II,101

Caesar, suspecting a cheat, sent one of his freedmen, Celadus, who had known Alexander well, to conduct the youth into his presence. When Celadus saw the pretender, he knew at once that this was not the real Alexander, because his body was coarse and rough compared to Alexander's, which had been softened by luxury. He confronted him as an imposter, but promised that Caesar would spare his life if he would point out the man who had concocted the scheme.* The false Alexander agreed and went with Celadus to Caesar, identifying his instructor. Caesar was amused by the affair, and, seeing that the pretender was a strong young fellow, he made him an oarsman in one of his galleys. But he put to death the scoundrel who had induced him.

Archelaus assumed the ethnarchy of Judea and splendidly rebuilt the palace at Jericho, adding a palm tree plantation. But he transgressed the law in marrying Glaphyra, Alexander's widow, for marrying a brother's wife [unless she is childless] is abhorrent among Jews. Archelaus also ruled with such cruelty that in the tenth year of his reign, both the Jews and the Samaritans accused him before Caesar. After hearing his defense, Cae-

---

* Thus the version in *War*. In *Antiquities*, it is Augustus himself who unmasks the imposter.

sar banished Archelaus to Vienne, a city in Gaul, and con-
A.D. 6 fiscated his property.

Before he had been summoned to Rome, Archelaus dreamed
that ten thick ears of wheat were being eaten by oxen, and no one
could interpret the dream except a certain Essene named Simon.
He told Archelaus that the oxen signified suffering; the ears the
number of years in his reign, which was now at an end. Five
days later, Caesar's summons arrived.

Roman Judea

A XVIII,1   Judea now became a province, and Coponius, a Roman of the
W II,117 equestrian order, was sent out as procurator with full authority,
including administration of capital punishment. Quirinius, a
Roman senator of consular rank, was also sent by Caesar to be
governor of Syria and assessor of property there and in Judea,
where he was to sell Archelaus' estate. While the Jews reluctantly agreed to register their property, a certain Judas of
Gamala claimed that this was tantamount to slavery, so he and a
Pharisee named Saddok called for revolution, starting a fourth
philosophy which led to ruin. Let me describe the various
schools of thought among the Jews.

The Pharisees regard observance of their doctrine and commandments as of most importance, and they believe that souls
have power to survive death and receive rewards or punishments. They are very influential among the townspeople, and
all rites of worship are performed according to their exposition.

The Sadducees teach that the soul dies along with the body,
and they observe no tradition apart from the [written] laws.
Whenever they assume office, however, they submit to the
formulas of the Pharisees, because the masses would not tolerate
them otherwise.

The Essenes believe in the immortality of the soul and strive
for righteousness, but they use a different ritual of purification
for their sacrifices and so are barred from the temple sanctuary.
The 4,000 in this sect hold their property in common, and do not
bring wives or slaves into the community, but live off by themselves.* Always dressed in white, they do not change their
clothes until they are worn threadbare. They deem oil defiling,
and purify themselves in cold water. A candidate joins their
order only after a three-year probation, and they are also ex-

---

* Probably at Qumran, the community at the northwest corner of the Dead Sea,
where the Dead Sea Scrolls were discovered in 1947.

Excavations at Qumran, near the northwestern corner of the Dead Sea, site of the Essene community which wrote and later hid the famed "Dead Sea Scrolls." The scrolls were discovered by accident in the caves of the Judean escarpment to the west (background).

The hole in the rock near the center of the photograph marks Cave 4 in the Judean escarpment overlooking Qumran, where some of the Dead Sea Scrolls were discovered.

traordinarily interested in ancient writings. So strictly do they observe the Sabbath that they will not even defecate on that day.

The fourth philosophy [the Zealots'] agrees with the Pharisees except that they have an overwhelming desire for liberty with the conviction that God alone is their leader. They will easily endure any sort of pain or death so long as they do not have to call man their master. These, then, are the philosophies among the Jews.

A XVIII,26   Having liquidated Archelaus' estate, Quirinius appointed Ananus, the son of Seth, as high priest.* Meanwhile, Herod Antipas and Philip were administering their tetrarchies. Herod fortified Sepphoris, while Philip improved Panias at the source of the Jordan and called it Caesarea [Philippi]. He also raised Bethsaida on Lake Gennesaritis [Sea of Galilee] to city status by adding townspeople.

During the Roman procurator Coponius' administration in Judea, the priests, as was their custom, threw open the gates of the temple at midnight during Passover. But some Samaritans, who had slipped into Jerusalem, scattered human bones in the porticoes and throughout the temple. As a result, from then on, the priests excluded everyone from the temple [sanctuary].

Coponius returned to Rome and was succeeded by Marcus Ambivulus and then Annius Rufus, during whose administra-
A.D. 14   tion Caesar [Augustus] died at age 77, having ruled 57 years. The third emperor** was Tiberius, son of Caesar's wife Julia [Livia], who dispatched Valerius Gratus to succeed Rufus as procurator over the Jews. Gratus deposed Ananus from the high priesthood and made three more changes before appointing Joseph Caiaphas to the office. Having stayed eleven years in
A.D. 26   Judea, Gratus retired to Rome and was succeeded by Pontius Pilate.

The tetrarch Herod, meanwhile, had attained a high place among the friends of Tiberius. He built a city on Lake Gennesaritis and named it Tiberias, settling a mixed population there, mainly Galilean, as well as slaves whom he liberated. Their freedom was on condition that they not move away, since the city was built on the site of tombs, which would render the settlers unclean.

---

* The Annas of the New Testament Gospels, who was high priest from A.D. 6 to 15.

** Tiberius was actually the second emperor but the third "Caesar."

Statue of Tiberius, second Roman emperor (Vatican Museum, Rome).

A two-by-three-foot stone, discovered at Caesarea in 1961, records the name of Pontius Pilate. The left facing of the stone had been chipped away for reuse, so that only "TIVSPILATVS" remains of Pilate's name in the middle line (Israel Museum, Jerusalem).

Pontius Pilate

Pilate, having been sent by Tiberius as procurator of Judea, moved his troops from Caesarea to winter quarters in Jerusalem. But by night he brought into the city busts of the emperor that were attached to the military standards, when our law forbids the making of images. For this reason, the previous procurators used standards that had no such ornaments. The next morning, the Jews were indignant and hurried to Pilate in Caesarea, imploring him to remove the images. When he refused, deeming it an insult to the emperor, they prostrated themselves around the palace for five days and nights. On the sixth, Pilate took his seat on the tribunal in the stadium, and when the Jews again pleaded, he gave a signal. The people were suddenly surrounded with a ring of troops three deep, their swords drawn, and Pilate threatened death if they did not stop the tumult. But they bared their necks, declaring that they would rather die than transgress the laws. Astounded at such religious

A XVIII,55
W II,169

zeal, Pilate immediately transferred the images from Jerusalem to Caesarea.

Later, he spent money from the sacred treasury to construct an aqueduct to bring water into Jerusalem. But the people were

A section of the aqueduct constructed by Pontius Pilate to improve Jerusalem's water supply. This segment runs at ground level through an olive orchard near Bethlehem.

angry at this enterprise and surrounded Pilate's tribunal when he visited Jerusalem. Anticipating the riot, Pilate had ordered many of his troops to mingle with the crowd, disguised as civilians, and on his signal, they clubbed the abusive Jews. Although Pilate had ordered them not to use swords, a large number were killed, some from the blows, others in the stampede which followed.

Jesus

A XVIII,63 At this time there was a wise man called Jesus, and his conduct was good, and he was known to be virtuous. Many people among the Jews and the other nations became his disciples. Pilate condemned him to be crucified and to die. But those who had become his disciples did not abandon his discipleship. They reported that he had appeared to them three days after his crucifixion and that he was alive. Accordingly, he was perhaps the Messiah, concerning whom the prophets have reported wonders. And the tribe of the Christians, so named after him, has not disappeared to this day.*

Scandals at Rome

Paulina, a virtuous lady of noble descent at Rome, was married to the equally-reputable Saturninus. But an equestrian named Decius Mundus was so in love with her that he offered her 200,000 Attic drachmas if they could share a bed a single time. When she refused, Mundus' freedwoman, Ida, bribed the priests of Isis—of whom Paulina was a devotee—to inform her that the god Anubis had fallen in love with her and invited her to share his table and bed at the temple, which she did. After supper, when the doors were shut and the lights extinguished, a hidden Mundus was not refused when he sought intercourse with her. Indeed, she performed a night-long service for him, assuming that he was the god. Two days later, when Mundus informed her that he had adopted the name Anubis and saved a substantial sum to boot, she told her husband of the horror, and he informed the emperor. Tiberius crucified both the priests and Ida, razed the temple, and ordered the statue of Isis thrown into the Tiber. Mundus received only exile, because his was a crime of passion.

The Jews of Rome suffered at this time. Four Jewish scoundrels encouraged Fulvia, a woman of high rank who became a Jewish proselyte, to send purple and gold to the temple in

A XVIII,65

---

* This, the most famous passage in Josephus, is also the most controversial. The standard text of *Antiquities* XVIII,63 reads as follows:

> About this time lived Jesus, a wise man, if indeed one ought to call him a man. For he was the achiever of extraordinary deeds and was a teacher of those who accept the truth gladly. He won over many Jews and many of the Greeks. He was the Messiah. When he was indicted by the principal men among us and Pilate condemned him to be crucified, those who had come to love him originally did not cease to do so; for he appeared to them on the third day restored to life, as the prophets of the Deity had foretold these and countless other marvelous things about him. And the tribe of Christians, so named after him, has not disappeared to this day.

Although the passage is so worded as early as Eusebius (c. A.D. 324), scholars have long suspected a Christian interpolation, since Josephus would not have believed Jesus to be the Messiah or in his resurrection and have remained, as he did, a non-Christian Jew. In 1972, however, Professor Schlomo Pines of the Hebrew University in Jerusalem announced his discovery of an Arabic manuscript by the tenth-century Melkite historian Agapius, in which this Josephan passage is expressed in a manner appropriate to a Jew, and which corresponds so precisely to previous scholarly projections of what Josephus originally wrote that it is substituted in the text above. While the final sentence is not in Agapius, Pines justifiably concludes that it was in the original Josephan text.

Jerusalem, which they promptly stole for themselves. Fulvia's husband reported this to his friend, Tiberius, who then banished the whole Jewish community from Rome. The consuls drafted 4,000 of them for military service and sent them to the island of Sardinia.

Pilate's Recall

A XVIII,85   The Samaritans too were not exempt from troubles. A demagogue persuaded them to go with him to Mount Gerizim, where he would show them the sacred vessels which Moses had supposedly buried there. A great multitude arrived at the mountain armed, but Pilate blocked their route of ascent with infantry and cavalry. In the clash that followed, some were killed and the rest scattered or taken prisoner. Pilate then executed the ringleaders.

After the uprising was quelled, the Samaritan council went to Vitellius, the governor of Syria, and accused Pilate of massacre. Vitellius sent Marcellus, one of his friends, to take charge of Judea, ordering Pilate to return to Rome and defend himself before the emperor against the Samaritan charges. And so Pilate, having spent ten years in Judea, hurried to Rome in obedience to Vitellius' orders. But before he reached Rome,
A.D. 37   Tiberius had already died.

Vitellius was received magnificently in Jerusalem, where the Jews were celebrating the Passover. He reduced some of the taxes and transferred the vestments of the high priest from the Antonia to the temple. He also removed Joseph Caiaphas from that office and appointed Jonathan, son of Ananus, in his place.

After his return to Antioch, Vitellius negotiated an agreement with Artabanus, king of Parthia. This took place on a bridge over the Euphrates, after which Herod [Antipas] the tetrarch feasted them in a luxurious pavilion. But Herod rushed the news of the successful negotiations to Tiberius, preceding Vitellius' report. Vitellius was furious with Herod and would get his revenge on the accession of Gaius [Caligula].

Herod and John the Baptist

A XVIII,106   Herod's brother, Philip, died at this time, a moderate ruler who dispensed justice on an itinerant basis. Since he died childless, Tiberius annexed his territory to the province of Syria. Herod himself now quarreled with Aretas, king of Petra, whose daughter he had married. But Herod had since fallen in love with Herodias, wife of his half-brother [also named] Herod, and he promised to marry her and dismiss Aretas' daughter.

However, she heard about the agreement, and asked Herod for permission to visit Machaerus. From there she hurried on to her father in Arabia, and told him of Herod's plans.

This and a boundary dispute led Aretas to attack Herod, whose whole army was destroyed. Herod wrote about this to Tiberius, who was furious, and ordered Vitellius, governor of Syria, to declare war on Aretas. But to some of the Jews, Herod's disaster seemed to be divine vengeance for his treatment of John, surnamed the Baptist. Although John was a good man and exhorted the Jews to lead righteous lives and practice justice toward their colleagues and piety to God, Herod had put him to death. John taught that baptism must not be employed to obtain pardon for sins committed, but as a consecration of the body, implying that the soul was already purified by proper behavior. When others also joined the crowds around John and were greatly aroused by his preaching, Herod grew alarmed that such eloquence could lead to rebellion. Therefore, he decided that it would be better to strike first and get rid of him, rather than wait for an uprising. Although John was brought in chains to Machaerus and put to death in that stronghold, the Jews decided that the destruction of Herod's army was God's vindication of John.

Vitellius, meanwhile, prepared for war against Aretas and was planning to march two legions through Judea. But he re-routed their course after Jewish leaders appealed that he not bring military standards bearing images on their soil. He and Herod the tetrarch, however, offered sacrifice in Jerusalem, where they received the news of Tiberius' death. This caused Vitellius to call off his war with Aretas, and he returned to Antioch.

Herod Agrippa and Caligula

Agrippa was the son of the Aristobulus who had been stran- A XVIII,143
gled by his father, Herod [the Great]. Agrippa had spent huge W II,178
amounts of money cultivating friends in Rome, and returned to Judea in poverty. He was contemplating suicide until his sister Herodias and Herod the tetrarch gave him a job as market-supervisor in Tiberias. Tiring of that, he borrowed great sums and returned to Rome and the good graces of Tiberius, who had moved to the island of Capri. Agrippa became a close friend of his young grand-nephew Gaius [Caligula]. One day, while they were out riding on Capri, Agrippa expressed the hope that Gaius would soon succeed Tiberius as emperor, since he was much worthier.

The island of Capri, where Agrippa and Caligula waited for Tiberius to die. The imperial palace crowns the summit of the precipice to the left.

This was overheard by the chariot driver and eventually reported to Tiberius, who angrily had Agrippa arrested. While he waited in chains in front of the palace, a horned owl alighted on the tree on which he was leaning. Another prisoner, a German, predicted that Agrippa would soon be released and attain the highest point of honor and power. "But remember," he continued, "when you see this bird again, your death will follow within five days."

Antonia, Tiberius' sister-in-law, took a special interest in Agrippa and tried to make him as comfortable as possible during the six months he spent in prison. Then Tiberius died, having A.D. 37 appointed Gaius as his successor. One of Gaius' early acts was to put a diadem on Agrippa's head and appoint him king over the tetrarchy of Philip. He also gave him a golden chain equal in weight to the iron one that had bound him, and Agrippa returned home in triumph.

Extremely jealous over the success of her brother, Herodias

prodded her husband Herod to embark for Rome and petition for the kingship also. He resisted as best he could, but finally gave in, and they sailed to Italy, where they met the emperor at Baiae. During their interview, Gaius was reading letters from Agrippa, in which he indicted Herod for conspiring with Sejanus, a Roman prefect, against Tiberius and for being in alliance now with Artabanus of Parthia against Gaius. As proof, Agrippa cited 70,000 pieces of armor stored in Herod's armories. Gaius asked whether the arms were there, and when he received an affirmative, he took away Herod's tetrarchy and added it to Agrippa's kingdom, banishing Herod to Lyons in Gaul.* He would have permitted Herodias to return and enjoy her property, but she chose exile with her husband.

Caligula's Statue

Meanwhile, the Jews and Greeks of Alexandria had engaged in civil strife. Both sides sent three delegates to present their case before Gaius, who was now overcome with delusions of A XVIII,257 W II,184
divinity. The Greeks' spokesman, Apion, scurrilously attacked the Jews for neglecting to honor the emperor with altars, statues, and temples as the rest of the empire had done. Philo, representing the Jews, began his defense but was angrily cut off by Gaius, who would now avenge himself on the Jews.

Gaius dispatched Petronius as legate of Syria to succeed Vitellius, and ordered him to lead an army into Judea and set up a statue of Gaius inside the temple of God. When Petronius arrived with his army at Ptolemais, he was met by many thousands of Jews who pleaded with him to respect their laws and not erect the statue. He then went on to Tiberias,

Bust of Gaius "Caligula" (Louvre, Paris).

where he received the same response from all the Jews. They

---

* According to *War*, II,183, Herod was banished to Spain, where he died in exile.

declared that they would rather die than see their laws transgressed, and even now prepared to leave their land untilled.

Struck by their resolve, Petronius decided to risk Gaius' anger rather than drench the country in blood. Convening an assembly of Jews in Tiberias, he told them that he would try to dissuade the emperor from carrying out his plan. And if he failed, he would endure suffering himself rather than see so many of them destroyed. He then told them to resume their agriculture and dismissed the multitude, who invoked many blessings on him. After returning to Antioch, he wrote to Gaius, reporting on his expedition into Judea, and added that unless the emperor wished to destroy both the country and its inhabitants, he ought to revoke his order.

King Agrippa, meanwhile, had treated Gaius to a lavish dinner in Rome, after which the emperor offered him any gift he desired. After declining repeatedly, he interceded for the Jews and asked Gaius not to erect his statue in Jerusalem. The emperor acceded to the request, but when Petronius' letter arrived, he grew irate again and ordered Petronius' suicide for being so slow in executing his commands. Yet it so happened that the messengers carrying Gaius' dispatch to Petronius were detained by stormy weather. However, later messengers, announcing the subsequent death of Gaius, had a favorable voyage. So Petronius marveled at the providence of God in not receiving Gaius' letter until nearly a month after he had learned of his death.

[Here Josephus introduces a long description of the massacre of Mesopotamian and Babylonian Jews by Parthians and Syrians.]

A XIX,1 Gaius' contempt of the Jews was typical of what he inflicted on the entire Roman empire. He terrorized all classes of citizens, putting some to death for their wealth, and insisted on his own divinity, calling Jupiter "brother." He pillaged the Greek temples of sculpture, and built a pontoon bridge across the gulf at Misenum just for his chariot. At the races, people shouted for a tax reduction, but Gaius had them executed before the spectators. He even had sexual intercourse with his own sister.

Three conspiracies attempted to assassinate him. One group was at Cordova in Iberia, the second was led by the tribune Cassius Chaerea [at Rome], and the third by Annius Vinicianus. Chaerea was particularly insulted by the effeminate or obscene passwords Gaius would give him, and the reaction of his men when he had to pass them on. Chaerea and his conspirators met him in an alley that led to the palace baths and cut Gaius down, in the fourth year of his reign. A.D. 41

Agrippa and Claudius

Gaius' uncle, Claudius, was kidnapped by praetorian guards- A XIX,212 men, who declared him emperor—they distrusted democracy— W II,206 but the Senate was ringing with oratory in favor of liberty, and opposed the succession of Claudius. King Agrippa happened to be in Rome at this time, and became a mediator between the praetorian camp and the Senate. Finding that Claudius was perplexed and about to yield to the Senate, he incited him to bid for the empire. Agrippa then went to the Senate and diplomatically persuaded many of its members to withdraw their opposition to Claudius' succession, while the soldiers moved the rest. Chaerea and several of his accomplices were put to death, and Claudius became emperor.

Claudius now confirmed Agrippa as king and added to his domain Judea and Samaria as well—all the lands formerly ruled by his grandfather, Herod [the Great]—but also Abilene, which had been governed by Lysanias. He then celebrated a treaty with Agrippa in the middle of the Roman Forum. After this the king returned to Jerusalem to offer sacrifices of thanksgiving in the temple, where he hung up the golden chain Gaius had given him on his accession.

From such huge territories, Agrippa began to amass great

Marble statue of Claudius (Vatican Museum, Rome).

wealth. He spent some of it fortifying the north walls of Jerusalem, and would have made them impregnable had not Marsus, the governor of Syria, notified Claudius about it. Claudius, in turn, wrote Agrippa to stop, suspecting revolution. Marsus also broke up a gathering of kings whom Agrippa was entertaining at Tiberias, greatly offending the king.

The reconstructed theater at Caesarea, with the Mediterranean in the background. The "Pilate" stone was discovered here, and this is also the site of Herod Agrippa's sudden seizure preceding his death five days later.

After his seventh year of rule, Agrippa came to Caesarea to celebrate games in honor of Caesar. At daybreak, he entered the theater, dressed in a garment of woven silver which gleamed in the rays of the rising sun. His flatterers started addressing him as a god, but then he looked up and saw an owl perched on a rope overhead and was struck with intense pain. "I, whom you called a god," he cried, "am now under sentence of death!" A.D. 44 Five days later he died, at age 54.*

The Procurators

A XX,1 Agrippa left three daughters, Bernice, Mariamme, and Dru-
W II,220 silla, and one son, Agrippa. Since the last was only seventeen,

---

* Another account of this scene occurs in Acts 12:20 ff., which accords well with Josephus' version.

Claudius again reduced the kingdom to a province, and sent Cuspius Fadus as procurator. Fadus punished some robber bands in Judea, and ordered the high priest's vestments returned to the Antonia. But the Jews sent envoys to Claudius, who countermanded that order, allowing the Jews to keep the vestments.

[At this point, Josephus introduces a lengthy report on the conversion of Helena, queen of Adiabene, and her son, Izates, to Judaism. Both were buried near Jerusalem.]

An imposter, named Theudas, persuaded the masses to take their possessions and follow him to the Jordan, where, as a prophet, he would part the river and provide them easy passage. Fadus, however, attacked them with his cavalry and captured Theudas himself, whose head was cut off and brought to Jerusalem.

Tiberius Alexander succeeded Fadus as procurator, and he crucified James and Simon, the sons of Judas the Galilean who had aroused the people to rebellion when Quirinius was taking the census in Judea. Herod, the brother of King Agrippa who ruled Chalcis, now died, and Claudius assigned his kingdom to the younger Agrippa.

When Cumanus came as successor to Tiberius Alexander, an uprising occurred in Jerusalem at the Passover. One of his troops who was standing on the porticoes of the temple for riot control uncovered his genitals and showed them to the multitude.* In rage, some of the people started hurling stones at the soldiers, and Cumanus marched reinforcements to the Antonia. This frightened the masses, and in their rush to escape through narrow exits, some 20,000 were trampled to death. So there was mourning, instead of feasting. A XX,105 W II,224

Some of the revolutionaries then robbed Stephen, a slave of Caesar, as he was traveling on a public highway, and Cumanus sent troops to sack neighboring villages in retribution. One of them found a copy of the laws of Moses, which he publicly tore in half while blaspheming. Infuriated, the Jews went to Caesarea and asked Cumanus for vengeance in behalf of God, and he beheaded the soldier who had outraged their laws.

At the time of a festival, the Galileans regularly passed through Samaritan territory on the way to the Holy City, but one group was attacked by Samaritans and many were killed. When the Galileans protested to Cumanus, he did nothing to avenge them, having been bribed by the Samaritans. So they took

---

* Thus the version in *Antiquities*. In *War*, the indecent soldier turned his backside to the Jews and broke wind.

matters into their own hands and set fire to some Samaritan villages. Cumanus then clashed with the rebels, killing many, and the survivors were persuaded by magistrates from Jerusalem to lay down their arms or bring Rome's vengeance down on the nation.

The Samaritan leaders appealed to Ummidius Quadratus, governor of Syria, and demanded the punishment of those Jews who had ravaged their country. The Jews, in turn, accused the Samaritans of creating the disturbance by committing murder, and principally Cumanus, for taking bribes. Quadratus crucified the Samaritan and Jewish rebels, and sent to Rome some of the leading Samaritans and Jews to plead their case before Claudius Caesar, as well as Cumanus and Celer, his tribune. Claudius was about to decide in favor of the Samaritans when Agrippa the Younger, who was in Rome, urged Agrippina, wife of the emperor, to intercede. Claudius then heard the case more thoroughly and put the Samaritan delegation to death, condemned Cumanus to exile, and ordered Celer to be dragged around Jerusalem and put to death.

A.D. 52   Claudius now sent Felix, the brother of Pallas, to take charge of Judea, and removed Chalcis from Agrippa but gave him the tetrarchy of Philip. Felix fell in love with Agrippa's sister, Drusilla, who surpassed all other women in beauty. He sent a Jewish magician named Atomus to lure her away from her husband and into Felix's arms. They married, and she gave birth to a son named Agrippa, who, with his wife, were later buried in the eruption of Mount Vesuvius. Bernice, another sister of Agrippa the Younger, was rumored to have had a liaison with her brother.

Nero, Felix, and Festus

A XX,148   Claudius Caesar died after a reign of almost fourteen years. He
W II,250   was poisoned by his wife, Agrippina, to insure the succession of
Nero, her son by a previous marriage, rather than Claudius' own
A.D. 54   son Britannicus. Subsequently, Nero poisoned Britannicus and openly murdered his own mother, Agrippina. But since many historians have written about Nero, I will return to the fate of the Jews.

In Judea, where matters were going from bad to worse, Felix had to capture imposters and brigands on a daily basis. When the high priest Jonathan continually urged him to improve his administration, Felix hired *sicarii* ["dagger-men", i.e., terrorists] to murder him. When they remained unpunished, the *sicarii* boldly attacked their enemies with hidden daggers, even in the temple area. This is why, in my opinion, God Himself turned away from our city and brought the Romans upon us.

An Egyptian imposter promised his followers to make the walls of Jerusalem fall down at his command. Felix attacked them on the Mount of Olives and killed 400, taking 200 prisoners, although the imposter escaped. At Caesarea, a quarrel broke out between Jews and Syrians over equal civil rights. The Jews claimed precedence because Herod had founded the city, while the Syrians asserted that the place had been Strato's Tower before Herod, without a single Jew living there. When both sides started stoning each other, Felix intervened with his troops and many Jews were killed. He then sent leaders of both parties to argue their case before Nero in Rome.

Bust of Nero (Uffizi, Florence).

When Porcius Festus replaced Felix, the Jewish leaders accused the latter before Nero, and he would have been punished had not his brother Pallas interceded. Festus, meanwhile, had to contend with: the *sicarii* who were plundering Judea, assorted imposters, and a newly erected western wall of the temple which blocked Roman surveillance as well as Agrippa's view. King Agrippa [II] had the right to appoint high priests, and enjoyed watching what went on inside the temple as he dined high in the Hasmonean palace to the west. The priests therefore built a high wall to block his view, which both he and Festus ordered demolished, but they appealed to Nero. Poppaea, Nero's wife, was sympathetic to the Jews and gained his permission to let the wall stand.

Jesus' Brother James and Albinus

Upon Festus' death, Caesar sent Albinus to Judea as procurator. But before he arrived, King Agrippa had appointed Ananus to the priesthood, who was the son of the elder Ananus.* This

A XX,197
W II,272

---

* The Annas of the New Testament Gospels.

elder Ananus, after he himself had been high priest, had five sons, all of whom achieved that office, which was unparalleled. The younger Ananus, however, was rash and followed the Sadducees, who are heartless when they sit in judgment. Ananus thought that with Festus dead and Albinus still on the way, he would have his opportunity. Convening the judges of the Sanhedrin, he brought before them a man named James, the brother of Jesus who was called the Christ, and certain others. He accused them of having transgressed the law, and condemned them to be stoned to death.

The people of Jerusalem who were considered the most fair-minded and strict in observing the law were offended by this. They secretly urged King Agrippa to order Ananus to desist from any further actions of this sort. Some of them even went to meet Albinus, who was on his way from Alexandria, and informed him that Ananus had no authority to convene the Sanhedrin without his permission. Albinus angrily wrote to Ananus, threatening vengeance. King Agrippa, because of this action, deposed Ananus from the high priesthood, which he had held for three months. He replaced him with Jesus, son of A.D. 62 Damnaeus, and Jesus son of Gamaliel after that.

These two high priests feuded as a result, and their partisans hurled stones at each other, typical of the lawless confusion in the city. When Albinus heard that Gessius Florus was coming to replace him, he cleared the prisons by executing those who deserved death. But he released—for a bribe—those guilty of lesser offences, thus infesting the land with brigands. He also stole private property, burdened the nation with excessive taxes, and committed every sort of villainy.

Just now, too, the temple was finally completed, leaving 18,000 workers unemployed, although they did pave Jerusalem with white stone. [At this point, Josephus lists the Jewish high priests from Aaron on.]

Conclusion of *Jewish Antiquities*

A XX,252 Gessius Florus, whom Nero sent as successor to Albinus,
W II,277 made the latter look like a paragon of virtue by comparison. Joining in partnership with the brigands to receive a share of the spoils, he virtually paraded his lawless wickedness before the nation. He stripped whole cities, ruined entire populations, and compelled us to go to war with the Romans. The war, in fact, began in the second year of his procuratorship and in the twelfth A.D. 66 of Nero's reign. The details may be read in the books that I have written on *The Jewish War*.

Here, then, is the end of my *Antiquities*, which records Jewish history in Egypt, Syria, and Palestine from man's creation to Nero's twelfth year. No one else, either Jew or gentile, would have been equal to this task. God-willing, I will in the future write of the later events in our history up to the present day, which is the thirteenth year of Domitian Caesar and the fifty-sixth of my life.*

[A list of the rulers of Judea and the Roman emperors during the first century A.D., as well as their dates, is found on page 391.]

---

* A.D. 93–94. The envisioned work was never completed. Although Josephus' earlier work, The Jewish War, is captioned at this point for chronological purposes, introductory material in the War—more than two books' worth— has already been coalesced into this condensation from Antiochus Epiphanes' assault on the temple (c. 170 B.C.) to this point. All marginal references from here on are from The Jewish War.

PART II

THE
JEWISH WAR

20

HOSTILITIES ERUPT

When Cestius Gallus, governor of Syria, visited Jerusalem at the Passover, a huge throng surrounded him, denouncing Florus as having ruined the country. Florus, who was at his side, scoffed at the protests, but Cestius promised the people greater moderation from Florus in the future and returned to Antioch. Florus accompanied him as far as Caesarea, scheming all the while to drive the Jews into open revolt. For he was afraid that if peace continued, they would accuse him before Caesar, whereas war would conceal his atrocities. W II,280

An incident at Caesarea touched off the war. The Jews had a synagogue there, but the adjoining land was owned by a Greek. The Jews had often offered a much higher price for his lot than it was worth, but he refused to sell. Now to insult them, he started to erect some workshops on the site, leaving the Jews only a narrow approach to their place of worship. Some hotheaded youths interrupted the builders, but Florus stopped their violence. The Jews then bribed Florus with eight silver talents to stop the builders, and he promised to do so. But, money in hand, he set out for Sebaste, leaving the riot to take care of itself. c. May, A.D. 66

On the following Sabbath, when the Jews came to the synagogue, they encountered a local troublemaker who had placed a pot beside the entrance, bottom-side-up, on which he was sacrificing birds. A certain passionate youth, furious at this outrage, attacked the Caesareans, who were expecting a clash and had arranged the mock sacrifice. Jucundus, master of horse under Florus, removed the pot and tried to quell the tumult. The Jews snatched a copy of their Law and fled to Narbata, about seven miles away. There they sent a delegation to Florus in Sebaste, imploring his assistance and reminding him of the eight talents. But Florus threw them into prison for having taken a copy of the Law from Caesarea!

This news outraged Jerusalem, although the people restrained their feelings. But Florus, determined to drive them to revolt, extracted seventeen talents from the temple treasury, claiming government necessity. The infuriated people rushed to the temple, shouting their contempt for the procurator. Some passed around a basket, begging coppers for the "poor beggar Florus."

Florus marched on Jerusalem, thinking this a good chance to pillage the city, but he should have gone to Caesarea instead, to

The Roman aqueduct at Caesarea delivered water to the city from Mount Carmel to the northeast.

extinguish the flames of war there. The citizens of Jerusalem, in order to shame him from his purpose, came out to applaud his army. Florus, however, sent a centurion ahead with 50 horsemen to order the people to return and not to mock with pretended courtesy one whom they had reviled. Dismayed at this message, the crowd went home and spent the night in anxiety and dejection.

Florus Ravages the People

Florus stayed at the palace, and in the morning summoned the W II,301
chief priests and leaders before him. He demanded that they
hand over those who had insulted him, or face his vengeance.
They asked his pardon for any who had spoken disrespectfully,
blaming a few indiscreet youths who were impossible to identify. If he wanted to preserve the city and the peace of the nation,
they said, he should forgive the few offenders on behalf of the
many who were innocent.

Florus became all the more incensed, and shouted to his
soldiers to plunder the upper market and kill any they met. The
troops not only sacked the market, but broke into the houses
and massacred the occupants. The city ran with blood, and
3,600 men, women, and children were cruelly slaughtered or
crucified.

King Agrippa was away in Egypt, but Bernice, his sister, was
in Jerusalem fulfilling a religious vow. Horrified at the awful
sights around her, she continually sent messengers to Florus,
imploring him to stop the carnage. She finally came before him
herself, barefoot in supplication. But he was deaf to her requests, and the queen had to retreat quickly into the palace to
save her own life.

The next day, the multitude gathered in the upper market to
lament their dead and shout curses against Florus. But the chief
priests and leaders begged them to keep quiet and not to pro-
voke Florus again. Out of respect for those exhorting them, the
crowd complied.

Florus was disappointed that the disturbance stopped, and to
relight the flames, he sent for the chief priests and leaders. He
told them that the one way to prove their peaceful intentions
was for the people to go out and welcome two cohorts of troops
that were advancing from Caesarea. Florus then sent word to
those cohorts not to return the greetings of the Jews, and if they
ridiculed him, to attack them.

The priests found it difficult to make the outraged people obey
this command, but they warned them that otherwise their country would be pillaged and their temple profaned. The people
finally agreed and were led out to meet the troops, whom they
saluted. When no response came from the cohorts, some of the
Jewish rebels started shouting against Florus. The troops surrounded them and beat them with clubs, while the cavalry
pursued and trampled those that fled. Many fell under the blows
of the Romans, but many more were crushed to death in the
stampede at the city gates when they all tried to get back inside.
The troops rushed in with the people, trying to seize the temple

and the Antonia fortress. Florus and his men burst out of the palace and also tried to reach the fortress. But they were prevented by the people who so blocked the streets that they could not cut their way through, while others assaulted the Romans from the roofs.

Florus retreated to the palace, but the Jewish rebels, fearing that he might return and use Antonia to capture the temple, cut off the porticoes that connected the two structures. Now unable to plunder the temple's treasures, Florus told the city leaders that he would be leaving. On the promise that they would keep the peace, he left one cohort with them and returned with the rest of his forces to Caesarea.

Agrippa Attempts to Avert War

W II,333   To establish a reason for new hostilities, Florus sent a report to Cestius Gallus, falsely accusing the Jews of revolt and charging them with the very crimes from which they themselves had suffered. The Jerusalem magistrates also wrote of the outrages committed by Florus, as did Bernice.

Cestius sent one of his tribunes, Neapolitanus, to investigate affairs in Jerusalem. On the way, he met King Agrippa at Jamnia, who was returning from Egypt, and informed him of his mission. A deputation of priests and leaders also arrived at Jamnia to welcome the king back. After paying their respects, they lamented their misfortunes and reported the cruelty of Florus. Agrippa, although he sympathized with them, skillfully concealed his compassion in order to divert them from revenge.

When Agrippa and Neapolitanus approached Jerusalem, the people poured out to meet them. The widows of those who had been killed ran to them first, wailing and lamenting. The rest pleaded with Agrippa to relieve them and reported to Neapolitanus the miseries they had endured under Florus. On entering the city, they showed how the market place was desolate and the houses sacked. Neapolitanus passed through the city, and, finding it peaceful, he went up to the temple and commended the people for their loyalty to the Romans, urging them to maintain the peace. Then he took part in the temple worship from the permitted area and returned to Cestius.

W II,342   The people now pressured Agrippa and the chief priests to send ambassadors to accuse Florus before Nero. Agrippa did not encourage this mission, since he wanted to discourage the people from war. He assembled them at Xystus, and, placing his sister Bernice conspicuously on the roof of the Hasmonean palace, he delivered a long and eloquent speech. Granting that some of the procurators were brutal, he said, "It does not follow that all Romans are unjust to you. They do not intentionally send us oppressive governors, and can not in the west see their officers in the east.'' After due complaint, he continued, moderate successors should follow. But their hopes of gaining independence were too late. If they could not resist part of the Roman forces under Pompey, how could they expect to be successful now when the Romans ruled the world? When so many great nations had been conquered, how could the Jews hope to be victorious? Finally, he described the horrors of war, and the destruction that would surely fall on Jews throughout the empire as well as on themselves, their city, and the temple.

He burst into tears at the end, as did his sister, and the people were touched. Yet many cried out that they had not taken up arms against the Romans, only against Florus. Agrippa replied, ''By your actions you are already at war with Rome: you have not paid the tribute to Caesar, and you have destroyed the galleries communicating with the Antonia. If you wish to clear yourselves on the charge of insurrection, repair the porticoes and pay the tribute.''

Accepting this advice, the people went with the king and Bernice to the temple and started rebuilding the galleries. The magistrates went out through the villages to levy the taxes, and in a short time, 40 talents were collected. The danger of war seemed past. But when Agrippa tried to persuade the people to obey Florus until Caesar sent a successor, they grew exasperated and abusive at the king, and banished him from the city. Some of the rioters even threw stones at him, and the infuriated Agrippa withdrew to his own dominions.

A party of the most rebellious spirits now attacked the fortress W II,408 Masada, and killed the Roman guards after capturing it. At the temple, meanwhile, Eleazar, son of Ananias the high priest, persuaded those who conducted the worship to accept no gift or sacrifice from a foreigner. This was the basis of war with Rome, since sacrifices offered in behalf of the emperor and Rome were now suspended. The chief priests and leading Pharisees pleaded with them not to abandon the customary offerings, since it was impious to prevent strangers from offering worship to God. They then presented the priests who were experts on tradition, and they stated that all their ancestors had received the sacrifices of foreigners.

But the revolutionary party would not listen to anything, nor would the temple priests. The leading citizens, then, saw that they could not check the rebellion and that they would be the first to suffer Rome's vengeance. In order to exonerate themselves, they sent a deputation to Florus and another to Agrippa, requesting both to bring an army to the city and crush the rebellion. Florus rejoiced at the news, but dismissed the delegation without a reply. Agrippa, anxious to save the city and the temple, immediately sent 2,000 cavalry to help those opposed to insurrection.

Menahem

W II,422   Encouraged by these reinforcements, the leading men, the chief priests, and all who favored peace seized the upper city, for the lower city and the temple were in the hands of the rebels. For seven days the two parties fought each other without either gaining any advantage. The next day was the festival of wood-carrying, when everyone brought wood to keep the sacred altar fire burning continually. The rebels excluded their opponents from this ceremony, but admitted into the temple the *sicarii* with their hidden daggers. A fierce attack was made on the royal troops, who were overpowered and retreated from the upper city. The victors then set fire to the residence of the high priest, the palace of Agrippa, and the public archives, where the bonds of creditors were registered. The chief priests and leaders now hid in sewers or fled with the royal troops to the upper palace [of Herod] and shut the gates.

c. Aug., A.D. 66   The next day, the rebels attacked the Antonia. After capturing it in two days, they killed the garrison and then set fire to the fortress. Following this, they assaulted the upper palace, where the royal troops threw missiles at the attackers, killing many. But the siege went on night and day.

Menahem was the son of Judas the Galilean, who had rebelled against Quirinius and had upbraided the Jews for obeying the Romans when they had God as master. Menahem took his followers to Masada, where he stripped the armory of Herod to equip his colleagues and other outlaws. Returning like a king to Jerusalem, he became leader of the rebellion, and directed the siege of the palace, in which the garrison soon sued for terms. The rebels granted safe passage to the royal troops, who withdrew, leaving their Roman allies despondent until the Romans retreated to the three strong towers built by Herod [the Great], known as Hippicus, Phasael, and Mariamme. Menahem's men then rushed into the palace, killed anyone left, and set fire to the garrison.

W II,441   The next day, Ananias the high priest and his brother Ezechias were discovered hiding near the canal in the palace grounds and were put to death. Menahem, inflated by his success, became an unbearable tyrant. Eleazar and his party decided that, having revolted from the Romans for liberty, they ought not sacrifice this freedom to a despot born lower than themselves. This party attacked Menahem in the temple, where he had gone to worship, dressed in royal robes. All who were caught were put to death, among them Menahem, who was dragged from a hiding place and publicly executed after all manner of torture. A few were able to escape to Masada, including another Eleazar, a relative of Menahem and subsequently despot of Masada.

The people hoped that Menahem's death would end the revolt. But Eleazar and his party pressed the siege so vigorously that Metilius, the commander of the Roman garrison, offered to exchange arms and property for their lives. This was agreed to, and Metilius marched his men down. But as soon as they had laid down their arms, they were all brutally massacred, despite their shouts of "The agreement!" and "The oaths!" Metilius alone escaped by promising to become Jewish and be circumcised. This horrible act made war inevitable, and the moderates realized that they would have to suffer for the insurgents' crime. The atrocity was all the more horrible because it took place on the Sabbath.

Cestius Invades

On the same day and hour, as if by the hand of Providence, the Caesareans slaughtered the Jews who resided in that city. In one hour over 20,000 were massacred, and Caesarea was emptied of Jews. The whole Jewish nation was infuriated, and they ravaged neighboring Syrian towns and villages, slaughtering a great number of the inhabitants. The Syrians similarly killed all Jews in the towns they captured, and the whole province was a scene of indescribable horror. W II,457

So far the Jews had been fighting against foreigners, but when they invaded Scythopolis, they found their own people living there armed against them in defense of the city. But the Scythopolitans mistrusted their Jewish allies, and asked them to retire with their families into a nearby grove. Three nights later, the Scythopolitans attacked these Jews, butchering 13,000 of them.

Other cities followed the example of Scythopolis, killing or imprisoning their Jewish inhabitants, except for Gerasa, Antioch, Sidon, and Apamea, which spared their Jews. In Egypt, meanwhile, Jews were massacred in Alexandria by Greek inhabitants and resident Roman forces.

The rebels took the fortress Cypros near Jericho, massacred the garrison, and demolished its defenses. At the same time, the local Jewish population forced the Roman garrison at Machaerus to evacuate that fortress, which they then occupied.

Cestius, knowing it was time to intervene, led out a large army from Antioch in order to crush the insurrection. Agrippa accompanied him, as did Soaemus [king of Emesa], each supplying additional forces. After advancing on Caesarea, Cestius sent part of his army to attack Joppa. They took it, slaughtered the inhabitants, and ravaged the countryside. Another detachment subjugated the province of Galilee.

Oct., A.D. 66   Cestius then proceeded towards Jerusalem, interrupting the Jews who were celebrating the feast of the Tabernacles. Although it was the Sabbath, the Jews attacked the enemy with such fury that they broke their ranks. If the cavalry and some infantry had not relieved the broken line, Cestius and his whole army would have been in severe danger. They lost 515 men to only 22 for the Jews, who withdrew into the city.

W II,523   Agrippa now tried to negotiate with the Jews. He sent two of his friends to offer amnesty in the name of Cestius if the Jews would lay down their arms. But the rebels, fearing that the whole multitude would accept the proposal, attacked the emissaries, killing one and wounding the other. Those citizens who protested were stoned and beaten.

Cestius, taking advantage of this dissension, attacked and scattered the Jews, pursuing them to Jerusalem. For three days he suspended operations, hoping to receive an offer of surrender, but on the fourth led his troops against the city. The rebels, awed by the discipline of the Romans, abandoned the suburbs and withdrew into the inner city and the temple. Cestius took the upper city and camped opposite the palace. Had he at that moment forced his way within the ramparts, the city would have fallen and the war ended. But his camp prefect, Tyrannius Priscus, bribed by Florus to prolong the war, diverted him from the attempt. Many of the leading citizens promised to open the gates for Cestius, but he hesitated out of suspicion. The rebels finally discovered the collaborators and pulled them down from the ramparts, stoning them into their houses.

For five days the Romans pressed the assault without success. On the sixth, Cestius, with a large group of picked men, attacked the north side of the temple. At first repulsed by the Jews, the Romans returned, and those in the front rank fixed their shields firmly against the wall. The second rank joined theirs to these, and the rest did the same, forming what they call "the tortoise." When the projectiles fell they glanced off harmlessly, while the soldiers undermined the wall and prepared to set fire to the gate of the temple.

Cestius Retreats

Panic now overcame the rebels, and many slipped out of the W II,538 city, thinking it was on the verge of capture. Encouraged by their flight, the collaborating Jews pressed nearer the gates in order to admit Cestius as a deliverer. Had he only persisted with the siege he would soon have taken the city. But for some reason Cestius suddenly recalled his troops and withdrew from the city. The rebels immediately grew bold again, and rushed out behind him, killing some of his cavalry and infantry.

The following day, as Cestius continued to retreat, they harassed his rear, and, advancing on either side of his route, hurled their javelins into his flanks. The Romans did not attempt to beat off the attackers because they were afraid of breaking their ranks, while the Jews, being lightly armed, dashed in and out, slaughtering the enemy. After numerous casualties, the Romans reached their former encampment at Gibeon, where Cestius halted for two days, perplexed as to what course he should pursue.

But on the third day, with the numbers of the surrounding enemy increasing, he accelerated his retreat, killing all beasts of burden, except those that carried the javelins and engines of war. When they entered the pass at Bethoron, the Jews attacked them from all sides. Some blocked their egress in front, others drove the rear down into the ravine, while the main body of Jews shot down showers of arrows from above. The Roman infantry was hard pressed, while the cavalry was in still greater jeopardy, unable to charge up the slopes or avoid the precipices and ravines in flight. The entire Roman army would have been captured if night had not fallen. The Romans took refuge in Bethoron, while the Jews controlled all the surrounding points.

Cestius now selected 400 of his bravest men and stationed them on the roofs. They were to shout out the watchwords so that the Jews would think the entire army was still there, while he and the rest of his forces moved silently ahead. At daybreak, the Jews discovered the trick, and rushed upon the 400 who had deceived them, killing them with javelins, and then hurried in pursuit of Cestius.

The Jews were unable to overtake the Romans, but in their flight the Romans abandoned their battering rams, catapults, and other war engines, which now were taken by the Jews. With songs of triumph, they returned to the capital, having suffered very little loss, while killing 5,300 infantry and 480 cavalry of Nov., A.D. 66 the Romans and their allies.

Josephus *versus* John of Gischala

W II,556 After the disaster of Cestius, many distinguished Jews abandoned the city, including Costobar and Saul, two brothers in the royal family, who joined Cestius. At their request, Cestius sent them to Nero, who was in Achaia, and told them to alert him to their emergency and blame the war on Florus, thus deflecting any risk from himself.

When the people of Damascus learned of the Roman disaster, they massacred the 10,500 Jews whom they had imprisoned in their gymnasium. The only impediment to their butchery might have been the wives of the Damascans, who, with few exceptions, had secretly converted to Judaism.

On returning to Jerusalem, the Jews called an assembly in the temple, and appointed generals for the war. Joseph, the son of Gorion, and Ananus, the [ex-] high priest, were given supreme authority in the city. Eleazar, the son of Simon, was passed over, because he was suspected of tyranny. But in time, since he controlled much of the public treasure, Eleazar would gain supreme command. They sent out generals for the various districts, including Josephus, son of Matthias,* who was sent to command in Galilee. He ruled his district through 78 appointed magistrates to promote harmony among the inhabitants. Fortifying all the defensible places, he raised an army of 100,000 men, among whom he introduced Roman military discipline.

A crafty native of Gischala, named John, schemed to replace Josephus as commander of Galilee, ravaging the land with a band of 400 lawless men. Josephus was at first taken with the man's flair and energy, and permitted him to furnish oil to the Jews living in Syria, for they would not use oil supplied by non-Jews. Buying the oil cheap and selling it to the foreign Jews for a very high price, he soon made an enormous fortune, which he now used against Josephus. He circulated reports that Josephus was about to betray the state to the Romans, and tried in every way to ruin his commander.

Some youths ambushed the steward of King Agrippa as the steward passed through Galilee, and plundered his baggage, which contained some valuable treasures he was bringing to the king. Unable to dispose secretly of the booty, the robbers brought it to Josephus, who was then at Tarichaeae. He censured them for the robbery, and put the plunder in charge of one of the magistrates of Tarichaeae, to be restored to Agrippa at the first opportunity. The robbers became very angry at this, and went about denouncing Josephus as a traitor.

---

* The present historian.

The next dawn, 100,000 men in arms assembled in the hippodrome at Tarichaeae, instigated by John, and they denounced Josephus. Some demanded that he be stoned, others that he be burned alive, and all but four of his friends and bodyguard fled in terror. Josephus woke from his sleep when his enemies were about to set fire to the house. The four friends urged him to flee, but he tore his clothes, and, with ashes sprinkled on his head, hurried out to face the crowd. This appearance of humility was only a scheme to produce dissension among his opponents, some of whom now sympathized with him. Promising to make a full confession, Josephus spoke as follows: "I intended neither to return this money to Agrippa nor keep it for my own use. But since your city, citizens of Tarichaeae, needed walls for defense, and I feared that the people of Tiberias and other cities had their eye on these spoils, I decided to keep quiet possession of the money in order to surround you with a wall. If you do not approve, I will produce what was brought me and let you raid it. But if I did well, do not punish your benefactor."

At these words, the Tarichaeaens applauded, while the Tiberians and people from other towns threatened him. The two parties now began to quarrel among themselves, until most of them left. But about 2,000 remained to attack Josephus, who retreated to his home and had to resort to a second stratagem. He went up to the roof and asked them to send a delegation to confer quietly with him. When some of the leading rioters arrived, Josephus ordered them dragged to the most secluded part of the house and had them whipped to the bone. Suddenly opening the doors, he ejected the men, all covered with blood. The sight so shocked the rioters that they threw down their arms and fled.

John next devised a second plot against Josephus. While W II,614 Josephus was addressing the people of Tiberias, John secretly sent some troops to kill him, but the people, seeing them draw their swords, shouted an alarm. Josephus jumped down from his podium to the beach, leaped into a boat, and escaped to the middle of the lake. John fled to Gischala, his native town, and many Galileans wanted to avenge Josephus and burn John as well as Gischala. But Josephus merely gave John's adherents five days to abandon his cause or see their property seized and their houses burned. Three thousand of John's party immediately joined Josephus.

John now sent emissaries to Jerusalem, warning that Josephus would appear at the capital as a tyrant unless he was resisted. Some of the leaders, envious of Josephus, secretly supplied John with money and recalled Josephus from command, sending 2,500 men into Galilee against him. Sepphoris, Gabara, Gischala, and Tiberias supported John's cause, but Josephus regained the cities without resorting to arms, and the troops returned to Jerusalem.

W II,632 Several days later, Tiberias again revolted, appealed to King Agrippa for aid, and excluded Josephus from the city. When this defection was reported to him at Tarichaeae, Josephus again resorted to a stratagem, since he had sent his army off on a foraging excursion, and any delay would have enabled the king's troops to occupy the town. He collected all the boats on the lake—there were 230, put only four sailors in each, and set sail with this fleet for Tiberias. Letting them sail far enough offshore so the townspeople could not see that the ships were unmanned, he himself, attended by seven of his guards, drew close enough to shore to be recognized. His adversaries, thinking the fleet full of troops, waved olive branches and implored him to spare the city.

Josephus reproached them for rebellion, but promised to pardon any who would assist him in securing the town. Ten of the leading citizens came down to him, and he put them on board one of his vessels. He sent for 50 more and put them on the other boats, repeating the procedure using various pretexts. Finally the entire council of 600 as well as 2,000 of the people were drawn out of the city and shipped to Tarichaeae, where they were put into prison.

The remaining citizens identified a certain Cleitus as prime instigator of the revolt. Josephus, determined to put no one to death, ordered one of his guards to go ashore and cut off the hands of Cleitus, but the guard was afraid. Seeing Josephus fuming with anger and ready to do the job himself, Cleitus pleaded from the beach to spare one of his hands. Josephus agreed on condition that he himself would cut off the other. Cleitus drew his sword with his right hand and severed the left—such was his dread of Josephus.

Galilee was now quiet, and the Jews turned to preparing for the struggle against Rome. In Jerusalem, Ananus, the [ex-] high priest, and his leaders repaired the walls and constructed engines of war. In every quarter, weapons and armor were forged, and the young were trained. The moderates, however, were despondent, foreseeing an impending disaster.

In his toparchy, Simon, son of Giora, mustered a marauding band of revolutionaries who caused such havoc that Ananus sent an army against him. Simon fled with his band to Masada and plundered Idumea instead, where the people had to raise an army to protect themselves.

VESPASIAN 21
CONQUERS GALILEE

When Nero learned of the reverses in Judea, he pretended an air of disdain. "These unpleasantries are due to poor generalship," he said, "and not the valor of the enemy." Inwardly, however, he was very disturbed. Accordingly, he sent Vespasian, a veteran general with victories in Germany and Britain, to assume command of the armies in Syria and subdue the rebellious Jews. From Achaia, where he attended Nero, Vespasian dispatched his son Titus to Alexandria to bring up the Fifteenth legion stationed there, while he himself proceeded to Syria. There he collected the Roman forces and auxiliary troops from the neighboring princes.

The Jews, meanwhile, elated by their conquest over Cestius, marched on Ashkelon, a city rather weakly garrisoned by Roman troops and situated about 65 miles from Jerusalem. But Antonius, the Roman commander of the city, learned of their approach and was ready for them, attacking with a squadron of cavalry. The Jewish forces, entirely on foot, were novices, and could not cope with their skilled adversaries, who dispersed and easily slaughtered them. Night finally put a stop to the awful carnage, leaving 10,000 Jews dead, including two of their generals, John and Silas. Niger, the one surviving Jewish general, escaped with the remainder, most of whom were wounded, to a town in Idumea called Chaallis.

In spite of this disaster, the Jews, even before their wounds had time to heal, collected their forces and made another assault upon Ashkelon. Antonius placed ambushes in the passes and surrounded the Jews with his cavalry before they had time to form for battle, killing 8,000 of them. Niger retreated, and, being

Statue of Flavius Vespasian, the first Roman commander-in-chief in the Jewish War and later emperor (Uffizi, Florence).

hard pressed, took possession of a strong tower in a village called Belzedek. Antonius set fire to the tower and withdrew, exulting in the belief that Niger had died in it. But Niger leaped down from the burning tower and crept into a cave in the interior of the fortress, where he was found three days later by friends who were searching for his dead body to bury it. The Jews were filled with joy, believing that God had preserved him for future battles.

Meanwhile, Vespasian led his army out of Antioch, where he W III,29
had found King Agrippa with his whole force waiting to join Spring,
him, and pushed on to Ptolemais. Here he was met by the a.d. 67
citizens of Sepphoris in Galilee, who, seeking their own safety,
came to assure him of their fidelity to Rome. Vespasian gave
them 1,000 cavalry and 6,000 infantry to defend their city
against the Jews, since Sepphoris was the largest city in Galilee
and strongly fortified, guarding the entire province. [Josephus
here provides a geographical description of Galilee, Perea, Samaria, and Judea.]

The Roman force sent to Sepphoris, under command of Placidus the tribune, ravaged the surrounding country, causing
Josephus and his men serious difficulties. Josephus did attempt
an assault on Sepphoris, but was repulsed. This provoked fierce
hostilities from the Romans, who spread fire and blood over all
of Galilee, killing any who were capable of bearing arms. The

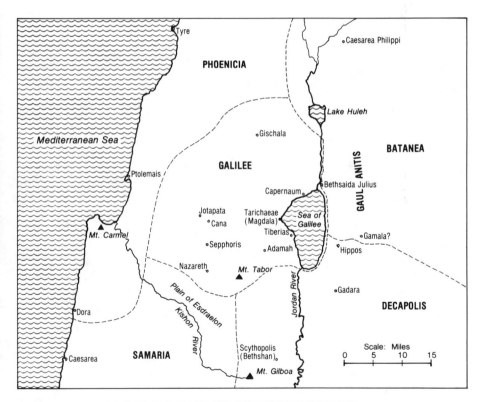

GALILEE AND ENVIRONS IN THE FIRST CENTURY A.D.

only places of security were those cities that had been fortified by Josephus.

The Roman Army

W III,64   Titus quickly arrived from Alexandria, bringing the Fifteenth legion, and joined his father at Ptolemais, where Vespasian waited with the Fifth and Tenth legions, which were the most distinguished of all. Twenty-three cohorts accompanied the legions, as well as auxiliaries furnished by Kings Antiochus, Agrippa, and Soaemus, as well as the Arab Malchus. The total strength of Vespasian's forces, horse and foot, including the kings' contingents, amounted to 60,000, not counting the many servants and camp followers, who also had military training.

The Romans never wait for war before training their army. Rather, as if they had been born with weapons in their hands, they practice maneuvers also in peacetime, so that battle never shocks them. Their camps are model cities, well fortified, and

Ruins of one of the Roman camps at the siege of Masada. Both the square outlines of the camp and its streets, as well as the surrounding siege wall, have survived for nineteen centuries without archaeological intervention.

their tents erected along streets laid out symmetrically, with the headquarters of the commander-in-chief in the center. At daybreak, the men report to their respective centurions, the centurions salute the tribunes, and the tribunes wait on the commander-in-chief, who gives them the password and orders for the day. The infantry are armed with breastplate, helmet, a sword on the left, and a long dagger on the right. The cavalry, additionally, carry a pike as well as a quiver with long arrows. Perfect discipline welds the army into a single body, compact in ranks, alert in movements to the right or left, and prompt in responding to orders. Small wonder that the Roman empire has extended its boundaries to the east as far as the Euphrates, in the west to the ocean, in the south to Libya, and in the north to the Rhine. This is not to extol the Romans so much as to console those whom they have vanquished, and to deter others who may be tempted to revolt.

While Vespasian consolidated his forces in Ptolemais, Placidus continued to overrun Galilee. He observed that the fighting men always took refuge in the fortified cities, so he advanced against the strongest of them, Jotapata. He thought that by a sudden assault he could easily capture it, after which the other towns would surrender in fear. But he was greatly deceived, for the people of Jotapata, aware of his approach, ambushed him outside of the town, fighting eagerly for their wives and children, and quickly scattered them. Placidus, finding that he was too weak to capture the town, retreated.

Vespasian now marched his forces out of Ptolemais in the customary Roman order: light-armed auxiliaries and archers went in advance to repel any ambushes, followed by heavy infantry and cavalry; surveyors and road builders were next, preceding Vespasian and his officers with their equipment; then followed legionary cavalry, the mules bearing siege towers and other machines of war; next came the junior officers and the standards surrounding the eagles of the legions, followed by the trumpeters, a solid column of infantry, the servant corps, and mercenaries; finally, a rearguard of infantry and cavalry closed in the forces.

When he reached the frontiers of Galilee, Vespasian halted awhile to display his forces and intimidate the enemy into reconsidering and deserting. Josephus' troops, who were camped at a town called Garis, learning that the Romans might attack at any moment, dispersed and fled before they had even seen their enemy. Left with a few companions, Josephus saw that his forces were not sufficient to cope with the Romans, so he and the remnant of his troops took refuge in Tiberias.

W III,132   Vespasian advanced on the city of Gabara and conquered it at the first assault. On entering the town, the Romans put to death all males who were of age and set fire to the city and all the villages around it, so bitter was their memory of Cestius' defeat.

Josephus' retreat to Tiberias filled its inhabitants with alarm, for they felt—correctly—that he would never have fled there unless he had lost all hope of success. Indeed, he foresaw the final catastrophe toward which the Jews were heading, but he would not betray his command. He therefore wrote to the Jerusalem authorities and informed them of the exact state of affairs, advising them either to negotiate or to send him an army able to cope with the Romans.

June, A.D. 67   When Vespasian heard that most of the enemy had fled to Jotapata, he was impatient to capture it. He sent a force to level the road leading to it, which was a stony mountain trail, difficult for infantry and impassible for cavalry. In four days the work was completed, and a broad highway opened for the troops. Josephus now hurried from Tiberias to Jotapata, and his arrival encouraged the Jews there.

Vespasian found this news a godsend, for Josephus, the man reputed to be the wisest of his enemies, had thus imprisoned himself. Vespasian camped at Jotapata on a hill about a mile from the town, selecting a site as conspicuous as possible to intimidate the enemy. Weary from a full day's march, the Romans did not launch an immediate attack, but surrounded the city with a double cordon of infantry and a third of cavalry, cutting off every hope of escape. This, however, inspired the Jews with the valor of necessity.

The Siege of Jotapata

W III,150   The next day the attack began. Vespasian ordered his archers and slingers to shoot, while he himself led the infantry up a slope that led to the least defensible part of the wall. Josephus rushed there with the entire garrison and drove the Romans from the ramparts. Great feats of daring were performed by both sides until night parted the combatants. The following morning and for the next five days, the Romans continued to make their assaults, while the Jews resisted bravely from their battlements.

Jotapata is surrounded by deep ravines on three sides, and is accessible only from the north, where there is a descending ridge of mountain. But Josephus had also enclosed this part within his wall to prevent an enemy from occupying the spur that commanded it. Vespasian and his officers decided to raise an embankment against the most accessible part of the wall. The whole army was sent out to procure materials, and they stripped all the surrounding mountains of timber and stone, and proceeded to build the earthworks. In order to protect themselves from projectiles hurled at them by their assailants, they spread screens of interlaced vines over props. Under this protection, they worked safely, although the Jews impeded the workers with great boulders.

Vespasian now brought out his artillery engines, 160

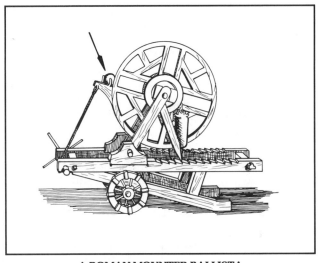

A ROMAN MOUNTED BALLISTA
The machine is poised to hurl a stone projectile (at arrow). The ratcheting adjusts for the weight of various missiles.

in all, and aimed them at those who defended the battlements. The catapults shot a huge volley of lances, and the stone-projectors hurled great blocks of enormous weight. There was also a

BALLISTA
The Roman ballista shot stones, up to 160 pounds in weight, at an angle of about 50° over an average range of 300 to 500 yards.

hail of firebrands and arrows, all of which soon cleared the battlements of the enemy. The Jews, however, rushed out in guerilla groups, stripping off the shelters and attacking the workers before setting fire to the props and screens. Vespasian noticed that the spaces between the earthworks provided openings for attack, so he united all the shelters and thus prevented these destructive raids.

The embankment was now rising and almost reached the level of the battlements. To offset this, Josephus directed masons to raise the height of the wall, but they said that it would be impossible to build under such a shower of projectiles. Josephus then ordered tall stakes driven into the top of the wall, and stretched fresh rawhides of oxen across them. Against this shielding curtain, the stones fell back harmless and the moisture of the hides quenched the firebrands. Thus screened, the builders raised the wall to a height of twenty cubits and crowned it with a strong parapet. The Romans, who thought they were already masters of the town, were struck with dismay at the ingenuity of Josephus and the bravery of the besieged.

W III,181   Inspired with fresh confidence by their new fortification, the Jotapatans again rushed out in bands to harass the Romans and burn their works. Vespasian finally decided to stop fighting and resort to a blockade to starve the city into surrender, so he kept all exits from the city strictly guarded. The besieged were well supplied with grain and other provisions, except salt, but they lacked water. Since there were no springs within the town, the inhabitants depended on rainwater, but it rarely rains there in summer, the current season. From the first, therefore, Josephus had put them on water rations. When the Romans on higher slopes saw the besieged all flocking to one spot to have water doled out to them, they aimed their catapults on that spot and killed some of them.

Vespasian thought that the cisterns would soon be dry and the city forced to surrender, but to crush this hope, Josephus hung dripping garments from the battlements, so that the whole wall suddenly streamed with water. The Roman general, losing hope of conquering the city through thirst, reverted to force, which was just what the Jews desired, for they preferred to die in battle rather than by thirst and famine.

Josephus devised another scheme to obtain supplies. A gully led down to the western ravine, which the Romans neglected to guard, but through which Josephus sent letters to the Jews outside and received in return supplies for the city. The messengers crept past the sentries on all fours with fleece on their backs, so that they might look like dogs, but the Roman guards eventually detected them and blocked the gully.

Josephus now began to think of his own safety, and debated with the leading citizens about escaping. But the people, learning of his intention, begged him to remain, as their one hope of being saved. He replied that he could do more for them on the outside by mustering the Galileans and creating a diversion to draw the Romans from their walls.

Unmoved by these arguments, the people only clung to him more closely, old men, women, and children falling in tears before him. Moved with compassion at their distress, Josephus decided to remain, and said, "Now is the time for combat, when there is no hope of safety. To exchange life for great deeds handed down in the memory of posterity is glorious!" He then burst out with the bravest of his troops, scattering the sentries. Forcing his way to the Roman camp, he tore away the skins which sheltered the men on the embankments and set the works on fire. Josephus repeated these attacks over the next days until Vespasian warned his troops not to engage with men bent on death.

The Ram

Now that the embankment was approaching the ramparts, Vespasian had the battering ram advanced into position. The

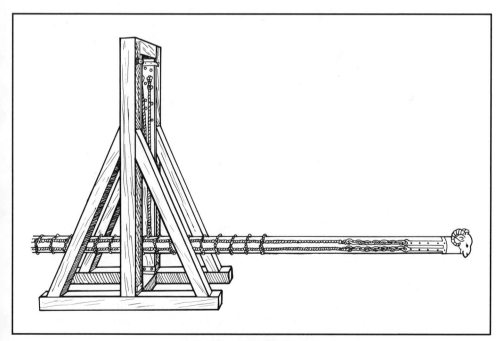

ROMAN BATTERING RAM
Suspended from a vertical frame, the ram was capable of enormous horizontal thrust. A protective canopy was often erected over the frame to ward off enemy missiles.

ram is composed of a large beam, like the mast of a ship, on one end of which is a mass of iron in the shape of a ram's head, whence its name. It is suspended by ropes and hung from a beam above, which is supported at both ends by upright posts. A large group of men first pull the ram backward, then heave it forward so that it batters the wall. No wall or town can withstand its repeated assaults.

The Romans now swept the battlements with a continual discharge from their artillery engines, as well as from their archers and slingers, so that the Jews could not obstruct the advance of the ram. At the first blow of the ram, the wall was shaken, and a fearful shriek arose from the town, as if it had already been taken. Seeing that repeated battering at the same spot would collapse the wall, Josephus ordered sacks filled with chaff let down by ropes at the spot where the ram battered, so that they would deflect the head and cushion its force. But the Romans then used long poles with scythes at the ends to cut down the sacks, so that the ram recovered its efficiency, and the wall began to give way. As a last resort, Josephus and his comrades grabbed all the dry wood they could find and rushed out to set fire to the machines and shelters of the besiegers. The Romans, astounded at this audacity, were beaten by the flames, which consumed in one hour the effort of many days.

On this occasion, a Jew named Eleazar lifted an enormous stone and hurled it at the ram with such force that he broke off its head. Leaping down from the wall, he carried off his prize to the base of the ramparts. Though transfixed with five arrows, he scaled the wall, displayed his trophy to all, but then, writhing under his wounds, fell headfirst with the ram.

W III,235   The Romans again set up the ram, and went on battering the wall at the same place. Just then, an arrow hit Vespasian in the sole of his foot, which caused great alarm among the Romans, especially Titus. But Vespasian easily relieved their fears, and incited them to fight that night more fiercely against the Jews. Although many of them now fell, they continued to heave down stones and fiery combustibles on the besiegers.

Towards morning, the wall, after incessant battering, fell before the ram. The defenders, however, set up defenses opposite the breach before the Romans could fix their scaling ladders. To open the breach, Vespasian ordered his bravest cavalry to dismount and storm through it the moment the escalade was ready. After them he marshaled the elite of his infantry, while archers and artillery were posted to the rear. He also ordered scaling ladders placed against parts of the wall that were still intact, to draw defenders away from the breach.

Josephus, seeing his design, placed the old and fatigued to guard these sections of the wall, but stationed his bravest to defend the breach. He told his men to ignore the war cry of the legions and wait until the archers had emptied their quivers. But when the Romans fixed their scaling gangways they should jump on them and fight to avenge their city. "Place before your eyes," he said, "your fathers and children and wives about to be butchered, and, anticipating the rage you will feel, let it loose on the ones who seek to kill them!"

When the women and children saw their city encircled and the enemy with sword in hand at the breach, and the mountainside above them glittering with arms, they raised a great shriek. But Josephus shut the women inside their homes so they would not discourage the men, and commanded them to be silent. He then took his post at the breach and awaited the attack.

The trumpets of the invaders sounded simultaneously and the Romans, with a terrific war cry, rushed to attack. Josephus' comrades covered their ears from the noise, and their bodies from the volleys. But the moment the scaling planks were laid, they dashed out on them before the Romans could cross, attacking them gallantly. Yet the Romans were able to pour fresh troops on the Jews and drove them back as they grew exhausted. W III,265

As they now climbed the ramparts, Josephus had a large quantity of boiling oil poured over the Romans, who rolled down the bulwarks in excruciating agony, for the burning oil trickled through their armor and penetrated to the skin. Writhing in anguish, they tumbled off the scaling bridges, and those who tried to escape were blocked by their comrades who were pressing forward.

But the Romans, undaunted by the tortures of their companions, continued to advance on the battlements. The Jews, however, poured boiled fenugreek* over the gangways, causing the Romans to slip and slide. Some were trampled to death, while others fell down on the embankment and were pierced by Jewish arrows.

Toward evening, Vespasian recalled his troops, who had suffered many casualties, and later had them raise the embankment. He then built three towers on it, 50 feet high and covered on all sides with sheet iron, so that they would be both firm and fireproof. In these he placed his slingers, archers, and the lighter artillery engines, which poured projectiles on the Jews, who were unable to harm their assailants protected inside the towers. Although they had to abandon the wall, the Jews rushed out against any who tried to renew the escalade. Jotapata thus continued to hold out, although its defenders were falling day after day, unable to retaliate against the enemy.

---

* A legume grown in Palestine for fodder, which would have been in flower during the month of July.

Other Rebellions

W III,289   At this time, Vespasian dispatched Trajan,* commander of the Tenth legion, with 1,000 horse and 2,000 footmen, against a town in the vicinity of Jotapata, called Japha, which was in revolt. As Trajan approached Japha, the inhabitants advanced against him, but he soon chased them inside the first of their double ring of walls, with his troops at their heels. But when they reached the inner wall, their fellow citizens shut the gates, thus excluding both their friends and enemies. Trapped between the two walls, the Galileans were slaughtered within sight of their friends, begging them all the while to open the gates. But the people inside were afraid of letting the enemy in. Meanwhile the fugitives, crushed by the disloyalty of their friends, did not resist and were killed, 12,000 in all.

Trajan sent a message to Vespasian, requesting that his son Titus be dispatched to complete the victory. Accordingly, Titus led the assault on the city with an additional force. When the Galileans quickly abandoned the walls, Titus and his troops scaled the ramparts and mastered the city. Inside, however, a desperate struggle took place, with men attacking the Romans in the alleys, while the women pelted them from the houses. But eventually the men were all killed, and only infants and women were spared, who were then sold as slaves.

Misfortunes also befell the Samaritans. They had not joined in the revolt, but had not learned from the failure of their neighbors, for they were thinking of rebellion and had collected a great force at their sacred Mount Gerizim. In order to nip this rebellion in the bud, Vespasian sent Cerealis, commander of the Fifth legion, with an armed force against the Samaritans. Cerealis surrounded the base of the mountain during the whole torrid day. It was midsummer, and the Samaritans, who had taken no provisions, were short of water, and several died of thirst while others deserted to the Romans. Assuming that the Samaritans were now greatly weakened, Cerealis ascended the mountain, surrounded the enemy, and offered them pardon if they surrendered. But when the overtures were rejected, he attacked and massacred them, 11,600 in all.

W III,316   Meanwhile, Jotapata was still holding out, but on the forty-seventh day of the siege, the Roman earthworks topped the wall. A deserter now informed Vespasian that those left inside the town were reduced in numbers and in strength, and could not resist a vigorous assault. In the early morning, he said, the

---

* Father of the future emperor.

sentinels were falling asleep at their posts from sheer exhaustion, and that would be the time to attack.

Vespasian doubted the deserter because of the faithfulness of all the other Jews to their cause. But what he said appeared probable, and no serious harm could come from making the attack. So he marshaled his army for the assault, and early in the morning the Romans approached in silence and under cover of a dense fog. Titus was the first to mount the wall, followed by a tribune and a few soldiers who killed the sentries, and then Placidus and Cerealis came over with their troops. The citadel was taken and the city captured before the inhabitants knew it, for most were asleep or enveloped in the thick mist. Remembering what they had suffered during the siege, the Romans showed no mercy to the defenders. They ruthlessly slaughtered the Jews, and many of Josephus' men chose suicide to capture. On the following days, the Romans searched the hiding places, butchering all but women and children, of whom 1,200 were taken prisoner. The capture and siege had claimed 40,000 Jewish lives, and Vespasian ordered Jotapata razed, reducing all its forts to ashes.

The Capture of Josephus

The Romans instituted a search for the body of Josephus, but W III,340 during the massacre he had slipped away into a deep pit, in the side of which was a large cavern invisible from above. Here he found 40 distinguished people in hiding, with considerable provisions. During the day he lay hidden, but at night he attempted to escape from the city. Since every exit was closely guarded, however, he had to return to the cavern. For two days he escaped detection, but on the third a woman who had been in the cave was captured and betrayed the secret.

Vespasian at once sent two tribunes with orders to offer Josephus protection and induce him to come up. They failed to persuade him, and Vespasian sent another tribune, Nicanor, who was a friend of Josephus. Nicanor assured Josephus that because of his valor he was rather an object of admiration than of hatred to the commanders. Vespasian, he said, would never have sent a friend for the purpose of deceiving him, and wanted to save a brave man.

While Josephus was hesitating, the Roman troops in their rage tried to throw fire into the cavern, but their commander, anxious to take the Jewish general alive, restrained them. Josephus suddenly recalled those nightly dreams in which God had foretold to him the fate of the Jews and the destinies of the Romans. He now silently prayed, "Since you have chosen me to announce what is to come, I will consent to live, but I call you to witness that I go, not as a traitor, but as your servant.''

But when he was about to surrender, the Jews in the cavern pointed their swords at him and threatened to kill him as a traitor if he submitted. Josephus tried to persuade them that it was right to save one's own life when it could be done without dishonor, and it was a great sin to throw it away unless in open warfare against an enemy. But they ran at him from all sides, and, with their blades at his throat, he finally warded them off with his general's authority. "If we must die," he then said, "let it not be by our own, but by each other's hands. Let us draw lots, and the one who draws the first lot will be killed by him who draws the second, and so on through our entire number, so that no one escapes.''

They readily agreed, and he drew lots with the rest. Each one in turn bared his throat to the next, until—should one say by fortune or by the providence of God?*—Josephus and one other remained alone. Josephus persuaded this man to surrender along with himself to Nicanor, who brought him before Vespasian. The Romans crowded around him on all sides, those at a distance shouting that he should be killed, but those near him thought of his exploits and pitied him. Titus in particular was struck by Josephus' nobility in misfortune, and Titus' intercession with his father was the main reason the prisoner was spared. Vespasian ordered that he be closely guarded, however, intending to send him to Nero.

W III,399   Josephus asked for a private interview with Vespasian, and all withdrew except Titus and two of his friends. "You think, Vespasian,'' Josephus said, "that you have a mere captive in Josephus, but I come to you as messenger of a greater destiny. Why send me to Nero? Do you think he will continue in office? You, Vespasian, will be Caesar and emperor—you and your son here. For you are master not only of me, but of sea and land, and of the whole human race.''

Vespasian at first discounted this declaration of Josephus as flattery, but gradually came to believe it. One of the friends of Titus who was present expressed his surprise that Josephus had been unable to predict either the fall of Jotapata or his own captivity, but Josephus replied that he had predicted both these things. Vespasian privately questioned the prisoners regarding these statements, and finding them true, began to believe that Josephus really was a prophet. Although he kept him in chains, he presented him with clothes and other articles, and treated him with kindness.

---

* One should probably say, "by the manipulation of Josephus.'' His veracity here is open to question.

PIRATES, 22
REBELS, AND VICTIMS

Vespasian now marched to Caesarea, where the army and its W III,409 commander were received cordially, mainly because of their hatred of the vanquished. Accordingly, they loudly demanded the punishment of Josephus, but Vespasian refused. He remained with two of his legions in Caesarea for the winter, and sent the third—the Fifteenth—to Scythopolis.

Meanwhile, some displaced Jews had rebuilt Joppa, which had been destroyed by Cestius, and constructed a fleet of pirate ships to raid the traffic between Syria, Phoenicia, and Egypt, making navigation there quite impossible. Vespasian sent a force against Joppa, which, finding the city unguarded, entered it by night. The inhabitants fled in terror to their ships, where they passed the night beyond reach of the enemy's missiles.

Joppa has no safe harbor, only a crescent-shaped roadstead with two stony reefs. The next morning, a fierce wind, called by sailors the "Black Norther," dashed the ships against each other or into the rocks. They could neither escape to the open sea, nor make for land, on account of the Romans, and so they foundered among the billows or were shattered on the shoals. Anyone swept to shore was immediately massacred by the Romans, and the blood of 4,200 corpses turned the sea red. Joppa was razed to the ground, but the citadel was garrisoned by the Romans, so that it would not again become a pirates' nest.

When rumors of the fall of Jotapata reached Jerusalem, they W III,432 were at first discounted, since no eyewitness had confirmed them. But when the truth was established and Josephus was reported to have been killed, Jerusalem was filled with profound sorrow. Yet when it was learned that he had surrendered to the Romans, the wailing for Josephus gave way to the fiercest indignation. He was cursed as a coward and a traitor, and the people were driven more fiercely to vengeance against both Rome and Josephus.

Vespasian, however, had gone to visit Agrippa's realm, since the king wanted to entertain him, while also using Vespasian's troops to quell disorders in his own kingdom. Vespasian marched to Caesarea Philippi, where the army rested for twenty days. When he learned that Tarichaeae had revolted and Tiberias was on the verge, he advanced with three legions and camped near Tiberias. He sent forward Valerian, a decurion, at the head of 50 horse to propose negotiations to the citizens, for Vespasian had heard that the people wanted peace, but had been compelled to revolt by a rebellious party. When Valerian came near the city, he and his troops dismounted, but before any talks, the rebel leaders, led by a certain Jesus, charged out at them. Not wanting to fight without orders from his general, Valerian and five others fled on foot, while Jesus' men seized the steeds and led them back in triumph.

Dreading the consequences of this affair, the leading citizens hurried to the Roman camp and implored Vespasian not to punish the entire city for the crime of a few, since the majority, they said, were friendly to the Romans. Because Agrippa was very concerned for the town, Vespasian yielded to these entreaties. Jesus and his party, thinking it no longer safe to remain at Tiberias, fled to Tarichaeae. The next day, Vespasian led his army into Tiberias and was received with acclamations. In compliment to Agrippa, he did not allow his soldiers to plunder the city, and because the king guaranteed the future fidelity of the inhabitants, the walls were not destroyed.

The Fate of Tarichaeae

W III,462   Vespasian then advanced upon Tarichaeae, where many insurgents had fled, relying on its strength. It had been fortified by Josephus, and was situated on the lake called Gennesar,* where they could embark on ships if defeated on land. While the Romans were entrenching their camp, Jesus and his band boldly rushed out. Dispersing the workmen, they leveled part of the structures, falling back before they sustained any loss. The Romans pursued them to their ships, but the rebels sailed out only far enough to leave the Romans in range and attacked them by sea.

---

* The Sea of Galilee.

The Sea of Galilee, looking northwest toward Tarichaeae (Magdala).

When Vespasian learned that a huge number of Jews had assembled on the plain outside Tarichaeae, he sent his son against them with 600 elite cavalry. Titus sent back for reinforcements, but, noting that many of his men were anxious to charge at once while some were dismayed at the immense size of the enemy, he urged them to secure the victory before the reinforcements arrived to share the glory. He inspired his men with such ardor that they were not pleased when Trajan arrived with 400 horse to assist them. Vespasian also dispatched 2,000 archers to the side of a hill opposite the town in order to keep the enemy on the ramparts from giving any assistance to the army outside. Titus now led the charge against the enemy, who withstood the attack for a short time, but were soon dispersed and fled towards the city. The Romans pursued, making lanes of dead through the bunched masses of Jews, while the rest escaped into town.

But here a fierce contention awaited them. The residents, anxious to protect their property, had disapproved of the war from the first, whereas the rebels from the outside wanted to maintain it. The two parties were on the point of coming to blows when Titus, who overheard the commotion, cried out, "Now is the time to attack, while they are torn by discord!"

W III,497   He leaped onto his horse, led his troops into the lake,* rode through the water, and entered the town. Terror-struck at his daring, those on the ramparts abandoned them without a fight, while many who rushed to the lake were killed by the advancing Romans. In the town itself there was mass slaughter until Titus, having punished the guilty, took pity on the natives and stopped the massacre. When those who had taken refuge on the lake saw the city taken, they withdrew as far as possible from the enemy. Titus sent word of this victory to his father, who was delighted and came there immediately. He ordered rafts built to pursue the fugitives, and these were soon constructed.

The lake of Gennesar has sweet, excellent water, perfectly pure, and the lake ends in pebbly or sandy beaches everywhere. It has a cooler temperature than river or spring water, and contains species of fish different in taste and appearance from those found elsewhere. The Jordan runs through the middle of the lake, with its source apparently at Panion but in reality at Philale, passing through a subterranean channel to Panion. Skirting the lake is a region of fertile soil and natural beauty, growing every species of plant—the walnut thriving next to the palm, the fig, or the olive—with fruits produced ten months of the year. The country is supplied by a very fertile spring, called Capernaum.

When his rafts were ready, Vespasian embarked his troops and ordered them to attack the fugitives. In their small skiffs, the Jews could not cope with the well-armed Romans on the rafts, and merely threw stones at them from a distance, which rattled off their armor. The Romans boarded their vessels, or killed them from the rafts with arrows or long lances. If any clung to the side of a raft, their hands or their heads were cut off. The survivors were driven to the shore, where they were killed by the Romans lining the beaches, so that not a man escaped. The lake was red with blood, the shores strewn with wrecks and swollen carcasses, which, in following days, polluted the district with a horrible stench. The dead, including the number who had fallen defending the city, totaled 6,700.

W III,532   After the battle, Vespasian set up a tribunal in Tarichaeae. He sat in judgment over the immigrant rebels, whom he had separated from the native inhabitants, consulting with his generals on whether their lives also should be spared. The officers, however, were in favor of putting them all to death as desperate

---

* Taking an aquatic route, since the town had no wall facing the lake.

men, who, if let loose, would stir up rebellion wherever they went. But if Vespasian then massacred Tarichaeae, he feared it would incite the inhabitants to rebellion. He therefore granted them amnesty, but ordered them to leave town only by the road which led to Tiberias. Promptly believing what they fondly hoped for, the wretches set out confidently along the permitted route, while the Romans lined the road to cut off any escape, and shut them inside Tiberias.

Soon afterwards, Vespasian entered Tiberias and had them all moved to the stadium, where the old and unserviceable, some 1,200, were put to death. From the youth he selected 6,000 of the most robust and sent them to Nero at the isthmus,* while the rest, numbering 30,400, he sold as slaves, except for some who were subjects of Agrippa. These were sold by Agrippa himself. Sept., A.D. 67

The Siege of Gamala

After the fall of Tarichaeae, nearly all the garrisons and towns of Galilee submitted to the Romans, except for Gamala, Gischala, and a rebel force on Mount Tabor. Gamala belonged to the kingdom of Agrippa, and was built on a rugged mountain spur that slopes downward at each end and rises into a middle ridge like the hump of a camel, whence its name. Its sides plunge into inaccessible ravines, and the only approach is where the "tail" hangs on to the mountain, but here a deep trench had been dug to impede access. The houses were built one above the other on the steep slopes, and the whole city seemed as if it would fall down upon itself. Josephus had rendered it still more impregnable with walls, mines, and trenches, so that, although the garrison was not as large as that which had defended Jotapata, the people felt secure and had already held out for seven months against the troops of Agrippa. W IV,1

Breaking camp, Vespasian advanced on Gamala, and since he could not surround it with troops, he stationed sentries where feasible and occupied the mountain that overhung it. Next he started earthworks at the tail with two legions, while the third filled up the trenches and ravines. During these operations, King Agrippa approached the ramparts and tried to persuade the people to surrender, but he was struck with a stone on the right elbow by a slinger, and was immediately surrounded by his troops. The Romans were enraged, and pressed the siege with renewed vigor.

---

* Of Corinth, where Nero himself broke ground for a planned canal, see Suetonius, *Nero*, 10.

The embankments were quickly completed, and the siege engines brought into position. Chares and Joseph, the Jewish commanders in Gamala, readied their forces, who manned the ramparts, and for a while kept at bay those who were advancing the engines. But the catapults and stone-projectors drove them back into the city. The Romans now applied the battering rams at three different points and broke through the wall. Rushing into the breach with trumpet blasts and a battle cry, the Romans stormed into the defenders. For a time the Jews repulsed the Romans, until, overpowered by numbers, they retreated to the upper town. Here, turning on their assailants, they drove the Romans down the slopes and killed them as they struggled up the steep passages.

Since the Romans could not repel the enemy above them, nor retreat against comrades pressing on them from below, they took refuge on the roofs of the houses, which rose one above the other on the slopes. The houses could not bear the weight of so many soldiers and gave way, one house collapsing several others below it in its fall, which, in turn, brought down others beneath it. Many Romans were buried in the ruins or died of suffocation from the dust. The men of Gamala seized the advantage to attack their besiegers, the debris supplying them plenty of boulders and the enemy's dead providing them with weapons. The Romans who tried to flee often killed their own comrades in the confusion, or were finished off by the Jews.

Vespasian himself had fought his way to the highest quarter of the town, where he found himself in the thick of danger, with only a few followers around him. Even Titus was absent, having just been sent off to Mucianus in Syria.* But Vespasian linked his comrades together with enveloping shields and retreated step by step, not turning his back until he was outside the ramparts.

W IV,39   The Romans were depressed at the disaster and ashamed that they had allowed their general to be exposed to such danger. But Vespasian encouraged them, saying that the reverse was merely due to careless fighting on difficult ground.

The people of Gamala momentarily gained confidence from their impressive success, but when they reflected that now they were cut off from any hope of terms, and that their supplies were giving out, they grew dejected. Yet the bravest continued to guard the breaches, and the rest manned what remained of the wall. But while the Romans were completing their embankment

---

* The legate of Syria who would become one of the strongest supporters of Vespasian in his drive for emperorship.

and preparing for another assault, the people started to run out of town down pathless ravines, where no sentries were posted, or through underground passages.

Gamala Falls

As a diversion from the siege, Vespasian sent Placidus with W IV,54 600 horse to attack the rebels on Mount Tabor. Finding ascent of the mountain unfeasible, Placidus made peace overtures to trick them down into the plain, where he could capture them. The Jews came down, but with the intention of attacking Placidus when off guard. Placidus' strategy, however, succeeded, for when the Jews assaulted, he pretended to flee. When he had drawn his enemies down into the plain, Placidus' cavalry wheeled around and scattered his pursuers with mass slaughter, cutting off their retreat to the mountain. Those who escaped fled to Jerusalem, while the natives surrendered the mountain to Placidus, under promise of protection.

Gamala still resisted, although the people were escaping or dying of famine. Early one morning, three Roman soldiers stole up and undermined an enemy tower without being noticed by the sentries. They rolled away five of the supporting stones and jumped back just before the tower fell with a tremendous crash, carrying the sentries headlong with it. Many were killed by the Romans as they tried to escape, among them Joseph. Chares [the other commander] was sick in his bed, but died of terror. The Romans, warned by their former disaster, did not attack at once.

Titus, who had now returned, was angry at the loss which the W IV,70 Romans had sustained during his absence, and entered the city with 200 horse and a body of infantry. The people grabbed their families and fled to the citadel or were killed without mercy, their blood flowing down the slopes of Gamala. Vespasian now entered the town with his entire force to aid the attack against the citadel. The rock on which it stood was surrounded on all sides by precipices, and from its summit the Jews hurled rocks and missiles on their assailants.

But to seal their destruction, a storm arose that blew in the faces of the Jews, and accelerated the Roman arrows while rendering theirs harmless. The Romans mounted the crag and quickly surrounded and slaughtered them. Savage because of their former defeat, they spared no one, not even infants, whom they flung from the citadel. Multitudes threw themselves headlong down the precipices, and their despair was even more fatal than the rage of the Romans, since the Romans killed 4,000 while over 5,000 hurled themselves over the cliffs. No one

Nov.,   escaped except two women who had hidden themselves. **Thus**
A.D. 67 Gamala fell.

Gischala

W IV,84   Only Gischala, a small town in Galilee, now remained in revolt. The inhabitants, an agricultural people, were inclined to peace, but the charlatan John commanded malcontents in the town who incited the people to defiance. Vespasian sent Titus with 1,000 horse against the town, and directed the Tenth legion to proceed to Scythopolis. Vespasian himself, with the other two legions, returned to Caesarea in order to rest his men before attacking Jerusalem.

Riding up to Gischala, Titus saw that it could easily be captured. But because he wanted to shed as little blood as possible, and knowing that many of the people wished to submit, he promised them pardon if they surrendered. Since the brigands had completely occupied the wall, the citizens were not allowed to ascend it as these terms were offered. John replied that he was satisfied with the proposals, but because it was the Sabbath, when Jews could neither fight nor make a treaty of peace, he asked Titus to wait until the next day. Titus agreed.

That night, John, seeing no Roman guard around the town, escaped with his band towards Jerusalem, followed by many non-combatants with their families. After some distance, however, he abandoned the women and children in his flight. They fell from fatigue and were trampled or screamed to their husbands and relatives to wait for them. But John cried, "Save yourselves, and have your revenge on the Romans if they catch any we leave behind!" So the men hurried onward, leaving the women and children alone in the darkness.

When day broke, Titus appeared before the walls [of Gischala] to conclude the treaty. The people threw open the gates and hailed him as a liberator, but informed him of John's flight. Titus immediately sent a squadron of cavalry to pursue John, but he escaped safely to Jerusalem. Of those who fled with him, however, 6,000 were killed, and the Romans brought back nearly 3,000 women and children. Although he was mortified at failing to punish John, Titus entered the city to general acclaim. He merely threatened offenders with future punishment should they disturb the peace, leaving a garrison to secure the town. Galilee was now entirely subdued, having provided the Romans substantial training for the coming Jerusalem campaign.

THE ZEALOTS IN JERUSALEM 23

When John entered Jerusalem, he and the fugitives were sur- WIV,121
rounded by vast crowds eagerly asking for outside news. The
newcomers, still hot and gasping, put on a boastful air and said
they had not fled from the Romans, but had come to defend the
capital, thinking it reckless to risk their lives for defenseless
little towns like Gischala. When, however, they mentioned the
fall of Gischala, their hearers understood that their "retreat"
meant "flight," and had a premonition of their own impending
capture.

John, however, went around inciting groups to war, portraying the Romans as weaklings, who, even if they had wings,
could never clear the walls of Jerusalem. They had already
experienced difficulty in subduing the villages of Galilee, he
claimed, and had worn out their engines against these walls.
The young believed him and were incited to take up arms, but
the old and prudent mourned over the future. Jerusalem was
now divided into two hostile factions: the enthusiasts for war
and the friends of peace. Indeed, the whole province [of Judea]
was torn by civil dissension, as the parties for peace and war
fought for supremacy in every city. Whenever the people had a
respite from the Romans, they attacked each other, leaving
families and friends divided.

In the country, bands of outlaws gathered to ravage the district, since the [Roman] garrisons in the towns provided little or
no protection to the distressed. Finally satiated with pillage, the
brigands gathered together in one band and stole into Jerusalem,
for this city, according to ancient custom, received any of Jewish
blood. They eventually ruined the city, consuming those supplies which might have been sufficient for the combatants, and
bringing on the people the miseries of sedition and famine.

315

The bandits grew so bold that they committed robberies and murders in broad daylight, with distinguished citizens as victims. Their first was Antipas, a man of royal birth and treasurer of the city. They arrested and imprisoned him as well as other leaders, while panic seized the people, each frightened for his personal safety. Since the outlaws feared that an attempt might be made to rescue the prisoners, they sent an assassin of theirs named John with ten men to execute the captives. Having butchered them, the brigands claimed that the prisoners had discussed surrender with the Romans, and they had therefore slain those who would betray their liberty.

W IV,147   Next, the robbers rose to such a height of madness that they assumed authority to appoint to the high priesthood, selecting ignoble and low-born individuals for that office to gain accomplices in their impious crimes. Moreover, by slanderous stories, they set at odds officials in authority, and so increased their own power by creating divisions.

At last the people were ready for rebellion against the Zealots, instigated by Ananus, the eldest of the chief priests. The Zealots had taken refuge in the temple of God and turned it into a fortress, making the Holy Place their headquarters. They pretended that, according to ancient law, the high priest should be chosen by lot, although the succession was hereditary. Casting lots, the office fell on a coarse clown named Phanni, who scarcely knew what the high priesthood meant, yet they dressed him in the sacred vestments and taught him how to act. This shocking impiety, which to them was a subject of merriment, drew tears from the other priests, who grieved over this mockery of their law.

Such an outrage was more than the people could stand. Some of their outstanding leaders convened a general assembly against the Zealots, for so these heretics styled themselves, as if they were zealous in the cause of virtue instead of vice in its most extravagant form. Ananus addressed the multitude, his eyes filling with tears as he looked at the temple, and reproached them for enduring a tyranny worse than that of the Romans. It was a cause for bitter tears to see the votive offerings of the Romans at the temple on the one hand, and the spoils taken by their own countrymen on the other, who killed some of their own people whom even the Romans would have spared! The Romans had never overstepped the limits at the temple, but those who called themselves Jews strolled freely inside the Holy Place, their hands still hot with the blood of their countrymen.

W IV,193   The people demanded that he lead them against the Zealots, but while Ananus was mustering his forces, the Zealots rushed out of the temple and spared none who came in their way.

Ananus hastily collected the citizenry, who, though superior in numbers, were inferior to the Zealots in training. Both sides fought with the greatest fury, and the slaughter was enormous. The Zealots finally had to retreat into the temple, Ananus and his party rushing in with them. Losing the outer court, the Zealots fled into the inner and closed the gates. Ananus decided it was wrong to attack the sacred gates and introduce unpurified crowds, and instead stationed 6,000 armed men to guard the porticoes.

The ruin of Ananus and his entire party was due to John, whose flight from Gischala has been related. This crafty man, always plotting for despotic power, pretended to side with the populace. He daily attended the councils of Ananus and the leaders only to betray their secrets to the Zealots. To allay any suspicion, he was obsequious to Ananus and the leaders, but so overacted his part that he came under suspicion when the people found out that the Zealots knew of their plans. Yet it was not easy to punish John because he had many followers, with officials among them. They decided, therefore, to bind him by oath to keep good faith. Without any hesitation, John swore that he would be true to the people. Relying on his oath, Ananus and his party now admitted him without suspicion to their deliberations, and even sent him to negotiate with the Zealots.

John, however, as if he had sworn allegiance to the Zealots instead of against them, told them of the dangers he had incurred in rendering them secret service. He reported that Ananus had sent an embassy to surrender the city to Vespasian and appointed a purification service the next day so that Ananus' followers might enter the temple and attack the Zealots. Against so many opponents, John reported, the Zealots must either appeal for pardon or obtain some external aid, and hinted at help from the Idumeans. The Zealot leaders, learning that Ananus had invited the Romans to assist him—another of John's libels—finally resolved to call the Idumeans to their aid. They sent some swift messengers to report that Ananus was about to betray the city to the Romans, and that the Zealots had revolted in the cause of freedom, but were now imprisoned in the temple. Unless they received immediate help, they continued, they would soon be overcome and the city surrendered to the Romans.

The Idumeans Invade

A turbulent and chaotic people, the Idumeans mustered their forces and marched to Jerusalem with an army of 20,000. Ananus, who heard of their coming, closed the gates, but he W IV,231 favored persuasion rather than hostility. Thus Jesus, the chief priest next in age to Ananus, addressed the Idumeans from an adjacent tower. He denied any negotiations with the Romans and asked the Idumeans to do one of three things: unite with them in punishing the scoundrels, or enter the city unarmed and act as judges between the two parties, or depart and let the city settle its own affairs.

But the Idumeans would not listen to Jesus' proposals, and Simon, one of their leaders, replied that they had come as true patriots against men who were in a conspiracy to betray the land to the Romans. "Here before these walls," he said, "we will remain in arms until the Romans are tired of listening to you, or you convert to the cause of liberty!"

The Idumeans loudly applauded these words, and Jesus withdrew in dejection. The Idumeans were angry at being excluded from the city, and when they received no aid from the Zealots, whom they supposed stronger, many were sorry they had come. Still they were ashamed to return having accomplished nothing, so they camped before the walls. That night there was a terrific storm of wind and rain, lightning and extraordinary thunder. The Idumeans huddled together to keep each other warm, and overlapped their shields to keep off the rain. Concerned about their allies exposed to this terrible storm, the Zealots debated means of relief. The impetuous among them wanted to force their way through the sentries and open the gates to the Idumeans. But the more prudent objected, since the sentries were at full strength and angered against the Idumeans, while Ananus would be inspecting them at all hours. This *had* been his practice on other nights, but not on this one. As the night advanced, the sentries at the colonnade fell asleep. Meanwhile, the Zealots took some of the temple saws and severed the bars of the gates first at the temple and then of the city, the wind and thunder preventing them from being heard.

The Idumeans, supposing that Ananus and his party were attacking them, grasped their swords until they recognized their visitors and entered the city. At the request of those who had let them inside, the Idumeans first marched to the temple to liberate the Zealots. Some of the sentries were killed in their sleep and then the entire force was roused and snatched up their arms in defense. As long as they thought only the Zealots were attacking, the guards fought with spirit, but when they discovered that the Idumeans had invaded, most of them threw down their arms and gave way to lamentation. A few of the younger ones, however, fencing themselves in, gallantly fought the Idumeans, and, for a time, protected the weaker crowd, whose cries alerted the rest of the city. But the people were too frightened to help them, as the Zealots joined in the battle cry of the Idumeans, a din that added to the howl of the storm.

Atrocities in the City

The Idumeans spared none, slaughtering all the guards, and W IV,310 day dawned on 8,500 corpses. The invaders then rushed on the city, looting all the houses and killing any who came in their way. The chief priests Ananus and Jesus were killed, and their bodies thrown out without burial, although the Jews are usually so careful about funeral rites that even felons who have been crucified are taken down and buried before sunset.* The capture of the city virtually began with the death of Ananus.

The Zealots and the Idumean hordes now butchered the people as if they were a herd of unclean animals, while youths of noble birth they threw into prison, hoping some would join their party. Not one, however, listened to their proposals, all preferring to die rather than unite with these felons against their country. They were scourged, racked, tortured, and finally killed—12,000 of the young nobility—and their relatives did not dare to weep openly for them, but only behind closed doors.

Weary of slaughter, the Zealots now set up mock trials and courts of justice. They wanted to get rid of Zacharias, son of Baris, one of the most distinguished citizens, because he loved liberty and was also rich, and they wished to plunder his wealth. Accordingly, they summoned 70 of the non-Zealot leaders to the temple to play the role of judges (although with no authority) and accused Zacharias of treasonable correspondence with Vespasian. They brought no proof or evidence, but insisted that he should be convicted on their charges alone.

Zacharias boldly ridiculed their charges, and in a few words refuted the accusations against him; then he recited all the atrocities of his accusers. Stung by his taunts, the Zealots could hardly resist drawing their swords, but they let the farce play out, anxious to test the judges. The 70, however, preferred to die with the defendant rather than be responsible for his death and so brought in a unanimous verdict of acquittal.

The Zealots roared, and two of them rushed over and killed Zacharias in the middle of the temple, jesting over his prostrate body, ''Now you have our verdict, and a more effective release!'' They then threw him from the temple into the ravine below. The Zealots beat the judges with the backs of their swords, and drove them in disgrace into the city.

---

* Deuteronomy 21:22–23, and the familiar case of Jesus of Nazareth, John 19:31.

W IV,345   The Idumeans, offended at this barbarism, began to regret that they had come. One of the Zealots came to them privately and exposed the crimes of those who had invited them. He urged the Idumeans to return home and no longer support, by their presence, the murders and atrocities of the Zealots, who had duped them into becoming their accomplices by misrepresenting Ananus and his party as guilty of treason. Acting on this advice, the Idumeans first liberated about 2,000 prisoners, who fled from the city to Simon [the son of Giora], of whom we shall soon speak, and then returned home.

The people assumed that they were relieved of their enemies, but the Zealots acted as if freed from their critics rather than deprived of allies. They became all the more audacious, massacring the brave and the nobility out of fear and envy, respectively. They thought that their own safety depended on leaving no one in authority alive. They murdered Gurion, for example, a liberal democrat, and even Niger, that gallant veteran, who pointed to his scars as he was dragged through the city, but finally asked only that they bury him. Denied this, Niger called down on the Zealots the vengeance of the Romans, famine, pestilence, and civil strife—all of which were ratified by God. The only penalty for the most serious or most trivial charge was death. No one escaped but those whose humble birth put them beneath notice.

W IV,366   Hearing of the dissensions inside Jerusalem, many of the Roman officers urged Vespasian to attack the city. He replied that this would instantly reunite the Jews against the common enemy. If, however, they were left alone, they would go on destroying each other and give the Romans an easy victory. God was a better general than he, Vespasian continued, and was conferring victory on the Romans without risk.

Every day people fled Jerusalem, although all the exits were guarded, and anyone caught was killed unless he paid a bribe, in which case he was released. The wealthy, then, purchased escape and only the poor were slaughtered. The dead lay in heaps along the highways, since the Zealots impiously forbade the rites of burial, polluting the Deity by letting the dead decay in the sun. Whoever interred a relative was put to death. The Zealots trampled every human law and scoffed at the oracles of the prophets as fables of imposters. Yet they brought down on their country the fulfillment of an ancient prophecy: it stated that when sedition broke out in the city and natural hands defiled God's sanctuary, the temple would be burned to the ground and the city taken.

Division Among the Zealots

Aspiring to despotism, John [of Gischala] gathered a group of W IV, 389
the more depraved and withdrew from the coalition. Those who
scorned submission to a former equal or dreaded monarchial
rule formed an opposite party. The two groups seldom fought
each other, as both were rival plunderers of the populace. The
capital was thus afflicted with the three greatest evils—war,
tyranny, and factionalism—but the people found war the mild-
est, and many fled to the Romans for security.

But a fourth tragedy was underway to complete the nation's
ruin. Not far from Jerusalem was a fortress of great strength,
called Masada, erected by the ancient kings as a treasury for
their wealth and a refuge during war. The *sicarii* had taken
possession of it, but so far they had confined themselves to raids
on surrounding districts. But when they learned that the Roman
army was inactive and that Jerusalem was distracted by sedition
and tyranny, they attempted more daring exploits. And so at the
feast of Unleavened Bread, these assassins swooped down by
night on a small town called Engedi, scattered the men before

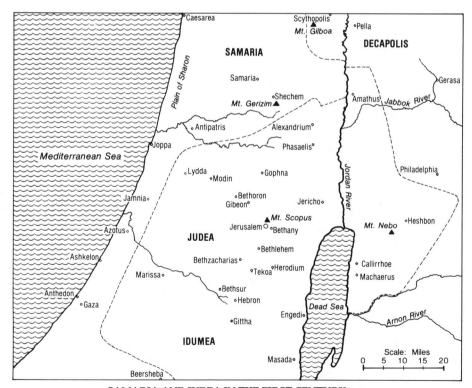

SAMARIA AND JUDEA IN THE FIRST CENTURY A.D.

they could grab their arms, and killed 700 women and children. They then ransacked the houses, took their crops, and carried off the booty to Masada. Many renegades flocked to them daily from every quarter, as other robber bands revived elsewhere until all Judea became a scene of plunder and ruin.

W IV,410   The Jewish refugees who had fled to Vespasian urged him to march on the capital and rescue its inhabitants, who, they said, were in great danger for their loyalty to the Romans. Vespasian thought it best to reduce the rest of the country first, and so broke camp to march on Gadara, the capital of Perea. The leading men of Gadara, who wanted to save their property, had sent a delegation to offer surrender. Gadara's rebels, at first unaware of this, killed the town's leaders who had originated the embassy and then fled when the Romans appeared. The Gadarenes threw open their gates to Vespasian, and welcomed him with acclamation. He left them a garrison for protection against the fugitives, for the Gadarenes had demolished their own walls to prove their love of peace.

The Romans Advance

March,   Vespasian sent 500 cavalry and 3,000 foot soldiers under
A.D, 68   Placidus to pursue those who had fled from Gadara, while he himself returned with the rest of his army to Caesarea. The fugitives swarmed into a village called Bethennabris, where they armed the young men and rushed out against the troops of Placidus. The Romans feigned a retreat, in order to lure them further from their walls, but then surrounded and killed many of them with javelins. The remainder of the fugitives fled back to the village, so closely pursued by the Roman cavalry that the Romans nearly entered the town with them. Placidus led the assault and by evening overcame the wall and the village. The inhabitants were slaughtered, and Bethennabris was reduced to ashes. But some fugitives escaped, creating panic across the countryside by claiming that the entire Roman army was advancing.

The whole population now fled to Jericho, where they hoped for safety. Placidus pursued them to the Jordan, killing all whom he overtook, but the river was swollen and unfordable, so [the Pereans] were compelled to stand and fight. Placidus charged them with his cavalry and drove multitudes into the river, where they drowned, killing 15,000 in battle and capturing about 2,200. The Romans took an immense booty of asses, sheep, camels, and oxen—the greatest blow that had befallen the Jews. Following up his good fortune, Placidus rapidly took town after town, and soon reduced the whole of Perea as far as Machaerus and Lake Asphaltitis. Here he embarked troops on shipboard to capture those who had taken refuge on the lake.

Meanwhile, Vespasian received news of the rebellion in Gaul, W IV, 440 and that Vindex had revolted from Nero. He foresaw the civil dissensions which threatened the empire, and decided that he had better end the Jewish war soon to calm the anxious Italians. During the winter, therefore, he garrisoned the villages and towns that he had conquered, but when spring broke he marched to Antipatris. Spending two days there to restore order, he advanced to Lydda, Jamnia, and Emmaus, where he left the Fifth legion. Then he marched into Idumea, where he massacred more than 10,000 and finally reached Jericho. He was June, joined there by Trajan. A.D. 68

Jericho lies in the Great Plain [Jordan Valley] between two barren ranges, and in summer is scorched and dry. Near Jericho, however, is a beautiful spring, which originally blighted fruit and caused women to miscarry. But the prophet Elisha, treated with much hospitality by the people of Jericho, cast a clay jar full of salt into the spring. Raising his right hand to heaven, he then implored that its waters be sweetened, and now they nourish many varieties of crops, date palms, balsam, and cypress. The climate, moreover, is so mild that the people wear linen when snow is falling throughout the rest of Judea.

The waters of Lake Asphaltitis [Dead Sea] are bitter and unproductive, but very buoyant. When Vespasian visited it, he ordered some who could not swim to be flung into deep water with their hands tied behind them, and they all bobbed to the surface and floated. The waters produce black masses of bitumen that float on the surface, which is useful for caulking ships and as

Arab women still draw water from Elisha's Spring at Jericho, which continues to serve the modern city.

an ingredient in medicines. Next to the lake is the land of Sodom, which was consumed by thunderbolts, and signs of the divine fire and faint traces of five cities are still visible.

W IV,486   Before the Romans arrived at Jericho, the inhabitants had escaped to the hill country near Jerusalem, so the city was deserted. Vespasian placed a garrison here, and another at Adida, in order to cover Jerusalem on all sides. He also sent Lucius Annius against Gerasa. Annius assaulted and won the city, killing 1,000 of its youth, plundering the property, and setting it on fire before advancing against surrounding villages.

Bust of Galba, Nero's successor (Louvre, Paris).

The whole country was now overrun, and all exit from Jerusalem prevented. Those who wanted to desert were closely watched by the Zealots, while those who did not yet favor the Romans were confined by the army, which hemmed in the city on all sides.

While Vespasian was preparing to march on Jerusalem, news reached him of Nero's violent death, so he delayed his expedition and waited anxiously to learn who would be the new emperor. When he heard that Galba had acceded, he sent his son Titus to receive his orders regarding the Jews, and Agrippa embarked with him. But while they were en route, Galba was assassinated and Otho succeeded as emperor, so Titus returned to his father at Caesarea without going to Rome. While the empire was in such flux, they refrained from carrying on the war, thinking it unwise to attack a foreign country while in anxiety over their own.

Simon, Son of Giora

W IV,503   But another war now threatened Jerusalem. Simon, son of Giora and a native of Gerasa, was not as cunning as John, who was now master of Jerusalem, but Simon was superior in physical strength and daring. These qualities had led Ananus the high priest to expel Simon from Acrabetene, after which he joined the brigands who had seized Masada. At first they regarded him with suspicion, but gradually he gained their confidence and joined them in raiding the surrounding country. He could not, however, tempt them to larger exploits, so Simon withdrew to the hills, where, by proclaiming freedom for slaves and rewards for others, he attracted villains of every sort. Soon he was spurred on to descend to the lowlands, and was joined also by men of rank in growing numbers. Simon fortified a village called Nain* as his headquarters, and deposited spoils and provisions in caves nearby, making it evident that he would soon attack Jerusalem.

Alarmed at his intentions, the Zealots marched out from Jerusalem to attack Simon, but were scattered and driven back into the city. He did not, however, attempt to take the city yet, but marched instead to Idumea with 20,000 men. The Idumeans mustered 25,000 and met Simon at the frontier, where a day-long battle was fought, but neither side gained the victory. Later, Simon returned with a larger force, and the Idumeans, alarmed at Simon's strength, decided to survey his forces before risking battle. James, an Idumean officer, volunteered his services and went to Simon, promising to betray the Idumeans in return for a post of honor under him. Simon consented, and James returned to his own people, frightening them with stories about the great numbers of the enemy, and advising surrender. He then sent a message to Simon, inviting him to advance. When Simon's army approached, James sprang on his horse and fled from the Idumeans, followed by accomplices he had corrupted. Seized with panic, the Idumean army dispersed before a blow was struck.

Simon captured Hebron, where he gained much booty, and advanced through Idumea, laying waste the entire country. Besides his regular forces, he had 40,000 followers, but his supplies were not sufficient for such a multitude. They therefore stole all they could find, and passed through the area like a swarm of locusts, leaving nothing but desert behind them.

The Zealots, afraid to meet Simon again in open warfare, placed ambushes in the passes, and captured his wife with her attendants. He advanced to the walls of Jerusalem, venting his rage on everyone Simon could capture outside the city. Old, unarmed men who ventured outside to gather herbs or wood were seized, tortured, and put to death. Others Simon sent back into the city with their hands cut off, and the message that unless his wife was returned at once, he would break down the wall and inflict a similar punishment on every resident. These threats so terrified even the Zealots that they sent his wife back to him.

---

* Not the Galilean village of the New Testament.

W IV,550   Vespasian, meanwhile, had left Caesarea, advancing on those places in Judea which had not yet submitted, and then rode with his cavalry up to the walls of Jerusalem. His officer Cerealis also invaded upper Idumea and took its towns, including Hebron. Every fortress was now conquered except Herodium, Masada, and Machaerus, which were held by the brigands, and Jerusalem itself.

Simon [son of Giora] now marched to Jerusalem and again camped outside its walls, killing any he caught going out into the country. The citizens thus found Simon outside more formidable than the Romans, and the Zealots inside more oppressive than either. The Galilean contingent among the Zealots, who had raised John [of Gischala] to power, were allowed by him to commit every excess. They looted the homes of the wealthy, murdered men, violated women, and assumed the dress as well as the passions of women, devising illegal pleasures and polluting the entire city. Those who fled the tyranny of John were massacred by Simon, and so there was no escape.

But the Idumean segment of John's army, envying his power and hating his cruelty, mutinied and attacked the tyrant, killing many of the Zealots. The rest were driven into the temple, from which John prepared to lead them against the people and the Idumeans. The latter feared that the Zealots might steal out of the temple by night, murder them, and set fire to the city. A council was therefore held with the chief priests, and they devised a remedy worse than disaster: to overthrow John, they decided to admit Simon, begging to introduce a second tyrant over their heads!

Spring,   Acclaimed by the people as their savior and guardian, Simon
A.D. 69   was admitted, and, after collecting plunder left in the city by John, he attacked the temple. The Zealots posted themselves on the colonnades and battlements and beat off their assailants, inflicting many casualties on Simon's ranks from their higher ground. To increase this advantage they erected four huge towers so that they could hurl their projectiles from a still greater height. On these they put their catapults and stone-throwers, as well as archers and slingers. These created havoc among Simon's troops, reducing their attacks, although they still held their ground.

Vespasian Proclaimed Emperor

W IV,585   In Rome, meanwhile, the emperor Galba had been murdered, and Otho succeeded, but Vitellius was chosen emperor by the legions of Germany. Conquered by the troops of Vitellius, Otho

committed suicide, and Vitellius marched in triumph to Rome. A.D. 69
But he converted Rome into a camp for his army, and his troops
plundered the citizenry. Vespasian, who had returned to Caesarea, was furious at this news, and his army even more so. His
men thought that Vespasian, a great leader, was the very anti-
thesis of the childless wretch Vitellius, for Vespasian had two
sons to succeed him and a
brother who was in charge of
the city of Rome.* Accor-
dingly, his troops proclaimed
Vespasian emperor, and urged
him to save the endangered
empire. Vespasian, however,
declined, but his officers
pressed him, while his troops
gathered around him and drew
their swords, threatening him
with death if he refused. Failing to convince them with additional arguments, Vespasian
finally yielded.

Mucianus, legate of Syria,
and other commanders sided
with Vespasian, who now
seized Egypt because it was the
granary of the empire, and a
starving Roman citizenry
would force emperor Vitellius

*Statue of the gluttonous emperor Vitellius, the
immediate predecessor of Vespasian (Uffizi, Florence).*

to surrender. The governor of
Egypt, Tiberius Alexander, im-
mediately declared for Vespasian, as did the legions there and in
Moesia and Pannonia.

Vespasian suddenly recalled the predictions of Josephus, who
had dared, even in Nero's lifetime, to address him as emperor,
and was shocked to think that he was still his prisoner. When
Vespasian ordered Josephus liberated, Titus advised that the
chains be severed, not opened, for this is the custom when
someone is put in irons unjustly. Vespasian approved, and
Josephus' chain was split with an axe.

Vespasian sent Mucianus to Italy with an army, where he was
joined by Antonius Primus from Moesia and his Third legion,

---

* Titus and Domitian, while T. Flavius Sabinus, his brother, was "prefect of
the city."

and they overcame the forces of Vitellius. Meanwhile, Vespasian's brother Sabinus seized the Capitol at Rome, but was executed by Vitellius; Primus arrived one day too late to save him. Vitellius emerged from a palace banquet, gorged and drunk, and was dragged through a mob and finally butchered, having ruled eight months. At last free from Vitellius' terrors, the Roman people acclaimed Vespasian emperor. He received the good news in Alexandria, from which he would sail to Rome. Meanwhile, he sent his son Titus with elite troops to crush Jerusalem.

Dec.,
A.D. 69

TITUS **24**
BESIEGES THE CITY

After a desert march from Egypt, Titus arrived at Caesarea, WV,1 where he organized his forces. Meanwhile, civil strife in Jerusalem had reached a new climax when another faction was bred within a faction, like some raving beast, preying on its own flesh. Eleazar, who had caused the Zealots to withdraw into the sacred precincts, could not stand submission to John [of Gischala], a tyrant younger than himself. And so he seceded with a considerable number of Zealots, seizing the inner court of the temple. They were well supplied, but with fewer numbers than John's, and they confined themselves to their retreat, where they could easily repel his attacks. Although he lost heavily, John, in his rage, made continual assaults on them, and the temple was defiled with the slaughter.

Then there was Simon, son of Giora, who was now master of the upper and a large part of the lower city. He attacked John with greater vigor, seeing that John was also assailed by Eleazar from above. But John had the same advantage over Simon that Eleazar had over John. From his superior height he easily repelled attacks from below with hand weapons, reserving his machines for hurling projectiles against the party above him.

The missiles shot by the catapults, stone-throwers, and "quick-firers"* flew all over the temple, killing priests and worshipers at the very altar itself. For despite war, the sacrifices went on, and those who had journeyed from all over the world to worship there sprinkled the altar with their own blood.

The three warring camps regularly rushed out and burned WV,21

---

* A special catapult for discharging arrows. The *lithoboloi* ("stone-throwers") in Greek equate to *ballistae* in Latin.

each others' food supplies. Thus the area around the temple became a mass of ruins, and great stores of grain, which would

Statue of Titus, who succeeded his father Vespasian both as commander in the Jewish War, and as Roman emperor (Capitoline Museum, Rome).

have supplied the besieged for years, were destroyed, and the city would fall to self-imposed famine. Terrorized by the bloody contentions of the three factions, many prayed that the Romans might come and deliver them from the internal strife. There was no other hope of escape, since the three parties, disagreeing on everything else, united in putting to death any who favored peace with Rome.

Day after day the factions fought, each party devising new ways to destroy the other. John stole some sacred timbers which

Agrippa had brought from Lebanon before the war to raise the sanctuary, and converted them into towers for attacking Eleazar's group. But before he put his impiously constructed towers into operation, the Romans appeared at the walls of Jerusalem.

Titus had marched from Caesarea with the three legions that his father had commanded, and also the Twelfth, which had formerly been defeated under Cestius and now burned for revenge. Besides these, he had troop contingents and auxiliaries from allied kings, as well as Tiberius Alexander, the former governor of Egypt, distinguished for his wisdom and loyalty, who would serve Titus as his military adviser.

Titus camped with his army about four miles from Jerusa-

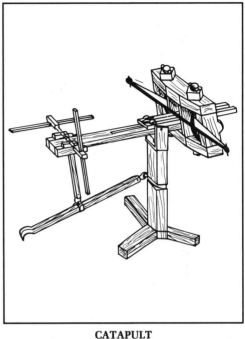

CATAPULT

The Roman catapult ("quick-firer") was used to shoot shafts of various kinds—arrows, pikes, fire missiles—but not stones, for which the ballista was used. The range of the catapult averaged 350 yards.

lem near Gibeah. Taking 600 horsemen with him, he rode forward to reconnoiter the city's strength and ascertain the mood of the Jews, for he had learned, as indeed was the fact, that the people wanted peace but were dominated by the rebels. While Titus was riding along the high road that led to the wall, no one appeared outside the gates. But when he diverged towards the tower Psephinus, the Jews suddenly rushed out in great numbers and broke through his ranks. Then the Jews placed themselves in front of the troops who were still advancing along the road and prevented their joining their comrades who had left the road, thus isolating Titus with only a handful of men.

Titus could not advance—the ground was cut by trenches for gardens and divided by walls and fences—nor could he rejoin his own men because the enemy intervened and his comrades were retreating, not knowing their prince's danger and assuming he had turned back with them. Titus wheeled his horse around, called to his companions to follow, and charged fiercely into the enemy, struggling to cut his way back to his own men. Although he wore neither helmet nor breastplate, none of the hail of arrows aimed at him touched his body, while he slashed the Jews on all sides, riding his horse over fallen enemies. Titus' men formed around him as best they could, and finally they cut their way through to reach the camp safely. Two of their number, however, were killed, while the Jews were elated at the success of their first clash, and inspired with much confidence for the future.

W V,67   Joined during the night by the legion from Emmaus, Titus advanced the next day to an elevation called Scopus [the Lookout] where the first view of the city, a mile away, is afforded. Here he formed a camp for two legions,* and stationed the Fifth to the rear. While the troops were entrenching, the Tenth legion arrived from Jericho and camped on the Mount of Olives, which rises to the east of the city and is separated from it by a deep intervening ravine called Kedron.

The Mount of Olives, east of Jerusalem, site of one of the Roman camps as well as a very dangerous Jewish sally.

---

* The Twelfth and Fifteenth.

The factions in the city watched in dismay as the Romans formed the three camps unmolested, and started to feel the necessity of uniting against the common foe. "Are we courageous," they exclaimed, "only against ourselves, while the Romans, through our dissension, make a bloodless conquest of the city?" Uniting forces, they seized their weapons and suddenly burst out, racing across the ravine with a terrific shout, and attacked the Tenth legion while they were working on their fortifications. The Romans had laid aside most of their arms— they had no idea that the Jews would dare attack—and were therefore thrown into disorder. Some instantly retreated, while many, who ran for arms, were slaughtered before they could turn on their assailants.

The Jews, meanwhile, were continually reinforced by others who were encouraged by the success of the first assault. Accustomed to fight only in orderly ranks, the Romans were confused by this wild kind of warfare, and were finally driven from the camp. The entire legion would probably have been defeated had not Titus instantly come to their aid. Censuring their cowardice, he rallied his fugitives, and, falling on the Jewish flank with his elite fighters, drove them headlong down the ravine. Rallying on the other side of the brook, however, the Jews renewed the combat, and the battle raged on until about noon. Then Titus deployed his reinforcements to repel any further sallies, and dismissed the rest of the legion to resume their fortification on the ridge.

The Jews, however, mistook this movement for flight. A watchman on the battlements gave a signal, and a fresh crowd of Jews rushed from the city with the fury of wild animals. The Romans, as if struck by an artillery engine, broke their ranks and fled up the mountainside, leaving Titus with a few followers halfway up the slope. These implored him to retreat and not risk his valuable life against the mad courage of the Jews. But Titus seemed not even to hear them as he confronted and killed the Jews rushing at him, and drove them back down. Yet still the Jews rushed up the hill on both sides of him to pursue those who were fleeing. Meanwhile, the troops fortifying the camp above saw their comrades below in flight and scattered in panic. They assumed that Titus himself was among the fugitives, since they thought the rest would never have fled while he held his ground. Then, seeing the general in the thickest part of the fight, they shouted his danger to the whole legion. Shame at deserting their general rallied the Romans, and they drove the Jews down the hill into the valley. The Jews contested the ground as they retreated, but the Romans, having the advantage of a higher position, drove them all into the [Kedron] ravine.

Titus, still pressing on those who opposed him, ordered the legion back to resume their fortifications, while he and his band kept the enemy in check. Thus Caesar* twice personally rescued the entire legion from jeopardy and enabled them to entrench their camp unmolested.

Jewish Stratagems

W V,98   During a lull in the war, factionalism resumed inside the
A.D. 70 walls. On the day of Unleavened Bread, Eleazar and his party opened the gates to admit citizens who wished to worship in the temple, but John made the festival a cloak for his treachery. Arming his followers with concealed weapons, he got his men inside the temple, where they threw aside their garments and appeared in arms. Eleazar's party, knowing the attack was against them, scattered and took refuge in the vaults of the temple. The rest cowered around the altar, and some were killed over private grudges, while others were trampled underfoot or mercilessly clubbed. But while the innocent were brutalized, John's intruders granted a truce to the criminals as they emerged from the vaults. Now in possession of the inner temple and all its supplies, John and his partisans could challenge Simon. The three-part factionalism was thus again reduced to two.

Meanwhile, Titus leveled the ground from Scopus to the city walls, removing all garden fences and felling every fruit tree while filling in the gullies. At this time, the Jews contrived the following stratagem. A group of rebels came out of the gates, as if they had been expelled from the city by advocates of peace, and stood cowering alongside one another close to the wall, as if fearing an attack from the Romans. Others stationed themselves on the wall and shouted "Peace!," promising to open their gates to the Romans. They also pelted their own men outside the walls with stones, as if to drive them from the gate.

The Roman rank and file were taken in by this trick, and thinking the gates would be opened to them, they were about to charge in until restrained by the wary Titus. (Only the day before, through Josephus, he had invited the Jews to terms, but met with no reasonable response.) Some who were stationed in front, however, had already snatched up their arms and rushed towards the gate. The sham "outcasts" at first retreated, but when the Roman troops were between the towers of the gate the Jews turned on them, while others darted out and surrounded

---

* Josephus uses this term proleptically for Titus, since his father was Caesar at this time.

them from the rear, and those on the wall threw stones on their heads. After many soldiers were killed and wounded, the Romans finally repelled the Jews and retreated.

The Jews jeered at the Romans for having become such easy dupes; flaunting their shields, they danced and shouted for joy. The Roman soldiers who had escaped were received with threats from their officers and a furious Caesar. "These Jews," Titus huffed, "who have no leader but Despair, do everything with foresight and precaution as they plot ambushes and strategies, while Romans, whom fortune has always served because of their steady discipline, have become so rash as to venture into battle without command." He then threatened them with the law that punished such disobedience with death. But when the other troops pleaded for their fellow soldiers, Titus pardoned the offenders, warning them to be wiser in the future.

The approach to the city was now complete, and opposite the northern and western wall Titus arranged his forces seven ranks deep: three of infantry in front and of cavalry to the rear, with a line of archers in the middle. The Jewish assaults were held in check by this formidable array, and the beasts of burden with the camp followers arrived securely. Titus himself camped about a quarter mile from the ramparts, near the tower Psephinus. Another division entrenched at the tower Hippicus, while the Tenth legion continued to occupy its position on the Mount of Olives.

Description of Jerusalem

Three walls fortified the city, except where impassable ra- WV,136 vines bordered it. The first was erected by David, Solomon, and their successors, and the last by King Agrippa to enclose the northern additions to Jerusalem. The third wall boasted 90 towers, the middle wall 14, and the old wall 60, while the circumference of the city was about four miles. Inside were two hills, that of the [western] upper city was much higher, and was separated from the [eastern] hill or citadel of the lower city by the Valley of the Cheesemakers [Tyropoeon], which extends down to Siloam, a spring of sweet and abundant water. Deep ravines and steep cliffs render the city inaccessible.

The tower Psephinus at the northwestern corner was octagonal and 70 cubits high, providing a view as far as Arabia and the sea. Herod had built three towers near this into the old wall: Hippicus, named after a friend; Phasael, after his brother; and Mariamme, for his wife, each with reservoirs and opulent residential quarters. Phasael soared 90 cubits in altitude, resembling the Pharos lighthouse at Alexandria, and it had now become the headquarters of Simon's tyranny. The towers were built of white marble blocks, each 20 cubits in length, 10 in width, 5 in depth, and so perfectly joined that each tower seemed like one natural rock.

The three great towers in western Jerusalem constructed by Herod the Great, which guarded his palace immediately to the south. They were named (l to r): Phasael, Hippicus, and Mariamme (model by M. Avi-Yonah).

Adjoining these towers was the king's palace, which surpasses all description. A wall 30 cubits high completely enclosed it, broken by ornamental towers at equal distances. Inside were immense banquet halls and bedrooms furnished in gold and silver for 100 guests. Groves, promenades, colonnades, canals, ponds, and statuary surrounded it—all ravaged by the brigands' fire, for it was not the Romans who burned it to the ground but conspirators at the beginning of the revolt, as we have already noted.

WV,184   The platform for the temple and its courts required an immense amount of fill as well as massive foundations for the structure itself, some blocks of stone 40 cubits long. [Here

Josephus provides a detailed description of the porticoes, courts, gates, structure, facade, and veil of the temple, some of which appeared earlier in his *Antiquities,* as did his portrayal of the interior of the sanctuary and its chambers, altar, priests, and vestments.] The innermost recess of the temple measured 20 cubits and was screened from the outer portion by a veil. Nothing whatever stood here: it was called the Holy of Holy— unapproachable and invisible to all.

The exterior of the temple was covered with massive plates of gold which brilliantly reflected the sun. From a distance it

The southeastern corner of the temple platform in Jerusalem, with great blocks of Herodian masonry nearly to the top. The walls also plummet underground in a vast substructure 24 meters below the present surface.

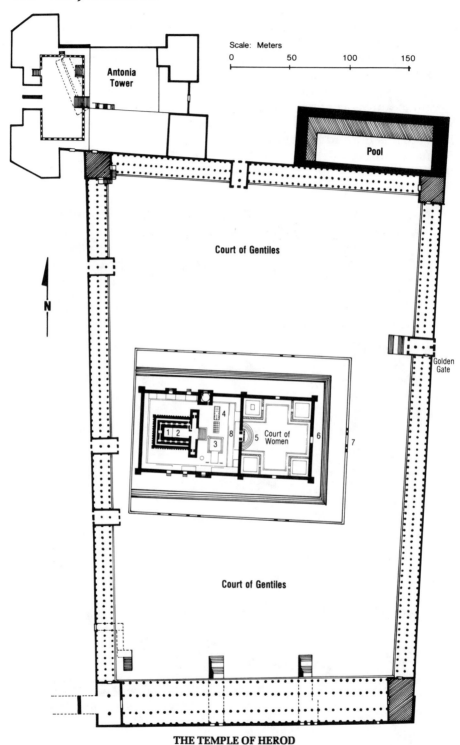

THE TEMPLE OF HEROD

1. Holy of Holies 2. Temple sanctuary 3. Altar 4. Court of the Priests 5. Nicanor Gate 6. The Beautiful Gate 7. Balustrade warning Gentiles not to enter the sacred precincts 8. Court of the Israelites.

appeared like a snow covered mountain, since whatever was not plated with gold was of purest white. Sharp golden spikes protruded from its apex to prevent birds from alighting and polluting the roof.

The Tower Antonia lay at the northwestern corner of the temple's outer court. Built by King Herod, it rose 40 cubits from a rock base 50 cubits in height, and its interior resembled a palace in its spaciousness and furnishings, with accommodations and broad courtyards also for troops. Towers rose at each of its four corners, the one at the southeast reaching 70 cubits in height and commanding a view of the entire temple area. Stairs led down to the temple porticoes where they impinged on the Antonia*, by which the guards descended. A Roman cohort was quartered there permanently, and posted around the porticoes at the festivals to watch the people and repress any rebellions. For if the temple controlled the city, the Antonia dominated the temple, while the upper city had its own fortress: Herod's palace.

The number of combatants and rebels in the city was as WV,248 follows: Simon, son of Giora, had an army of 10,000, not counting his allies, the Idumeans, who numbered 5,000. John had 6,000 when he seized the temple, but these were now joined by 2,400 led by Eleazar and his Zealots. The factions soon relapsed into their former hostilities, and it was this party strife that subdued the city, which suffered nothing worse from the Romans than what the partisans inflicted on each other.

Titus, meanwhile, rode around the wall to see where he could best attack. He determined to make the assault at a point opposite the tomb of John [Hyrcanus], the high priest, for here the outer wall was lower, and there was easier access to the two inner walls. While Titus was riding around the city, his friend Nicanor, who had approached too near to the walls with Josephus, was wounded by an arrow as they were trying to negotiate peace with those on the ramparts.

Angry at this, Titus gave the legions permission to destroy the suburbs and erect earthworks. He defended these with javelin-men and archers between the embankments, and artillery engines in front. Although John's partisans were impatient to clash with the enemy outside, John, through fear of Simon, did not stir. Simon, however, being nearer the besiegers, was not inactive. He mounted on the ramparts the artillery engines which had formerly been taken from Cestius or captured from the Antonia. But these weapons did little damage, since the

---

* Paul stood here when he addressed the Jews after his arrest, Acts 21:40.

Jews did not know how to work them well. However, they attacked the builders with stones, arrows, and raids, although the Romans were protected by wicker-work screens and artillery engines.

All the Roman engines were well built, but those belonging to the Tenth legion were most powerful. Their stone-projectors hurled boulders weighing a talent* a quarter mile, and the Jews set lookouts on the towers to spot the fired stones which, being white, shone and whizzed as they flew. When they saw the stone discharged, these watchmen would call out, "Sonny's coming!"**—at which those in the line of fire dropped down to let the stone pass through harmlessly. When it occurred to the Romans to blacken them, the stones were more effective, destroying many with a single shot.

W V,275   When the embankments were completed, the battering rams were brought up, and the artillery moved closer to the walls to protect those working the rams. Suddenly, at three different sectors, they began their thundering, and a shriek rose from those inside. The factions themselves were alarmed, and the two parties shouted to each other that for the present, at least, they had to stop fighting and unite against the Romans.

Simon proclaimed an amnesty to all John's followers who wanted to leave the temple and man the wall. John, though still suspicious, gave his permission, and the two parties, burying their differences, fought side by side. They hurled showers of firebrands against the machines and kept those who worked the rams under constant fire. The more courageous dashed out in bands, tore the screens off the engines, and assaulted those who fired them off. Titus always came to relieve those who were hard pressed, placing horsemen and archers on either side of the engines, and beating back the raiders. The wall, however, did not yield to the battering rams except for the corner of one tower.

W V,284   The Jews paused for a while in their attack, but when the Romans, who thought the Jews had withdrawn through fear and fatigue, were off guard, they suddenly dashed out through a hidden gate, carrying firebrands to burn the works. The daring of the Jews at first prevailed over the discipline of the Romans. They would soon have succeeded in burning the Roman engines had not the elite troops from Alexandria bravely held their ground until Titus, at the head of his cavalry, charged the enemy. With his own hand he killed a dozen of the Jewish leaders as the rest retreated, and then rescued the works from the flames.

---

* c. 75–85 pounds.

** "The stone" in Hebrew is *ha-eben*, which is easily corrupted to *ha-ben*, "the son."

One of the Jews taken prisoner in this engagement was crucified before the walls, on Titus' orders, in the hope that this sight would lead the rest to surrender in horror. After the retreat, John, the general of the Idumeans, while talking with a soldier in front of the ramparts, was shot in the breast by an arrow and killed on the spot. His death caused much grief to the Jews, for he was a man of gallantry and sound judgment.

The First Wall Breached

That night, the Romans were suddenly awakened by a crash, W V,291 which threw the troops into a panic, as they feared a Jewish assault. Titus had ordered three siege towers to be built on the respective embankments, and one of these fell accidentally in the middle of the night. But Titus quickly ordered this news generally spread, and so allayed the alarm.

The archers and stone-throwers placed in the towers did great damage to the Jews, while they themselves were high out of

A seventeenth-century reconstruction of the Siege of Jerusalem, illustrating the metal-plated siege towers used by the Romans (from the 1613 edition of Polybius' Greek and Roman Militia).

range. Nor could the Jews set fire to the towers because they were plated with iron. The battering rams, with their constant pounding, were gradually taking effect, and the wall began to totter before the largest ram, which the Jews themselves called Victor. Worn out with fatigue and having become somewhat careless, the Jews abandoned their posts and retreated to the second wall, while the Romans poured through the breach Victor had made. The Romans demolished much of the outer wall and the northern quarter of the city. Titus now shifted his camp to a position before the second wall just out of bowshot. The Jews, dividing their forces, made a vigorous defense from the wall: John and his party fighting from the Antonia and the northern portico of the temple, while Simon guarded the rest of the wall as far as a gate through which an aqueduct passed to the tower Hippicus. The Jews made continual raids, which were driven back by the discipline of the Romans. Both sides spent the night armed, the Jews afraid to leave the wall defenseless, the Romans dreading a sudden attack.

Simon inspired his men with such awe and reverence that they were ready to take their own lives at his command. The Romans were also incited to valor by Titus, who always rewarded bravery. Once, when the Jews were preparing for a raid, Longinus, a Roman soldier, dashed into their phalanx, single-handedly broke their ranks, and killed two of their bravest before retreating in triumph to his own lines. He gained distinction for his valor, and many emulated his gallantry.

W V,317   Titus now applied the battering ram against the central tower of the north wall, which the defenders abandoned except for a crafty Jew named Castor and ten others. When the tower began to totter, Castor stretched his hands out to Titus and begged for mercy in a pitiful voice. Titus stopped the ram, forbade the archers to shoot, and told Castor to speak his wishes. When he said that he wanted to come down under pledge of protection, Titus congratulated him and said he would gladly offer security to the whole city if it surrendered. Five of the ten Jews joined in the sham supplication, while the rest cried out that they would never be slaves of the Romans, and a dispute seemed to arise, during which the assault was suspended.

Castor, meanwhile, sent word to Simon that he had time to arrange his defense, since he could fool the Romans for some time longer. All the while he seemed to be urging the unwilling five to accept the proferred pledge until they "plunged" their swords into their breastplates and fell down as if dead. Castor was struck near his nose with an arrow, which he drew out and showed to Titus, complaining of unjust treatment. Caesar sternly rebuked the archer, and directed Josephus, who was at

his side, to offer his hand to Castor. But Josephus, convinced
that the petitioners meant no good, declined to go. Aeneas, a
deserter, however, said that he would go, and when Castor
called for someone to catch the money which he was bringing
out, Aeneas ran forward with open robes to receive it. But Castor
hurled a boulder at him, which Aeneas dodged, and it wounded
a soldier instead. His eyes opened, Caesar angrily applied the
battering ram more vigorously. The tower giving way, Castor
and his companions set fire to it, and seemed to jump into the
flames. The Romans were impressed with their courage, but in
fact the Jews jumped into a vault below.

The Romans Repulsed

On the fifth day after capturing the first wall, Caesar stormed W V,331
the second, and, since the Jews had fled from it, he and his men
entered the new town district. Without widening the breach in May,
the wall, Titus gave orders to kill no one or set fire to any of the A.D. 70
houses. He promised to restore their property to the people, for
his goal was to preserve the city and the temple. The people
indeed had long been ready for peace, but the rebels mistook the
humanity of Titus for weakness, and assumed that his overtures
proved his inability to take the rest of the city. Threatening
death to any who mentioned surrender or peace, they attacked
the Roman division that had entered both in the streets and from
the houses. The Jews, at a great advantage because they knew
the streets, drove the Romans back with their charges. Because
the breach was so narrow, the Romans could not retreat at once,
and all would probably have been annihilated had Titus not
stationed his archers at the ends of the streets and kept the
enemy at bay with a torrent of arrows until his soldiers had
withdrawn.

Thus the Romans, after gaining possession of the second wall,
were driven out. The spirits of the war party in the city soared at
this success, but they did not know that the forces still available
to the Romans far outnumbered those ejected, or that famine was
slowly approaching. Many were already failing for lack of supplies, but the rebels considered it a good riddance. As for the
breach, they walled it with their own bodies for three days, but
on the fourth they were unable to withstand Titus' assault and
fell back to their former refuge. Master of the wall a second time,
Titus immediately razed much of it and laid plans for attacking
the third wall.

Titus suspended the siege for a few days to see if loss of the W V,348
second wall or famine might induce any to surrender. He used

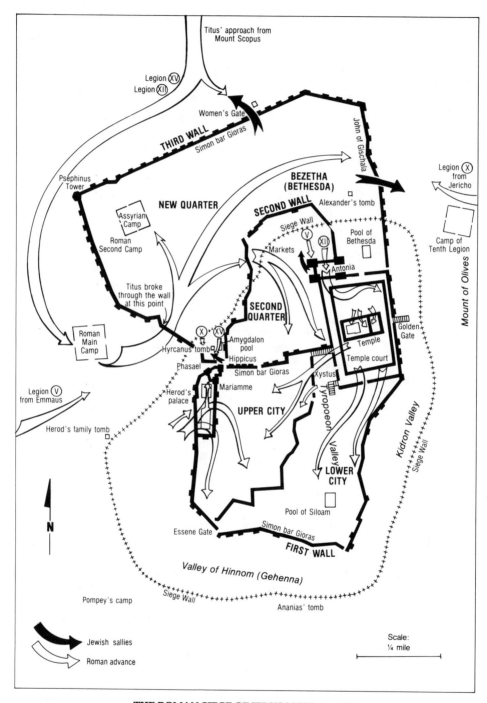

Titus' approach from
Mount Scopus

Legion ⓧⓋ
Legion ⓍⒾⒾ

Women's Gate

THIRD WALL
Simon bar Gioras

John of Gischala

Psephinus
Tower

NEW QUARTER

BEZETHA
(BETHESDA)

SECOND WALL
Alexander's tomb

Legion Ⓧ
from
Jericho

Assyrian
Camp

Siege Wall

Pool of
Bethesda

Camp of
Tenth Legion

Roman
Second Camp

Markets

Ⓥ

ⓍⒾⒾ

Antonia

Titus broke
through the wall
at this point

SECOND
QUARTER

Temple

Golden
Gate

Mount of Olives

Roman
Main
Camp

Ⓧ　ⓍⓋ

Amygdalon
pool

Temple court

Hyrcanus' tomb

Hippicus

Phasael

Simon bar Gioras

Xystus

Legion Ⓥ
from Emmaus

Herod's
palace

Mariamme

UPPER CITY

Tyropoeon

Herod's family tomb

Kidron Valley

Siege Wall

Valley

LOWER
CITY

Pool of Siloam

N

Essene Gate

Simon bar Gioras

FIRST WALL

Valley of Hinnom (Gehenna)

Pompey's camp

Siege Wall

Ananias' tomb

Jewish sallies

Roman advance

Scale:
¼ mile

THE ROMAN SIEGE OF JERUSALEM, A.D. 70

the time to review his troops and pay them their salaries. They appeared as a gleaming parade of shining arms which filled the throngs of Jewish observers with awe and dismay. In four days the Roman legions had all received their pay. On the fifth, since the Jews had not requested peace, Titus started raising embankments both at the Antonia and at John's monument in order to capture the temple and the upper city, respectively. Simon and his troops impeded those at work beside the monument by raids, while John and the Zealots obstructed those at the Antonia. With daily practice, the Jews had now become skilled in the use of artillery engines, and their 300 quick-firers and 40 stone-throwers seriously retarded the Roman earthworks.

Titus, anxious to preserve the city from destruction, sent Josephus to negotiate with the Jews in their native tongue. Josephus therefore went around the wall, keeping out of range of projectiles and yet within earshot, and implored the people to spare themselves, their country, and their temple. Their forefathers, men far superior to them, had yielded because they knew God was on the Roman side, and it was now hopeless to fight famine and the imminent conquest. [Here Josephus adds page after page of lessons his hearers should have learned from history, and then concludes with a final appeal.]

During his address, many on the ramparts derided and cursed Josephus, while others threw missiles at him, and they did not yield to his tearful appeal. The people, however, decided to desert. They would swallow gold coins to elude the rebels, and, after escaping to the Romans, they had ample supplies after discharging their bowels. Titus released most of them, which further encouraged desertion, but the partisans of John and Simon kept a sharp lookout for such refugees and slaughtered any suspects.

25

HORRORS AT JERUSALEM

Famine now raged in the city, and the rebels took all the food W V,424 they could find in a house-to-house search, while the poor starved to death by the thousands. People gave all their wealth for a little measure of wheat, and hid to eat it hastily and in secret so it would not be taken from them. Wives would snatch the food from their husbands, children from fathers, and mothers from the very mouths of infants. Many of the rich were put to death by Simon and John, while the sufferings of the people were so fearful that they can hardly be told, and no other city ever endured such miseries. Not since the world began was there ever a generation more prolific in crime than this bastard scum of the nation who destroyed the city.

Meanwhile, as Titus' earthworks were progressing, his troops captured any who ventured out to look for food. When caught, they resisted, and were then tortured and crucified before the walls as a terrible warning to the people within. Titus pitied them—some 500 were captured daily—but dismissing those captured by force was dangerous, and guarding such numbers would imprison the guards. Out of rage and hatred, the soldiers nailed their prisoners in different postures, and so great was their number that space could not be found for the crosses.

But the rebels dragged to the walls the relatives of the deserters and any who wanted peace and showed them how the Romans treated suppliants—not captives. Until the truth became known, this restrained many who wanted to desert. Titus then ordered the hands cut off several of the captives so they would not be mistaken for deserters, and sent them to John and Simon to urge them not to compel him to destroy the city, but to save their lives, their city, and the temple. But the Jews abused

Caesar from the ramparts, cursing him and his father, and saying that they preferred death to slavery, and that as long as they breathed they would continue to damage Romans in every way possible.

W V,466   After seventeen days of continuous work, the Romans completed four huge embankments and brought up the engines. But John had secretly undermined the earthworks at the Antonia, and supported the tunnels with props to leave the embankments suspended. But now he set fire to the props, and the earthworks fell in on the collapsing tunnels with a tremendous crash, and the engines and embankments were either buried or burned up.

Two days later, three bold members of Simon's party rushed out against the machines in that sector and set them on fire, although the Roman guards tried to prevent them. The flames spread, and the Romans rushed from their camp to the rescue, while the Jews attacked them with great fury. The Romans tried to drag the rams away from the fire, but the Jews would not let go of them even though the iron was red-hot. From there the fire spread to the earthworks, overcoming the Roman defenders. Surrounded by flames, the Romans gave up any hope of saving the works, and retreated to their camp. Flushed with success, the Jews dashed forward, and, advancing to the very entrenchments, grappled with the sentries. These men bravely held their ground, because Roman sentinels were punished with death if they quit their posts, but so fierce was the Jewish attack that the Roman forces began to waver.

At this moment Titus arrived from the Antonia, where he had been inspecting a site for new earthworks, and he and his men charged the enemy in the flank. The Jews turned and faced him bravely, but blinding dust and deafening noise soon obscured friend from foe, and the Jews retreated into the city. Their earthworks demolished, the Romans were profoundly dejected, because in one short hour they had lost the fruits of their long labor; many lost hope of ever taking the city by ordinary means.

The Roman Siege Wall

W V,491   Titus held a council of war, and some of his officers advised him to commit his entire army to take the wall by storm. Others were for rebuilding the earthworks, while still others proposed a blockade to reduce the city by famine. Titus knew that it would be useless to fight against desperate men who would soon destroy each other, and that it would be difficult to get enough materials to restore the earthworks. He thus decided to surround the city with a wall, blocking every possible exit, in order to compel the Jews to either surrender or starve.

Accordingly, he set his legions to work, and they built so enthusiastically and quickly that the project was finished in three days. This was an incredibly short time, considering that the wall was five miles long, and had thirteen forts attached to its outer side. In these Titus placed garrisons, while sentries patroled the intervals between the forts throughout the night.

All hope of escape and all food supplies were now cut off from the Jews, and famine devoured thousands upon thousands. The alleys were choked with bodies, the survivors not having enough strength to bury the dead and even falling into graves with them. No mourning was heard in Jerusalem, for famine stifled all emotions, and an awful silence shrouded the city. The rebels at first ordered the bodies buried at public expense, finding the stench unbearable, but then flung them into the ravines when they became too numerous.

When Titus, as he made his rounds, saw these valleys choked W V,519 with dead bodies oozing decay, he groaned, and, lifting up his hands, called God to witness that this was not his doing. His army, meanwhile, was in the highest spirits with plenty of food, and many of the Roman troops would approach the ramparts displaying these quantities to accentuate the enemy's hunger. Titus, pitying the people and anxious to save the survivors, ordered new earthworks raised. Timber for them was scarce and had to be brought from ten miles away, since all the trees around the city had been cut down for the previous embankments. The new mounds were raised at four points opposite the Antonia, and were much larger than before.

Even their own sufferings failed to make the outlaws feel any W V,525 remorse, but, like dogs, they mauled the people even after death. Simon actually turned on Matthias, one of the chief priests who had persuaded the people to let Simon into the city to oppose John. Accusing him of Roman sympathies and without allowing him any defense, Simon condemned Matthias to death, along with three of his sons. Matthias begged that he might be put to death before his sons were, but Simon ordered the sons butchered before Matthias' eyes and in full view of the Romans, before Matthias himself was killed. After these, a priest named Ananias, and Aristeus, the secretary of the council,* and fifteen other leaders were executed, while the father of Josephus was put into prison. The outlaws further forbade by edict any gathering in the city or any mourning in groups.

Judes, one of Simon's officers in charge of a tower, called ten of his most trusted subordinates and said, "How long will we tolerate these crimes? Or what prospect of saving ourselves do

---

* The Sanhedrin.

we have by obeying this villain? The Romans are all but in the town, so let's surrender the ramparts, and save ourselves and the city!'' The ten agreed, and the next morning Judes called to the Romans from the tower [in surrender], but they were suspicious. While Titus was advancing to the wall with some troops, Simon learned of the plot, seized the ten, and killed them in full view of the Romans, throwing them over the ramparts after mutilating their bodies.

W V,541   As Josephus was making his rounds, urging surrender, he was struck on the head by a stone and knocked unconscious. The Jews rushed out and would have dragged him into the city had Caesar not sent a rescue party. During the conflict that followed, Josephus was carried away, hardly knowing what had happened. Assuming they had killed Josephus, the rebels shouted for joy. Rumors of his death spread through the city and reached his mother, who was in prison. But she was not long distressed, for Josephus quickly recovered from the blow and shouted to his enemies that he would soon have his revenge.

Some of the deserters jumped from the ramparts, while others started out carrying stones, as if for a skirmish, then fled to the Romans. When they arrived, swollen with hunger, many of them gulped down so much that they burst, but some learned that they had to eat moderately at first for stomachs unused to food. But even these were doomed, because one of the refugees in the Syrian ranks was found picking gold coins out of his excrement. After this the Arab and Syrian rabble cut open the refugees and searched their intestines, and in one night 2,000 were cruelly ripped open.

On hearing of this outrage, Titus was on the point of putting his allies to death, but refrained because they far outnumbered their victims. However, he threatened with death any daring to repeat the crime, and ordered his legionaries to identify any such culprits in their ranks. Still, greed drove the barbarians rather than fear of punishment, so they now did their outrages in secret. They went forward to meet deserters and killed them where they could not be seen by the Romans, but few bowels contained any significant money. This disaster drove many of the deserters back.

When John had plundered the people of all they possessed, he began to strip the temple itself. He took its golden vessels, bowls, tables—some of them gifts of Augustus and his consort—and even the sacred wine and oil and gave them to his followers to use. But why do I need to describe the sufferings? One refugee, who had been in charge of a single gate, told Titus that 115,880 corpses had been carried out in an eleven-week period. Other leaders reported that 600,000 bodies of the lower classes had been thrown out, and it was impossible to number the rest. A measure of wheat now sold for a talent, and when it was no longer possible to gather herbs after the city was walled in, some searched the sewers for offal or ate old cow dung. Yet the rebels were relentless.

The Antonia Assaulted

The Romans finished their earthworks in 21 days, having W VI,1 stripped the whole district of its trees for eleven miles around, and the once beautiful suburbs of the city looked like a wilderness. The new embankments caused anxiety to both the Romans and the Jews. Jews were afraid that if they failed to burn these too, the city would be taken. The Romans feared that if these mounds were also destroyed, they would never take the city, and they were depressed by the invincible Jewish spirit.

Before the rams were brought up, John and his party inside the Antonia tried to destroy the Roman works. But the attempt was unsuccessful, since they rushed out in small, unmotivated groups with no united plan. The Romans also screened the works and stood firmly at their posts, knowing that all their hopes would be cut off if they burned. The artillery engines helped them against the raiding parties, and, with each fallen Jew blocking the way for the man behind him, the Jews soon July, retreated. A.D. 70

The Romans now brought up the siege engines, although they were attacked from the Antonia with stones, fire, iron [arrowheads], and every kind of projectile the Jews could throw. But the wall of the fortress resisted battering. The Romans then locked their shields over their heads for protection against boulders and worked with hands and crowbars to undermine the foundations, and succeeded in dislodging four stones. Night suspended the labor, but in the course of it, the wall suddenly fell in, for it had been shaken by the rams at the point where John had dug beneath it while undermining the former earthworks. Yet the joy of the Romans was dampened by seeing a second wall, which John had built inside. Although this wall appeared to be weaker than that of the Antonia, no Romans ventured to mount it, for death surely awaited the first attackers.

Titus called his bravest together and urged them to scale the W VI,33 wall, promising rewards to the man who led the assault. When they all hesitated, an auxiliary named Sabinus, a Syrian by birth, volunteered. His skin was black and emaciated, and anyone would have thought him unfit to be a soldier, but in that slender body lived a heroic soul. He rose and said, "I gladly

The Tower Antonia, constructed by Herod on a rise northwest of the temple area, and named in honor of his patron, Mark Antony (model by M. Avi-Yonah).

offer myself to you, Caesar. I am the first to scale the wall, and if I die, know that for your sake I willingly give up my life!''

He then lifted his shield over his head, drew his sword, and advanced towards the wall. Only eleven men had the courage to follow him. The defenders hurled their javelins from the ramparts, showered them with arrows, and rolled down enormous boulders which crushed some of the eleven. But Sabinus never slackened his pace until he had reached the summit and scattered the enemy, for the Jews, shocked at his boldness and thinking that more had followed him, turned and fled. But at the very moment of his triumph, Sabinus slipped and stumbled over a rock, falling headlong with a loud crash. The Jews turned and, seeing Sabinus alone and prostrate, attacked him from all sides. Rising on his knee and screening himself with his shield, he kept them at bay for a while, wounding many who approached, but was soon buried under the missiles. Three of his comrades were crushed by the stones, while the rest were carried back to the camp, wounded.

Two days later, twenty of the guards stationed at the earth- w VI,68 works, together with a standard-bearer, a trumpeter, and two auxiliaries crept silently toward the Antonia in the dead of night. They scaled the wall, killed the sentinels as they slept, and then ordered the trumpeter to sound. The other guards woke up from their sleep and fled before any had noticed the numbers of the enemy, for the trumpet led them to suppose they had mounted in force. Titus immediately ordered the troops to arms, and, with his group of elite men, was the first to mount. The Jews fled to the temple, where the forces of John and Simon made a desperate defense. The Romans pressed on to take possession of the temple, the Jews thrusting them back to the Antonia. Arrows and spears were useless to both sides. Drawing their swords, they resorted to hand-to-hand combat, and fought so closely and fiercely that the combatants found it hard to tell on which side they were fighting.

At length, after fighting from 3 A.M. to 1 P.M., the Jews suc- ceeded in driving the Romans back. They had the advantage in numbers—only a portion of the Roman army had come to attack—and so the Romans were satisfied to hold the Antonia for the time being. But Julianus, a heroic Bithynian centurion, sprang forward and single-handedly drove the Jews back to the corner of the inner temple, killing all he overtook. The multi- tude ran away from him, regarding such strength and courage as supernatural. But, like any other soldier, his shoes were thickly studded with pointed nails, and while running across the pave- ment, he slipped and fell on his back. The loud clash of his armor made the fugitives turn and thrust him with spears and swords. Julianus defended himself gallantly, wounding many of his enemies, until he himself was hacked to pieces. Mean- while, the Romans were again shut inside the Antonia, deeply moved by Julianus' heroism.

The Antonia Destroyed

In order to prepare an easy ascent for his whole army, Titus w VI,93 ordered the fortress Antonia torn down to its foundations. Learning that the daily sacrifice in the temple had stopped for lack of men [or lambs], and that the people were therefore Aug., dejected, Titus sent Josephus to tell John that he would allow A.D. 70 him to come out of the temple and fight somewhere outside, so they would no longer pollute the Holy Place. John also had Titus' permission to perform the interrupted sacrifices with the help of any Jews he might choose.

Josephus, standing where not only John but also the multitude could hear him, delivered Caesar's message in Hebrew, urging the Jews to spare their country and their temple. But the tyrant John cursed Josephus repeatedly, and said that he did not fear capture, because the city was God's.

Josephus countered, "It is God Himself who is using the Romans to purge His temple with fire, and exterminate a city so choked with pollution!" As Josephus broke down in sobs, many of the upper class were moved by his words, and some chief priests and nobles deserted to the Romans. Caesar received them courteously and sent them to Gophna,* promising to restore their possessions after the war. When these were happily secure at Gophna, the rebels spread a report that they had been slaughtered by the Romans, and this lie temporarily kept the people from deserting.

W VI,118   Titus, however, recalled the men from Gophna and ordered them to walk around the wall with Josephus to let the people see them, and great numbers fled to the Romans. Standing in front of the Roman line, the refugees implored the rebels with tears to surrender, or at least withdraw from the temple and save it from ruin, since the Romans would not set fire to the holy places unless compelled.

But the rebels only shouted curses on the deserters, and mounted their artillery engines over the sacred gates, so that the temple looked like a fortress. They rushed in arms around the holy places, and shocked even the Roman soldiers by their impiety. Again Titus rebuked John and his followers: "Wasn't it you, abominable wretches, who placed this balustrade in front of your sanctuary, with slabs in Greek and in your own language warning that no one may pass the barrier? And didn't we allow you to put to death any who passed it, even if he were a Roman? Why, then, do you now trample corpses underfoot within it? I call the gods of my fathers to witness, and any deity who once guarded this place—for now I believe there is none—I call on my army, the Jews within my ranks, and on yourselves, to witness that it is not I who force you to pollute these precincts. Fight in any other place, and no Roman shall profane your holy places. Rather, I will save the sanctuary for you, even against your will!"

Josephus translated this message for the Jews, but the rebels and their tyrant scorned it. Titus, therefore, reluctantly resumed hostilities. He could not make the assault with his whole army, because the approaches to the temple were too narrow, and so selected the 30 best men out of each century, placing Cerealis in command, with orders to attack at around 3:00 A.M. He would

---

* Twelve miles north of Jerusalem.

*A fragment of one of the thirteen signs surrounding the inner temple area —
cited in Titus' speech — which threatened death to any Gentile who penetrated
the sacred precincts. Part of the Greek word for "death" appears near the
bottom (Rockefeller Museum, Jerusalem).*

himself have led the attack had his officers not persuaded him
that it would be wiser to watch and guide his troops from the
Antonia, in order to reward the brave and punish the cowardly.

Before dawn, the Romans attacked, but they did not find the W VI,136
guards asleep as they had hoped, for they sprang to arms with a
shout. The Romans at first had the advantage in the fight,
because they remembered the password in the darkness, while
the Jews often attacked each other in the confusion. But
when morning broke, the Jews maintained their defense in

better order. The battle raged on until 11 A.M., with neither side victorious.

The rest of the army, meanwhile, overturned the foundations of the Antonia, and within a week prepared a broad ascent to the temple, where they erected embankments against four places in the outer court. These were built with great difficulty, because the Romans had to bring the timber from a distance of over twelve miles, and the Jewish attacks had become even more daring. Some of the Roman cavalry, when they went out to collect wood or food, turned their horses loose to graze while they were foraging, and the Jews often charged out in bands and stole them. Determined to make them more careful of their steeds by setting a severe example, Titus put to death one of his troops who had lost his horse. Man and beast were inseparable after that.

W VI,157   Suffering from famine, the rebels suddenly attacked the Roman wall on the Mount of Olives at supper time, hoping to find their enemies off guard. But the Romans saw them coming, hurried to the spot from adjacent forts, and prevented their attempts to scale the wall or cut through it. A fierce contest took place, but the Jews were finally repulsed and driven down the ravine.

The Jews now set fire to the portico leading from the Antonia to the temple, and then hacked away a 30-foot opening by hand. Two days later, the Romans set fire to the adjoining colonnade and burned about 20 feet more. The Jews then cut away the roof and destroyed all connection between themselves and the Antonia.

One day, a mean looking little Jew named Jonathan appeared across from the monument of the high priest John and challenged the best of the Romans to single combat. For some time he yelled his insults without the Romans taking any notice of him. But finally an auxiliary named Pudens, disgusted at his impudence and thinking he could easily whip so puny a fellow, came forward to accept the challenge. He was getting the best of the fight, when suddenly he slipped and fell down. Jonathan immediately ran him through with his sword and then danced in glee, jeering at his Roman spectators, until a centurion bent his bow and shot him with an arrow. Writhing with pain, he fell on the body of his foe, demonstrating that in war undeserved success brings instant vengeance on itself.

THE DESTRUCTION OF TEMPLE AND CITY   26

The rebels in the temple, meanwhile, thought up the follow- W VI,177 ing trick. Along the western portico, they filled the space between the rafters and the ceiling with dry tinder, bitumen, and pitch, and then, as if worn out, they retreated. At this, many of the rash legionaries chased them, mounting the portico with ladders. The more prudent, however, suspicious of the withdrawal, remained. When the portico was filled with those who had climbed up, the Jews set fire to the whole structure. The flames roared up on every side, and some of the Romans jumped down into the city, others into the midst of the enemy, while many fractured their limbs jumping to friends. Most, however, died in the flames or commited suicide, anticipating the fire.

Caesar, although angry at all who had mounted the portico without orders, was still touched with pity when he saw them, and urged his men to make every effort to rescue them, though nothing could be done. A few got back to the wall of the portico, which escaped the flames, but they were surrounded by the Jews and killed after a valiant resistance. The last of them, a youth named Longus, was offered his life by Jews below if he would come down and surrender. But his brother called up to him not to tarnish Roman arms, so Longus raised his sword in view of both armies and killed himself.

Among those enveloped in flames, a certain Artorius saved himself by his cunning. He shouted to a comrade below with whom he shared a tent, "Lucius! I'll leave you heir to my property if you come and catch me." Lucius ran up, and Artorius threw himself down upon him and was saved. But Lucius was smashed against the pavement by Artorius' weight and killed on the spot.

The Romans were depressed by this disaster, but it made them all the more cautious against Jewish schemes. The Romans set fire to the northern portico, destroying it up to the northeast corner, which was built over the Kedron ravine.

Porticoes which surrounded the temple in Jerusalem, site of many encounters between Romans and Jews (model by M. Avi-Yonah).

The Excruciating Famine

W VI,193   In the meantime, countless thousands of Jews died of hunger. In every house where there was the least morsel of food, relatives fought over it. Gaping with hunger, the outlaws prowled around like mad dogs, gnawing at anything: belts, shoes, and even the leather from their shields. Others devoured wisps of hay, and then there was the incredible horror of Mary of Bethezuba.

Distinguished in family and fortune, Mary had fled to Jerusalem from Perea, but her property had been plundered by the tyrants during the siege, and her food by the daily raids of their followers. Maddened by hunger, she seized the infant at her breast and said, "Poor baby, why should I preserve you for war, famine, and rebellion? Come, be my food—vengeance against the rebels, and the climax of Jewish tragedy for the world." With that, she killed her infant son, roasted his body, and devoured half of it, hiding the remainder.

Instantly the rebels arrived, sniffing the unholy smell and threatening her with death if she did not produce what she had prepared. She had reserved a fine portion for them too, she replied, uncovering the remnants of her baby. They stood paralyzed with horror. "This is my child and my action," she said. "Help yourselves, for I've had my share. Don't be weaker than a woman or more compassionate than a mother! But if you're squeamish and disapprove of my sacrifice, then leave the rest for me."

They left trembling, and the whole city rocked with this abomination, while the Romans were horrified, and Caesar declared himself innocent of this crime in the sight of God. He swore, however, to bury this atrocity of infant cannibalism beneath the ruins of the country.

When some of the earthworks were finished, Titus ordered W VI,220 the battering rams to be brought up opposite the western hall of the outer temple court. Others tried to undermine the foundations of the northern gate, but failed. Instead the Romans applied ladders to the porticoes, but as soon as they reached the top, the Jews threw them down headlong, or killed the Romans before they could defend themselves with their shields. They pushed aside, from above, several ladders filled with armed men, hurling all the soldiers to the ground. All who had mounted fell, and even the Roman standards were captured. Realizing that his effort to spare a foreign temple led only to the slaughter of his troops, Titus ordered the gates set on fire.

At this time two of Simon's lieutenants deserted to Titus, hoping for pardon because they surrendered at a moment of success. Titus was inclined to put them to death, because he thought that they had surrendered only to save themselves from the disaster they had brought on their city. Nevertheless, his good faith resulted in their release.

The Roman troops set the gates on fire, and the flames spread quickly to the porticoes. When the Jews saw the circle of fire surrounding them, they lost all spirit and stood gaping at the flames, without trying to put them out. Through the whole day and the following night the fire continued to burn.

The next morning Titus gave orders that the fire should be W VI,236 extinguished and a road made to the gates to facilitate entry of the legions. He then called his generals together to debate the fate of the temple. Some wanted to destroy it at once, because it would always be a focus for Jewish rebellion. Others advised that if the Jews would leave the temple it should be spared, but if they used it as a fortress, it should be burned. But Titus declared that, whatever happened, so magnificent a work as the temple ought to be spared, because it would always be an ornament to the empire. Three of his principal generals agreed with him, and the council was dissolved.

The next day the Jews made a furious raid against the guards posted in their outer court. The Romans closed up their ranks, locked their shields together like a wall, and withstood the attack. But the Jews poured in with such numbers that Titus, who was watching from the Antonia, hurried his elite cavalry to assist his troops. The Jews could not withstand their charge, and retreated to the inner court of the temple.

Burning of the Temple

W VI,249   Titus then withdrew into the Antonia, intending the next dawn to attack with his entire force and overwhelm the temple. But on that day—the tenth of Lous [August 30]—the structure
A.D. 70   was doomed, the very day on which the former temple had been destroyed by the king of Babylon. When Titus withdrew, the rebels again charged the Romans, and conflict took place between the Jewish guards of the sanctuary and the Roman troops who were trying to put out the flames in the inner court. The Jews were scattered and pursued up to the sanctuary. At this moment, a soldier, neither waiting for orders nor awed by so dreadful an act, grabbed a burning brand. Hoisted up by one of his comrades, he threw the brand through a small golden door on the north side which gave access to chambers surrounding the sanctuary. As the flames caught, a fearful cry welled up from the Jews, who rushed to the rescue, caring nothing for their lives.

Titus was resting in his tent when a messenger rushed in with the news. Jumping up just as he was, he ran to the temple to stop the flames. But there was such noise and confusion that the soldiers either could not or would not hear the commands of their general, or obey the waving of his hand. Nothing could hinder the fury of the troops, and many were trampled by their own comrades at the entrances. Falling among the burning ruins, they shared the fate of their enemies.

Mad with rage and pretending not to hear the orders of their general, the soldiers rushed on, hurling their torches into the sanctuary. The rebels now were helpless, and made no attempt at defense, for on every side was slaughter and flight, civilians being butchered the most. Around the altar were heaps of corpses, while streams of blood flowed down the steps of the sanctuary.

When Caesar could not restrain the fury of his soldiers, he and his generals entered the structure and viewed the Holy Place of the sanctuary, and all the splendors it contained. Since the flames had not yet reached the interior, but were still feeding on the chambers surrounding the temple, Titus made one last effort to save it. Rushing out, he appealed to his troops to put out the flames, ordering one of his centurions to club anyone disobeying his orders. But respect for their general and fear of punishment were overwhelmed by their raging hatred of the Jews and hope of plunder. Seeing that all the surroundings were made of gold, they assumed that the interior contained immense treasure. And when Titus ran out to restrain the troops, one of those who had entered with him thrust a firebrand into the hinges of the gate [of the inner temple], and flame shot up in the interior. Caesar and his generals withdrew, and thus, against his wishes, the sanctuary was burned.

While the temple was in flames, the victors stole everything W VI,271 they could lay their hands on, and slaughtered all who were caught. No pity was shown to age or rank, old men or children, the laity or priests—all were massacred. As the flames roared up, and since the temple stood on a hill, it seemed as if the whole city were ablaze. The noise was deafening, with war cries of the legions, howls of the rebels surrounded by fire and sword, and the shrieks of the people. The ground was hidden by corpses, and the soldiers had to climb over heaps of bodies in pursuit of the fugitives. The Jewish brigands forced their way through the Romans into the outer court of the temple, and then into the city. Some of the priests at first tore up spikes from the sanctuary and hurled them at the Romans, but afterwards, retreating from the flames, they withdrew to the wall.

Prophets and Portents

The Romans now set fire to all the surrounding buildings, the W VI,281 remains of the porticoes and gates, and the treasury chambers, where vast sums of money had been deposited. They then moved on to the one surviving portico at the outer court, where 6,000 women and children had taken refuge. They had gathered there because of a false prophet, who had told them that God commanded them to go to the temple where they would receive guarantees of deliverance. Before Caesar had made up his mind what to do with these people, the soldiers set fire to the colonnade, and not a soul escaped.

Numerous false prophets deluded the people at this time. They were hired by the tyrants to urge the people to wait for help from God, and so keep them from deserting. Before the siege, however, portents had appeared, foretelling the impending devastation, but the Jews had disregarded these warnings of God. A star resembling a sword hung over the city, and also a comet which lasted a year. And just before the revolt, when the people were coming together for the feast of Unleavened Bread, a bright light shone around the altar during the night and brightened the sanctuary for half an hour. The people thought this a good omen, but the sacred scribes told them the contrary. A cow gave birth to a lamb in the temple court, and the eastern gate of the inner court, which was fastened with iron bars and so heavy that it took twenty men to move it, flew open on its own during the night. And at the feast of Pentecost, when the priests entered the inner court of the temple, they heard a great noise, and after that the voices of a multitude, saying, "We are leaving this place!"*

W VI,300   But another portent was even more alarming. Four years before the war, while the city was enjoying prosperity and peace, a rude peasant named Jesus, son of Ananias, came to the feast of the Tabernacles. He stood up in the temple, shouting, "A voice from the east, a voice from the west, a voice from the four winds, a voice against Jerusalem and the sanctuary, a voice against bridegrooms and brides, a voice against all the people!" Day and night he walked the streets with this cry. Some of the leaders arrested the fellow and beat him, but he only kept on shouting as before. The magistrates brought him before the Roman governor, who had him whipped to the bone, but he neither begged for mercy nor shed a tear, only crying at each stroke, "Woe to Jerusalem!" When Albinus, the governor, asked him who he was, where he came from, and why he uttered these cries, he did not reply, but only repeated his dirge, "Woe to Jerusalem!" For seven years and five months, continuing through the war, he maintained this cry, until, making his rounds on the wall during the siege, he shouted with his piercing voice, "Woe once more to the city, to the people, and to the temple!" Then he suddenly added, "And woe to me also!" and was immediately struck dead by a stone hurled from a ballista.

But what most incited the Jews to war was an ambiguous oracle, which predicted that someone from their country would become ruler of the world. This they interpreted as someone from their own race, but the oracle actually signified Vespasian, who was proclaimed emperor on Jewish soil.**

---

* For a parallel account of these portents, indeed, of Titus' whole campaign, although in less detail, see Tacitus, *History*, v,11 ff.
** So also Tacitus, *History*, v, 13, and Suetonius, *Vespasianus*, 4.

Titus Takes the Upper City

Now that the rebels had fled into the city, the Romans pitched W VI,316 their standards inside the temple court and offered sacrifice, acclaiming Titus as imperator. The troops were so glutted with spoils that gold was depreciated to half its former value throughout Syria.

From among the priests still perched on the walls of the sanctuary, a boy called to the Roman guards that he was suffering from thirst, and asked their protection while he came down and got a drink of water. Taking pity on him, they agreed, and so he came down, quenched his thirst, filled a jar with water, and raced back to the priests before the guards could catch him. When they cursed his treachery, the boy replied that he had not broken his word, not having promised to stay with them. The Romans were astonished at having been outwitted by so young a boy.

Five days later, the priests became so hungry that they came down and surrendered to Titus, begging him to spare their lives. But he said that the time for pardon had passed: that for which he might have spared them was gone, and so he executed them, saying it was only fitting that they should perish with their temple.

Seeing that there was no hope of escape, the Jewish tyrants W VI,323 and their followers now invited Titus to a parley. Since he wanted to save the city, Titus spoke to them through an interpreter at the western gates of the outer courts of the temple, where they opened onto a bridge leading to the upper city. He reminded them in detail of all the past favors Rome had conferred on them, which were repaid only by rebellion, intransigence, and a wretched cruelty that had led to the destruction of their temple. "However," Titus concluded, "I will not imitate your frenzy. Throw down your arms in surrender, and I grant you your lives. As a lenient master, I will punish only the unruly and spare the rest for my own use."

To this they replied that they could not accept his pledge because they had sworn not to do so. They asked for permission to pass through his lines, with their wives and children, and withdraw into the wilderness, leaving the city to him. Titus was furious that virtual captives were offering proposals as if they were victors. He warned them not to hope for terms any longer, but to fight to save themselves as best they could, because from now on he would be governed by the laws of war. He then gave his troops permission to burn and sack the city, and flames soon consumed the Archives, the Acra, the council chamber, and many homes.

W VI,358   The rebels now rushed to the royal palace [of Herod in the upper city] where many had deposited their wealth, beat off the Romans, and killed 8,400 people who had gathered there. Looting the money, they also captured two Roman soldiers, one a cavalryman, the other a foot soldier. The latter they slaughtered on the spot and dragged his body around the city. The horseman pretended to have a suggestion for their safety, and so was brought to Simon, but, having nothing to say, he was handed over to execution. The officer bound his hands behind his back, put a bandage over his eyes, and led him out to be beheaded in view of the Romans. But while the Jew was drawing his sword, the prisoner managed to escape to the Romans. After such an escape, Titus could hardly put the officer to death for being taken alive, and dismissed him from the legion instead.

The next day the Romans drove the Jewish outlaws from the lower city, and set it on fire as far as Siloam. Cooped up in the upper city, the rebels dispersed themselves and lay in ambush amid the ruins, executing all who attempted to desert. As a last hope, they planned to find refuge in the underground passages, where they would hide until the city was entirely destroyed and the Romans had departed.

Because the ascent to the upper city was steep, Caesar ordered earthworks, even though the land for twelve miles around had been stripped of timber. But the legions raised one embankment on the west side of the city opposite the royal palace, while the auxiliaries and other units threw up another from the Xystus and bridge.

W VI,378   The Idumean chiefs now met secretly to discuss surrendering themselves, and sent five delegates to Titus to ask his protection. Titus, hoping that if the Idumeans defected the Jewish tyrants would also surrender, sent the men back, agreeing to spare them. But while the Idumeans were preparing to leave, Simon learned of the plot and immediately put to death the five emissaries and threw the chiefs into prison. The Idumean soldiers, helpless at the loss of their leaders, were watched by Simon, who stationed more vigilant sentries on the walls.

Still, these guards could not prevent desertion, for although many were killed trying to escape, a far larger number fled to the Romans. Mercifully disregarding his former orders, Titus received them all, freeing some 40,000 citizens and selling the rest as slaves.

At this time, one of the priests received a promise of protection on condition of delivering certain treasures of the temple which he had secured. And so he handed down from the wall of the sanctuary two candlesticks, tables, bowls, and platters—all of solid gold—as well as the veils, vestments of the high priests with precious stones, and other articles. Another priest pointed out where similar treasures were hidden, and so obtained the pardon awarded refugees.

The earthworks were finished in eighteen days, and the siege W VI,392 engines were then brought up. Some gave up all hope and retired from the ramparts to the Acra. Others crept down into the caverns, yet many endeavored to repel the Romans from the walls, but were easily driven back. When part of the wall and some of the towers were battered down by the rams, the defenders fled and the tyrants themselves panicked. Those fierce Jewish leaders, previously so proud of their daring crimes, now stood trembling and afraid, or fell on their faces, mourning their fate and unable to flee. Then the tyrants, of their own accord, left the three towers [of Herod] which would have defied every siege engine and where they could have held out until reduced by famine. Abandoning these—or rather driven down from them by God—they took refuge in the ravine below Siloam. Afterwards, when Simon and his followers had recovered a little from their panic, they tried to break out of the wall the Romans had built around the city and escape. But when the guards beat them back, they crept down into the subterranean passages.

Jerusalem is Destroyed

Now conquerors of the city wall, the Romans planted their W VI,403 standards on the towers in jubilation over their victory, finding the end of the war an easier task than its beginning. They could hardly believe they had surmounted the last wall with no bloodshed and had found no defenders inside. Pouring into the streets [of the upper city], they massacred everyone they found, burning the houses with all who had taken shelter in them. So great was the slaughter that in many places the flames were put out by streams of blood. Towards evening the butchery ceased, but all night the fires spread, and when dawn broke, all Jerusalem was Sept. 26, in flames. A.D. 70

As Titus entered the city he was astonished at its strength, and especially the towers which the tyrants had abandoned. Indeed, when he saw how high and massive they were, and the size of each huge block, he exclaimed, ''Surely God was with us in the war, who brought the Jews down from these strongholds, for what could hand or engine do against these towers?'' Titus then freed all those imprisoned by the tyrants, and when he later destroyed the rest of the city and razed the walls, he left the towers standing as monuments of his fortune.*

Since the soldiers were growing tired of slaughter, Caesar ordered them to kill only those who were found armed and offered resistance, and to capture the rest. Still the troops killed

Base of the Tower Phasael in Jerusalem today, the largest of the three towers at the northern end of the Palace of Herod. The lower six courses of stone are original Herodian masonry, which were intentionally left intact by Titus to demonstrate how formidable Jerusalem's defenses were.

the old and feeble, but drove those in the prime of life and fit for service into the Court of the Women at the temple. Titus placed a guard over them, and ordered his friend Fronto to decide what should be done with them. While Fronto was sorting them out, 11,000 died of starvation, some because the guards, through hatred, would not give them food, others because they refused the food when offered. Fronto executed all the rebels, reserving the tallest and most handsome of the youths for the triumph. Of the rest, those over the age of seventeen were sent to the mines in

---

* The lower courses of Phasael, the largest tower, still stand in Jerusalem today.

Egypt or presented to the provinces to be destroyed by sword or beast in the theaters. Those under seventeen were sold.

The total number of prisoners taken during the war was W VI,420 97,000, and those who died during the siege 1,100,000. The greater part of these were of Jewish blood, but not natives of the city, because just before the siege, people had flocked into Jerusalem from all parts of the country for the feast of Unleavened Bread. They found themselves engulfed in the war and overcrowding that produced pestilence and famine. That the city could hold so many is clear from a count taken under Cestius, when the priests, during a Passover sacrifice, counted 255,600 animal victims. Allowing an average of ten diners per victim, we have a total of 2,700,000.* All of these were pure and holy, since those afflicted with leprosy or gonorrhea, or menstruating women were not permitted to participate.

The Romans now went down into the subterranean passages and killed all they found, discovering 2,000 who had died from violence or famine. The stench was horrendous. John and his followers, dying of hunger in the caverns, begged the Romans for that protection he had so often spurned. He was condemned to life imprisonment. The Romans set fire to the outlying quarters of the city and demolished the walls to the ground.

Thus Jerusalem was taken in the second year of Vespasian's reign, on the eighth of Gorpiaeus.** It had been captured five times before, and was now for the second time destroyed. Shishak, king of Egypt, Antiochus, Pompey, and then Sossius with Herod had taken the city but preserved it. Before then it had been laid waste by the king of Babylon, 1,486 years and six months from its foundation. Its original founder was a prince of Canaan, called Melchizedek, or "Righteous King," for such, indeed, he was. He was the first priest of God, and the first to build the temple; he named the city Jerusalem, which was previously called Solyma.

The Canaanites were driven from Jerusalem by King David, who established his own people there. The Babylonians destroyed it 477 years and six months later, and Titus 1,179 years after David, or 2,177 years since its foundation. So ended the siege of Jerusalem.

---

* Because the total, obviously, should be 2,556,000, either the text or Josephus' arithmetic is faulty. In any case, the number is too large.
** September 26, A.D. 70.

FROM 27
ROME TO MASADA

Caesar ordered the entire city and the temple smashed to the W VII,1 ground, leaving only the tallest of the towers standing— Phasael, Hippicus, and Mariamme—and part of the western wall to show posterity the strong defenses which had yielded to the Romans. He now gathered his army in order to commend them for their achievements and confer rewards on those who had particularly distinguished themselves. A high tribunal was erected in the center of the camp, and Titus mounted it with his principal officers. He thanked the army for their magnificent efforts and praised them for their obedience and courage. The officers then read out names of those who had performed any noble feat during the war. Calling up each of them, Titus applauded as they came forward, placed crowns of gold on their heads, presented them with golden neckchains, little golden spears, and silver standards, as well as booty, and promoted each to higher rank. When all had been rewarded, he stepped down from the tribunal, receiving thunderous applause, and sacrificed a great number of oxen in thanksgiving for his victory, giving them to the troops for a banquet.

For three days Titus joined in celebration with his officers, and then dismissed his army. The Tenth legion, however, he left to guard Jerusalem. Because the Twelfth had been defeated under Cestius, he banished it from Syria altogether, and sent it to the Euphrates. The Fifth and the Fifteenth legions he retained until his arrival in Egypt. With them he descended to Caesarea-on-the-sea, where his prisoners were kept in custody, because the winter season prevented his sailing to Italy.

The base of the Western (or "Wailing") Wall of the temple platform in Jerusalem exhibits the size of the Herodian ashlars used in its construction. Some have been eroded from many generations of Jews weeping for the destruction of the temple and the city.

W VII,23   Titus and his troops now went to Caesarea Philippi and remained there for some time, staging a variety of exhibitions. Many of the prisoners were thrown to wild animals in these games, or were compelled to fight each other in combat. It was here that Titus learned of the capture of Simon, son of Giora, which was accomplished as follows.

During the siege of Jerusalem, Simon and his faithful friends, along with some stonecutters and their tools, had descended into one of the subterranean passages, with provisions for many days. Advancing until they had reached the end of the passage, they then tried to dig their way beyond the walls and escape. But the mining went so slowly that the provisions gave out. Simon then decided to scare the Romans. Dressing himself in white tunics and purple mantle, he rose out of the ground at the very spot where the temple had stood. Bystanders were shocked at first, and then came nearer to ask him who he was. Simon refused to tell them, but had them call their general. When Terentius Rufus appeared, who had been left in command, Simon told him the whole truth. Rufus put him in chains and wrote Titus of Simon's capture, a surrender for which Simon himself had put many to death on false charges of desertion to Rome! On Titus' return to Caesarea-on-the-sea, Simon was sent to him in chains, and was kept prisoner for the triumph which Titus was planning to celebrate in Rome.

Victory Games

While Titus remained at Caesarea, he celebrated his brother Domitian's birthday with great splendor, putting over 2,500 prisoners to death in games with beasts and flames. After this he moved to Berytus,* a Roman colony in Phoenicia, where he celebrated his father's birthday by killing many more captives at elaborate exhibitions. W VII,37 Nov., A.D. 70

Titus had been overjoyed to learn of the excellent manner in which his father Vespasian had been received by all the Italian cities, and how the people of Rome poured out in crowds to hail him as their emperor. The city was hung with garlands, and the multitudes feasted, offering libations to their gods that the empire of Vespasian might long be preserved. Vespasian's son Domitian put down revolts in Gaul and Germany, while others did the same in Moesia.

Titus left Berytus and marched towards Antioch, passing through the cities of Syria, in which he gave more exhibitions, during which his Jewish captives acted out their own destruction. When he reached Antioch, the people hurried out to receive him enthusiastically and at the same time petitioned him to expel the Jews from town.

Now, there were many Jews in Antioch, who had enjoyed equal rights with the native Syrians. But at the time war had first broken out, hatred of the Jews was everywhere at its height. A Jew named Antiochus, son of the chief magistrate of the Jews in Antioch, falsely charged the Jews (among them his own father) with planning to burn the whole city by night. Furious, the

---

* Beirut.

Antiochenes massacred many Jews, after which Antiochus, aided by Roman troops, lorded it over his fellow Jews, and would not even allow them to rest on the Sabbath.

Subsequently, a fire broke out in the marketplace, which burned down a number of public buildings, and Antiochus accused the Jews of setting it. The citizens again attacked the Jews maniacally until Gnaeus Collega, the deputy governor, intervened and investigated the affair. He found out that the Jews were not to blame, but rather some scoundrels who owed large debts and thought that if they could destroy the public records office they could escape having to pay them. Still, the inhabitants hated the Jews, and now begged Titus to drive them from the city. Titus, however, replied, "Jews ought to be banished to their own country, but this has been destroyed and no other land will receive them." Failing in this request, the Antiochenes then asked that the rights of the Jews be taken away from them. But this Titus also refused, leaving the status of the Jews in Antioch unchanged.

W VII,112   On his way to Egypt, Titus passed by Jerusalem, and, as he surveyed the ruins, he could not help thinking of the beautiful city that had formerly stood there. He felt sorry for its destruction and cursed the criminal authors of the revolt. He then hurried to Egypt, crossing the desert quickly, and soon reached Alexandria. Here he dismissed his two legions and set sail for Italy. The two Jewish leaders, Simon and John, with 700 of the Jewish captives selected for their height and appearance, were sent off immediately that they might grace Titus' triumph in Rome.

A Roman Triumph

After a favorable voyage, Titus received as enthusiastic a welcome in Rome as Vespasian had. His father and [Domitian, his younger] brother came out to meet him, and the citizens were overjoyed to see the three princes united. They decided to celebrate their success by one common triumph, although the Senate had decreed a separate triumph for each. When the day arrived, the entire city poured out to view the pageant of victory.

Before sunrise, all the military forces marched out in companies and divisions under their officers, and gathered near the temple of Isis. When dawn broke, Vespasian and Titus appeared—crowned, laureled, and clothed in the traditional purple robes, and they ascended a tribunal which had been erected for them. Instantly, loud cheering erupted from the troops, which Vespasian acknowledged, and signaled for silence. He now rose, covered his head with his cloak, and, together with

Titus, recited the customary prayers. Vespasian then made a short speech to the soldiers, and dismissed them for a traditional breakfast the emperors provided.

The princes then sent the procession on its way through the Triumphal Gate, driving via the theaters to give the crowds a better view. Words cannot describe the magnificence of the procession and the articles displayed: gold, silver, and ivory, all wrought in various forms; beautiful tapestries, worked in Babylon; jewels and crowns of gold; and images of gods made of costly materials. Animals of many species were led along by men clad in purple, and even the horde of captives was well dressed.

But nothing in the procession excited so much wonder as the moving stages, some of them three or four stories high, many enveloped in tapestries and each vividly representing some episode of the war. Here was to be seen a prosperous country laid waste, and there an enemy slaughtered. Others portrayed huge walls demolished by siege-engines; fortresses battered down; an army storming over ramparts; houses thrown down over their owners; hands of the defenseless raised in supplication; temples set on fire; and other scenes of blood and famine. On each of these floats was placed the general of one of the captured cities in the same posture in which he had been taken. A number of ships also followed. W VII,139

Then the spoils were displayed in confused heaps, and above them all were those taken from the temple at Jerusalem, including a golden table, a candelabrum with seven branches, and a copy of the Jewish Law. Next came a large group carrying images of victory made of gold and ivory, and finally Vespasian himself, driving his chariot, followed by Titus, while Domitian rode beside him in magnificent apparel, mounted on a steed.

The procession ended at the temple of Jupiter Capitoline, where they waited until Simon, son of Giora, had been put to death. He had been part of the parade and now had a halter thrown over him, and he was whipped and executed at the spot adjoining the Forum where malefactors are executed. After the announcement that Simon was no more, the people gave a shout of joy, and the princes offered sacrifices, after which they withdrew to the palace for a banquet.

When the triumph was over, Vespasian decided to erect an elegant temple to Peace, adorning it with masterpieces of sculpture and painting taken from different countries. Here he placed also the golden vessels taken from the temple of the Jews, but the purple hangings of the sanctuary and their Law he kept in his own palace.

The Roman Forum, site of Vespasian's and Titus' triumph. The cavalcade wound its way along the Vi
Senate house, under what (later!) would be the Arch of Septimius Severus to its left,   and then up to th

acra which runs along the upper (northern) route in this photograph, past the reconstructed squarish summit of the Capitoline hill.

The Fortress Machaerus

W VII,163   Lucilius Bassus had been sent to Judea as legate, and, taking over command from Cerealis, had captured the fortress of Herodium. He now gathered the Roman forces throughout Judea, together with the Tenth legion, and marched against Machaerus. It was absolutely necessary to destroy this, lest its very strength should induce the Jews to revolt.

It was built on a high crag, surrounded on all sides by deep ravines which could not be easily crossed and were impossible to climb. The valley to the west of it ends at Lake Asphaltitis, seven miles away. Noting the natural advantages of the site, Alexander [Janneus], king of the Jews, first erected a fortress there, but this was destroyed by Gabinius in his war with Aristobulus. When Herod became king, he founded a city there with ramparts and towers, and at the summit he raised a wall with high towers at each corner. In the center of the enclosure he built a spacious palace with cisterns to receive the rain and maintain a water supply in case of siege, for which he also stocked weapons and engines.

W VII,190   After Bassus had examined the place from every side, he decided to fill up the eastern ravine, and his men worked rapidly on the embankment. The Jewish inhabitants now separated themselves from the aliens there, compelling them to defend the lower town while they occupied the citadel. Daily the Jews raided those building the embankments, with much loss of life on both sides. These clashes, however, did not decide the fate of the town, but a surprising incident did.

Among the besieged was a bold youth named Eleazar, who participated in the raids and created havoc in the Roman ranks. Always the last to retreat, he remained alone outside the gates after one of the battles, chatting with some friends on the ramparts. Suddenly, an Egyptian called Rufus, who was serving in the Roman army, rushed up behind Eleazar, picked him up, armor and all, and succeeded in carrying him off to the Roman camp.

The Roman general ordered Eleazar stripped and taken to a spot where he would be most visible to onlookers in the town and whipped there. The Jews all burst into lament, and when Bassus observed this, he thought he could trick the town into surrendering. He ordered a cross erected, as if he were about to crucify Eleazar. Those in the fortress reacted with piercing shrieks, and Eleazar himself pleaded [with his compatriots] not to allow him to undergo so horrible a death but to yield to the Romans, who had conquered everyone else. Overcome by his appeals, the Jews quickly sent a delegation, offering to surrender the fortress if they were allowed to depart in safety and take Eleazar with them.

Bassus agreed to these conditions. When the people in the lower town heard of the agreement, they decided to steal away quietly during the night. But as soon as the gates were opened, the Jews informed Bassus, who attacked those intent on escaping. He killed 1,700 men and enslaved the women and children, although a few of the bravest managed to cut their way through the Roman forces and escape. According to the agreement, Bassus allowed those who had surrendered the fortress to depart, along with Eleazar.

Bassus then marched to a forest, called Jardes, and proceeded W VII,210 to surround it, for many of those Jews who had escaped from sieges in Jerusalem and Machaerus had gathered here. Bassus posted his cavalry around the forest, and then had the infantry begin chopping down the trees, among which the fugitives had taken refuge. Compelled to fight, the Jews concentrated their forces and attacked the troops hemming them in. But the Romans, well-armed and prepared, lost only twelve, while no Jew escaped and 3,000 died, including their general Judas, son of Ari.

At this time, Caesar sent instructions to Bassus and Laberius Maximus, the procurator, to lease out the whole Jewish territory, for Titus reserved the country as his own private property, except that he assigned to 800 discharged veterans the town of Emmaus, about four miles [northwest of] Jerusalem. And on all Jews, wherever resident, he imposed an annual tax of two drachmas for the support of the Capitol, the amount they had formerly contributed to the temple in Jerusalem.

[Josephus here reports the unjustified attack on Antiochus, king of Commagene, by Paetus, the Roman governor of Syria, and the subsequent reconciliation of the king and his sons with Vespasian in Rome.]

The Fortress of Masada

Bassus died in Judea, and was succeeded as governor by W VII,252 Flavius Silva. Since the whole country was subdued except for one fortress, Masada, he collected all his forces and marched against it. Masada was occupied by *sicarii* and their commander Eleazar, a descendant of Judas [the Galilean]. Judas had induced many Jews to refuse to enroll themselves when Quirinius was sent as censor to Judea, and plundered the property of those who submitted to Rome for surrendering Jewish liberty. But this was only a pretext used by his successors to conceal their cruelty and

The fortress Masada, viewed from the Dead Sea plain in the east. The whitish line scaling the summit is the eastern "Snake Path."

greed, since the people *did* join them against Rome, only to suffer still worse atrocities from the rebels.*

A.D. 73   Flavius Silva immediately built a wall around Masada and guarded it with sentinels to prevent the besieged from escaping. Masada stood on a high rock, which was surrounded by deep ravines. It could be reached by only two narrow and difficult paths, from Lake Asphaltitis on the east and from hills to the west. The former path they call "the Snake," since it resembles a reptile in its narrow windings back and forth along breathtaking precipices, until it finally reaches a plain at the summit on which Masada stood.

---

* Here, one last time, Josephus vents his fury against the *sicarii* and their successors: John of Gischala, Simon bar-Giora, the Idumeans, and the Zealots, all of whom suffered, yes, but much less than what they inflicted, in his estimation.

View northward across the Dead Sea from Herod's Northern Palace at Masada. The Corinthian capitals originally stood on columns here.

Flavius Silva, the Roman commander, stationed his camp to the northwest of Masada, just above a precipice. The walls of the camp, his own quarters within it, and the siege wall surrounding Masada all remain clearly visible after nineteen centuries.

The fortress was first built by the high priest Jonathan, but Herod later surrounded the summit with a high wall, fortified by 37 towers, and built a palace at the northwestern corner. He also cut in the rock a number of cisterns so that residents would never lack water. The fortress was nearly impregnable, since the eastern path could not be used by an attacking party, while that on the west was barred by a huge tower built at the narrowest point.

The fortress was well-stocked with provisions—enough grain, wine, oil, legumes, and dates to last for years—and enough arms for 10,000 men, along with unwrought iron, brass, and lead. King Herod had provided this fortress as a refuge for himself in case of a revolt among his Jewish subjects, and also because he feared Cleopatra, since she was always asking Antony to kill him and give her the throne of Judea.

W VII,304   Silva now applied himself to the siege, and started to construct earthworks, 200 cubits in height, over a rock that jutted out below called "White [cliff]", which is behind the tower that barred the western path. He then covered this ramp with a second embankment, made of enormous stones, which was built as a platform. On this a high tower was raised and completely encased with iron, from which the Romans shot missiles and arrows by means of their artillery engines, clearing the ramparts of Masada.

Silva brought up a battering ram, which hammered against the wall until it made a breach. But in the meantime, the *sicarii* had erected another wall inside built of wood and earth, which, being soft, cushioned the blows of the ram and even became firmer from the blows. Silva then ordered his soldiers to throw burning torches on it, and the wood soon caught fire. But before long, a north wind blew the flames in the faces of the Romans, and they were afraid that their siege engines would be burned. Yet suddenly the wind shifted and blew fiercely from the south,* driving the flames against the wall and setting it ablaze from top to bottom. The Romans returned rejoicing to their camp, intending to attack the enemy on the following day. During the night they kept a tighter watch lest any of the besieged escape.

The Fall of Masada

W VII,320   Eleazar, however, did not intend to flee, nor would he allow anyone else to do so. When he saw the wall in flames, he

---

* Even though the western gate at the Masada excavations is somewhat angled to give these wind directions credibility, north*east* and south*west* wind systems seem far more likely for the effect Josephus describes.

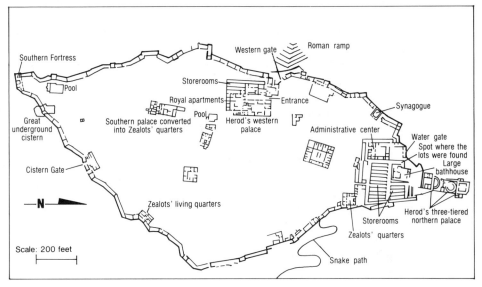

EXCAVATIONS AT MASADA

thought it would be nobler for all to die than fall into Roman hands, and so he assembled his bravest comrades. "Long ago we decided to serve neither Roman nor anyone else except God," he said, "and now the time has come to verify that resolution by action. We, who were the first to revolt and are the last in arms against the Romans, must not disgrace ourselves by letting our wives die dishonored and our children enslaved. We still have the free choice of a noble death with those we hold dear. When they are gone, let us render a generous service to each other. But first we must destroy our property and the fortress by fire, sparing only our provisions, so that the Romans will know it was not hunger that subdued us, but that we preferred death to slavery."

Some of his hearers were eager to respond, but others could not bear the thought of putting their wives and children to death, and tears stole down their cheeks. Seeing them wavering, Eleazar addressed them again, asserting that "life, not death, is man's misfortune, for death liberates the soul from its imprisonment in a mortal body. Why, then, should we fear death who welcome the calm of sleep?" Indian philosophers happily greeted the purifying flames, he added, and then told of the tortures they could expect from the Romans, who would also violate their wives. "Let us die as free men with our wives and children," he concluded, "and deny the Romans their joy of victory! Let us rather strike them with amazement at our brave death!"

W VII,389   While Eleazar was still speaking, he was cut short by his hearers, who were filled with zeal to comply. They rushed away like possessed men, and began the bloody work. While they embraced their wives and took their children in their arms, clinging in tears to their parting kisses, they killed them.

When all were put to death, they gathered together their effects and set fire to them. Then they chose by lot ten of their number to kill the rest. They lay down beside their dead wives and children and, flinging their arms around them, offered their throats to those who slaughtered them all. The ten then cast lots, and he on whom it fell killed the other nine. He then looked about to see that all were dead, set fire to the place, and finally drove his sword through his body, falling beside his family. Two women and five children, however, escaped by hiding in an underground aqueduct during the massacre. The victims numbered 960, and the tragedy occurred on the fifteenth of Xanthicus.*

Early the next morning, the Romans advanced to the wall over gangways, expecting fierce resistance. But no enemy appeared, and an awful silence hung over the place. They finally shouted in their perplexity, to arouse anyone. Hearing the noise, the two women who had saved themselves came out of hiding and informed the Romans of what had happened, one of the two lucidly reporting Eleazar's speech itself. At first they could hardly believe the story, until, putting out the flames, they cut their way into the palace and there found the mass of bodies. Instead of rejoicing over their enemies, the Romans admired the nobility of their determination.

The general left a garrison at Masada and departed with his army for Caesarea. Not an enemy remained in the country, all of it now subdued by this protracted war.

The Temple in Egypt

W VII,408   Later, some of the *sicarii*, who had fled to Egypt, tried to incite a revolt among the Jews in Alexandria, claiming that they should assert their independence and regard God alone as their master. Some of the Jewish leaders in Alexandria opposed the *sicarii* and were murdered by them.

---

* May 2, A.D. 73.

Looking eastward over Masada toward the Dead Sea. The Roman ramp still rises almost to the summit at the center of the fortess' western face.

Noting the fanaticism of the *sicarii*, the leaders of the council of elders among the Jews called the people together and exposed their madness. "These men," they said, "knowing they will be put to death by the Romans if recognized, want to make us all share their danger, who have not shared their crimes." They urged the people to turn the villains over to the Romans, and thus keep peace with them. The people then rushed on the *sicarii*, and 600 were captured. All the rest who escaped from the city were pursued and arrested. They were put under various tortures [by the Roman governor] to force them to acknowledge Caesar as lord, but not one submitted, astonishing everyone. Even their little children preferred to die rather than call Caesar lord.

Lupus, who was then in charge of Alexandria, reported this commotion to the emperor, who ordered him to destroy the temple of Onias, so that the Jews, with their penchant for revolution, would not collect there and raise another revolt. This

W VII,420
C. A.D. 73

temple had been built in former times by Onias, one of the chief priests of the temple at Jerusalem, who had fled to Alexandria at the time that Antiochus, king of Syria, was at war with the Jews. Onias was well received by Ptolemy [VI Philometor], who hated Antiochus, and Onias promised to make the Jewish nation an ally of the Egyptian king if he gave his permission to build a temple in Egypt. Since Antiochus had destroyed the temple in Jerusalem, the Jews would flock to Egypt for freedom of worship, Onias claimed.

Ptolemy then gave Onias a tract of land 23 miles from Memphis in the nome of Heliopolis, where Onias built a fortress and temple that was not like the one in Jerusalem. Indeed, he resented the Jerusalem Jews for his exile, and hoped his rival temple would lure Jews away from them. The king also gave him extensive territory for revenue collection so that the priests might be sustained in the service of God.

When Lupus received Caesar's order, he went to this temple, took away some of the offerings, and shut the building up. When Lupus died, his successor Paulinus stripped the temple, forbade anyone from worshiping in it, and blocked up the entrance—243 years after its founding.*

Sedition in Cyrene

W VII,437   Like a disease, the madness of the *sicarii* also infected the cities around Cyrene. A scoundrel named Jonathan, who had found refuge in that city, persuaded a multitude of the lower classes to follow him out into the desert, promising to show them great signs and wonders. But the men of rank among the Jews of Cyrene reported the exodus to Catullus, governor of the Libyan Pentapolis. Catullus dispatched a body of horse and foot soldiers that easily overpowered the unarmed crowd, the majority of whom were killed, and the rest brought back to Cyrene. Jonathan managed to escape capture for a while, but finally was taken. When brought before Catullus, he falsely claimed that the wealthiest of the Jews had ordered the scheme.

Catullus pretended to believe the charges, because he hated the Jews and wished to make the affair appear as dangerous as possible so that he too might seem to have won a Jewish war. He even made Jonathan name Alexander, a Jew with whom he had quarreled, and Bernice, his wife, as being in on the plot. He then killed 3,000 of the wealthiest Jews and confiscated their property for the imperial treasury.

---

* The standard text is likely corrupt, claiming 343 years, or a century too long for the period c. 170 B.C. to A.D. 73.

To prevent Jews elsewhere from exposing his crime, Catullus had Jonathan and his associates charge the leading Jews in Alexandria and Rome with promoting the rebellion. Among those insidiously accused was Josephus, the author of this history. Catullus went to Rome with his "witnesses," but Vespasian investigated the affair and discovered that all the charges were false. Jonathan was tortured and then burned alive. Catullus was reprimanded, but soon after was afflicted with a terrible disease that affected also his mind, which was haunted by ghosts of his murdered victims. When his bowels ulcerated and fell out, he died, another evidence of God's punishment of the wicked.

Conclusion of *The Jewish War*

Here we close the history, in which we promised to relate W VII,454 accurately how this war was waged by the Romans against the Jews. My readers may judge its style, but as to truth, this has been my aim throughout.

Inner relief of the Arch of Titus commemorates the destruction of Jerusalem. The seven-branched candlestick — the Menorah — and other items from the temple are paraded by the triumphant Romans as booty.

The Arch of Titus commands the eastern entrance of the Roman Forum to the present day. The Latin inscription across its top is translated: "The Senate and the Roman People to the divine Titus, son of the divine Vespasian, and to Vespasian Augustus."

APPENDICES

Reconciling Josephus' chronology for the kings of Israel and Judah with that in the Old Testament and, in turn, with records from surrounding countries is extemely difficult. Father-son coregencies, as well as varying use of the accession-year system for calculating the monarchs' years of rule, also contribute to the problem of why numbers for the length of some reigns do not always accord perfectly with the chronology indicated on the next pages. The following dates, however, reflect the current scholarly consensus.

THE KINGS OF THE UNITED KINGDOM

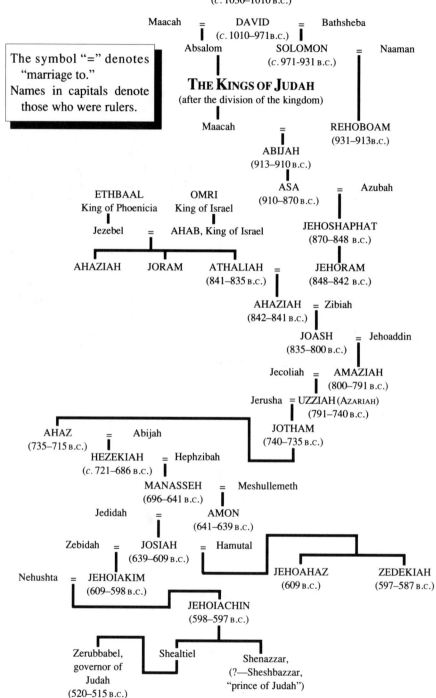

SAUL
(*c*. 1030–1010 B.C.)

Maacah = DAVID = Bathsheba
(*c*. 1010–971B.C.)

Absalom SOLOMON = Naaman
(*c*. 971-931 B.C.)

The symbol "=" denotes "marriage to."
Names in capitals denote those who were rulers.

THE KINGS OF JUDAH
(after the division of the kingdom)

Maacah = REHOBOAM
(931–913B.C.)

ABIJAH
(913–910 B.C.)

ASA = Azubah
(910–870 B.C.)

ETHBAAL OMRI JEHOSHAPHAT
King of Phoenicia King of Israel (870–848 B.C.)

Jezebel = AHAB, King of Israel

AHAZIAH JORAM ATHALIAH = JEHORAM
(841–835 B.C.) (848–842 B.C.)

AHAZIAH = Zibiah
(842–841 B.C.)

JOASH = Jehoaddin
(835–800 B.C.)

Jecoliah = AMAZIAH
(800–791 B.C.)

Jerusha = UZZIAH (AZARIAH)
(791–740 B.C.)

AHAZ = Abijah JOTHAM
(735–715 B.C.) (740–735 B.C.)

HEZEKIAH = Hephzibah
(*c*. 721–686 B.C.)

MANASSEH = Meshullemeth
(696–641 B.C.)

Jedidah = AMON
(641–639 B.C.)

Zebidah = JOSIAH = Hamutal
(639–609 B.C.)

Nehushta = JEHOIAKIM JEHOAHAZ ZEDEKIAH
(609–598 B.C.) (609 B.C.) (597–587 B.C.)

JEHOIACHIN
(598–597 B.C.)

Zerubbabel, Shealtiel Shenazzar,
governor of (?—Sheshbazzar,
Judah "prince of Judah")
(520–515 B.C.)

THE KINGS OF ISRAEL
(AFTER THE DIVISION OF THE KINGDOM)

DYNASTY OF JEROBOAM

JEROBOAM I -- *c.* 931-909 B.C.

NADAB --- 909-908 B.C.

DYNASTY OF BAASHA

BAASHA --- 908-885 B.C.

ELAH --- 885-884 B.C.

ZIMRI -- 884 B.C.

TIBNI -- 884-881 B.C.

Dynasty of Omri

OMRI --- 881-873 B.C.

AHAB --- 873-852 B.C.

AHAZIAH -- 852-851 B.C.

JORAM --- 851-841 B.C.

DYNASTY OF JEHU

JEHU --- 841-814 B.C.

JEHOAHAZ --- 814-798 B.C.

JEHOASH -- 798-782 B.C.

JEROBOAM II --- 782-745 B.C.

ZECHARIAH --- 745 B.C.

SHALLUM -- 745 B.C.

DYNASTY OF MENAHEM

MENAHEM --- 745-736 B.C.

PEKAHIAH --- 736-735 B.C.

PEKAH --- 735-732 B.C.

HOSHEA -- 732-724 B.C.

THE MACCABEES (HASMONEANS)

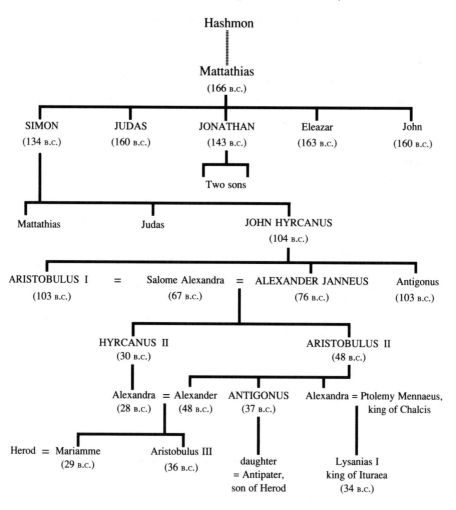

Hashmon

Mattathias
(166 B.C.)

SIMON	JUDAS	JONATHAN	Eleazar	John
(134 B.C.)	(160 B.C.)	(143 B.C.)	(163 B.C.)	(160 B.C.)

Two sons

Mattathias	Judas	JOHN HYRCANUS
		(104 B.C.)

ARISTOBULUS I   =   Salome Alexandra   =   ALEXANDER JANNEUS   Antigonus
(103 B.C.)   (67 B.C.)   (76 B.C.)   (103 B.C.)

HYRCANUS II   ARISTOBULUS II
(30 B.C.)   (48 B.C.)

Alexandra = Alexander   ANTIGONUS   Alexandra = Ptolemy Mennaeus,
(28 B.C.)   (48 B.C.)   (37 B.C.)   king of Chalcis

Herod = Mariamme   Aristobulus III
(29 B.C.)   (36 B.C.)   daughter   Lysanias I
                                                = Antipater,   king of Ituraea
                                                son of Herod   (34 B.C.)

Names in capitals denote those Hasmoneans who
  were rulers.
The dates following (unless otherwise indicated)
  are the dates of death.
The symbol "=" denotes "marriage to."

THE RULERS OF JUDEA

Herod (king) -- 37 – 4 B.C.
Archelaus (ethnarch) ---4 B.C. – A.D. 6

PREFECTS

Coponius -- A.D. 6 – 9
Marcus Ambivius -- A.D. 9 – 12
Annius Rufus --- A.D. 12 – 15
Valerius Gratus --- A.D. 15 – 26
Pontius Pilatus -- A.D. 26 – 36
Marcellus -- A.D. 37
Marullus --- A.D. 37 – 41

Herod Agrippa I (king) --- A.D. 41 – 44

PROCURATORS

Cuspius Fadus --- A.D. 44 – 46
Tiberius Julius Alexander --- A.D. 46 – 48
Ventidius Cumanus -- A.D. 48 – 52
Antonius Felix -- A.D. 52 – 59
Porcius Festus -- A.D. 59 – 62
Albinus -- A.D. 62 – 64
Gessius Florus -- A.D. 64 – 66

ROMAN EMPERORS
OF THE FIRST CENTURY A.D.

THE JULIO – CLAUDIAN DYNASTY

Augustus (Octavian) ---------------------------------------31 B.C. – A.D. 14
Tiberius --- A.D. 14 – 37
Gaius (Caligula) --- A.D. 37 – 41
Claudius -- A.D. 41 – 54
Nero --- A.D. 54 – 68
Galba -- A.D. 68 – 69
Otho --- A.D. 69
Vitellius --- A.D. 69

THE FLAVIAN DYNASTY

Vespasian --- A.D. 69 – 79
Titus --- A.D. 79 – 81
Domitian -- A.D. 81 – 96
Nerva -- A.D. 96 – 98

THE HERODS

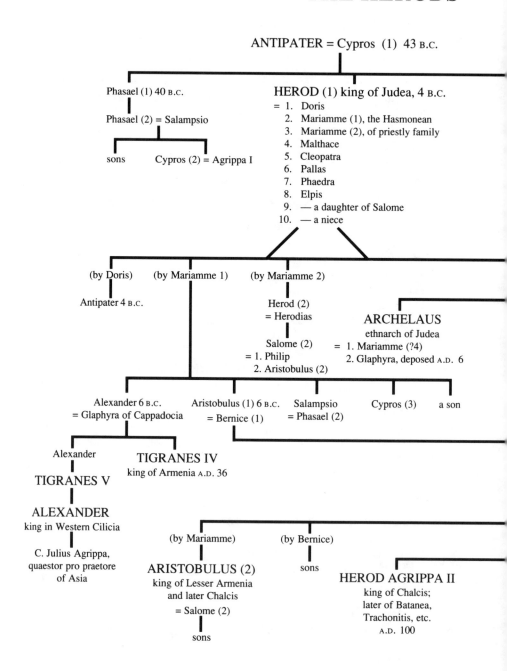

OF JUDEA

Names in capitals denote those who were rulers. The dates following (unless otherwise indicated) are the dates of death. The symbol "=" denotes "marriage to."

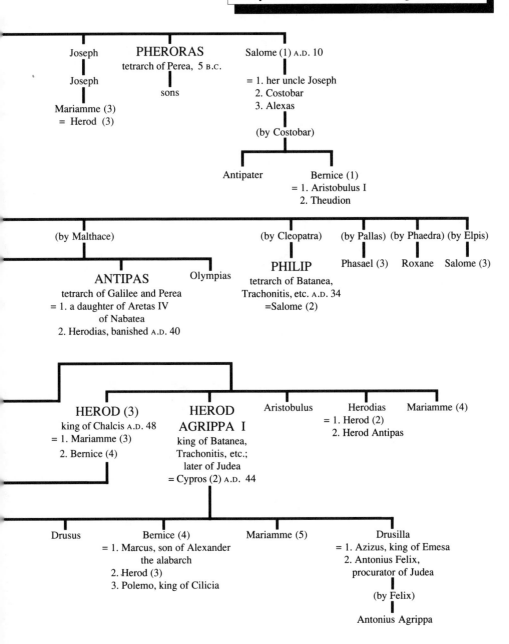

Joseph

Joseph

Mariamme (3)
= Herod (3)

PHERORAS
tetrarch of Perea, 5 B.C.

sons

Salome (1) A.D. 10

= 1. her uncle Joseph
2. Costobar
3. Alexas

(by Costobar)

Antipater

Bernice (1)
= 1. Aristobulus I
2. Theudion

(by Malthace)

ANTIPAS
tetrarch of Galilee and Perea
= 1. a daughter of Aretas IV
of Nabatea
2. Herodias, banished A.D. 40

Olympias

(by Cleopatra)

PHILIP
tetrarch of Batanea,
Trachonitis, etc. A.D. 34
=Salome (2)

(by Pallas) (by Phaedra) (by Elpis)

Phasael (3)   Roxane   Salome (3)

HEROD (3)
king of Chalcis A.D. 48
= 1. Mariamme (3)
2. Bernice (4)

HEROD
AGRIPPA I
king of Batanea,
Trachonitis, etc.;
later of Judea
= Cypros (2) A.D. 44

Aristobulus

Herodias
= 1. Herod (2)
2. Herod Antipas

Mariamme (4)

Drusus

Bernice (4)
= 1. Marcus, son of Alexander
the alabarch
2. Herod (3)
3. Polemo, king of Cilicia

Mariamme (5)

Drusilla
= 1. Azizus, king of Emesa
2. Antonius Felix,
procurator of Judea

(by Felix)

Antonius Agrippa

BIBLIOGRAPHY

Aside from the various editions of Josephus cited in the Introduction, the following studies are valuable. Only comparatively recent works published in English are listed here.

Beall, Todd S. *Josephus' Description of the Essenes Illustrated by the Dead Sea Scrolls.* (New York: Cambridge, 1988).

Bernstein, Leon. *Flavius Josephus, His Time and His Critics.* (New York: Liveright, 1938).

Coburn, Oliver. *Flavius Josephus: The Jew Who Rendered Unto Caesar.* (London: Dobson, 1972).

Cohen, Shaye J. D. *Josephus in Galilee and Rome.* (Leiden: Brill, 1979).

Farmer, William R. *Maccabees, Zealots, and Josephus: An Inquiry into Jewish Nationalism in the Greco-Roman Period.* (New York: Columbia, 1956).

Feldman, Louis H. *Josephus and Modern Scholarship.* (Berlin and New York: W. de Gruyter, 1984); *Josephus: A Supplementary Bibliography.* (New York: Garland, 1986).

_____, *Josephus, the Bible, and History.* (Detroit: Wayne State U. Press, 1989).

_____, and Hata, Gohei, eds. *Josephus, Judaism, and Christianity.* (Detroit: Wayne State U. Press, 1987).

Foakes-Jackson, F. J. *Josephus and the Jews.* (New York: R.R. Smith, 1930).

Frankman, Thomas W. *Genesis and the Jewish Antiquities of Flavius Josephus.* (Rome: Pontifical Institute Press, 1979).

Pines, Schlomo. *An Arabic Version of the Testimonium Flavianum and its Implications.* (Jerusalem: The Israel Academy of Sciences and Humanities, 1971).

Rajak, Tessa. *Josephus—The Historian and His Society.* (Philadelphia: Fortress, 1984).

Rengstorf, Karl H. *A Complete Concordance to Flavius Josephus.* (Leiden: Brill, 1973).

Shutt, R. J. H. *Studies in Josephus.* (London: S.P.C.K., 1961).

Thackeray, Henry St. John. *Josephus, the Man and the Historian.* (New York: Ktav, 1968).

Ulrich, Eugene C. *The Qumran Text of Samuel and Josephus.* (Missoula: Scholars Press, 1978).

Villalba i Varneda, Pere. *The Historical Method of Flavius Josephus.* (Leiden: Brill, 1986).

Williamson, Geoffrey A. *The World of Josephus.* (Boston: Little, Brown, 1964).

Zeitlin, Solomon. *Josephus on Jesus.* (Philadelphia: Dropsie College, 1931).

INDEX

PHOTOGRAPHS

MAPS AND
ILLUSTRATIONS